REFERENCE

The Entrepreneur's
ALMANAC
2008-2009

W9-CNB-910

Entrepreneur
MAGAZINE'S

The Entrepreneur's
ALMANAC

2008-2009

Fascinating FIGURES, FUNDAMENTALS and FACTS You Need to Run and Grow Your Business

JACQUELYN LYNN

Ep
Entrepreneur.
Press

Editorial Director: Jere L. Calmes
Cover Design: Beth Hansen-Winter
Production and Composition: Eliot House Productions

This publication is designed to provide accurate and authoritative information in regard to the subject matter covered. It is sold with the understanding that the publisher is not engaged in rendering legal, accounting or other professional services. If legal advice or other expert assistance is required, the services of a competent professional person should be sought.

Library of Congress Cataloging-in-Publication Data

Lynn, Jacquelyn.
    The entrepreneur's almanac: fascinating figures, fundamentals and facts at your fingertips/by Jacquelyn Lynn
and Entrepreneur Press.
       p.   cm.
   ISBN-13: 978-1-59918-139-4 (alk. paper)
   ISBN-10: 1-59918-139-8 (alk. paper)
      1. Small business—Management—Handbooks, manuals, etc.. I. Title.

HD62.7.L96 2007
658.02'2—dc22   2007013848

Printed in Canada
12 11 10 09 08 07   10 9 8 7 6 5 4 3 2 1

Contents

CHAPTER 10

Customer Service 89

CHAPTER 11

Human Resources: Policies, Procedures, and Great Ideas 99

SECTION III

Marketing, Advertising, Sales, and Public Relations

CHAPTER 22
Sales. 211

CHAPTER 23
Public Relations, Media
Relations, and Publicity. 219

SECTION IV
The Role of the Internet
in Your Business

CHAPTER 24
Online Sales and Marketing. 233

SECTION V
Protecting Your Business

Appendices

Preface

This is a small-business book unlike any other small-business book you'll ever read. It's not an instruction manual or a step-by-step how-to guide—although it has a wealth of advice on starting and running a successful business. It's not a book of lists—although it has plenty of lists. It's not a book of resources—although the resources it contains are abundant.

Historically, almanacs have offered seasonal weather forecasts, puzzles and other amusements, and practical household hints. Technological advances have rendered the weather forecasts contained in almanacs superfluous and there are plenty of resources for entertainment today. But the practical hints are still in demand and it seems clear that business owners could use them as much as homemakers, farmers, and any other group that has been targeted by almanacs in the past.

The *Entrepreneur's Almanac* is not designed to be read sequentially from beginning to end. Of course, you could read it that way—but you'll get just as much out of it if you use the table of contents to go to the topics that are of immediate interest and concern to you and your company.

My goal was *not* to create a "gee whiz" book—that is, a book you read, say "gee whiz" or even "gee whiz, that was interesting," then put it down and forget about it. Rather, I wanted to write a book that would give you strategies and techniques you could use immediately—whether you're just thinking about starting a business or you have a successful operation or you're somewhere in between.

This is a perfect reference volume for your desktop or any convenient place, including a bedside table, the breakfast table for a quick read with morning coffee, by the phone for reading while on hold—even the bathroom. The idea is to provide today's busy business owner/manager with a few minutes of ideas, advice, and even inspiration every day in small, easy-to-digest chunks.

I know you're busy, so let's get started.

—*Jacquelyn Lynn*

✣ ✣ ✣

THE STATE OF SMALL BUSINESS

The small business landscape is ever-changing. There are certain constants, but perhaps the most constant is change. The state of small business is different today than it was 100 or 50 or even 10 years ago, and it will be different again just a few years from now.

So, what does the small business picture look like today? And what does this mean for you and the business you have or would like to start?

❖ ❖ ❖

CHAPTER 1

Small Business Today

SMALL-BUSINESS FACTS

- There were approximately 25.8 million businesses in the United States in 2005.
- Small firms with fewer than 500 employees represent 99.9 percent of the 25.8 million businesses.
- For research purposes, a small business is defined as an independent business having fewer than 500 employees.
- Small businesses represent 99.7 percent of all employer firms.
- Small businesses employ half of all private sector employees and pay more than 45 percent of total U.S. private payroll.
- There are nearly 17,000 large businesses in the United States.
- Estimates for businesses with employees indicated that there were 671,800 new firms and 544,800 closures in 2005.
- Small businesses have generated 60 to 80 percent of net new jobs annually over the last decade.
- Small businesses create more than 50 percent of nonfarm private gross domestic product (GDP).
- In 2005, small firms supplied more than 23 percent of the total value of federal prime contracts.
- Small firms produce 13 to 14 times more patents per employee than large patenting firms. These patents are twice as likely as large firm patents to be among the 1 percent most cited.
- Small businesses employ 41 percent of high-tech workers, such as scientists, engineers, and computer workers.
- In 2004, small firms made up 97 percent of all identified exporters and produced 28.6 percent of the known export value.
- Two-thirds of new employer establishments survive at least two years, and 44 percent survive at least four years.

Source: U.S. Small Business Administration

The best advice I've ever received came from my dad and several others, and it's this: It's better to work for yourself than for somebody else!

Words of Wisdom

—PAUL A. CURASI, D.V.M., OWNER, UNIVERSITY ANIMAL HOSPITAL

DEMOGRAPHICS OF THE SELF-EMPLOYED

Overall, self-employment (as a primary occupation and including incorporated ventures) rose 12.2 percent from 1995 to 2004, with 10.2 percent of the 2004 work force choosing self-employment. Overall, the number of self-employed declined somewhat from 1995 to 2000, and then increased considerably from 2000 to 2004. Over the 1995-2004 decade, about 0.3 percent of adults per month became primarily self-employed.

Women's self-employment rate was below the overall rate but increased more than men's self-employment over this period. Men represented two-thirds of the self-employed in 2004.

Large self-employment gains occurred in all non-white race and ethnic origin categories; however, self-employment rates remained low for black and Hispanic populations. By 2004, white Americans still constituted most of the self-employed—88.3 percent.

Trends in business ownership among military veterans moved in the opposite direction, with large declines in self-employment—22 percent over the 1995-2004 decade—but a high self-employment rate of 14.8 percent in 2004. Most of the declines in veterans' self-employment were over the 1995 to 2000 period.

Individuals with disabilities that restrict or prevent some types of work sought self-employment opportunities at rates higher than the national average. These business owners had a 14.3 percent self-employment rate. The number that were self-employed changed little over the 1995 to 2004 period, gaining 3.8 percent.

In the period from 1995-2004, patterns in the age of the self-employed population matched findings from years past: Few younger workers are self-employed; self-employment rates increase with age; most of the self-employed are middle-aged; in line with population shifts, self-employment is climbing substantially in the older age categories.

❧ ❧ ❧

Remember that time is money.
—Benjamin Franklin

Words of Wisdom

WORTH KNOWING

Major factors in the survival of a small business include an ample supply of capital; being large enough to have employees; the owner's education level; the owner's reason for starting the firm in the first place, such as freedom for family life or wanting to be one's own boss.

NOT ALL BUSINESS CLOSURES ARE FAILURES

New firms are believed to have high closure rates and these closures are believed to be failures, but such assumptions may not be justified. U.S. Census Bureau data sources show that about a third of closed businesses were successful at closure. The significant proportion of businesses that closed while successful calls into question the use of "business closure" as a meaningful measure of business outcome. It appears that many owners may have executed a planned exit strategy, closed a business without excess debt, sold a viable business, or retired from the work force. It is also worth noting that such inborn factors as race and gender played negligible roles in determining survivability and success at closure.

Source: Headd, Brian, Redefining Business Success: Distinguishing Between Closure and Failure, U.S. Small Business Administration

THE IMPACT OF REGULATIONS ON SMALL FIRMS

To comply with federal regulations, very small firms, with fewer than 20 employees, spend 45 percent more per employee than larger firms, according to the SBA. These very small firms spend 4.5 times as much per employee to comply with environmental regulations, and 67 percent more per employee on tax compliance than their larger counterparts.

Table 1.1 Cost of Federal Regulations by Firm Size, All Business Sectors (Dollars)

Type of Regulation	Cost per Employee for Firms with:	
	Less than 20 Employees	500+ Employees
Environmental	3,296	710
Economic	2,127	2,952
Workplace	920	841
Tax compliance	1,304	780
Total	$7,647	$5,282

Source: The Impact of Federal Regulations on Small Firms, a study by W. Mark Crain, Sept. 2005.

WOMEN IN BUSINESS

Women's business ownership has greatly influenced the economy in general and women's economic well-being in particular. Women constitute more than 51 percent of the American population and nearly 47 percent of the labor force. According to data released in 2006 by the U.S. Census Bureau, in 2002, women owned 6.5 million or 28.2 percent of nonfarm U.S. firms. More than 14 percent of these women-owned firms were employers, with 7.1 million workers and $173.7 billion in annual payroll. Yet, in that same year, almost 80 percent of women-owned firms had receipts totaling less than $50,000.

Between 1997 and 2002, the numbers of women-owned firms overall increased by 19.8 percent. Women-owned firms with employees increased by 8.3 percent. Firms owned by women increased employment by 70,000.

More than half of women-owned businesses provide services. Of the total women-owned businesses, an estimated 14 percent are in the professional, scientific, and technical services industries; about 16 percent are in health care and social assistance. Wholesale trade and manufacturing account for approximately 4 percent of women-owned businesses. About 15 percent are in retail trade.

The Center for Women's Business Research has made the following projections from the Census Bureau data and other research:

- Nearly 10.4 million firms are owned by women (50 percent or more), employing more than 12.8 million people and generating $1.9 trillion in sales.
- For the past two decades, majority women-owned firms have continued to grow at around two times the rate of all firms.
- From 1997 to 2004, the greatest growth among majority women-owned firms has been in wholesale trade; healthcare and social assistance services; arts, entertainment, and recreation services; and professional, scientific, and technical services. Industries that saw a decline in majority women-owned firms include mining; transportation and warehousing; construction; agriculture, forestry, fishing, and hunting; information; manufacturing.
- Women-owned businesses spend an estimated $546 billion annually on salaries and benefits.
- Women of color own an estimated 1.4 million firms, employ nearly 1.3 million people, and generate $147 billion in sales (as of 2004).
- Eighty-one percent of women-owned firms do not have employees (75 percent of all firms have no employees) and these firms generate more than $167 billion in annual sales. Sales revenue increased for these firms 66 percent from 1997 to 2004, compared to 42 percent for all such firms.

✤ ✤ ✤

NUMBERS TO **KNOW** In the face of higher costs of federal regulations, the research shows that small businesses continue to bear a disproportionate share of the federal regulatory burden. The research finds that the cost of federal regulations totals $1.1 trillion; the cost per employee for firms with fewer than 20 employees is $7,647.

WORTH KNOWING

Women business owners are prepared to face risk. Most (66 percent) are willing to take above-average or substantial risks for business investments.

Source: Center for Women's Business Research

GENDER OF OWNERSHIP OF U.S. NONFARM FIRMS 2002

Number of Businesses

Race or Ethnicity of Firm Ownership	Women-Owned	Men-Owned	Equally Men/ Women-Owned	Total*
Total*	6,492,795	13,185,703	2,691,722	22,370,220
Hispanic	540,909	921,963	111,287	1,574,159
White	5,580,524	11,916,049	2,398,250	19,894,823
African American	547,341	571,670	78,978	1,197,989
American Indian and Alaska Native	79,637	119,567	6,922	206,126
Asian American	340,556	641,032	123,740	1,105,328
Pacific Islander	11,673	18,189	2,437	32,299

Gender Share of Total (percent)

Race or Ethnicity of Firm Ownership	Women-Owned	Men-Owned	Equally Men-/ Women-Owned
Total*	29	59	12
Hispanic	34	59	7
White	28	60	12
African American	46	48	7
American Indian and Alaska Native	39	58	3
Asian American	31	58	11
Pacific Islander	36	56	8

*The sum of all racial and ethnic groups does not equal the U.S. total, as multiple counts occur across racial and ethnic groups.

Source: U.S. Small Business Administration, data made available in 2006

RECEIPTS SIZES OF ALL WOMEN-OWNED BUSINESSES 2002

	Number of Firms	Percent of All-Women-Owned Firms	Receipts (thousands of dollars)	Percent of Receipts
All women-owned firms	6,489,483		$940,774,986	
Less than $5,000	1,831,238	28.2	$4,371,785	0.5
$5,000–$9,999	1,167,913	18.0	$7,876,084	0.8
$10,000–$24,999	1,405,378	21.7	$21,641,615	2.3
$25,000–$49,999	731,950	11.3	$25,408,375	2.7
$50,000–$99,999	495,519	7.6	$34,580,259	3.7
$100,000–$249,999	422,596	6.5	$66,300,101	7.0
$250,000–$499,999	197,309	3.0	$69,001,805	7.3
$500,000–$999,999	121,510	1.9	$84,699,002	1.9
$1,000,000 or more	117,069	1.8	$626,895,960	66.6

Source: U.S. Small Business Administration, data made available in 2006

NUMBERS TO KNOW

In 1989, households owning more than one small business constituted about 16 percent of all small-business-owning households; however, they earned more than 30 percent of total household income and held more than 38 percent of the wealth of small business owners. In 2004, they constituted nearly 18 percent of all small-business-owning households; however, at that point, they earned nearly 35 percent of total household income and held 47 percent of the wealth of small-business-owning households.

Source: Small Business Administration

MOST COMMON REASONS FOR STARTING A BUSINESS:

- Be your own boss.
- Financial independence.
- Creative freedom.
- Fully use your skills and knowledge.

WORTH KNOWING

Is there a disadvantage in being a woman in a non-traditional industry? No, say 85 percent of women business owners in non-traditional industries, and it can actually be beneficial.

Source: Center for Women's Business Research

NUMBERS TO KNOW

According to a study on veteran business ownership, about 22 percent of veterans in the U.S. household population were either purchasing or starting a new business or considering purchasing or starting one in 2004, and almost 72 percent of these new veteran entrepreneurs planned to employ at least one person at the outset of their new venture.

Source: U.S. Census Bureau

ENTREPRENEURIAL CHARACTERISTICS: BLESSING OR CURSE?

The very characteristics that are the mark of an entrepreneur are also characteristics that can cause trouble in companies and personal lives. Recognizing and understanding this reality can go a long way toward preventing problems with which many entrepreneurs struggle.

For example, entrepreneurs are notorious for being good at starting but bad at running a business. The difference between the entrepreneur and the manager is that the entrepreneur has a talent and gift in the creation process, while the manager has the ability to organize the details. Entrepreneurs need to either develop their management skills, or hire a manager to run their company.

Entrepreneurs are frequently accused of being too optimistic, which can set them up for failure. Their line of reality gets swayed by their passion for their idea. Step back and set reasonable goals, and then create a practical plan to reach those goals.

Along with realistic goals, entrepreneurs need to be realistic about the originality of their ideas. Entrepreneurs have a desire to create something, and often think it's new and different when it's actually not. Pay attention to what market research and your advisors tell you.

Finally, entrepreneurs can get so wrapped up in their business that their personal relationships suffer. They don't even realize how their business is affecting their families. Schedule time every week to look at other issues in your life, to be with your family and to take care of your personal needs.

> **FAST FACT**
>
> A National Federation of Independent Business (NFIB) poll found that only 51 percent of small employers wanted to grow their firms; fewer than 10 percent aspired to become "growth firms." This 10 percent is a small percentage of all firms, but certainly the group of firms largely responsible for changing the competitive nature of markets and developing new markets.
>
> *Source: U.S. Small Business Administration*

FEDERAL CONTRACTING WITH SMALL FIRMS IN 2005

In fiscal year 2005, federal government awards exceeded those in the previous banner year of FY 2004, when the federal government awarded a total of $299.9 billion in contracts for the purchase of goods available for small business participation. Of the $314 billion total in FY 2005, small businesses were the recipients of more than $79.6 billion in direct prime contract dollars, up from $69.2 billion in FY 2004. The small business share of the dollars available for small business competition was 25.36 percent—it had been 23.09 percent in FY 2004.

Source: U.S. Small Business Administration

❧ ❧ ❧

For more statistics and information of the state of small businesses, visit the Small Business Administration's web site at www.sba.gov for the most recent edition of *The Small Business Economy: A Report to the President.*

CHAPTER 2

Best Places to Be in Business

THE PERFECT CITY FOR YOUR BUSINESS

What makes for an entrepreneur-friendly environment? "There's a real kaleidoscope of factors," says Andy Levine, president of Development Counsellors International, a national public relations firm that specializes in economic development marketing, "and the biggest mistake people make is focusing on just one or two of them. An area may offer tremendous tax incentives, for example, which helps in the short term, but the longer-term profit picture may be a problem because the transportation system isn't so good, or you can't find the right kinds of workers there." Levine cautions that sometimes governments use incentives as a way of masking business problems in the community.

To find the right location for your growing business, you have to understand the basic profit factors that are really important for your business. "Number one in importance is access to your markets and customers; you want to be as close to them as possible," says Levine. "Next is access to the type of labor your business needs. If you're a high-technology business, for example, you're looking for a place with access to the research departments of major universities, like the Triangle region in North Carolina." Not only can you get help with your research and development, says Levine, but prominent universities graduate exactly the types of employees you want to attract. Also, university communities tend to have the cultural amenities (such as museums and performing arts centers) that will attract highly educated workers.

Levine warns to beware of stereotypes. For instance, if you're a manufacturing business looking for low operating costs, "the Northeast that would seem a poor choice. But there are areas in the Northeast, such as Buffalo, New York, where you can operate just as effectively as in some Sunbelt states."

When getting started, look for areas with "clusters" of businesses like your own. "If you see a lot of similar businesses clustering in a particular area or region, there are probably some very good reasons for that," advises Levine. As an example, he cites DCI's success in Tacoma, Washington. A sister city to Seattle, for years, Tacoma struggled to attract high-technology businesses. "Years ago, Tacoma's image was that of a blue-collar town dominated by pulp and paper mills," recalls Levine. "Residents joked about the 'Tacoma Aroma.'" But all that changed when Tacoma brought DCI on board. "The first thing we did," says Levine, "was to establish a marketing plan. Every town, city, or state should have a unique selling proposition that encapsulates what that area is about. We learned that Tacoma had built the largest city-owned telecommunications network in the country. So we developed the theme that Tacoma was 'America's #1 Wired City.'"

Within two years of launching the Tacoma campaign, about 80 growing businesses have located in the area, mostly e-commerce and internet-oriented businesses that have a high need for the bandwidth that fiber-optic cables provide. "Interestingly enough, some of these businesses relocated from Seattle," says Levine.

Once you've decided on a few "target" regions for your business, get in touch with the economic development organizations in each area. This can best be done on the internet. Go to your favorite search engine, and type in the name of the target community or region followed by the words "economic development" or "growth." "If you're looking at a particular region, start with the largest organizations you can find, the umbrella groups that represents the largest geographic area," advises Levine. Generally, these groups have the word "greater" in their title, such as the Greater Cleveland (Ohio) Growth Association, or the Greater Phoenix (Arizona) Economic Council. "They can help you target more particular communities and areas within the region, and make the introductions for you."

Finally, Levine cautions that you have to manage your expectations when choosing the right location for your business. "No area is going to be Nirvana," he says. "If you're looking for places that will solve all your problems, they don't exist."

Source: Cliff Ennico, "Finding that Perfect City,"
Entrepreneur.com

WORTH KNOWING

From statistics gathered covering the period from 1989 to 2004, multiple business owners appeared to be the most prosperous small business group, with nearly three-fourths of them classified as high income and nearly one-half classified as high wealth.

Source: Small Business Administration

HOT CITIES FOR ENTREPRENEURS

Large Cities

Overall Rank	City/Metro Area/State	Young Company Rank	Rapid Growth Rank
1	Phoenix-Mesa, AZ	1	2
2	Charlotte-Gastonia-Rock Hill, NC-SC	3	1
3	Raleigh-Durham-Chapel Hill, NC	5	3
4	Las Vegas, NV-AZ	2	8
5	Austin-San Marcos, TX	6	5
6	Washington-Baltimore, DC-MD-VA-WV	8	4
7	Memphis, TN-AR-MS	4	12
8	Nashville, TN	13	7
9	Norfolk-Virginia Beach-Newport News, VA-NC	17	6
10	San Antonio, TX	14	9

Midsized Cities

Overall Rank	City/Metro Area/State	Young Company Rank	Rapid Growth Rank
1	Mobile, AL	1	4
2	Charleston-North Charleston, SC	3	3
3	Birmingham, AL	2	5
4	El Paso, TX	4	2
5	Tucson, AZ	9	1
6	Madison, WI	10	8
7	McAllen-Edinburg-Mission, TX	5	12
8	Columbia, SC	6	11
9	Knoxville, TN	12	6
10	Omaha, NE-IA	13	9

Small Cities

Overall Rank	City/Metro Area/State	Young Company Rank	Rapid Growth Rank
1	Auburn-Opelika, AL	2	1
2	Green Bay, WI	1	8
3	Yuma, AZ	4	4
4	Laredo, TX	3	19
5	Huntsville, AL	5	11
6	Casper, WY	16	2
7	Las Cruces, NM	7	9
8	Missoula, MT	19	3
9	Dothan, AL	8	14
10	Lincoln, NE	20	6

HOT CITIES FOR ENTREPRENEURS, continued

Counties

Overall Rank	City/Metro Area/State	Young Company Rank	Rapid Growth Rank
1	Mecklenburg, NC	2	2
2	Fairfax, VA	3	1
3	New York, NY	1	4
4	Wake Forest, NC	5	3
5	Du Page, IL	4	7
6	Maricopa, AZ	6	5
7	Travis, TX	7	6
8	Fulton, GA	9	9
9	Clark, NV	8	13
10	Franklin, OH	10	11

States

Overall Rank	City/Metro Area/State	Young Company Rank	Rapid Growth Rank
1	Arizona	1	1
2	Virginia	5	2
3	Alabama	2	5
4	New Jersey	3	4
5	South Carolina	4	6
6	Delaware	7	11
7	North Carolina	8	12
8	Tennessee	11	8
9	Maryland	12	7
10	Nevada	6	18

Hot Cities Ranking Definitions

Overall Entrepreneurial Activity Rank: Averages the young company rank and rapid grower rank to identify the best places to start and grow a company.

Young Company Rank: Number of companies within an area that started 4 to 14 years ago and have at least 5 employees today.

Rapid Growth Rank: Measurement of a company's job growth accounting for both absolute and percent change in employment.

Source: Entrepreneur and NPRC's 2006 ranking

TOP SPOTS FOR WOMEN-OWNED BUSINESSES

Top 10 States that Have the Most Women-Owned Businesses

1. California
2. New York
3. Texas
4. Florida
5. Illinois
6. Pennsylvania
7. Ohio
8. New Jersey
9. Michigan
10. Georgia

Top 10 States for Fastest Growth in Majority Women-Owned Firms

1. Florida
2. Arizona
3. Hawaii
4. Georgia
5. New York
6. Virginia
7. New Hampshire/New Jersey (tie)
9. Rhode Island
10. Nevada

Top 10 Metro Areas for Majority Women-Owned Firms

1. Los Angeles
2. New York
3. Chicago
4. Washington DC
5. Atlanta
6. Boston/Houston (tie)
8. Philadelphia
9. Santa Ana-Anaheim
10. Dallas/Detroit (tie)

Top 10 Metro Areas for Fastest Growth in Majority Women-Owned Firms

1. Fort Lauderdale/West Palm Beach (tie)
3. Tampa
4. Orlando
5. Miami/Phoenix (tie)
7. New York
8. Atlanta/Suffolk County-Nassau County (tie)
10. Virginia Beach

Source: Center for Women's Business Research

The future will be owned and operated by the entrepreneurially minded.

—MARK VICTOR HANSEN

IF WHERE YOU WANT TO BE ISN'T THE BEST PLACE

Are you thinking of starting a business in a town that sports rows of faceless storefronts and "Going Out of Business" signs and more graffiti than graphics? While appearances are dismal, your prospects for profit needn't be. The area where you hope to build your business doesn't have to be in Podunk, USA, to be considered a "losing" town. There are pockets within almost every city and town that beg for either renovation or a wrecking ball. You could be smack in the middle of Los Angeles and still wonder whether consumers will find you, buy your product or service, and make a success of your idea.

The fact that you've chosen the site you have shows that you hope to be part of a solution. And while the disadvantages are obvious, there can be some major strategic advantages to your choice of location. You might qualify for substantial tax credits and benefits, lower lease or rent rates, low interest loans, and even expedited city permits. Find out by calling the local SBA office, Economic and Resource Development Department, or Community Redevelopment Agency.

"But No One Has Any Money to Spend Around Here"

People at least need the basics, yes? Look around your area and notice the quality of businesses. Junky displays, homemade signs, high prices, and poorly kept businesses do not a confident consumer make. Who wants to spend money where they feel like they're getting taken? Give residents a place they would be proud to frequent, and offer fair prices for products and services they want and need.

Says Diem Van Groth, founder and CEO of ZGyde Inc., a Los Angeles-based urban-focused business and technology development company, "These [economically depressed] areas are proving to be some of the hottest targets for savvy redevelopment mavens." According to Van Groth, the economically depressed areas are untapped gold mines for the motivated entrepreneur.

Still, starting any new business requires hard work, lots of forethought, and a great amount of moxie. If you're in a depressed area, you'll have more to prove—not just to your negative adversaries—but also to your lender, your suppliers, and your potential customers. On the other hand, securing financing for your venture shouldn't be any more of a process because you're in an economically depressed area. If your business plan covers all the bases (strong idea, targeted market, a plan to reach that market, and a responsible fiscal plan), lenders should be just as willing to be repaid by you as by any other entrepreneur.

In an underserved community, members will be suspicious of the "newest thing in town," especially if they've been expected to pay high prices in the past for poor service and product choices. They will want to know whom you are and that you have their interests at heart.

What's Your Deal?

It's possible that your business is replacing another that didn't make it. What will you do differently? Can you learn from their mistakes? How will you convince your consumer base that your business is worth creating a relationship with? Will what you are offering be enough for them to shift their buying habits in your direction?

In a down economy or depressed area, many are reluctant to change what they know and what feels comfortable, especially when it comes to their pocketbooks. They don't want to establish a new buying habit if they're not sure you'll be in business in a year. It's important that you offer the "over and above" kind of service, because in a tight community, people talk. And your reputation may count on how well you meet the needs and desires of those who have taken a chance on you.

Source: Carrie Schmeck, "Winning in a Losing Town,"
Entrepreneur.com

WHAT ELEMENTS CONTRIBUTE TO A BUSINESS-FRIENDLY (OR UNFRIENDLY) CITY?

- Business and personal tax burden
- Strategic location
- Economic vitality and cost of living
- Programs supporting emerging businesses
- Transportation, services, and technology infrastructure
- Cost of property/business space and available labor pool
- Education, cultural, and other community resources
- Crime rate

TOP 10 STATES IN ENTREPRENEURIAL DYNAMISM FOR 2005

1. Massachusetts

2. California

3. New Mexico

4. Virginia

5. Maryland

6. Washington

7. Colorado

8. Utah

9. New York

10. Rhode Island

Source: U.S. Small Business Administration

FAST
FACT

New entrants in local economies at first harm, then help, already existing firms. In the first year of entry, the effect on existing firms' financial performance (return on assets) is negative. However, after three years the effect on performance reverses and becomes positive. This means that, in the short term, new entrants are competitive foes, but in a few years, the old and new learn to cooperate with each other and increase profits due to positive spillover.

Source: Office of Advocacy of the U.S. Small Business Administration

STATE SMALL BUSINESS PROFILES

The Small Business Profiles for the States and Territories uses the latest federal government statistics to detail small business' contribution to the economy of the states, District of Columbia, the nation, Puerto Rico, and the U.S. territories. Citing a variety of sources, data is updated annually and documents the number and type of businesses, ownership demographics including minority and women-owned statistics, employment and financing data, and other business information. Small Business Profiles for the States and Territories from 2002 to the present may be found at www.sba.gov/advo/research/profiles.

STATE BUSINESS TAX CLIMATE INDEX

The ten best states for business taxes:

1. Wyoming
2. South Dakota
3. Alaska
4. Nevada
5. Florida
6. Texas
7. New Hampshire
8. Montana
9. Delaware
10. Oregon

The ten worst states for business taxes:

1. Minnesota
2. Maine
3. Iowa
4. Nebraska
5. California
6. Vermont
7. New York
8. New Jersey
9. Ohio
10. Rhode Island

Taxes matter to business. They affect location decisions, job creation and retention, international competitiveness, and the long-term health of a state's economy. The most competitive tax systems are typically found in states that raise sufficient tax revenue with economically neutral and simple tax systems. The least competitive are typically found in states with complex, multi-rate corporate and individual tax codes; above-average sales tax rates that exempt few business-to-business transactions; high state tax collections; and few institutional restraints on the level of taxation or spending.

Source: Tax Foundation, www.taxfoundation.org

❧ ❧ ❧

CHAPTER 3

Great Business Ideas

HOW TO EVALUATE ANY BUSINESS INVESTMENT DECISION

A re you considering a particular type of business? Have you been asked to invest in someone else's operation? Before you make a decision, ask yourself these questions:

1. What is my total investment of time and money?

2. What can I realistically expect the return on my investment to be, and is the gain sufficient?

3. What are all the upsides of this investment?

4. What are all the downsides?

5. What is the best case scenario?

6. What is the worst case scenario?

7. Can I handle the worst case scenario?

You have to find something that you love enough to be able to take risks, jump over the hurdles and break through the brick walls that are always going to be placed in front of you. If you don't have that kind of feeling for what it is you are doing, you'll stop at the first giant hurdle.

—GEORGE LUCAS, FILM PRODUCER

THE MOST POPULAR BUSINESS TRENDS FOR 2007

Green Products

Even Wal-Mart sells organic-cotton T-shirts these days, but you definitely don't have to

FAST FACT

be a retailing behemoth to take your business in a green or organic direction. In fact, entrepreneurs have an advantage when it comes to reaching customers who care about the cause as well as the products. A study by the Organic Trade Association shows that nonfood organic product sales reached $744 million in U.S. consumer sales in 2005, with supplements, personal care, and household products leading the charge.

Alternative Energy

Some major alternative-energy growth areas include solar, hydrogen, bio-fuel, fuel cells, and energy-conservation technologies. Development, installation, and creative application of these technologies are all possibilities for entrepreneurs. Research firm Clean Edge expects the worldwide market for clean energy to reach $167 billion within a decade, up from $40 billion in 2005. Entrepreneurs will have to find their niches and build flexible companies that can react as the energy market changes.

Dessert-Only Restaurants

A clear indication of America's growing sweet tooth is in consumers' dining habits. According to Hudson Riehle, senior vice president of research at the

National Restaurant Association in Washington, DC, nearly one in three fine-dining operators reported that consumers bought more desserts this year than two years ago. Fine-dining operators also indicated the strongest growth in desserts.

Chocolate

The verdict is in: Chocolate has officially gone from sinful to unstoppable. In fact, trend-watching firm Datamonitor named chocolate "the new coffee" in a list of the top 10 trends to watch. But that's not all: Studies have come out demonstrating the health benefits of flavanoids often contained in dark chocolate. Sales are soaring (dark chocolate sales were up 40 percent in 2006, according to Mintel International), and entrepreneurial opportunities are rich with promise. Dark, artisanal, organic, socially responsible, and nutraceutically enhanced chocolates are especially hot varieties. Opportunities also exist in chocolate cafés, chocolate fountains, and chocolate education, such as tastings. And you can't go wrong with basics like chocolate snacks or a shelf-stable ganache.

Burger Restaurants

Americans always have a buck for a burger. Ivan Brown, brand manager of ground beef at Cargill Meat Solutions, a producer of ground beef in Wichita, Kansas, says 8.5 billion burgers were served in commercial restaurants during the 12 months ending March 2006. Entrepreneurs can "beef" things up with upgrades, customization, and flavor. Give consumers high-end toppings, the freedom to create, and ethnic and untraditional flavor options, and this is one item certain to keep the grill red-hot.

Healthy Food

America has a growing appetite for all things healthy. From zero trans-fat snacks to fortified foods with added health benefits; if it's good for the consumer, it's most likely good for business. Even candy is being loaded with omega-3 fatty acids, healthy extracts, and vitamin C. But the real buzzword is organic. According to the Organic Trade Association, based in Greenfield, Massachusetts, organic food sales in the U.S. totaled nearly $14 billion in 2005, with double-digit growth expected from 2007 to 2010. Not sure there's room for more competitors on the organic playing field? Have no fear. Opportunities abound, especially in niche areas like alcohol (according to the Organic Trade Association, organic beers grew from $9 million in 2003 to $19 million in 2005), candy, condiments, and sauces, not to mention food for kids, babies, and pets.

Wine

As long as grapes bud from vines, the wine business will be bursting with flavorful opportunity. Estimated at $26 billion, with a 115 percent increase since 1995, the wine industry is unlikely to be sobering up anytime soon. Wine has such appeal that a variety of businesses can be seen cropping up— from wine bars and wine stores to educational in-home tastings and ancillary products that enhance the overall wine experience. And now that new laws legalizing online wine sales have uncorked the industry, entrepreneurs are finding a worldwide market to conquer. Attracting the masses means keeping your wines inexpensive and drinker-friendly. Also growing in popularity are wines packaged in single-serving bottles, and bottles topped with a screw cap.

Coffeehouses

Whether it's a drip, a latte, or a cappuccino, Americans are addicted to their coffee. If a coffeehouse isn't for you, think products like Java Juice— a liquid extract straight from the bean. Other niches include aftermarket products like Coca-Cola Blak and products that incorporate coffee for its health benefits—caffeine's been linked to decreasing the risk of diabetes, liver cirrhosis, Parkinson's disease, and even gallstones.

Social Networking

The hot social spots these days aren't in the hip clubs—instead, they're online, where users connect, share information, and make friends and business contacts. Not all social networking startups will survive and thrive. Businesses that aim to be the next MySpace should probably reconsider. Smart entrepreneurs will avoid the saturated areas and head for niche markets, such as seniors, music fans, groups of local users, pet owners, or dating groups. If you're planning to catch this blazing bandwagon, now is the time.

Bluetooth Gear

Bluetooth is turning out to be the little technology that could. With an estimated install base of at least 1 billion devices by the end of 2006, it's a veritable tidal wave of blue. For entrepreneurs, feeling blue can be a good thing. Bluetooth is showing up in cell phones, PDAs, cars, digital cameras, and billboards. Billboards? Yep. "Push advertising" that sends product messages to passersby is a new market with a lot of potential.

Look into wirelessly pushing information (like new menu items, coupons or train times), and you have a new market for creative uses of the technology—and new entrepreneurial opportunities related to Bluetooth services and device creation. Services might include push advertising, information transmittal, remote control capabilities, or mobile commerce.

Virtual Economies

Virtual games and worlds are spawning virtual economies. Entrepreneurs will have to look beyond potions and battle helms for opportunities, though. Think virtual real estate speculation, content creation, and even ultra-interactive online learning spaces for 3-D collaboration.

Home Automation and Media Storage

A Jetsons-style home may not be that far off. Increasingly, home is where the high-tech is, and there's a need for entrepreneurs to pitch in to this burgeoning market. Broadband is rampant, networking technology has matured, and consumer devices and desires are ramping up. Some red-hot areas in the home automation and media storage market: lighting control, security systems, energy management, comfort control, entertainment systems, and networked kitchen appliances. There's room for creative product-development ideas, but entrepreneurs should also investigate the service side. Once homes are relying on all these technology items, consumers will need someone to make sense of it all, install equipment, and maintain and service the systems.

Nanotechnology

Good things come in small packages. Really, really small packages. There's a lot happening in both the development of nanotechnology and in practical applications. For some entrepreneurs, nanotech will be their business. But a wider pool of companies will want to use nanotechnology to improve their existing products. Nanotech is already out there in the form of pants that won't stain and shirts that won't wrinkle, but that's just the tiny tip of what's to come. The National Science Foundation estimates that by 2015, the United States will command about 40 percent of the $1 trillion worldwide market for nanotech products and services.

Nonmedical Health Care

According to the Census Bureau, 13 percent of the population will be over the age of 65 by 2010. By 2030, the figure will jump to 19.6 percent. Many older people want to remain in their family home as long as they can, so savvy entrepreneurs are rushing in to provide a range of nonmedical home care services that help them age in place.

Transition Services

Even though many seniors want to live in their own homes as long as they can, others need, or want, to move on to one of the many residential options ahead. But that transition is often a daunting one, leaving many seniors and their families reeling from the challenges. This is a chance for entrepreneurs to do well while doing good.

Education and Tutoring

Colleges keep getting more competitive, and parents want to give their children every possible edge. Add to that the No Child Left Behind Act, which requires schools to provide tutoring services if their programs don't meet performance standards, and you have a solid market in education and tutoring. According to data from Eduventures LLC, an educational market research and consulting firm in Boston, revenue in the tutoring, test-preparation services, and supplemental content industry for kindergarten through 12th grade grew 6 percent in the 2004–2005 school year, reaching $21.9 billion.

Online tutoring—a $115 million market—is one of the hottest areas, especially for high school and middle school students, notes Eduventures senior analyst Tim Wiley. Selling tutoring services to schools is also sizzling, though Wiley notes entrepreneurs in this arena should be prepared to meet all the local, regional, and state school requirements. For grades three through eight, reading and math tutoring is always in high demand, but look to science tutoring as a growth area in the next few years. Preschool education, too, is expected to grow exponentially, says Steven Barnett, director of the National Institute of Early Education Research at Rutgers University in New Brunswick, New Jersey—especially as more states mandate preschool for all children.

Sports Education

Kids' sports—from baseball and soccer to basketball and volleyball—are hot, and entrepreneurs jumping into the sports education field are scoring big. With so many parents wanting to help their kids excel in their sport of choice, there's a big market willing to shell out good money to train young superstars-to-be.

Kids' Cooking

Americans' interest in cooking has drizzled down to the nation's kids. From cooking classes and kits to full-fledged cooking parties, this still-hot category even includes kids' cookbooks in the recipe for success. Whether a kids' cooking business takes a recreational bent or a more serious one—like teaching children about health and food preparation—the key, experts say, is to keep it fun and age-appropriate. Even kids as young as two can participate with doughy, cookie-type foods. Tweens (preteen youngsters between 8 and 12 years old) are a great entry point into the market, as are simple cooking parties. Look to regional food trends for what's hot with kids in your area.

Teen Party Planning

American teens, who number more than 70 million, want what's hot at their parties—from bar and bat mitzvahs to sweet 16s, quinceañeras, and other coming-of-age rites. Whether you start a new specialty, add teen parties to your existing event planning business, or specialize in peripheries like security or entertainment, teen parties have an angle for everyone.

Niche Gyms

The business model focuses not on the general consumer, but on one demographic and then builds the club and all its services around that profile. Popular target niches include kids, women, and over-50 folks.

Inclusive Design

Fifty million Americans have some sort of physical limitation that makes it hard for them to use tools or function in environments designed for the able-bodied. When they look for products that make their lives easier, they often find that those products are, in a word, hideous. From can openers to canes, the opportunities to fill a niche in this field with products that are both functional and stylish are everywhere.

Employee Screening

Employee screening is now a multibillion-dollar industry. The industry is trending toward one-stop shopping, offering pre-employment drug and alcohol testing as well as education verification, fingerprinting, credit and driving history reports, INS verification, and background checks for criminal or terrorist activities.

Staffing Services

According to the Bureau of Labor Statistics, staffing services will be one of the fastest-growing industries over the next five to ten years. If you know how to lasso talent for some high-demand professions, you might be a contender in this still-hot field. Entrepreneurs new to the business aren't likely to do well pitting themselves against the huge, full-service, staffing giants like Manpower. Rather, accountants, lawyers, nurses, mental-health professionals, engineers, and pharmacists, among others, are finding success using their connections and insider savvy to create niche staffing services for their own professions.

Specialty Apparel

Women are increasingly looking to specialty retailers to satisfy their appetites for hip, hard-to-find clothing. Even men are jumping onboard. Among women, growth areas include specialty athletic apparel, maternity wear, footwear, clothing for over-40s, and petite and plus sizes. Think high-end: Market research firm The NPD Group notes that loyal customers of upscale retailers buy more than 25 percent of their apparel at high-end stores and spend an average of $95 per shopping trip.

Plus-Size Products

The numbers don't lie. The average American woman is a size 12 to 16, and 30 percent of all U.S. adults are obese. Meanwhile, London-based researcher Mintel International Group Ltd. reports the plus-size clothing market reached nearly $32 billion in 2005. It's no wonder plus sizes are making waves. In fact, within the plus-size market, niches are cropping up for the underserved—including plus-size clothing for petite and pregnant women. Over-40 women, including plus sizes, are craving more variety. The NPD Group also reports that one-third of overweight children wear adult or junior size clothing for lack of properly fitting children's clothes. Nor are you limited to clothing: extra-large products like baby seats, doorways, caskets, furniture, and bath towels are also in demand.

Baby Boomer Career Counseling

Layoffs, health problems, and other challenges are pushing baby boomers out of their jobs earlier than they might have intended, spurring many to hunt for new employment or change career paths altogether. Entrepreneurs who want to provide them with career counseling must understand their varying needs.

Expanded Living Spaces

The slowdown in home sales has been accompanied by a surge in overall residential remodeling, which totaled an estimated $238 billion in 2006, according to the National Association of Home Builders. Many of these dollars are being used to enhance existing spaces rather than add more square footage. Garages are among the spaces getting extreme makeovers to be used for hobbies, parties, wine storage, and even cooking.

Remodeling fever has also hit the American backyard. Whether you provide the remodeling services or create the products, this opportunity has room to grow.

Home Party Sales

It's a party at your home—or better yet, at someone else's. Customers socialize, and you make money. Home parties now account for roughly 29 percent of the nearly $30 billion in U.S. direct sales, and 13.6 million Americans bought or sold goods from home in 2004. Direct sellers are hawking everything from organic gardening supplies to wine. Some are even hosting virtual parties online. And the numbers are growing. Be sure to thoroughly research any company you're considering, and make sure you love the products.

Source: Entrepreneur.com

> *When everyone is looking for gold, it's a good time to be in the pick-and-shovel business.*
>
> —MARK TWAIN

Words of Wisdom

25 PART-TIME BUSINESS IDEAS

Antiques

Make new money from old treasures and have fun doing it! Scout garage sales, estate auctions, and flea markets for great buys on antique furniture, toys, clothing, and other treasures from the past. Rent space at antique cooperatives, or set up booths at weekend fairs to sell your antiques.

Computer Tutor

Whether you're an expert at Windows or Linux, desktop publishing or Web research, HTML or word processing, you can help anyone enhance their computer skills. Start promoting your computer-training services by teaching classes through organizations in your community that offer adult education courses.

Custom Jewelry and Accessories

Put your creative talents to work designing custom jewelry and accessories. Whether you work with sterling silver or recycled metals, clay or papier-mâché, there's a market for your custom earrings, pins, bracelets, necklaces, and belt buckles at art shows, crafts fairs, and holiday boutiques.

Espresso Cart

Brew up profits day after day! Specialty coffee drinks generate gross profits of 55.1 to 61.5 percent per cup, says the Specialty Coffee Association of America. So, brush up on your coffee drinks, buy or rent an espresso cart, and head for sporting events, concerts, and farmers' markets in your community.

Garage and Attic Cleaning/Hauling Service

Nobody likes to spend a weekend cleaning out the garage, attic, or garden shed—it's dirty and time-consuming, and when it's done, there's still the task of hauling off all that discarded junk. But if you don't mind putting in the physical labor, a cleaning and hauling service can be a lot of fun. You can usually find a few treasures among the trash that most people are delighted to give away, and you can add to your income by recycling bottles, newspapers, and metal castoffs. You'll need a pick-up truck or other vehicle capable of carrying everything from cast-iron sinks to old timbers.

Handyman

If it's broke, you can fix it. Your phone will ring off the hook with calls from homeowners, senior citizens, and others who don't want to fix it themselves. Advertise in shopper publications and on bulletin boards, and drop off fliers at real estate offices. Then start repairing everything from leaky faucets to broken windows.

Home Inspection

Buyers need not beware when they hire a home inspector to conduct a complete physical checkup on their dream home. You'll inspect the house for structural problems and refer your clients to the contractors or handymen who can make the repairs. Knowledge of construction and your local building codes will get your business off the ground.

25 PART-TIME BUSINESS IDEAS, continued

Medical Transcription

Work as an important member of a medical team without leaving your homebased office. There's big demand by hospitals, doctors, dentists, chiropractors, and veterinarians who need outside help transcribing patient medical records. Training in medical terminology and linguistic skills will keep your business healthy.

Mobile Home-Entertainment Service

When it's dirty, disconnected, or in need of repair, you'll save the day for homeowners who want their stereo, compact-disc player, or videocassette recorder in working order. Brush up on your electrical and wiring know-how. Door-to-door fliers and calls to retail-store managers about your services will get your business off to a great start.

Mobile Window Tint

With some training and basic equipment, you'll be seeing plenty of green with your mobile window-tinting business. For best results, have a pager and van ready to help car, van, and truck owners prevent heat damage to their vehicles' interiors. Other hot markets: homes, high-rise condominiums, and office buildings.

Office and Home Organizer

Attention all neatniks: Help packrats, overworked executives, and other organizationally challenged individuals clean out messy closets, straighten files, and throw out the excess clutter. Putting your knack for neatness to part-time business use is bound to arrange some tidy profits for you.

Personal Chef

What's for dinner, honey? Great home-cooked meals for working parents and busy professionals who hire you as a personal chef. There's plenty of demand for this specialized service. So plan your menu, make out your shopping list, and go to work to satisfy your hungry clientele.

Personal Trainer

Pumping iron, pumping profits. Americans of all ages, sizes, and shapes want to keep fit, trim and healthy, and they're willing to hire their own personal coach to exercise correctly. Spread the word about your physical-fitness expertise at health spas, running, swimming, and biking clubs, and other athletic outlets.

Picture Framer

Get in the frame with a picture framing service. You can work with gallery owners, artists, portrait photographers, and individuals who've purchased a print, painting, or fine photo. If you aren't already a framing expert, read up, take classes at a local college or community center, then assemble your tools—including clamps, saws, miter boxes, glue, and a pneumatic or hand stapler. Establish relationships with local artists' groups, galleries, photographers, and print shops that can give you their business or refer their customers to you.

Plant Leasing and Maintenance

Got a green thumb and a delivery van? You're all set to service corporations, home builders, health clubs, and other businesses who want fresh greenery.

25 PART-TIME BUSINESS IDEAS, continued

Develop a steady clientele with a regular watering, pruning, and fertilizing program and a full replacement guarantee.

Records Search

Using specialized databases, you'll search public records on your computer to help your clients find lost loves, check out questionable suitors, track down debtors, verify a contractor's track record, or dig up facts on a business opportunity. Clients include attorneys, business owners, and individuals.

Restaurant Delivery

Whether it's macaroni and cheese or a five-course gourmet meal, at-home meal replacement is fast becoming the newest way to dine. When customers want their restaurant orders "to go," you'll be "on the go" with your restaurant delivery service. A great way to make your late afternoons and weekends extra-profitable!

T-Shirt Design

If you're an artist in search of a medium, why not make T-shirts your canvas? Paint, draw, bead, or appliqué your designs on plain T-shirts, and spend your weekends showcasing your art-to-wear at farmers' markets and crafts fairs.

Wallpaper Hanging

Help residential and commercial clients turn drab walls into works of art with your wallpaper-hanging skills. Build a growing business with great referrals and repeat customers. Drop off fliers at paint and wallpaper stores; also, advertise in shopper publications, in homeowner-association newsletters, and on bulletin boards at local supermarkets and malls.

Yoga and Tai Chi Instructor

In today's hectic, fast-paced world, parents, business owners, and students alike can benefit from the deep-breathing, relaxation, and centering techniques you can teach them. Get started by offering classes at health clubs, through your city's recreation and parks department, or on your own.

Source: Carla Goodman, "25 Part-Time Business Ideas,"
Entrepreneur.com

Words of Wisdom

Early on Robert and I went through a very difficult time financially and emotionally as we were building our first business together. We were broke and, for a short period of time, homeless. It would have been very easy for either of us to quit and go get a job. But we didn't quit. Instead we kept going ... and the rest is history.

—KIM KIYOSAKI, AUTHOR OF *RICH WOMAN*,
REAL ESTATE INVESTOR, AND A FOUNDER OF THE RICH DAD COMPANY

TOP TEN FRANCHISES FOR COMPUTER GEEKS

1. Geeks on Call

This franchise focuses on providing on-site computer services and is great for computer geeks. Computer experience is not required and training is provided, but computer geeks will especially love the Geeks on Call franchise because they are already passionate about computers. Total capital investment is $55,850 to $87,150 and liquid capital is only $50,000. Support, training, and financial assistance are provided. Geeks on Call was considered the best new franchise opportunity in 2006, so computer geeks should jump on this opportunity while it is hot!

2. CompuChild

An affordable franchise opportunity for computer geeks who also love kids. CompuChild requires an investment of $12,500 to $15,000. Financial assistance is not provided, but training and support is. This franchise prepares preschoolers with computer education for success in school in the future.

3. WSI Internet Consulting and Education

This franchise opportunity provides wonderful income opportunities and is one of the highest-ranking and fastest-growing franchises. WSI helps companies within a community profit from the internet. Capital investment is $49,700 or more and this is the same amount of liquidity required. Training and support are offered, financial assistance is not.

4. Secure Pay

Paying bills online has become the preferred method for many individuals. But what about those individuals without bank accounts, credit or debit cards? The answer is Secure Pay. This franchise allows such individuals to pay their bills in no time over the internet. The total capital investment is $12,975.

5. Concerto Networks

If you are a computer geek who likes making technology simple for other small businesses then a Concerto Networks franchise is for you. The total capital investment is $24,900 to $47,900 and the liquid capital required is $30,000. Third-party financial assistance is an option and training and support are provided.

6. Sir Speedy

This document and service center is one of the world's largest. From creating documents to online ordering Sir Speedy franchises offer document solutions to businesses worldwide. Computer geeks can really make their Sir Speedy franchise successful. All that is needed is a capital investment of $261,413 to $286,413 and a net worth of $300,000. Financial assistance is not offered, but support and training are.

7. Expetec

If you are a computer geek interested in the IT sector, then Expetec is the franchise opportunity for you. This franchise has received accolades for its success and it will be successful for you as well. The total capital investment is $71,800 to $111,500 and the liquid capital is $100,000. Third-party financing is available as are training and support.

8. Nerds to Go

Taking computer solutions to clients is the backbone of this franchise and it works extremely well. If you are a computer geek interested in providing computer solutions to clients then this is a great opportunity for you. Total capital investment is $40,000 and financing assistance is available, as are support and training.

9. CM/IT Solutions

Provide the IT solutions that so many businesses need with a CM/IT Solutions franchise. This proven model has a huge market that any computer geek can easily harness. Capital investment is $55,400 to $104,900 and liquid capital requirement is $60,000. Financing assistance is not available, but training and support are.

10. Fast Teks

Manage technicians who repair computers with a Fast Teks franchise. You don't need computer experience to be successful with a Fast Teks franchise, although computer geeks are especially prepared and interested in such a franchise. The capital investment is $19,500 plus and liquid capital requirement is $5,000 to $7,000. Training and support are provided.

Source: Raymond Lawrence, www.franchisegator.com

SIZE OF U.S. MARKETS BY INDUSTRY

	Estimated U.S. Business Revenue 2001 (in $ billions)
Professional and business services	$ 1,403.3
Information Industries	1,273.3
Health care and social assistance	539.2
Retail trade	3,435.5
Wholesale trade	2,376.3
Accommodation and food services	503.7
Other services	234.8
Construction	1,425.0
Utilities	612.7
Real estate	244.1
Rental and leasing services	117.1
Manufacturing	5,507.1
Transportation	598.2
Finance and insurance	3,962.9
Arts, entertainment, and recreation	123.6
Agriculture, forestry, fishing, and hunting	138.4
Mining	162.7
Totals—All Industries	**$22,594.1**

Source: BizStats, www.bizstats.com

SAFEST SMALL BUSINESSES

Rank	Type of Business	Industry	% with Profits	% with Losses
1	Surveying and mapping (except geophysical) services	services	93.7%	6.3%
2	Optometrists	health care	93.0%	7.0%
3	Dentists	health care	91.8%	8.2%
4	Certified public accountants	services	91.2%	8.8%
5	School and charter bus drivers	transportation	90.8%	9.2%
6	Special trade contractors	construction	88.2%	11.8%
7	Mental health practitioners and social therapists	health care	87.8%	12.2%
8	Physicians (except mental health specialists)	health care	87.1%	12.9%
9	Taxi and limousine service	transportation	86.3%	13.7%
10	Residential building construction	construction	85.9%	14.1%
11	Medical and diagnostic lab services	health care	85.4%	14.6%
12	Architectural services	services	85.1%	14.9%
13	Land subdivision and land development	construction	85.1%	14.9%
14	Child day-care services	health care	85.0%	15.0%
15	Legal services	services	84.6%	15.4%
16	Administrative and support services	services	84.6%	15.4%
17	Home-health-care services	health care	83.5%	16.5%
18	Physicians–mental health specialist	health care	83.1%	16.9%
19	Educational services	services	83.0%	17.0%
20	General freight trucking, local	transportation	82.8%	17.2%
21	Architectural, engineering, and related services	services	82.7%	17.3%
22	Drafting, building inspection, and geophysical survey	services	82.4%	17.6%
23	Support activities for mining	services	82.4%	17.6%
24	Motor vehicle towing and other transportation	transportation	82.0%	18.0%
25	Personal and laundry services	services	81.5%	18.5%

Source: BizMiner, www.bizminer.com

✤ ✤ ✤

BUSINESS OPERATIONS

One of the most critical keys to business survival and success is operations–that is, how you run your company. The greatest product and the best location will rarely be able to overcome bad management. But a strong operational structure can maximize your profits in good times and keep you afloat in a downturn. This section addresses a wide range of operational issues that most businesses are likely to face at one time or another.

✢ ✢ ✢

CHAPTER 4

Running Your Business

BEGIN EVERY YEAR BY LOOKING BACK

For a healthy operation, the New Year is a perfect time to conduct an annual checkup on your company or department. Take the time to step out of the trenches and look at where you've been and where you're going; what's gone right and what's gone wrong; how close you are to your original plan and whether you need to change what you're doing, or change the plan.

The multi-step process of conducting an annual checkup involves studying your history; forecasting for the future; communicating with vendors, customers, and other professional associates; organizing all of the elements of the exercise into a productive and useful format.

An effective annual review needs to be as thorough as possible. Take a look at these specific areas:

- *Mission statement.* Is your mission statement still valid? If not, revise it.

- *Business plan.* Compare what you planned to do with your actual results, and analyze why things worked the way they did—or didn't. Go through each section, updating as necessary to make the plan an accurate reflection of the company with a clear forecast for the coming years.

- *Employee compensation and benefit packages.* How do your pay scales and bonus plans compare with other employers in your area? Benefits play a major role in creating job satisfaction and employee loyalty; how satisfied are your workers with what you are offering? Could your benefit resources be realigned for improved employee relations?

- *Insurance.* Review all your policies with a line-by-line coverage and cost analysis. Let your agent know about any changes in your operation that could require changes in insurance, and ask about new insurance products that may be beneficial for you.

- *Security issues.* Consider safety: is exterior lighting adequate? Are locks sturdy? Are measures in place to protect late-night and solitary workers? Who has keys? Security experts recommend changing locks, alarm codes, and other security passwords at least once a year.
- *Professional relationships.* Be sure the people on whom you rely for advice—your attorney, accountant, financial planner, other consultants, etc.—have the knowledge and skills appropriate for your needs.

- *Financial relationships.* Review the details of your banking agreements, commercial loans, and leases. Renegotiate these contracts if you can get a better deal.

Other areas to examine include competitor information, customer satisfaction feedback, vendor terms and relationships, maintenance and service contracts, office furnishings and equipment, computer systems, freight, and telecommunications systems.

🌿 🌿 🌿

Words of Wisdom

Another increasingly important source of information that can be incredibly helpful to you at this stage of your entrepreneurial career will be tapping into and sucking the life out of the many blogs out there . . . . An enormous number of blogs are business based, and I can guarantee you, no matter what kind of empire you are intent on building, there are hundreds of bloggers out there doing something pretty similar to you. Most of them are more than happy to share their insights, screw ups, and all kinds of useful information with you.

—from *MadScam: Kick-Ass Advertising Without the Madison Avenue Price Tag* by George Parker

---

TEN STEPS TO WISE DECISION-MAKING

1. Define, as specifically as possible, what the decision is that needs to be made.
2. Brainstorm and write down as many alternatives as you can think of.
3. Think where you could find more information about possible alternatives, including friends, family, clergy, co-workers, state and federal agencies, professional organizations, online services, newspapers, magazines, books, and so on.
4. Check out your alternatives.
5. Evaluate your alternatives to see which ones could work for you.
6. Visualize the outcomes of each realistically workable alternative.
7. Do a reality check. Which of your remaining alternatives are most likely to happen?
8. Review those remaining alternatives and decide which ones feel most comfortable to you.
9. Make a decision and take action.
10. Review your decision at specified points. Remember, you can always change your mind and your direction.

PRINCIPLES FOR BUSINESS SUCCESS

Principle 1

When you find yourself in a hole, stop digging. Take a long, hard, objective look at everything you're doing. If it doesn't add value or maximize efficiency, stop doing it. If your customers don't care about it, stop doing it. Rethink every process. When you hear the words, "But we've always done it this way," ignore them. Change is hard, and it does upset numerous apple carts.

Principle 2

Take action—you can't afford to wait for all the facts. Knowing that uncertainty will always exist, be a confident decision maker. Don't fall prey to "analysis paralysis." Opportunities pass quickly, and if you don't grab them quickly, someone else will. Once you've made a decision, don't fret over it. No one has ever figured out how to turn back time and un-do anything. Even if 20/20 hindsight proves your decision was a mistake, well, mistakes are learning vehicles for all of us.

Principle 3

Get comfortable with ambiguity. The ambiguity I refer to here applies only to business decisions. There's no ambiguity about integrity, honesty, and the core values that provide a moral rudder. Those qualities must remain constant. However, when operating in a globalizing economy, there are few cut-and-dry rules; there is no clear right and wrong. Even if you don't make the wrong choice, you might not make the most "right" choice, either. Accept that fact.

Principle 4

Find your brilliance and leverage it relentlessly. Every company must decide what it does best—indeed, what it does better than anyone else—and infuse that brilliance into its entire operation.

Principle 5

Being all things to all people is the golden rule for failure. Trying to be all things to all people doesn't allow you to differentiate, it doesn't reward you for creativity, and it doesn't reward you for fashion leadership.

Principle 6

Cut the fat. Leave the muscle. Get lean!

Principle 7

Embrace globalization. Take advantage of what's best in the world, as long as it reinforces your strategy. You can and probably should use outsourcing on a selective basis.

Principle 8

Create a culture of trust. A culture of trust centers on authenticity: Don't pretend you know all the answers, and don't make promises you can't keep.

Principle 9

Foster a sense of ownership. How do you instill an entrepreneurial mindset in your employees? First, ensure that your employees literally own a stake in their company. But just as important, share your vision with your employees every chance you get. The only way to create organizational clarity is to communicate the same message at all levels of your company.

Principle 10

Hire and retain the very best people. You know the basic rules: Hire smart people, passionate people, people who fit your culture. These basics all still apply. But when you're hiring people who must do the near-impossible, that is, keep your American factories running in a tough global economy. You've got your work cut out for you. You look like a big risk. So make it a priority to convince the best and brightest that you have an environment in which they can do their best work. Learn how to play up your strengths. On the other end of the employment spectrum, don't be afraid to cut people loose when the passion isn't there. This isn't just for your benefit, it's for theirs as well.

Principle 11

Reward people for a job well done. Yes, financial rewards are always welcome. But don't forget the power of recognition and praise.

Principle 12

Innovate, innovate, innovate! Look outside the paradigm for new ideas. When you have an innovative culture, a culture filled with divergent thinkers who feel free to express their wildest ideas, you have something no competitor can steal.

Principle 13

Give customers what they really want. Are you giving your customers what they really want, or are you giving them what you want them to want? Just because you're in love with your own products and services doesn't mean the customer will be. Do continuous market research. Ask the customer what she wants. Keep an eye on emerging trends, and be mindful of how your company might leverage opportunities that arise from them. This is no guarantee of success, of course, but it does make success more likely.

Principle 14

Practice perpetual optimism. Some psychologists believe there's a strong connection between a person's mood and his conception of the future. Just the simple act of saying, "We have a plan" calms people and creates a positive mood in the organization—which, in turn, makes it more likely that the plan will be successful. To lead in an environment of ambiguity, you must defeat anxiety in yourself so you don't risk infecting the people around you. Strive to manage your moods—employees will follow your lead.

Principle 15

Never, ever be a victim. I refuse to be a victim, and I refuse to have victims working for me. I've read that Jack Welch fired the bottom 10 percent of his workforce every year. The people who comprised that 10 percent were "victim types" who could no longer effect change and drive the business forward. Jack was right—victims and other low performers bring everyone else down with them.

The message is clear: even as the world transforms itself, old-fashioned, strong leadership, superb quality, and uncompromising service still count.

Source: Robert J. Maricich, "16 Ways to Ensure Success: How Century Furniture is Beating the Odds and How You Can Follow Their Lead," Entrepreneur.com

---

The best advice I ever got was from Federal Express Founder and Chairman Fred Smith. He told me that not making a decision is, in fact, every bit as potent as any decision to take action can be.

Words of Wisdom

—RON BERGER, CHAIRMAN AND CEO, FIGARO'S ITALIAN PIZZA, INC.

SEVEN SIGNS OF TROUBLE IN YOUR BUSINESS

Watch for these seven symptoms of trouble and deal with them before they turn into a crisis.

 1. *Little or no revenue growth.*

Early-stage companies normally experience substantial growth. Then there is a leveling-off period when growth seems to slow and then stop. Look for ways to get back on the growth path. Flat growth lowers your profit and may begin to create a serious cash squeeze and imperil your ability to pay debts and keep up with needed equipment purchases or repair.

 2. *Deteriorating capital base.*

Periods of flat growth in revenue can cause a negative cash flow. You need a steady stream of profit to allow cash to pay principal debt service and allow for reinvestment in new technology, equipment, or new product development.

 3. *Equipment failures that threaten productivity.*

If your equipment is not operating properly, your production may be slower, or quality not what you need or expect. In addition, total breakdowns will stop production and cause employees to stand around not accomplishing any work. This will raise your direct costs and lower profits even further.

 4. *Poor employee morale.*

Having good employees is a contributing factor to the growth and success of your venture.

So it makes sense that when (and if) they feel negative, this will have a negative effect. The most immediate result will be diminished productivity. And remember, your employees are often the public face of your company. If they have gripes, that's where they may air them—in public.

 5. *Unpaid taxes.*

No business owner sets out to get into trouble with the tax collector. But it may start accidentally and grow quickly.

 6. *Failure or closing of a major customer.*

Most new businesses are warned about becoming dependent on a single customer or even a few. Avoiding this is easy in theory, but often difficult in practice. When a customer offers you a lot of business, it isn't easy to turn it down. If you are in an industry where there are only a few players of any size, this may be your reality. If it is and one of your major customers cuts back operations, files for reorganization, or closes, your entire business may be jeopardized. So, pay attention to what is happening within the industry as well as with your customers.

 7. *New technology creating pricing pressure.*

The years bring new technology: if older companies cannot afford to keep up, they are likely unable to compete.

Source: Suzanne Caplan, Second Wind: Turnaround Strategies for Business Revival

THE DRIVE TO SUCCEED

Larry H. Miller presides over a multimillion-dollar financial empire that includes automotive dealerships in several states, an entertainment and sports arena, a television station, and the Utah Jazz, a National Basketball Association franchise team. His formal education consists of high school and about ten weeks of college, and he says it hasn't mattered to his business that he didn't do well in subjects like trigonometry and geometry.

"All I need to worry about is two and two. It's simply adding and subtracting numbers," he says. When he wants to know more about something, he finds out. "It's very simple: the only stupid question is an unasked question. If something interests me and I don't know about it, I learn about it."

Though he isn't entirely comfortable wearing the mantle of millionaire, Miller believes he understands why he has been successful. First, he has learned that business is simple. "It is simply a function of having quality goods and/or services consistently delivered at a fair price." He says the message in Adam Smith's *The Wealth of Nations* is as applicable today as it was two centuries ago: "Supply and demand works." It's an approach that keeps him from becoming overwhelmed. "I take things one day at a time. It's one phone call, one experience, and one negotiation at a time."

Second, he found a niche for his business interests, particularly the auto dealerships, that suit his style and abilities.

Third, he is not afraid to fail. "I lost my fear of failure a long time ago," he says. "I learned that I was going to fail on some things, but that wasn't catastrophic. Failure is not the end of the world." He also learned to capitalize on the positives. "Successes give confidence, and strength leads to strength."

In Miller's opinion, the biggest challenge a growing business faces is managing growth. "I believe that a high percentage of business failures—probably as much as 80 percent—are not a result of lack of effort, or a bad product or service, but rather the result of outgrowing one's capital base and/or the ability to manage growth. Today's business world is dynamic, and when growth comes, it often comes very suddenly."

Miller says there's no substitute for hard work, but it needs to be smart work. "It's easy to confuse motion and progress. Progress always needs motion, but motion isn't always progress."

His solution? He repeats: Keep things simple. Don't get caught up in sophisticated or complex trappings. Pay attention to the basics. "I don't have to look at many numbers to know what's going on in any given store, whether or not we own it. Every department has two or three key numbers that tell the story. Focus on the simple things and then let yourself get more sophisticated. You can't lose sight of the core issues; if you do, you'll forget what made you great."

Words of Wisdom

When you make a mistake, don't look back at it long. Take the reason of the thing into your mind, and then look forward. Mistakes are lessons of wisdom. The past cannot be changed. The future is yet in your power.

—Phyllis Bottome, author

❧ ❧ ❧

PROFESSIONAL ETHICS: BUILD YOUR SUCCESS ON HONOR AND INTEGRITY

In today's business world, trust is hard to earn, easy to lose, and once lost, extremely difficult, if not impossible, to regain. Growing consumer skepticism is sending business owners and managers a clear message: organizations must maintain the trust of their customers, employees, suppliers, and communities if they hope to succeed—and doing that requires integrity.

Is success without integrity possible? That depends on how you define success. If your goal is strictly to make money and you're out for a quick buck, integrity might not be an essential element of your operation. But if your vision is a solid organization with a stable future, the opposite is true.

Business owners, managers, and employees are faced daily with ethical dilemmas for which there are often no easy answers. Complicating the issue is that not all the companies you compete against adhere to the same high standards. It's a good idea to articulate the company's values and ethics in a policy statement, and use that statement both as an operations guide and a marketing tool. A clear statement removes any doubt as to what is considered right and wrong.

To help resolve ethical dilemmas, hold your decision to the glaring light of publicity. How would you feel if your actions were reported on the front page of the newspaper? If the thought makes you cringe, the action you're considering is probably a mistake.

When it comes to your employees, be prepared to deal swiftly and decisively with any violation of your values statement, but temper your action with understanding. Consider the true motivation behind the behavior when deciding what action to take. Was the person's behavior thought-out and intentional, or was he trying to do the right thing and made a mistake in the process? In the case of the former, that's probably someone you don't want in your company. In the case of the latter, some counseling and education should prevent the mistake from being repeated.

When your organization does experience an ethical lapse, it's not the end of the world; recovery is possible. Begin by admitting what you've done to the affected parties. Take responsibility, then immediately put a plan in place to correct the situation. Of course, you may not be able to totally repair the damage. It could be like a marriage when infidelity has occurred: the relationship may survive, but it will never be exactly the same. Rebuilding trust takes time and effort—something you should consider before you take an ethical risk.

❧ ❧ ❧

Never stop looking at and working on the future of your business. Don't get bogged down in dealing with issues related to today or yesterday. Hire others to deal with those issues.

Words of Wisdom

—SHARON LECHTER, CO-AUTHOR OF *RICH DAD POOR DAD* AND A FOUNDER OF THE RICH DAD COMPANY

If you even think you have a problem, almost 100 percent of the time, you have a real problem. An entrepreneur needs to have a sixth sense for sniffing out problems. With a little focus, you can quickly spot the danger signs. When you dig in fast, you can usually keep a small problem from becoming a big one. If you ignore the danger signs, it only gets worse—usually, much worse!

—David Woods, CEO and
President, Adventures in Advertising Franchise, LLC

DEVELOPING A CODE OF ETHICS IN YOUR BUSINESS

When you are developing your ethics policy, you must decide what it is you want your company to stand for, put it in writing, and enforce it. According to Kenneth Blanchard and Norman Vincent Peale, authors of *The Power of Ethical Management*, you can base your policy on five fundamental principles:

- *Purpose.* A purpose combines both your vision and the values you would like to see upheld in your business. It comes from the top and outlines specifically what is considered acceptable or unacceptable in terms of conduct in your business.
- *Pride.* Pride builds dignity and self-respect. If employees are proud of where they work and what they are doing, they are much more apt to act in an ethical manner.
- *Patience.* Since you must focus on long-term vs. short-term results, you must develop a certain degree of patience. Without it, you will become frustrated and be more tempted to choose unethical alternatives.

- *Persistence.* Persistence means standing by your word. It means being committed. If you are not committed to the ethics you have outlined, then they become worthless. Stand by your word.
- *Perspective.* In a world where there is never enough time to do everything we need or want to do, it is often difficult to maintain perspective. However, stopping and reflecting on where your business is headed, why you are headed that way, and how you are going to get there allows you to make the best decisions, both in the short term and in the long term.

A company policy is a reflection of the values deemed important to the business. As you develop your ethics policy, focus on what you would like the world to be like, not on what others tell you it is.

Source: Small Business Administration

MAINTAIN A PROJECT AND SOLUTION ARCHIVE

Too many companies spend valuable time reinventing the wheel each day. "Every time you treat a known problem as a new problem that has to be solved again, you're wasting time and money," says David Kay, founder of DB Kay & Associates, a Los Gatos, California, knowledge management consulting firm. In fact, Kay says, it's four to ten times more expensive to relearn how to solve a problem than to have a solution ready to go.

Capturing knowledge starts by thinking about your business in small pieces—from IT to marketing—and then deciding where the core knowledge lies and which information is most likely to be reused, says Nabil Nasr, director of the Center for Integrated Manufacturing Studies at the Rochester Institute of Technology in Rochester, New York. Also, determine which information is most at risk. If you lost every employee tomorrow, where would it hurt most?

It's easy to think software will solve the problem, but don't build a database until you've decided which knowledge needs managing. The last thing you want is a dusty database no one uses. "Throwing tech at broken processes is a waste of time," says Kay, co-author of *Collective Wisdom: Transforming Support With Knowledge.*

Human nature is the biggest challenge companies face in managing knowledge. Some employees resist

> *Doug Van Arsdale, CEO of Lending.com, shared this with me: If it won't work small, it won't work big.*
>
> —RANDY PENNINGTON, PENNINGTON PERFORMANCE GROUP
>
> *Words of Wisdom*

sharing knowledge as a means of job security, or they see documentation as too much work. They might hate writing or not know how to explain things well. Keep your system as simple as possible so employees can pick it up. For example, employees can use brief summaries, such as bullet points, to describe how they solved a problem. Ultimately, capturing knowledge requires a cultural shift. "Capturing and reusing knowledge has to be seen as a part of the job," says Kay.

A collaborative approach is critical to increasing the company's knowledge base and making sure knowledge lingers as employees come and go. "You've got to ask, 'Where is the knowledge should we make redundant?'" says David DeLong, adjunct professor at Babson College and author of *Lost Knowledge: Confronting the Threat of an Aging Workforce.* "[And] what are the opportunities you're missing by not capturing knowledge?"

Source: Chris Penttila, "Keeping a Project Archive," Entrepreneur.com

> *You're only as successful as the last person you helped.*
>
> —ROBERT A. FUNK, FOUNDER AND CHAIRMAN, EXPRESS PERSONNEL SERVICES
>
>
> *Words of Wisdom*

STOP SOLVING PROBLEMS— PREVENT THEM INSTEAD

Rather than sharpening your problem-solving skills, consider concentrating on problem prevention. A proactive perspective of anticipating problems and taking steps to prevent them is far more beneficial than patching things up after-the-fact. Some thoughts:

- *Have good intuition and be pessimistic enough to imagine possible negative outcomes.* Continually size up situations and consider possible outcomes, both positive and negative. Pay attention to your hunches and work on developing your intuition.

- *Visualize worst-case scenarios.* Think about problems before they occur and plan for how you'll deal with them. For example, what happens if your computer crashes? In a large office with a technical support staff, you just call for help. But if you're by yourself in your home-based office, whom will you call to get your system back on-line quickly? Knowing that before you need it can prevent a lot of headaches. Or, what will you do if your initial sales projections fail to materialize? Do you have a financial contingency plan? This is not an exercise in negativity, but rather preparing in advance for dealing with manageable problems so they don't turn into major disasters.

- *Pay attention to early warning signals.* Look for little signs that could mean troubles ahead. If you're feeling anxious, figure out why. If sales dip, even slightly, be sure you understand the reason.

- *Avoid bad decision-making.* The most common error in decision-making is to accept the first good solution that comes along, rather than taking the time to find truly the best alternative. Also, never make decisions when you're emotional; delay action for a day or so, until you've calmed down and can think clearly.

GO OUTDOORS FOR YOUR NEXT COMPANY MEETING

Looking for a new place to hold your next company meeting? Try heading outside. A work session at a local park with plenty of fresh air and sunshine may be just what your staff needs to relax, get the creative juices flowing, and increase their productivity. But don't just grab a few cans of soft drinks and some carry-out food; an outdoor meeting takes as much, if not more, planning than one held inside. Some advice:

- *Reserve a spot with shelter.* True, the goal is to be outside, but you also want protection from too much sun and the possibility of rain. Reservations also ensure that your location of choice will be available.

- *Find out what else is going on.* Be sure that other events scheduled for the same day won't distract your group. Consider what other ambient noises and nearby activities might affect your meeting.

- *Arrange a comfortable work area.* Does the park have tables? Do you need to bring chairs or blankets? Also, be sure the restrooms are clean, conveniently located, and stocked with necessities.

- *Take advantage of recreational offerings.* Plan your agenda so participants can use the park's amenities at breaks or after the meeting.

- *Plan food carefully.* Make lists so you don't forget anything, and have plenty of coolers on hand so food won't spoil.

MAKE YOUR TIME COUNT

How can you reduce the amount of time you spend on activities that don't generate revenue? Take an inventory of how you're spending your time. Then go through your activities list one item at a time with these thoughts in mind:

- *Be sure the task is essential.* It's easy to get caught up, doing things that don't really need to be done. Will your business suffer if you aren't doing some of the things you've been doing? If not, then it's time to stop performing non-essential tasks and focus on essentials.

- *Systematize the task.* Once you've determined that the task is essential, turn it into an identifiable system. Analyze the procedure and create a step-by-step formula for getting it done. This forces you to think through the most efficient way of accomplishing the work. Once you understand that, create a system that can be implemented, monitored, and measured by anyone.

- *Delegate.* Systematizing makes delegating much easier and more effective. Look around within your organization for people who can take over systematized tasks, and give them the necessary responsibility and authority for getting the work done.

- *Outsource.* When you don't have the necessary skills for particular tasks within your company, and when hiring an employee with those skills isn't practical, outsource the work.

- *Consolidate.* When outsourcing, consider a source that can handle a number of related tasks. For example, you may look to your accounting firm to handle payroll and provide cash flow management assistance, as well as the standard financial reports and tax preparation. This allows the source to really get to know your company, and to act more as a consultant than as a simple task-performer. It also simplifies things for you, because you have a single contact for a variety of functions.

We live in a world of 'should-ofs', 'could-ofs,' and 'would-ofs' and I believe they just create more stress in our lives. I have made many mistakes in business but have learned valuable lessons along the way that have helped me get to where I am today.

Words of Wisdom

—SHARON LECHTER, CO-AUTHOR OF *RICH DAD POOR DAD* AND
A FOUNDER OF THE RICH DAD COMPANY

GUARD AGAINST BECOMING INSULATED

Regardless of its size, running a business is demanding. But as your company grows, the nature of those demands changes and you may find yourself losing touch with your customers and employees. It's a problem Stan Clark is well aware of. He and a partner were the only two employees when they bought Eskimo Joe's, a small bar in Stillwater, Oklahoma, in 1975. Today, the company has grown to a multimillion-dollar conglomerate.

Clark says simple awareness of the risk of becoming insulated goes a long way toward preventing the problem. But he also advises owners to be pro-active and look for ways to eliminate barriers that may arise between themselves and their employees and customers.

"There's no substitute for listening and interacting with the customers, and listening and interacting with the line people," he says. Though he has a regular meeting with senior managers every two weeks, he says, "That's not the same as being on the floor with the line employee, and it's certainly not the same as being face-to-face with the customer."

He visits every department and location of his organization regularly, sometimes just observing, other times pitching in when something needs to be done. He also personally conducts a new-hire orientation program. "They hear the history of the company, the core values, what my expectations are of them, and how important they are to the future of the organization," he says.

Clark says he views his company as an inverted pyramid, with himself at the bottom. "My role is to support all the managers, all the line people, and ultimately all the customers, who are the ones at the top of the inverted triangle," he explains. "The leader-as-servant mentality is so right. The bigger you get, the harder it is to stay close to the people you depend on for your company's success. There's no magic, no trick to it, you just have to do it."

MANAGING WORKPLACE NOISE

Ringing phones, other people's conversations, the whirring and grinding of machines—all common sounds in today's office, and all distractions that can have a negative impact on productivity. While technology and design trends may have changed the source and type of some noises, the fundamental problem is still there. Though there aren't many typewriters in offices these days, there are still plenty of computer keyboards clicking away. Laser printers are quieter than impact printers, but we've added other types of equipment, fax machines, paper shredders, sorters, etc., that generate their own noise. Open floor plans may encourage communication and enhance space efficiency, but the design also adds to office noise—and leaves staffers feeling as though their workplace lacks privacy. Finally, modern architectural trends often call for the use of sterile, hard surfaces that reflect rather than absorb sound. How can you deal with office noise?

First, identify the source(s) of the noise. Next, get rid of it, if possible. Move noisy equipment to a room that can be closed off. If a noise source can't be moved, look for a way to contain the noise behind a barrier. Finally, introduce sound-absorptive materials—such as acoustical ceiling tile—that will help dissipate noise. Because there are literally thousands of sound-absorbent materials that may or may not work in your environment, consider hiring a consultant to help you plan your noise reduction strategy. They can be found under "acoustical consultants" or "acoustical contractors" in your telephone directory. In just a few hours, a consultant can help you develop an effective and affordable plan; expect to pay $300 to $500 for the consultation. Be sure the consultant is an engineer and check their qualifications as you would any professional service provider.

USE NEGATIVE THINKING TO MAKE BETTER DECISIONS

The most important quality for success in entrepreneurship and in life is the quality of optimism. Optimists have an unrealistic expectation of success. As a result, they're willing to try far more things without becoming discouraged. In addition, because of their unrealistically positive attitude, they're willing to persist much longer than the average person. Optimism is a wonderful quality—as long as you have it under control.

In order to be successful in business, and in any activity where your money's involved, you must temper your optimism with negativism. You must be enthusiastic about the possible upside of the investment, but you must be skeptical, critical, suspicious, and demanding about all the different ways in which your money can be lost. Seek out and listen carefully to people who are negative towards your idea. Look for negative thinkers, because their viewpoints can be invaluable and save you a fortune in time and money. I have a friend who's a lawyer, and he gives advice to many people on investments. When someone comes to him and asks him about making an investment he's unsure about, he says, "All right, I want you to come to my office and I want you to sit behind my desk. Then I'm going to come in and present this investment to you, and I want you to critique as if you were me." He says that when his clients begin critiquing the investments they're considering making, when they start to become negative thinkers about the investments, they're astonished at how bad the investments really are. He said he's saved his clients millions of dollars by forcing them to be negative thinkers about their own ideas simply by switching roles and sitting in front of the desk while they sit behind it. It pays to act as your own negative thinker.

Conversely, don't be overly influenced by negative thinkers. Just take their viewpoints into consideration. There's a famous story of Mary Hudson, who started off with $200 in the middle of the Depression and leased a gas station that two men had gone broke running at two different times. From that location, she built a company called Hudson Oil, which is now the biggest independent distributor of gas and oil in the United States from a $200 investment, even though everybody told her she'd fail. So remember, listen to negative thinkers, seriously consider what they have to say, but don't necessarily accept their advice.

Source: Brian Tracy,
"Be a Negative Optimist," Entrepreneur.com

KNOW WHERE YOU HAVE LEVERAGE

Leverage is using your resources in a way that the potential positive or negative return is magnified. Your company could have leverage in these areas:

- Customer base
- Goodwill
- Cash
- Market position/leadership
- Reputation
- Momentum
- Human resources and key people
- Systems
- Responsiveness
- Intellectual property
- Suppliers
- Unique factors

BUY, DON'T RENT

If you're going to start a business in a commercial location, you may assume the best thing to do is to rent a facility. Children's Discovery Centers owner Lois Mitten Rosenberry suggests a different approach: If at all possible, purchase the facility your business is in.

Mitten Rosenberry personally owns all the buildings her child care centers are in and leases those properties to her company. This is a woman who started her business when her older daughter was on a free-school-lunch program and she now owns more than $3 million worth of real estate that will be paid for long before she's ready to retire.

"When you rent, you're paying money so the developer or landlord will have the money to make his own payments. At the end of 10 years, you have nothing, and the person who owns the real estate has some valuable income-generating property," she observes. "If you can get the down payment and qualify for a mortgage, you'll find your payments

The smartest thing I've done in my business is finding and purchasing property, developing it, and moving my practice to its current location.

Words of Wisdom

—PAUL A. CURASI, D.V.M.,
UNIVERSITY ANIMAL HOSPITAL

probably won't cost you any more than rent, and you're building equity."

If the idea of owning property is a little scary, Mitten Rosenberry thinks you should be more frightened of a lease. If you own the property and things aren't going well, you can sell; if you sign a lease, you probably won't be able to get out of it. Also, if you own the real estate, you're not at risk of hefty rent increases after you've improved the property and built a successful business.

Mitten Rosenberry says she makes more money from owning and leasing back the property than she takes in salary, which gives her a tax break along with financial security. "If I didn't own the real estate, I would not be where I am today," she says.

⚜ ⚜ ⚜

DOING IT RIGHT

Do you use a desktop computer in the office and a notebook on the road, and then get confused about which computer has the most recent files? One solution is to use only one computer—a notebook that can be plugged into a docking station (or port replicator) in the office for access to the company network and which you can take with you whenever necessary. Or set up your notebook so that, instead of working directly on that machine, you access the office computer when you're working remotely. An IT person can set up the connection for you, or you can use a service such as GoToMyPC.com.

TRUST YOUR INTUITION

Learn to trust your intuition, especially when you can back your hunches with logic. Robert Kiyosaki, founder of the Rich Dad Family of Companies, says he wishes he had realized that when he started his business. "Although my intuition didn't always lead me to the right answers, it did lead me to what I needed to learn," Kiyosaki says.

❧ ❧ ❧

CHAPTER 5

Business Etiquette and Relationships

COURTESY COUNTS

Believe it or not, minding your ps and qs really does make a difference in business these days. To illustrate: A client who recently hired us told me that he had spoken with a number of potential firms and that, while every one of them could do the job, in the end they picked us because our team had the best manners by far. He added, and I quote, "We always hire for manners because everything else can be learned on the job."

It's an interesting hiring strategy, to be sure. Wouldn't your mother be thrilled? (I know mine was.) Who would have thought that the unique value in the deal would be manners? Although business protocol wasn't actually taught in any business school I considered, maybe they should start.

So what can you do to incorporate a little Emily Post into your daily routine? It's not as hard as you think.

1. *Focus on the present.* We've all turned into multitasking machines: We talk on the phone, check e-mail, travel to the next meeting, and eat lunch—all at the same time. But juggling tasks is overrated and frankly unfulfilling for all involved. The person on the other end of the line can tell your mind is wandering as your voice trails off, the clicking of the keys in the background is annoying and distracting, you're about to sideswipe the guy on your left, and food is meant to be shared and enjoyed, not shoved down your throat as fast as possible. Slow down, focus, and put your full attention into everything you do. People notice and appreciate your interest.

2. *When you're on the phone, smile as you talk.* Smiling almost forces you to articulate more—it's harder to mumble and

slur your words when you smile. And a smile comes through in your voice and tone. I find it also helps to stand up or sit up in your chair because your voice projects better and sounds clearer. We once worked with a company that put millions of dollars into a fancy customer relationship management (CRM) system to help them "touch" their customers in meaningful ways. The funny thing is, when you call their main number, you get put into a phone tree that never seems to end. It's frustrating, and they no longer let you push "0" to reach an actual human being; they overrode that feature in the system because so many people were using it (which should have been a clue). You actually have to listen to several minutes of "Press 1 for X, press 4 for Y." My first recommendation for them was to have a real human being—preferably one who smiles—pick up the phone, at least during normal business hours. They can hire a lot of people for all the money they spent on the CRM system upgrades and training. Call me old-fashioned, but it really is nice when you can reach a smiling human being on the other end of the line.

3. *Listen to your phone's outgoing message.* I know a professional whose cell phone message barks, "I'm not here. Don't leave me a message on this phone!" And he's in sales. Would you buy from him? Not likely. Make it easy for people to find you and follow up with you, especially if you're in a people business. It's perfectly acceptable to say that you're traveling and unable to check messages regularly, or that you prefer people to leave messages at another number, or even to set your cell phone so that it doesn't accept messages at all. Announcing that you don't welcome voice messages makes

you seem unapproachable and cold—neither are desirable qualities in business.

4. *Apologize when you make a mistake.* It's the cover-up or denial in the first place, not the screw-up, that ultimately gets you in trouble. In the past year, I had two people not show up for scheduled meetings. One made excuses and said he would get back to me with dates for a lunch to make up for it (I'm still waiting for his call); the other sent the most beautiful flowers I've ever seen and called the following day asking when and where we could meet again. Everyone has emergencies or technology snafus. It's how you handle these situations that shows your character. People can become more loyal than they ever would have been if you rectify a bad situation by addressing the problem and making amends. "The dog ate my homework" didn't work in high school, and it won't work in business. Come clean and make good on your promises.

5. *Let the call go to voice mail.* Turn off your cell phone when you're in a meeting and forward your phone to voice mail when people are in your office. If you start responding to every incoming missive, you send a message that the person you're actually with just isn't important. People don't care how much you know until they know how much you care, so give them your full attention and be engaged in the conversation that's right in front of you. In a movie theatre, before the movie starts, they always show the "inconsiderate cell phone man" ad to remind people to turn off their phones. Do we really need to stoop that low in business now, too? Before I give speeches or workshops, I always ask everyone in the room to silence their phones, and I let them know that I'll collect $10 for every phone that rings

and donate the money to a local charity. That usually does the trick.

6. *Practice positive e-mail etiquette.* I call it *The New York Times* test: If you wouldn't want to see it on the front page of the newspaper, then don't send the message. It's amazing what gets passed around the office and left on the printer, and you can be sure that such information will fall into the wrong hands. So, before you hit "send" after a heated interchange, take a walk, get a cup of coffee, and then read it one last time to make sure you really want that message to go out.

7. *Acknowledge gifts.* A simple thank you is sufficient. It's embarrassing for both parties to have to follow up to make sure a gift was received. The person who sent the gift isn't fishing for a compliment—they just want to be sure their package was delivered. And the recipient knows they should have responded sooner. Save everyone the hassle and just drop a quick e-mail saying it arrived. Similarly, if someone is responsible for helping you find a new customer or getting you a meeting with an influential person, you should let them know you appreciate their help. In many ways, a customer or a meeting is a gift.

8. *Don't take it out on the receptionist or cashier.* When things aren't going your way, don't let the first person with whom you come in contact take the brunt of your anger. It reflects badly on you, and it's likely that whatever went wrong wasn't their fault. So, take the high road—you'll attract more bees with honey anyway.

Maybe all good manners just go back to the Golden Rule: Do unto others as you would have them do unto you. You may, in fact, find that good manners will turn into good money—I did. So, listen to your mother and mind your manners. It's the little things that add up to making a great impression with every encounter. Focus, smile, listen. It doesn't take much these days.

Source: Paige Arnof-Fenn, "Why You Should Mind Your Manners," Entrepreneur.com

---

Treat every person at all levels with courtesy and respect.

—CHRIS MURPHY, PRESIDENT, MURPHY LIGHTING SYSTEMS, INC.

Words of Wisdom

HOSTING A BUSINESS MEAL

Do your palms sweat when you think about hosting a business meal? Do you shrink in terror at the idea of choosing the wrong fork? Do you know what the proper seating arrangements are? With so many rules to keep straight, we went to Dana May Casperson, business etiquette expert and author of *Power Etiquette: What You Don't Know Can Kill Your Career* (Amacom), for practical tips to help you clear your worries clean off the table.

Before you even get to the restaurant, advises Casperson, have a few topics of conversation ready. An interesting tidbit about yourself can be a great opener, for example. "Plan some questions you can ask, because people like to talk about themselves," she says. Because it's improper to talk business until after the entrée dishes are cleared, make sure you're ready to discuss current events, good movies, business books, and the like before and during the meal.

Make sure you're ready to discuss current events, good movies, business books, and the like before and during the meal.

The right outfit is essential to any business lunch, dinner, or tea. For daytime meals, typical businesswear is appropriate (unless your daily attire is super casual, in which case you should step it up). In the evening, you should dress a bit more formally, though this can vary depending on the restaurant you choose. Casperson also recommends wearing an eye-catching tie or lapel pin to help spark conversation. "Wear something interesting up near your face," she suggests. "People will remember you."

Generally, seat your most important guest to your right. And if you've invited your guests, you're the host, adds Casperson. Make it clear upfront that you'll be paying. A quick statement before you sit down can avoid awkwardness at the end of the meal. Simply say, "You'll be my company's guest today." You can even arrange to pay the tab in advance or at least ask the wait staff to bring you the check.

Avoid ordering alcoholic drinks, because some companies frown on mixing business with alcohol. (If you are in the wine business, however, it would be appropriate.) After the entrée is cleared, it's time to start talking business. Now's the time to take out papers and other documents—keep them out of sight until then. Offer your guests coffee and dessert (it's OK to discuss business while enjoying these).

"Remember," says Casperson, "what people see across the table, how they see you handling your knife and fork, is how they see you handling business."

Source: By Nichole L. Torres, "Mind Over Manners," Entrepreneur.com

---

The solution to most problems is more communication, not less. And face-to-face is best.

—KIM KIYOSAKI, AUTHOR OF *RICH WOMAN*, REAL ESTATE INVESTOR, AND A FOUNDER OF THE RICH DAD COMPANY

Words of Wisdom

BUSINESS INTRODUCTION ETIQUETTE

Business is about relationships, and relationships begin with introductions. But the old social rules about gender and age don't apply to effective introductions in today's business world.

It's all based on precedence. In other words, rank rates. When you perform an introduction, the "less important" person is presented to the "more important" one. A key exception is in the case of clients and customers; they are considered more important than someone in your firm, even if the client has a lower rank than your colleague. And if you're unsure of the precedence, be guided by the respective agendas of the people you're introducing; treat the person with the most to gain from the contact as the "junior" person in the introduction.

Along with names, your introduction should include a brief bit of information about the individuals. Keep the details appropriate to the situation, perhaps giving a title or recent business accomplishment. Don't mention personal issues, don't try to be humorous, and never poke fun at an unusual name.

When you're the one being introduced, remember that custom calls for the senior person to initiate the handshake—if they don't, you should go ahead. The person who extends the hand first is at an advantage because they're taking the initiative.

What about introducing yourself? Never break in on two people, especially if they're in deep conversation. But for groups of three or more, simply wait for a lull in the conversation, ask if you can join them, introduce yourself, and shake hands all around. This forces everyone else to shake hands and say their name—and most people will be delighted that you had the courage to make the first move.

❧ ❧ ❧

ARE YOU USING PUBLIC PLACES AS A WORK SPACE?

In the Dilbertesque world of corporate etiquette, most people know it's rude to leave meatloaf decomposing in the office refrigerator. But for the swarms of entrepreneurs whose offices are local coffeehouses, what makes for good manners is often as murky as a mocha latte: "Coffeehouse-based" entrepreneurs with laptops hog tables near coveted outlets for hours at a time. They chide baristas to turn the shop's music down and bark into cell phones while ordering grande cappuccinos.

"It's just plain rude," complains Paige Kayner, owner of Aurafice Internet & Coffee Bar in Seattle, where freelance graphic designers and computer entrepreneurs work. Kayner was so irritated by her customers' noisy calls, she stuck a magnet on her espresso machine reading: "Your cell phone only makes you more annoying." Then someone stole it.

The basis of all good manners is the consideration of others, says etiquette expert Gloria Starr. For entrepreneurs using coffeehouses as offices, that means limiting your time at a table to an hour or two. It's also courteous to take cell phone calls outside or to cover the receiver with your hand so your conversation can't be heard. And if you're going to stay, it's polite to pay for your space by buying cups of joe. "You've got to feed the kitty," says David Story, an independent nonfiction TV producer in Los Angeles who works at his local Starbucks.

Life is not the way it's supposed to be. It's the way it is. The way you cope with it is what makes the difference.

Words of Wisdom

—VIRGINIA SATIR

But if you really want to be courtly, Peter Post, great-grandson of manners maven Emily Post, says you should only use coffeehouses as meeting places for cordial conversations with clients. In other words, don't make a public space your office, no matter how good the coffee is.

Source: Kelly Barron,
"Cup of Courtesy," Entrepreneur.com

> *The quality of a person's life is in direct proportion to their commitment to excellence, regardless of their chosen field of endeavor.*
>
> —VINCE LOMBARDI, FOOTBALL COACH

Words of Wisdom

LEAVING MESSAGES

If your phone calls don't always get returned, the problem may be with how you leave your messages. Here are some tips for leaving voice mail messages:

- Begin by stating your name, company, and telephone number—even if the person you're calling knows your number.
- Add the day, date, time, and time zone. Even though most voice-mail systems have an automatic time stamp, it's usually given before the message. People are more apt to hear it if you say it.
- Briefly explain the reason for your call. Do you need certain information? Are you calling to set up a meeting?
- If you are asking for a return call, say when you will be available. If you want information faxed or e-mailed, clearly state your fax number or e-mail address.
- Before hanging up, repeat your name and telephone number.
- Always speak clearly and slowly enough for the person listening to the message to take notes. Don't annoy people by forcing them to listen to your message several times to get all the information.

USE TRIAL LAWYERS' TECHNIQUES IN YOUR BUSINESS

When an attorney is in front of a jury, there's a lot at stake, which is why successful trial lawyers know how to purposely and effectively sway jurors. You can put the techniques they use to work in your own business. Noelle C. Nelson, Ph.D., author of *Winning! Using Lawyers' Courtroom Techniques to Get Your Way in Everyday Situations* (Prentice Hall), explains how:

- *Establish credibility with your employees.* Just as lawyers are careful to establish their credibility from the minute they walk through the door of the courtroom, you need to show your credibility with your employees by "walking your talk." Nelson says, "If you want your employees to be professional, come in on time, and respect certain ways of doing things, then you have to do that, too."
- *Make your employees your allies.* Certainly a trial is an adversarial situation, but the conflict

> *I destroy my enemies when I make them my friends.*
>
> —ABRAHAM LINCOLN

Words of Wisdom

is between the two sides, not between attorneys and juries. "Lawyers may point the finger all day at the other guy in court, but they sure don't do that to the jurors. Because the jurors are the ones who make the decision, not the other guy," says Nelson. "A lawyer works hard to create a relationship of trust with jurors, a feeling that we are in this together, we are allies. That's what you need to do with your employees." Approach issues from an allied position, Nelson advises. Don't surrender your authority, but put yourself on the same side as your employees. "Bring them together, and say, 'We have this project, we have this concern, we have a goal we need to accomplish. What's in the way?'" When they've identified the obstacles, they'll be ready to work on solutions.

- *Use a rousing theme.* Appeal to emotions with a theme that's relative to the issue; come up with a slogan or other appropriate message that will inspire people. "Make it specific to the issue, but something around which people can coalesce, look up to, and hold in their minds," Nelson says. "Rouse their hearts, then back it up with logic. The logic empowers people, and when they're empowered, they'll work hard."

But is it manipulative? Not at all, says Nelson. "Good lawyers aren't manipulative. They put it right out there for the jurors. They tell them what they want and why. There is no need to manipulate when you come from a position of strength and openness."

MIND YOUR E-MANNERS WITH PROPER E-MAIL ETIQUETTE

Are you using e-mail effectively and appropriately? These guidelines can help:

- Remember that an e-mail reader cannot hear your tone of voice or see your facial expressions and gestures. Write clearly, concisely, and in a manner that won't be open to misinterpretation.
- Keep your e-mail brief, preferably to one page.
- Return e-mails with the same promptness that you would return a telephone call.
- Use capitalization, punctuation, and grammar in the same way that you would in any other business document.
- Spell-check and proofread every e-mail before hitting "send."
- Write an appropriate and specific subject so the recipient knows what the e-mail is about before opening it.
- If you engage in a lengthy e-mail dialog and the subject changes, adjust your subject line accordingly.
- Write a salutation or greeting for each new subject e-mail. If you are exchanging several e-mails on the same topic, it is not necessary to include a greeting in each one; instead, treat it as though you were having a conversation— you wouldn't say "hello" each time you begin speaking.

- Remember that e-mails are public documents. Once you send an e-mail, you have no control over where it goes and who might see it, so never include anything in an e-mail that you would not want widely known.
- Don't send unnecessary attachments.
- If you are sending an attachment, title it in such a way that will make it easy for the recipient to recognize once it has been downloaded. In the content of your e-mail, explain why you are sending the attachment and what type of software was used to create it.
- Don't hit "reply all" unless it's essential that everyone on the initial distribution list see your reply.
- When sending a message to a large group of people, consider using the "blind copy" feature. This protects the privacy of the recipients by not revealing their e-mail addresses.
- Don't type in all caps; it means you're shouting.
- Don't type in all lower-case letters; you're not ee cummings.
- Include a signature line with your name, title, company, and telephone number so recipients know who you are and how to reach you.
- When replying to an e-mail, be sure to include a quote from the original message that can provide context for your response.
- Be careful with abbreviations and acronyms; if you're not absolutely certain your reader will understand them, spell things out.
- Avoid sending out junk e-mail—if an e-mail says to "forward this to everyone in your address book," don't.
- Never send an e-mail when you're upset or angry; wait until you've calmed down.
- Keep business e-mail on a business level—no jokes.

The value of a relationship is in direct proportion to the time that you invest in the relationship.

—Brian Tracy

YOUR MOTHER WAS RIGHT

Now that I'm older and a little wiser, I can't help but think about all the encouragement, support, and great advice my mom gave me that has helped me become a successful entrepreneur. Although she never started a company, my mother ran a tight ship for my siblings and me, and has managed an extended family as well as any CEO I've ever known.

Here are some valuable lessons she taught me that have helped me succeed in business today.

Watch Your Manners
Say please, write thank-you notes, and be polite. People notice and like being around you when you do these things, which is really important whether you're hiring a new team member or selling your product or service.

Dress for Success
Look the part. See what the movers and shakers are wearing for clues and find a style that suits you. My mom was a fashion-design major in college so this came much easier to her than to me, but you can never go wrong with a simple, classic style. When in doubt, err on the dressier, more professional side. You won't regret it.

YOUR MOTHER WAS RIGHT, continued

Do Your Homework

The best things in life are worth working hard for. There's no substitution for paying your dues. You have to learn the basics before things get interesting, so learn as much as you can as fast as you can because when you become the best at something is when the real fun begins.

Travel and Explore

Everyone in the world doesn't do things the same way you do. Open your mind and see a situation from another's perspective. Customs and norms are different in each culture, so understanding someone else's history adds texture and perspective you may have never considered before. Seeing different habits and practices can make you think more creatively about your own needs.

Be Financially Independent

Understand your finances and use your brain to figure out how to make a living while also making a difference. Don't spend money you don't have. Get in the habit of saving a little bit from every paycheck.

Reward Yourself

All work and no play is not a sustainable long-term strategy, so always make sure you leave time for some fun in your life. Take vacations; save room for dessert—life is short so enjoy something in every day.

Look Out for Others

As the oldest kid, it was my responsibility to make sure my siblings were safe and accounted for at all times. As an entrepreneur, you have people to watch out for as well: your customers, employees, partners, advisors, and other stakeholders. If you take care of them, they'll watch your back, too.

Respect Your Elders

You may not like those who came before you but you must show respect for their position. You can learn something from everyone (both positive and negative), so listen to their stories and learn from their experience.

My mom always told me I could be anything I put my mind to, and if that isn't great advice for an entrepreneur, I'm not sure what is. I'm certain there are important women in your life who have had great impact and influence on you and your career, so remember them and share those lessons generously as a tribute to them.

Source: Paige Arnof-Fenn, "Business Lessons from Mom,"
Entrepreneur.com

Too often we underestimate the power of a touch, a smile, a kind word, a listening ear, an honest compliment, or the smallest act of caring, all of which have the potential to turn a life around.
—LEO BUSCAGLIA, AUTHOR

Words of Wisdom

⚜ ⚜ ⚜

CHAPTER 6

Legal Structures and Taxes

YOUR COMPANY'S LEGAL STRUCTURE

One of the first decisions that you will have to make as a business owner is how the company should be structured. This decision will have long-term implications, so consult with an accountant and attorney to help you select the form of ownership that is right for you. Remember that your legal ownership structure is not the same as your operating structure. You may, for example, decide to form a corporation as your legal structure and still choose to run your day-to-day operations as a sole proprietor. In choosing your legal structure, you will want to take into account the following:

- Your vision regarding the size and nature of your business.
- The level of control you wish to have.
- The level of structure you are willing to deal with.

- The business's vulnerability to lawsuits.
- Tax implications of the different ownership structures.
- Expected profit (or loss) of the business.
- Whether or not you need to reinvest earnings into the business.
- Your personal need for access to cash from the business.

Sole Proprietorships

The vast majority of small businesses start out as sole proprietorships. Such firms are owned by one person—usually the individual who has day-to-day responsibilities for running the business. Sole proprietors own all the assets of the business and the profits generated by it. They also assume complete responsibility for any of its liabilities or debts. In the eyes of the law and the public, you are one and the same with the business.

Advantages of a sole proprietorship
- It is the easiest and least expensive form of ownership to organize.
- Sole proprietors are in complete control and, within the parameters of the law, may make decisions as they see fit.
- Sole proprietors receive all income generated by the business to keep or reinvest.
- Profits from the business flow directly to the owner's personal tax return.
- The business is easy to dissolve, if desired.

Disadvantages of a sole proprietorship
- Sole proprietors have unlimited liability and are legally responsible for all debts against the business. Their business and personal assets are at risk.
- A sole proprietorship may be at a disadvantage in raising funds and is often limited to using funds from personal savings or consumer loans.
- Sole proprietors may have a hard time attracting high-caliber employees or those that are motivated by the opportunity to own a part of the business.
- Some employee benefits, such as owner's medical insurance premiums are not directly deductible from business income (they are only partially deductible as an adjustment to income).

Federal tax forms for sole proprietorship
(This is only a partial list and some may not apply.)
- Form 1040: Individual Income Tax Return
- Schedule C: Profit or Loss from Business (or Schedule C-EZ)
- Schedule SE: Self-Employment Tax
- Form 1040-ES: Estimated Tax for Individuals
- Form 4562: Depreciation and Amortization
- Form 8829: Expenses for Business Use of Your Home
- Employment Tax Forms

Partnerships

In a partnership, two or more people share ownership of a single business. Like proprietorships, the law does not distinguish between the business and its owners. The partners should have a legal agreement that sets forth how decisions will be made, profits will be shared, disputes will be resolved, future partners will be admitted to the partnership, partners can be bought out, and what steps will be taken to dissolve the partnership when needed. Yes, it's hard to think about a breakup when the business is just getting started, but many partnerships split up at crisis times, and unless there is a defined process already in place, there will be even greater problems. Partners must also decide up-front how much time and capital each will contribute, etc.

Advantages of a partnership
- Partnerships are relatively easy to establish; however, time should be invested in developing the partnership agreement.
- With more than one owner, the ability to raise funds may be increased.
- The profits from the business flow directly through to the partners' personal tax returns.
- Prospective employees may be attracted to the business if given the incentive to become a partner.
- The business usually will benefit from partners who have complementary skills.

Disadvantages of a partnership
- Partners are jointly and individually liable for the actions of the other partners.
- Profits must be shared with others.

- Since decisions are shared, disagreements can occur.
- Some employee benefits are not deductible from business income on tax returns.
- The partnership may have a limited life; it may end upon the withdrawal or death of a partner.

Types of partnerships that should be considered

- General partnership. Partners divide responsibility for management and liability as well as the shares of profit or loss according to their internal agreement. Equal shares are assumed unless there is a written agreement that states differently.
- Limited partnership and partnership with limited liability. Limited means that most of the partners have limited liability (to the extent of their investment) as well as limited input regarding management decisions, which generally encourages investors for short-term projects or for investing in capital assets. This form of ownership is not often used for operating retail or service businesses. Forming a limited partnership is more complex and formal than that of a general partnership.
- Joint venture. Acts like a general partnership but is clearly for a limited period of time or a single project. If the partners in a joint venture repeat the activity, they will be recognized as an ongoing partnership and will have to file as such as well as distribute accumulated partnership assets upon dissolution of the entity.

Federal tax forms for partnerships

(This is only a partial list and some may not apply.)

- Form 1065: Partnership Return of Income
- Form 1065 K-1: Partner's Share of Income, Credit, Deductions
- Form 4562: Depreciation

- Form 1040: Individual Income Tax Return
- Schedule E: Supplemental Income and Loss
- Schedule SE: Self-Employment Tax
- Form 1040-ES: Estimated Tax for Individuals
- Employment Tax Forms

Corporations

A corporation chartered by the state in which it is headquartered is considered, by law, to be a unique entity, separate and apart from those who own it. A corporation can be taxed, it can be sued, and it can enter into contractual agreements. The owners of a corporation are its shareholders. The shareholders elect a board of directors to oversee the major policies and decisions. The corporation has a life of its own and does not dissolve when ownership changes.

Advantages of a corporation

- Shareholders have limited liability for the corporation's debts or judgments against the corporations.
- Generally, shareholders can only be held accountable for their investment in stock of the company. (Note, however, that officers can be held personally liable for their actions, such as the failure to withhold and pay employment taxes.)
- Corporations can raise additional funds through the sale of stock.
- A corporation may deduct the cost of benefits provided to officers and employees.
- A corporation can elect S corporation status if certain requirements are met. This enables the company to be taxed in a fashion similar to a partnership.

Disadvantages of a corporation

- The process of incorporation requires more time and money than other forms of organization.

- Corporations are monitored by federal, state, and some local agencies, and as a result may have to file more paperwork in order to comply with regulations.
- Incorporating may result in higher overall taxes. Dividends paid to shareholders are not deductible from business income; thus, they can be taxed twice.

Federal tax forms for regular or "C" corporations
(This is only a partial list and some may not apply.)
- Form 1120 or 1120-A: Corporation Income Tax Return
- Form 1120-W Estimated Tax for Corporation
- Form 8109-B Deposit Coupon
- Form 4625 Depreciation
- Employment Tax Forms
- Other forms as needed for capital gains, sale of assets, alternative minimum tax, etc.

Subchapter S Corporations

A tax election only, this enables the shareholder to treat earnings and profits as distributions and have them pass through directly to their personal tax return. The catch here is that the shareholder—if working for the company and if there is a profit—must pay him/herself wages, and must meet standards of "reasonable compensation." This can vary by geographical region as well as occupation, but the basic rule is to pay yourself what you would have to pay someone to do your job, as long as there is enough profit. If you do not do this, the IRS can reclassify all of the earnings and profit as wages, and you will be liable for all of the payroll taxes on the total amount.

Federal tax forms for subchapter S corporations
(This is only a partial list and some may not apply.)
- Form 1120S: Income Tax Return for S Corporation

- 1120S K-1: Shareholder's Share of Income, Credit, Deductions
- Form 4625: Depreciation
- Employment Tax Forms
- Form 1040: Individual Income Tax Return
- Schedule E: Supplemental Income and Loss
- Schedule SE: Self-Employment Tax
- Form 1040-ES: Estimated Tax for Individuals
- Other forms as needed for capital gains, sale of assets, alternative minimum tax, etc.

Limited Liability Company (LLC)

The LLC is a relatively new type of hybrid business structure that is now permissible in most states. It is designed to provide the limited liability features of a corporation and the tax efficiencies and operational flexibility of a partnership. Formation is more complex and formal than that of a general partnership.

The owners are members and the duration of the LLC is usually determined when the organization papers are filed. The time limit can be continued, if desired, by a vote of the members at the time of expiration. LLCs must not have more than two of the four characteristics that define corporations: Limited liability to the extent of assets; continuity of life; centralization of management; and transferability of ownership interests.

Federal tax forms for LLC
- Taxed as partnership in most cases; corporation forms must be used if there are more than two of the four corporate characteristics, as described above.

Source: Small Business Administration

In a general sense, all contributions imposed by the government upon individuals for the service of the state, are called taxes, by whatever name they may be known, whether by the name of tribute, tythe, tallage, impost, duty, gabel, custom, subsidy, aid, supply, excise, or other name.

*W*ords *of W*isdom

—JOSEPH STORY (COMMENTARIES ON THE CONSTITUTION, 1833)

KEEP PROFESSIONAL ADVICE IN PERSPECTIVE

Get good advice from professionals, but remember that this is *your* company and *you* make the decisions. "Don't let accountants and attorneys run your company," says Robert Kiyosaki, founder of the Rich Dad Family of Companies. Use their knowledge and guidance, but remember that in the end, the responsibility for your decisions rests with you and you alone.

BUSINESS TAXES

The form of business you operate determines what taxes you must pay and how you pay them. The four general types of business taxes are income tax, self-employment tax, employment taxes, and excise tax.

Income Tax

All businesses, except partnerships, must file an annual income tax return; partnerships file an information return. The form you use depends on how your business is organized.

The federal income tax is a pay-as-you-go tax. You must pay the tax as you earn or receive income during the year. An employee usually has income tax withheld from his or her pay. If you do not pay your tax through withholding, or do not pay enough tax that way, you might have to pay estimated tax. If you are not required to make estimated tax payments, you may pay any tax due when you file your return.

Self-Employment Tax

Self-employment tax (SE tax) is a social security and Medicare tax primarily for individuals who work for themselves. Your payments of SE tax contribute to your coverage under the social security system.

Social security coverage provides you with retirement benefits, disability benefits, survivor benefits, and hospital insurance (Medicare) benefits.

Generally, you must pay SE tax and file Schedule SE (Form 1040) if your net earnings from self-employment were $400 or more, or you work for a church or a qualified church-controlled organization (other than as a minister or member of a religious order) that elected an exemption from social security and Medicare taxes and you receive $108.28 or more in wages from the church or organization.

Employment Taxes

When you have employees, you have certain employment tax responsibilities that you must pay and forms you must file. Employment taxes include the following:

- Social security and Medicare taxes
- Federal income tax withholding
- Federal unemployment (FUTA) tax

Excise Tax

You may have to pay excise tax if you manufacture or sell certain products; operate certain kinds of business; use various kinds of equipment, facilities, or products; receive payment for certain services. Your tax advisor will be able to tell you if you are required to pay excise tax.

Source: Internal Revenue Service

TAX-DEDUCTIBLE BUSINESS EXPENSES

Business expenses are the cost of carrying on a trade or business. These expenses are usually deductible if the business is operated to make a profit.

What Can I Deduct?

To be deductible, a business expense must be both ordinary and necessary. An ordinary expense is one that is common and accepted in your trade or business. A necessary expense is one that is helpful and appropriate for your trade or business. An expense does not have to be indispensable to be considered necessary.

It is important to separate business expenses from the following:

- Expenses used to figure the cost of goods sold
- Capital expenses
- Personal expenses

Cost of Goods Sold

If your business manufactures products or purchases them for resale, you generally must value inventory at the beginning and end of each tax year to determine the cost of goods sold. Some of your expenses may be included in figuring the cost of goods sold. Cost of goods sold is deducted from your gross receipts to figure your gross profit for the year. If you include an expense in the cost of goods sold, you cannot deduct it again as a business expense.

The following are types of expenses that go into figuring the cost of goods sold.

- The cost of product or raw materials, including freight
- Storage
- Direct labor costs (including contributions to pensions or annuity plans) for workers who produce the products
- Factory overhead

Under the uniform capitalization rules, you must capitalize the direct costs and part of the indirect costs for certain production or resale activities. Indirect costs include rent, interest, taxes, storage, purchasing, processing, repackaging, handling, and administrative costs. This rule does not apply to personal property that you acquire for resale if your average annual gross receipts (or those of your predecessor) for the preceding three tax years are not more than $10 million.

Capital Expenses

You must capitalize, rather than deduct, some costs. These are a part of your investment in your business and are called capital expenses. Capital expenses are considered assets in your business. There are, in general, three types of costs you capitalize:

- Business start-up cost
- Business assets
- Improvements

Note: You can elect to deduct or amortize certain business start-up costs.

Personal versus Business Expenses

Generally, you cannot deduct personal, living, or family expenses. However, if you have an expense for something that is used partly for business and partly for personal purposes, divide the total cost between the business and personal parts; you can deduct the business part.

For example, if you borrow money and use 70 percent of it for business and the other 30 percent for a family vacation, you can deduct 70 percent of the interest as a business expense. The remaining 30 percent is personal interest and is not deductible.

Business Use of Your Home

If you use part of your home for business, you may be able to deduct expenses for the business use of your home. These expenses may include mortgage interest, insurance, utilities, repairs, and depreciation.

Business Use of Your Car

If you use your car in your business, you can deduct car expenses. If you use your car for both business and personal purposes, you must divide your expenses based on actual mileage.

Other Types of Business Expenses

- *Employees' pay.* You can generally deduct the pay you give your employees for the services they perform for your business.

- *Retirement plans.* Retirement plans are savings plans that offer you tax advantages to set aside money for your own, and your employees', retirement.

- *Rent expense.* Rent is any amount you pay for the use of property you do not own. In general, you can deduct rent as an expense only if the rent is for property you use in your trade or business. If you have or will receive equity in or title to the property, the rent is not deductible.

- *Interest.* Business interest expense is an amount charged for the use of money you borrowed for business activities.

- *Taxes.* You can deduct various federal, state, local, and foreign taxes directly attributable to your trade or business as business expenses.

- *Insurance.* Generally, you can deduct the ordinary and necessary cost of insurance as a business expense, if it is for your trade, business, or profession.

This list is not all-inclusive of business expenses that you can deduct. Check with your accountant, tax advisor, or the IRS for more information.

Source: Internal Revenue Service

Noah must have taken into the Ark two taxes, one male and one female. And did they multiply bountifully! Next to guinea pigs, taxes must have been the most prolific animals.

Words of Wisdom

—WILL ROGERS

STATE AND LOCAL TAXES

Every state levies some form of tax on small businesses, but some states levy little or no tax on some business structures (especially sole proprietorships). Local authorities may tax personal property like machinery, equipment, furniture, supplies, leased equipment, and even movable machinery used in a business. Some cities and municipalities also levy income taxes on any business operating within their borders.

To learn more about your state and local tax obligations, contact your state's department of revenue and your local county or municipality government.

A TAXING ALTERNATIVE

Politicians continue to struggle with alternatives to the current federal tax system. One for which support is growing is the FairTax Act, which would replace current federal taxes with a federal retail sales tax. Wages would no longer be subject to federal withholding and workers would take home 100 percent of their paychecks.

The FairTax would abolish all taxes on income and would repeal: individual income tax; alternative minimum tax (AMT); corporate and business income taxes; capital gains taxes; Social Security taxes; Medicare taxes; all other federal payroll taxes; self-employment tax; estate taxes; and gift taxes.

Under the FairTax, advocates say, the cost of goods and services will drop because the FairTax will remove embedded federal taxes and the cost

TAX-FAVORED HEALTH PLANS

As consumers take a more active role in health care choices and financing decisions, Congress has created tax-favored health plans that you may want to consider for yourself and/or your employees. When you check with your accountant to see what will work best in your operation, you can expect to hear one or more of these terms:

- *Health Savings Account (HSA).* A tax-advantaged medical savings account available to taxpayers who are enrolled in a high-deductible health plan.
- *Health Reimbursement Account (HRA).* A partially self-funded medical insurance plan with special tax advantages. Also called a Health Reimbursement Arrangement.

- *Medical Savings Account (MSA).* An account, generally associated with self-employed individuals, in which tax-deferred deposits can be made for medical expenses.
- *Flexible Spending Account (FSA).* A tax-advantaged account set up through an employer that allows companies to set aside a portion of their earnings to pay for qualified medical expenses (most commonly medical but often for dependent care and other expenses) as established in a cafeteria plan. Also called a Flexible Spending Arrangement.

A TAXING ALTERNATIVE

of managing and collecting them from prices. It's important to note that the FairTax would be levied against all new goods and services. Nothing will be exempt, and there will be no loopholes or special interest considerations—and everyone would be able to see exactly how much federal tax they pay with each purchase.

To protect low-income people, every taxpayer would receive a monthly "prebate" in an amount covering the amount of tax paid on the bare necessities of life. This means that no American will ever have to pay federal tax on essentials.

The FairTax would allow individuals and businesses to make financial decisions based on what's best for them without considering the tax consequences.

Millions of dollars previously spent on consulting with lawyers and accountants on tax strategies can instead be invested in economic growth. The millions of hours spent preparing tax returns can be used for more productive, or perhaps just more enjoyable, activities.

Finally, the FairTax would eliminate the so-called "underground" economy. Drug dealers, prostitutes, illegal aliens, and others who have avoided paying federal income tax would pay their fair share into the tax system through their retail purchases, as would the foreign tourists who come to the U.S. to shop and spend.

For more information about the FairTax, visit www.fairtax.org.

GLOSSARY OF TAX TERMS

Accelerated depreciation. A depreciation method that allows larger deductions in the early years of an asset's "life" and smaller deductions at the end of the period. (See "Straight-line depreciation.")

Accrual method (or accrual basis). One of two main accounting methods for determining when a transaction has tax significance. The accrual method says that a transaction is taxed when an obligation to pay or a right to receive payment is created (for example, at the time products are delivered, services rendered, billings sent, etc.). This method is used by all but the smallest of businesses. (See "Cash method" or "cash basis.")

Adjusted basis. The cost of property (or a substitute figure—see "Basis") with adjustments made to account for depreciation (in the case of business property), improvements (in the case of real estate), withdrawals or reinvestment (in the case of securities, funds, accounts, insurance, or annuities), etc. Adjusted basis is part of the computation for determining gain or loss on a sale or exchange and for depreciation.

Adjusted gross income. The amount of income considered actually "available" to be taxed. Adjusted gross income is gross income reduced principally by business expenses incurred to earn the income and other specified reductions (such as alimony).

Alternative minimum tax. An alternative tax system that says: your tax shall not go below this level. The alternative minimum tax works by negating (or minimizing) the effects of tax preferences or loopholes.

Amortization. The write-off of an amount spent for certain capital assets, similar to depreciation. This tax meaning is different from the common meaning of the term that describes, for example, payment schedules of loans.

Applicable Federal Rates (AFRs). Minimum interest rates that must be charged on various transactions that involve payments over a number of years. If the parties to a transaction do not adhere to these rates, the IRS will impute the interest. (See "Imputed interest.")

At-risk rules. Rules that limit an investor's deductible losses from an investment to the amount invested. Complications arise when investors finance their investment through loans for which they are not personally on the hook (nonrecourse financing). Without these rules, investors could raise their deduction limit considerably without being at risk for the actual loss.

Basis. The starting point for computing gain or loss on a sale or exchange of property or for depreciation. (See "Adjusted basis.") For property that is purchased, basis is its cost. The basis of inherited property is its value at the date of death (or alternative valuation date). The basis of property received as a gift or a nontaxable transaction is based on the adjusted basis of the transferor (with some adjustments). Special rules govern property transferred between corporations and their shareholders, partners and their partnership, etc.

Cafeteria plan. A plan maintained by an employer that allows employees to select from a menu of taxable and nontaxable benefits.

Capital expenditures. Amounts spent to acquire or improve assets with useful lives of more than one year. These expenditures may not be deducted but are added to the basis of the property (see "Adjusted basis") and, for business property, may be converted into deductions through depreciation or amortization.

Capital gain or loss. Gain or loss from the sale or exchange of investment property, personal property (such as a home), or other "capital asset," which is often entitled to preferential tax treatment.

Carrybacks and carryforwards. Deductions that may be transferred to a year other than the current year because they exceeded certain limits. These deductions are typically carried back to earlier years first and, if they exceed the limits for those years, are then carried forward to later years until the deduction is used up. Charitable contributions and net operating losses are examples of deductions that may be carried back or forward.

Cash method (or cash basis). One of two main accounting methods for determining when a transaction has tax significance. The cash method says that a transaction is taxed when payment is made. This method is used by most individuals. (See "Accrual method.")

Community property. A system governing spousal ownership of property and income that is the law in certain western and southern states and Wisconsin. The differences between community property and "common law" can change how federal tax law applies to spouses. For example: married taxpayers filing separately in a common law state do not have to report income earned by the other spouse. They do have to report income earned in a community property state.

Deferred compensation. An arrangement that allows an employee to receive part of a year's pay in a later year and not be taxed in the year the money was earned.

Depletion. A system similar to depreciation that allows the owner of natural resources (for example a coal mine or an oil well) to deduct a portion of the cost of the asset during each year of its presumed productive life.

Depreciation. A system that allows a business or individual to deduct a portion of the cost of an asset ("recover its cost") during each year of its predetermined "life" (or "recovery period").

Earned income. Income earned by working for it. Interest, dividends and other kinds of profits are examples of unearned income.

Earned income credit. A tax credit available to individuals with low earned income. An individual is entitled to the full amount of this credit even if it exceeds the amount of tax otherwise due.

Employee stock ownership plan (ESOP). A type of profit-sharing plan in which benefits come in the form of stock in the employer.

Estimated tax. Quarterly down payments on a year's taxes that are required (on April 15, June 15, September 15, and January 15) if the total year's taxes will exceed $1,000 and the amount is not covered by withholding.

Federal Insurance Contributions Act (FICA). Social security taxes (for both old-age, survivors, and disability insurance—OASDI—and Medicare).

Federal Unemployment Tax Act (FUTA). Unemployment taxes.

Filing status. One of four tax ranks determined by your marital status, your dependents, and the way you file your tax return: (1) single, (2) married filing jointly, (3) married filing separately, and (4) head of household. Filing status determines your tax rates and your eligibility for various tax benefits, such as alimony deduction, IRA deduction, standard deduction, etc.

First-in, first-out (FIFO). A rule that applies to the sale of part of a group of similar items (such as inventory, shares of the same stock, etc.) that assumes the first ones acquired were the first ones sold. This is important if the items in the group were acquired or manufactured at different times or for different costs. The rule may be overridden by identifying the specific item sold, if possible. (See "Last-in, first-out.")

Generation-skipping transfer tax. An extra tax on gifts or on-death transfers of money or property that would otherwise escape the once-per-generation transfer taxes that apply to gifts and estates. For example: a gift from a grandfather to a granddaughter skips a generation and might be subject to this tax.

Golden parachutes. Bonuses payable to key executives in the event control of their corporation changes, as in the case of a takeover. "Excess" golden parachute payments are subject to tax penalties.

Gross income. All income that might be subject to tax. Most "realized" increases in wealth are considered income. The main exceptions for individuals are gifts, inheritances, increases in value of property prior to sale, loan repayments, and some personal injury awards. For businesses, investments in their capital are not considered income.

Head of household. A filing status available to qualifying single parents (or others supporting certain dependents) that allows lower taxes than the normal rates for singles.

Imputed interest. A portion of a future payment that is treated as interest if parties to the transaction do not provide a stated amount of interest at a rate acceptable to the IRS. (See Applicable Federal Rates.) This prevents improper use of certain tax advantages (capital gains rates or tax deferral). For example: if a business sells an asset on the installment basis, part of all future payments is treated as interest whether the transaction states it or not.

Incentive stock option. A stock option that may be granted to an employee under tax-favored terms.

Itemized deductions. Personal deductions that may be taken if they total more than the standard deduction. (See "Standard deduction.") The following deductions are then itemized or listed on Schedule A of Form 1040: medical expenses, charitable contributions, state and local taxes, home mortgage interest, real estate taxes, casualty losses, unreimbursed employee expenses, investment expenses, and others.

Investment credit. A credit against tax available for investment in a limited range of business property. The general investment credit was repealed in 1986, but this type of credit has been enacted and repealed repeatedly throughout history.

Involuntary conversion. The conversion of property into money under circumstances beyond the control of the owner. For example: (1) property that is destroyed and "converted" into an insurance settlement, or (2) property that is seized by the government and "converted" into a condemnation award. Owners may avoid tax on any gain that may result (if the insurance settlement or condemnation award exceeds the adjusted basis of the property) by reinvesting in similar property within certain time limits.

Joint return. An optional filing status available to married taxpayers that offers generally (but not always) lower taxes than "married filing separately."

Keogh plan. A retirement plan available to self-employed individuals.

Last-in, first-out (LIFO). A rule that applies to the sale of part of a group of similar items in an inventory that assumes the last ones acquired were the first ones sold. This is important if the items in the group were acquired or manufactured at different times or for different costs. (See "First-in, first-out (FIFO).")

Like-kind exchanges. Tax-free swaps of investment property. Commonly used for real estate.

Limited liability company (LLC). A legal structure that allows a business to be taxed like a partnership but function generally like a corporation. An LLC offers members (among other things) protection against liability for claims against the business that is not available in a partnership.

Listed property. Property listed in the tax code or by the IRS that must comply with special rules before depreciation may be claimed. Cars and personal computers are examples of listed property. The special rules are designed to prevent deductions where the property is used for personal rather than business purposes.

Modified Accelerated Cost Recovery System (MACRS). The system for computing depreciation for most business assets.

Net operating loss. The excess of business expenses over income. A business may apply a net operating loss to get a refund of past taxes (or a reduction of future taxes) by carrying it back to profitable years as an additional deduction (or by carrying it forward as a deduction to future years).

Original issue discount (OID). The purchase discount offered on some bonds (and similar obligations) in lieu of interest. For example, zero-coupon bonds. OID is generally treated as interest income to the holder rather than as a capital gain.

Passive activity loss (PAL). Loss on an investment that is deductible only up to the limit of gains from similar investments. The limit mainly affects tax shelters and does not apply to stocks, bonds, or investments in businesses in which the investor materially participates. Special rules apply to investments in real estate.

Qualified plan. A retirement or profit-sharing plan that meets requirements about who must be covered, the amount of benefits that are paid, information that must be given to plan participants, etc. Qualified plans are entitled to tax benefits unavailable to nonqualified plans.

Real estate investment trust (REIT). A kind of "mutual fund" that invests in real estate rather than stocks and bonds.

Real estate mortgage investment conduit (REMIC). A kind of "mutual fund" that invests in real estate mortgages rather than stocks and bonds.

Recapture. The undoing of a tax benefit if certain requirements are not met in future years. For example: (1) The low-income housing credit may be recaptured or added back to tax if the credit property ceases to be used as low-income housing for a minimum number of years. (2) The alimony deduction may be retroactively lost or recaptured if payments do not continue at the requisite level for a minimum number of years.

Regulated investment company (RIC). A mutual fund.

Rollover. The tax-free termination of one investment and reinvestment of the proceeds. For example: An individual may roll over a lump-sum distribution from an employer's retirement plan into an IRA.

S corporation. A corporation with no more than 35 shareholders that is not taxed, but treated similarly to a partnership, if other requirements are met.

Savings Incentive Match Plan for Employees (SIMPLE plans). A simplified retirement arrangement for small businesses that comes in two varieties: one similar to a 401(k) plan and one that funds IRAs for employees.

Standard deduction. A deduction allowed to individuals instead of listing or itemizing deductible personal expenses. (See "Itemized deductions.") The amount depends on the individual's filing status. Additional amounts are available for taxpayers who are blind or are age 65 or over. Individuals may deduct either their standard deduction or the total of their itemized deductions, whichever is greater.

Straight-line depreciation. A depreciation method that allows equal deductions in each year of an asset's "life" or recovery period. (See "Accelerated depreciation.")

Swaps, tax-free. (1) Exchanges of like-kind property that result in no capital gains tax (commonly used for real estate). (2) Sales and repurchases of stock (or other securities) designed to realize a tax loss without discontinuing the investment. Transactions must comply with the wash sale rules to be effective. (See "Wash sales.")

Taxable income. What is left after all deductions are taken. This is the amount upon which tax is computed.

Taxpayer identification number (TIN). In the case of an individual, the Social Security number. In the case of a business (even an individual in business), the employer identification number.

Top-heavy plan. An employee retirement or profit-sharing plan that disproportionately benefits top executives.

Uniform capitalization rules (Unicap). A set of uniform rules for computing the cost of goods produced by a business that prevents current deductions for costs that must be capitalized (see "Capital expenditures") or added to inventory.

Wash sales. Simultaneous or near-simultaneous purchases and sales of the same property—usually stocks or bonds—made to generate deductible tax losses without discontinuing the investment. Losses on such transactions are ignored for tax purposes, unless a 30-day waiting period is observed between them.

Withholding allowances. Adjustments made to assure correct withholding on wages for individuals who may have unusually large deductions or who may be subject to other special circumstances.

Source: CCH Inc., Entrepreneur.com

❧ ❧ ❧

CHAPTER 7

Financial Management

KNOW THE NUMBERS

What are the most important numbers for every emerging business owner to know? Keep your eyes on these numbers to best manage the financial side of your business:

Working capital

Working capital is capital you have available to work with today. This is determined by subtracting current liabilities from current assets. A rule of thumb says you should have $1.50 to $2 of current assets for every $1 of current liabilities.

Revenues

Know your sales on a monthly, quarterly, and year-to-date basis. Compare these to your plan to see if you are behind or ahead.

Gross profit

Revenues less the direct costs of producing your product is your gross profit. In most cases, there should be 50 percent or more of your sales volume left over after you subtract your direct costs (cost of goods sold).

Profit margin

Subtract the total of your general and administrative expenses from your gross profit, then divide that number by your sales. This will tell you how profitable the business is. If the number is negative, you are losing money. Make sure the number is as good as or better than others in your industry. If the typical profit margin in your industry is 12 percent and yours is 5 percent, you are not managing your business as well as your competitors. Find out what you need to do to improve that margin.

General and administrative expenses

There are typically three biggies over which the business owner has a great deal of control. Know these numbers, and be prepared to adjust them to the current business environment. They are:

- *Compensation.* This is often one of the largest expenses for any business. When business slows, you need to be positioned to reduce compensation quickly and decisively. This isn't always fun, but it's a decision that a business owner who knows the numbers must make.

- *Marketing expenses.* The largest marketing expense is often advertising. You should be able to turn up or slow down your sales by adjusting your advertising expenditures. If there does not appear to be a correlation between advertising and sales, then there may be something wrong with your advertising strategy. The important point is that if you do not compare your advertising expenses and sales, how will you know the effectiveness of your advertising?

- *Research and development.* R&D effectiveness is not as easy to quantify as advertising. However, the savvy manager sets a budget based on anticipated costs necessary to achieve a certain goal. Be certain to periodically measure your progress by comparing the amount spent with the proximity to the goal. Like compensation and marketing, this is a variable number that must be monitored and adjusted quickly to meet current needs.

Source: Bill Fiduccia, "Know Your Numbers," Entrepreneur.com

RAISE PRICES WITHOUT LOSING CUSTOMERS

Price increases are never pleasant, but they are often the only way to maintain profitability when your expenses go up. Ease customers into your new pricing structure to make it as palatable as possible. Let them know that gradual increases are necessary for you to cover your costs, and that those increases will be reflected in future orders.

It's a good idea to avoid across-the-board price hikes. Increasing everything by the same amount at the same time can have a jarring impact on customers. Stagger the increases for a softer reaction.

If possible, don't raise prices to all customers all at once. First increase prices to your least-profitable customers. If you lose one of those accounts, you'll probably be better off; take it as an opportunity to find a new, more profitable buyer.

Even if you lose a better account because of higher prices, keep two points in mind: First, chances are your competitors are charging similar rates, so there's an excellent possibility those customers will come back. Second, the only way for your own company to grow and thrive is for your business to be profitable.

GREAT ADVICE

Remember the concept of perceived value and make it a policy to always get paid what you're worth. You may be tempted to offer a deep discount to a new client or as a favor to someone who can't afford your regular prices. If you are willing to charge so little for your work, why should the receiver value it any higher than you do? And why should they be willing to pay more later? The only exception is when you are clearly donating your products or services to a bona fide charity.

ACCOUNTING SYSTEM BASIS: CASH OR ACCRUAL?

Cash basis means that you show income when money is actually received. A credit sale will show up only when the cash comes in. On the other side, expenses are shown only when they are paid, not when they are incurred.

Accrual basis refers to the system that recognizes income as soon as it is earned, whether it is received or not, and expenses at the time they are incurred, whether they are paid or not. All obligations, including taxes, will be accounted for.

Most businesses use accrual basis accounting because, with only a few exceptions, the reports you generate will give you a more accurate view of how the company is doing.

Source: Suzanne Caplan, Second Wind: Turnaround Strategies for Business Revival *(Entrepreneur Press)*

Evaluation of the past is the first step toward vision for the future.
—CHRIS WIDENER

FIVE COMMON BUDGETING MISTAKES

1. Overstating projections.
Enron was not the first company to over-promise and under-deliver, and unfortunately, it won't be the last. Investors are occasionally fooled by numbers in the short term, but in the end the funded company almost always gets hurt. Realistic budgets and projections may lengthen your search for funding, but when the money does arrive, it will be honest money, and you should then have a profitable plan to follow for several years to come.

2. Ignoring your immediate budgetary needs.
On the other hand, if your plan shows that you need $50,000 to take a product to market, don't ask for only $30,000. Potential investors and bankers will only wonder why they should give you money for a project that will fail without additional funding. This was the sad lesson of the dotcom bubble. Companies burned through their initial seed money without coming close to profitability and then gave up. Investors have become more savvy and would rather spend $50,000 in a smart fashion than throw $30,000 out the window.

3. Assuming that the existence of revenue is indicative of being cash-flow positive.
In virtually every transaction, there is a lag time between the finalization of the deal and the completed cash collection. This is a fact of business and should not be a problem, assuming you are prepared. Unfortunately, many businesses are not prepared and run into serious cash-flow problems because they spend money they don't yet have. Perhaps what's most troubling is many of these purchases could easily have been delayed for 30 days, when the available money is finally in the bank. A

little wisdom, discretion, and foresight can go a long way toward corporate survival.

4. Forgetting about Uncle Sam.

End-of-the-day balances can often appear larger than they really are. Sales tax on revenues and employee withholdings may sit in your account temporarily but will ultimately be owed to the government. Your balance sheets should not count these finances as holdings, otherwise you run the risk of budgeting for future projects and costs that you will not be able to afford.

5. Mismanaging the advertising timeline.

It seems so elementary: advertising leads to sales. However, many budgets show advertising costs as a percentage of sales in the same period. To be truly effective, an advertising/marketing campaign will have to be initiated at least one period before sales can be expected. When the additional out-of-pocket costs are taken into account, a healthy advertising budget is needed before any revenue can be assumed. Failure to budget the appropriate items in a strategic time frame will under-utilize finances needed to achieve these sales goals and can lead to overspending in later months.

Source: Ian Benoliel, "5 Common Budgeting Mistakes,"
Entrepreneur.com

Words of Wisdom

"My other piece of advice, Copperfield," said Mr. Micawber, "you know. Annual income twenty pounds, annual expenditure nineteen six, result happiness. Annual income twenty pounds, annual expenditure twenty pounds ought and six, result misery."

—CHARLES DICKENS, *DAVID COPPERFIELD*

TOP TEN FINANCE TERMS ENTREPRENEURS NEED TO KNOW

1. Return on investment (ROI)

The only way to think about your business is with an ROI perspective. The entrepreneur has committed capital investment into a certain combination of assets, from which the company generates sales. Those sales cover the costs of operations and hopefully produce a profit. That profit, divided by the total funds invested in the company (the assets), equals the ROI to the entrepreneur. Think of it this way: Would you work all those hours and take on all that responsibility if your ROI was only 6 percent annually? The stronger the profit picture compared to the total funds employed in the enterprise, the higher the ROI.

2. Internal rate of return (IRR)

Every decision enacted by the entrepreneur must be viewed in terms of its internally generated return to the company. Unlike the simple division used to find the ROI, the IRR compares the net expected returns over the useful life of a project being reviewed by management to the funds spent on that decision (or project). All projects must meet a certain IRR in order to be acceptable for investment by the company. If a project cannot meet a minimum IRR, then don't invest in it.

3. Fixed asset base

This is the long-term base of the company's operation strategy, represented by all the equipment, machinery, vehicles, facilities, IT infrastructure, and long-term contracts in which the firm has invested to conduct business. From a finance perspective, these assets are the revenue generators. When the entrepreneur decides to invest in a certain fixed-asset configuration, that becomes the base from which the company functions week in and week out, doing business and serving its customers.

4. Working capital

Current assets are those short-term funds represented by cash in the bank; funds parked in near-term instruments earning interest; funds tied up in inventory; all those accounts receivable waiting to be collected. Subtracting the company's current liabilities from these current assets shows how much working capital (your firm's truest measure of liquidity) is on hand and your ability to pay for decisions in the short term. For example, if the firm has $500,000 in current assets and $350,000 in current liabilities, then $150,000 is free and clear as working capital, available for spending on new things as needed by the company.

5. Cost of capital

This is the true cost of securing the funds that the business uses to pay for its asset base. Some funds are from debt (less risky to the creditors, so it has a lower cost of capital to the firm), and some funds come from equity (more risky to the investors, so these have a higher cost of capital). The combination of lower-cost debt capital with higher-cost equity capital produces the next item in this list.

6. Weighted average (between debt and equity) cost of capital (WACC)

This is the firm's true annual cost to obtain and hold on to the combination of debt and equity that pays for the fixed-asset base. Every time the owners contemplate investing in a new project, the IRR for that project must be at least equal to the WACC of the funds used to do that project, otherwise it makes no sense taking on that new project, because its return cannot even cover the cost of the capital employed to make the project happen.

7. Risk premium

Entrepreneurs must understand that every decision they consider has an inherent level of risk associated with it. If project A is far riskier than project B, there should be a clear risk premium that could accrue to the firm if project A is enacted. But with that risk premium return, there will also be a risk premium cost to the company for the use of the funds. Business owners always have to decide whether the risk premium of additional potential return is commensurate with the additional risk costs that come with doing that investment project.

8. Systematic risk

Some risks facing the company are not unique to that business in that market, but are faced by all firms operating in the broader, general marketplace. These so-called "systematic" risks (such as changes in interest rate levels, the performance and direction of the U.S. economy or the availability of certain types of skilled labor) cannot be avoided.

9. Nonsystematic risk

The risks that are entirely unique to your company—products, buyers, promotional programs, billing, pricing, IT system—and so on are nonsystematic risks specific to your firm. Although there's little you can do to avoid or mitigate exposure to systematic risk, it is possible to use various diversification strategies to offset risks unique to your business. When working with risk premium—systematic risk and nonsystematic risk—the rule is that the expected return on the business operations will always be directly related to the amount of risk taken on: Lower risk decisions come with lower expected returns; higher risk decisions come with higher expected returns.

10. Option premium

A "call" is an option to buy something at a future date; a "put" is an option to sell something at a future date. On virtually every partnership contract, vendor deal, distributor arrangement, equipment lease or financing, personnel hire, and investment decision, there will likely be some kind of option offered to one party by the other. Entrepreneurs must always place a dollar value on any option premium they offer or have offered to them in these various deals. The value of having an option to either buy or sell, agree or disagree, accept certain terms or let them expire, should always be determined prior to signing any deal or contract or term sheet, and that value should always be treated as a tangible benefit when negotiating decisions with parties inside and outside the firm.

Source: David Newton, "Top 10 Finance Terms,"
Entrepreneur.com

WHAT A BANKER WILL WANT TO KNOW WHEN YOU APPLY FOR A LOAN

- Can the business repay the loan? (Is cash flow greater than debt service?)

- Can you repay the loan if the business fails? (Is collateral sufficient to repay the loan?)

- Does the business collect its bills?

- Does the business control its inventory?

- Does the business pay its bills?

- Are the officers committed to the business?

- Does the business have a profitable operating history?

- Does the business match its sources and uses of funds?

- Are sales growing?

- Does the business control expenses?

- Are profits increasing as a percentage of sales?

- Is there any discretionary cash flow?

- What is the future of the industry?

- Who is your competition and what are their strengths and weaknesses?

Source: Small Business Administration

❧ ❧ ❧

CHAPTER 8

Cash Flow Management

THE DIFFERENCE BETWEEN CASH FLOW AND PROFIT

Cash flow is your pattern of income and expenses typically measured over a given period and calculated after taxes and other disbursements. Profit is your return after all operating expenses have been met. One is tactical, the other is strategic. Both are essential, but cash flow is more important in terms of the short-term management of the business because, without cash in hand, the business will stop functioning.

SIX STEPS TO INCREASE CASH FLOW

1. Increase collection activity
2. Solicit advances on big jobs
3. Slow down payables
4. Draw on credit lines
5. Sell excess inventory
6. Decrease expenses using barter instead of cash payments

Source: Suzanne Caplan, Second Wind: Turnaround Strategies for Business Revival

CASH MANAGEMENT TOOLS

What's the secret to maintaining strong, positive cash flow? There isn't one. All it really takes is an awareness of effective techniques and consistent attention to detail. Try some of these cash flow management tools:

- *Sweep account.* This banking service lets you earn the maximum interest on all the money in your accounts, even if it's just overnight, without penalties or concerns about bouncing checks. The system is set up so funds are automatically moved—or swept—in and out of the appropriate accounts each day.
- *Lockbox.* Another bank service, a lockbox, works like this: your customers mail their payments to a post office box,

which your bank rents in your company's name. The bank sends a courier several times a day to clear out the box, checks are immediately deposited into your account—literally within hours of their arrival in the mail—and you get a report outlining all the transactions in as much detail as you want, as frequently as you want. You not only get your deposits made faster, you save the labor of having someone on your staff open envelopes, sort checks, and make the deposit.

- *Electronic payments.* Talk to your bank about the various options for accepting electronic payments. As technology advances, the available methods for electronic funds-transfer increase.
- *Establish and enforce payment terms.* Indicate the payment due date clearly and prominently on your invoice, and follow up immediately when payments aren't received on time. If your terms include a late fee, be sure to charge it.
- *Talk to your customers.* Ask what you can do to ensure prompt payment; that may include confirming the correct billing address and finding out what documentation may be required to help the customer determine the validity of the invoice. Keep in mind that many large companies pay certain types of invoices on certain days of the month; find out if your customers do that, and schedule your invoices to arrive in time for the next payment cycle.
- *Don't pay until you have to.* Unless there's an incentive to pay early, take the full term of the agreement—but don't pay late.

IMPROVE YOUR CASH FLOW

These tips can improve your cash flow:

1. Require a down payment on projects so that your customers fund the project, not you.

2. Set your terms to be payment in full upon completion. Don't extend out 30 or 60 days after you've completed your work. You don't get to use your hard-earned cash until payment is received from your clients, so get it as soon as you can.

3. Negotiate terms with your vendors for 30 days or more so you have an opportunity to complete the work, bill your customers, and receive payments prior to paying your vendor.

4. Have a collection process in place and follow through. When your customers delay payments, they're using your cash. You need to ensure that you're being diligent in collecting from your customers.

5. Set up a line of credit at your bank that you can use in case of emergency. Often lenders rates will be less than the late fees your vendors will charge. This line of credit will help you cover a lapse in cash flow for short periods of time.

6. Factoring of your receivables allows you to sell your receivables and get cash now instead of waiting 30 or 60 days. There's a fee for using a factoring service, so you need to ensure that the benefits of getting cash today exceeds the cost you'll pay for the expedience.

7. Minimize the amount of personal draws you take from your business. Each dollar you take from your company reduces the amount of cash flow you'll have available for the business to grow.

Source: Pam Newman, "7 Tips for Improving Your Cash Flow,"
Entrepreneur.com

WHEN YOU'RE STRAPPED FOR CASH

Talk to your bank.

It is in your bank's best interest for you to grow and be successful. You've seen the commercials about low-interest credit lines and free advice. They offer them for a reason, and it's to keep their customers afloat and happy. If you think your bank's not being accommodating enough, don't be afraid to look around. In most cities, there are probably at least five other banks that would love your business.

Incentivize your customers.

One of the hardest parts of running a business is getting your customers to pay on time. Unfortunately, too often they don't, and that can leave you very prone to a crunch. However, if you incentivize customers, not only do you increase your chances for getting paid on time, but you might even get paid early. For example, customers are usually given a 30-day grace period to pay a bill. However, what if a company were to offer an additional 2 percent off a future purchase for any customer who pays their bills within 10 days? The customer receives a discount for simply paying a bill that they were going to have to pay anyway. Meanwhile, not only does the company get paid, but it gets paid early—which helps to ensure positive cash-flow continuity and perhaps an additional 20 days of interest on capital. Furthermore, assuming the service was satisfactory, the 2 percent discount should incentivize the customer to purchase from the company again.

Sell and lease-back owned assets.

This is a trick that many companies utilize to survive a short-term cash crunch. They sell some of the assets they own outright and then immediately arrange to lease them back. This is almost the corporate equivalent to refinancing a home and can be coordinated through a bank or leasing company. The company receives what amounts to a favorable loan with a better payment structure while effectively retaining all their assets in a rather simple, painless manner.

Clear out excess inventory and unused equipment.

Take a look around and clean out your storage rooms. Guaranteed there are valuable, working products in your company's possession that are rarely, if ever, being used. With the internet, it has never been easier to find a willing buyer and receive immediate cash for a piece of equipment that is not benefiting your production in the least.

Don't panic.

Virtually all successful companies are destined to go through a crunch at one point or another. It is how they handle the crunch that separates the survivors from the might-have-beens. Take a deep breath and assess the situation, then review all your options and make a plan. A clear focus can go a long way toward crunching the crunch.

Source: Ian Benoliel, "Crunching the Cash Crunch,"
Entrepreneur.com

> *Words of Wisdom*
>
> *Cash flow is king—above and beyond profits. One of my professors in college spent about three days explaining the hows and whys of how cash flow, not profit, is what keeps a company running. We saw many detailed studies of how companies can run for extended periods of time not making any money as long as they have cash flow, and with skill, determination, and some luck, they return to being profitable.*
>
> —MICHAEL JANSMA, PRESIDENT, GEMAFFAIR.COM

❧ ❧ ❧

CHAPTER 9

Credit and Collections

WHY YOU SHOULD EXTEND CREDIT

Extending credit works in your favor in many ways.

- It increases customer loyalty.
- If you have credit applications for new customers to fill out, they know you plan to be around for a while and that you are interested in your customers. They feel like getting credit is a favor you do for them and they like that idea.
- It shows your business as financially stable; it tells your customers that you care and are serious about your money, success clientele, and future.
- It increases your sales, and therefore, your bottom line.
- Studies show customers will purchase more if they can pay later.
- It shows you are serious and smart about your business.
- You are not desperate, otherwise you would extend credit to anyone who walked in your door.

- It allows you to expand your customer base.
- Customers who are happy with your terms will tell other people about you. Word-of-mouth advertising is the best and cheapest advertising there is. Offer incentives or discounts for referrals of other credit-approved customers.
- It shows good customer service.
- It shows you are interested in your customers and want to help them by offering sales and discounts and a credit limit so they can buy more now and pay later.

Why Your Customers Want You to Extend Credit

- It is convenient—they can write one check a month, rather than every time they order something from you.
- They may not have the money right now but will soon and need your service or product now. We live in a world of "I

want it now." Credit allows us to fulfill this need.

- They feel it makes them an "official" customer. They go through a process to get credit from you, you know personal financial information about them, and you created an account for them in your computer. They also will feel that if they are not happy with something—such as customer service, delivery, or quality—they can withhold payment until the issue is resolved. They will believe themselves a valued customer to whom you will listen if they have an issue.
- It creates a paper trail.
- It delivers a message of value: when you extend credit, you extend faith in your customer.

Source: Entrepreneur Magazine's Ultimate Credit and Collections Handbook: The Check Is in the Mail! *by Michelle Dunn (Entrepreneur Press, 2006)*

EQUAL CREDIT OPPORTUNITY ACT: YOU CAN'T JUST SAY NO

If you deny credit to another business, you must follow certain federal guidelines when you tell them of your decision. The provisions of the Equal Credit Opportunity Act (ECOA) became mandatory for business creditors in 1990, and are designed to protect businesses from illegal credit discrimination.

Within 30 days, you must provide notice to an applicant who is denied credit. The notice must contain a statement of the action taken; the specific reason for the denial of credit; the name and address of the creditor; a copy of ECOA Notice 701(a), along with the name and address of the federal agency that administers compliance. Consider drafting a standard letter that includes these points, with the reasons listed with check boxes.

Some specific reasons for the denial of credit may include delinquent credit obligations; the need for additional references; unfavorable trade references; the inability to verify references. Do not cite your own internal company standards and policies or the applicant's failure to achieve a qualifying score on your scoring system as specific reasons for the adverse action.

You must maintain records on applicants for up to a year, depending on the size of their company and whether or not they have requested additional information from you about your decision. For complete information on your rights and obligations as both a business creditor and borrower, contact the Federal Trade Commission, www.ftc.gov

Text of ECOA Notice 701(a):

The Federal Equal Credit Opportunity Act prohibits creditors from discriminating against credit applications on the basis of race, color, religion, national origin, sex, marital status, age (provided the applicant has the capacity to contract); because all or part of the applicant's income derives from any public assistance program; or because the applicant has, in good faith, exercised any right under the Consumer Credit Protection Act. The federal agency that administers compliance with this law concerning this creditor is the Federal Trade Commission, Equal Credit Opportunity, Washington, DC 20580.

TIPS FOR IMPROVING YOUR COLLECTIONS PROCEDURES

- Explain your credit policy and/or terms of payment at the very beginning, before a customer actually becomes a customer. When payment is overdue, reiterate your policy.
- Always ask for payment when it is justly due.
- Never extend credit to a new customer without obtaining a complete credit application and going through your credit approval process.

- Once credit is extended, maintain accurate records on each account's payment history.
- Adhere to your collection policies no matter what. No exceptions.
- Keep current with trade reports pertaining to specific companies and industries so that you can spot potential collection problems before they become major issues.
- Change your collection letters frequently. Make them stronger and more action-oriented.
- Discourage payments on account or changes in payment terms. Too many payment plans or changed payment terms can impair your cash flow.
- When you receive payments "on account" be sure to follow up right away with a letter or phone call thanking the customer for the payment and stating the new balance and the date the next payment is due. Don't ask when the payment will be sent; *tell* the customer when to send it.
- On large accounts, call or send a reminder just a few days after terms if the account becomes delinquent.
- When making collection calls, ask to speak to a manager or owner rather than speaking to a secretary or receptionist. You should have this information on the credit application.
- If a customer disputes the quality of merchandise or service, price, or delivery, resolve the situation as quickly as possible. Insist that the portion of the bill not in dispute be paid while you are working out the problem.
- When all else has failed, refer the account to an outside collection agency. Yes, they keep a percentage of the amount they collect, but something is better than nothing.
- Update your records often (at least once a year) to be sure the telephone numbers, addresses, and contacts you have for your customers are current.

Source: Adapted from Michelle Dunn, "Debt Collection Tips," Entrepreneur.com

COMMON DEBT COLLECTION ERRORS

Avoid making these common mistakes when collecting on past due accounts:

- Not checking customers' credit history before extending credit.
- Not getting a credit application, agreement, or contract in writing and signed.
- Not being familiar with the Fair Debt Collection Practices Act (FDCPA) and unintentionally "harassing" a debtor.
- Overlooking small balances.
- Not asking for the money that is owed because you hate asking for money.
- Not knowing when it is the right time to turn a debt over to a collection agency.
- Not having a credit policy in place and enforcing it.
- Extending credit to anyone who walks in the door or calls on the phone because they "sound like they will pay."
- Not taking action on NSF notices or bad checks.
- Not using letters and forms to collect on past due accounts.
- Not having a credit application.
- Not pulling credit reports and checking references.
- Not understanding how to communicate with customers so they stay current.
- Not having a budget and controlling cash flow.
- Not knowing how to effectively do business online.
- Not using small claims court to your advantage.

- Not using discounts and incentives to persuade customers to pay early.
- Not educating yourselves with online resources and networking groups.
- Not understanding how a collection agency can work for you.
- Not knowing how to set up realistic payment arrangements with customers.
- Not knowing what to do if a customer dies or files for bankruptcy.
- Not training yourself or your staff.
- Waiting too long to use a collection agency.

Source: Michelle Dunn, "Debt Collection Tips,"
Entrepreneur.com

EVERY YEAR . . .

- 20 percent of business addresses will change
- 21 percent of CEOs will change
- 18 percent of telephone numbers will change

Source: Dun & Bradstreet

TIPS FOR COLLECTING MONEY

- Don't feel guilty asking for the money unless you like working for free.
- Develop a credit policy or "payment rules."
- Keep on top of late payers.
- Hire a credit manager or outsource your accounts receivables if you cannot do it yourself.
- Contact customers immediately if they become past due.
- Set up payment plans on the full amount due.
- Be firm and don't accept excuses.
- Be professional.

Source: Entrepreneur Magazine's Ultimate Credit and Collections Handbook: The Check Is in the Mail! *by Michelle Dunn (Entrepreneur Press, 2006)*

GUIDELINES FOR ACCEPTING CHECKS

Most business owners accept checks as a form of payment. Remember, taking a check is a courtesy you extend to your customer. You are not obligated to take a check if you don't feel it is in your best interest. Use these tips to help you avoid receiving bad checks:

- Make sure name, address, and phone number are imprinted on the check.
- Use the current date only (no post-dated checks).
- Compare an ID picture with that of the person cashing or writing the check.
- Make sure the signature matches the ID signature.
- Make sure the phone number is a working phone.
- Ask for a street address—do not accept checks with imprinted post office box numbers.
- Don't let the check writer rush you.
- Don't take any check, or person, for granted; *always* obtain proper ID.
- Don't accept pre-written personal checks. At least the signature should be written in your presence.
- Don't accept unsigned checks.
- Don't accept starter checks.
- Don't accept two-party checks.

You can accept checks in person, by mail, over the phone, by fax, or online. Check with your bank to see if they offer any program you can use, or visit www.checkman.com. You can order special checks from them and print the checks for deposit into your bank account.

Source: Entrepreneur Magazine's Ultimate Credit and Collections Handbook: The Check Is in the Mail! *by Michelle Dunn (Entrepreneur Press, 2006)*

BILL IN SYNC WITH YOUR CUSTOMERS' PAYABLE PROCEDURES

A simple, but often overlooked, technique for improving cash flow is to coordinate your billing system with your customers' payable procedures. Submitting your invoices at the right time with complete information will often speed up payment, particularly with larger companies. Consider these tips:

- When setting up a new account, find out what the company's payment procedures are. Ask what you can do to ensure prompt payment. Remember that if you are a sole proprietor, you will need to complete a W-9 for tax purposes.

- Be sure your invoice is easy to read and includes all necessary information. Clearly identify your products and services, your terms, where to send payment, and indicate any customer reference, such as a purchase order, that will help the accounts payable department determine the validity of your invoice.

- If you are billing on a retainer, find out when checks for your type of services are written, and time your invoices to arrive shortly before that date. Often large companies have particular days of the month when checks are written for certain types of payables. If you miss their cycle, you may have to wait weeks or another full month to get paid.

- Be sure you are sending your invoice to the correct person and location. Some companies, for example, may require the purchaser to approve invoices; others may pay faster if your bill goes straight to accounting.

- If possible, bill on delivery of the product or service. That's when the appreciation of your work is highest. When they're thinking about you in a positive way, they're more likely to process your invoice faster.

PHOTOCOPY CHECKS BEFORE YOU DEPOSIT THEM

"Collecting past-due accounts can be a nightmare, but you can increase your chances of getting what's due you if you photocopy checks before you deposit them," says Ron Z. Opher, a collection attorney in Philadelphia, Pennsylvania.

"Many accounts that end up in collection have some past payment history," Opher says. "If we had the bank name and account information, we would dramatically increase recovery in the post-judgment phase."

Do you need to copy every check you receive? No, says Opher, just do it often enough to maintain current information on each customer. "At the outset, you don't know who will pay or who won't in the long run, so it's always a good idea to record the bank information at first payment, and then review it upon subsequent payments for any changes."

GREAT ADVICE

If you're extending credit to a small business that's incorporated or a partnership or LLC, have the owner(s) personally guarantee the obligation. This means that if the business fails to pay, you can collect from the owner. If the owner is reluctant to make a personal guarantee, you may want to reconsider your decision to extend credit. Also, consider this: if the business does run into cash flow problems, it's likely that the debts the owner will try to pay first are the ones for which his personal assets are on the line.

WHEN A CUSTOMER DECLARES BANKRUPTCY

It's a legal notice every business owner dreads: a customer has filed bankruptcy, owing you money. What should you do, and what can you expect?

First, stop all collection activities. "The automatic stay [which is essentially a federal injunction that prohibits collection efforts while the case is pending] descends like an iron curtain and operates as an absolute bar to further collection activities," says David Gamache, an attorney in St. Louis, Missouri. "If the matter has been placed for collection, the attorney or agency should be notified immediately by telephone with a follow-up copy of the bankruptcy notice."

Next, read the notice of bankruptcy carefully. Gamache advises making note of important dates, such as the claims bar date, which is the deadline by which a proof of claim must be filed to allow a creditor to share in any distribution of funds; the date of the creditors' meeting, which is also called a "341" meeting; and the deadline for filing a non-dischargeability action, which is a petition to the court that the debt you are owed not be discharged in the bankruptcy. Also, make a note of the trustee and the location of the bankruptcy court.

"The claims bar date is particularly important, as failure to file a claim with the appropriate bankruptcy court in a timely fashion likely eliminates any chance of recovery," Gamache says. "The name and address of the trustee and of the bankruptcy court should be on the initial notice. Although the trustee cannot give legal advice, they can, in many cases, answer routine questions related to the status of the case, asset recovery, and important deadlines. Claims forms can be obtained from the court."

If you are unfamiliar with bankruptcy proceedings, Gamache suggests consulting a bankruptcy attorney to make sure you fully understand your options and can make a decision on the best course of action. Don't just assume that you'll never collect what's owed you. While that may happen, it's also true that many companies emerge from bankruptcy stronger than before and able to pay their bills, and many companies that are liquidated are able to pay creditors at least a portion of their debts.

COLLECTING BANKRUPTCY JUDGMENTS

Business bankruptcies are often lengthy, complicated procedures, and can take years to settle. If you are a creditor in a bankruptcy, don't just assume you'll never see your money; stay in touch with the bankruptcy trustee until the final distribution is made. This is especially important if you move because trustees don't have the time to search for creditors.

The payoff could be substantial. Every once in a while, a trustee will find hidden assets. It could be two years later, and suddenly a zero-asset case will yield a 45-cents on the dollar distribution. If creditors can't be found, the funds are simply deposited into the U.S. Treasury as unclaimed.

To notify the trustee of any change in your address, simply send a letter to the clerk of the court and the trustee in the appropriate jurisdiction and ask for an acknowledgement. It then becomes the responsibility of the trustee to see that you get your share when the bankrupt company's affairs are finally settled.

DEDUCTING A BAD DEBT

When a debt becomes uncollectible, it can be claimed as a deduction on your tax return. You do not have to wait until a debt is due to determine whether it is worthless. A debt becomes worthless when there is no longer any chance the amount owed will be paid.

It is not necessary to go to court if you can show that a judgment from the court would be uncollectible. You must only show that you have taken reasonable steps to collect the debt. Bankruptcy of your debtor is generally good evidence of the worthlessness of at least part of an unsecured and unpreferred debt.

If you receive property in partial settlement of a debt, reduce the debt by the fair market value of the property received. You can deduct the remaining debt as a bad debt if and when it becomes worthless. If you later sell the property, any gain on the sale is due to the appreciation of the property; it is not a recovery of a bad debt.

Source: Internal Revenue Service

CREDIT REPORTING SERVICES

Dun & Bradstreet
(800) 519-3111 or (816) 843-4299
www.dnb.com

Equifax
(888) 202-4025
www.equifax.com

Experian
(800) 588-3657
www.experian.com

TransUnion
(800) 916-8800
www.transunion.com

ESTABLISHING YOUR BUSINESS CREDIT SCORE

Business credit scores range on a scale of 0 to 100, with 75 or more considered an excellent rating. Personal credit scores, on the other hand, range from 300 to 850 with a score of 680 or higher considered excellent.

It's important to note that there are many factors that affect a credit score; it's based on more than just whether you pay your bills on time. Your score can be affected by the amount of available credit you have on bank lines of credit and credit cards; the length of time you've had a credit profile; the number of inquiries made on your credit profile, and more. The mistake many business owners make is using their personal information to apply for business credit, leases, and loans. By doing so, they risk having a lower personal credit score.

Why is that? The average consumer credit report gets just one inquiry per year and has 11 credit obligations, typically broken down as seven credit cards and four installment loans. Business owners are not your average consumer, however, because they carry both personal and business credit. By using their personal credit history to get business credit, they're not able to build their business score, which could help them attain critical business credit in the future.

Follow these basic steps to establish your business credit profile and score:

1. Form a corporation or LLC under which to operate your business and obtain an FIN (Federal Identification Number) or EIN (Employer Identification Number) from the IRS. You can apply for an EIN at the IRS website. Form a corporation or LLC as opposed to structuring your business as a sole proprietorship or partnership—with a sole proprietorship or partnership, your personal credit

information could be included on your business credit report, and vice-versa. In addition, as a sole proprietor or partner in a partnership, you're personally liable for the debts of the business and all your personal assets are at risk in the event of litigation. Corporations and LLCs, on the other hand, afford business owners liability protection, and you can build a business credit profile that's separate from your personal debts.

2. Register your company with the business credit bureaus.

3. Comply with the business credit market requirements. It's extremely important for businesses to meet all the requirements of the credit market in order to ensure a higher likelihood of credit approval. In fact, not being in compliance with the credit market can raise red flags with both credit bureaus and grantors. The red flags include such simple things as not having a business license or a phone line. Most businesses will not grant credit to another business that hasn't taken the steps to set up the company with the proper licenses and local, state, and federal requirements.

4. Prepare financial statements and a professional business plan. These documents are often required by many credit grantors.

5. Find companies willing to grant credit to your business without a personal credit check or guarantee. When a company grants your business credit, be certain they report the payment experiences you have with them to the business credit bureau to help build your business credit report and a financial foundation for your company.

6. Manage your debt so you don't fall into trouble making your payments, which will negatively affect your credit score.

7. Make monthly payments to credit grantors to keep your business credit profile active.

Source: David Gass, "The ABCs of Business Credit,"
Entrepreneur.com

THE UNHAPPY CLIENT OR CUSTOMER

When it comes to paying what they owe, "The happy customer pays quickly; the unhappy customer pays late (if at all)." So one way of improving your collections is to make sure your customers are satisfied. Here are a few ways to do that:

- *Use a written contract with your customers.* By clearly spelling out in writing what products and services you're providing and your payment terms, you'll help avoid misunderstandings.

- *Keep your customers well informed when it comes to their orders.* If there's a delay or some other problem, let them know how you plan to deal with it.

- *If a problem does arise, remember that "The customer is always right."* In other words, you can't win by arguing with an unhappy customer. Therefore, it's in your best interest to find a way to turn him or her into a happy customer. It's definitely a challenge, and one we've all faced, but if you're successful, think of the impact. How many people do you think your now-happy customer will tell about your first-rate customer service?

Source: Judy Gedge, "Does Your Collections System Need a
Check-up?" Entrepreneur.com

❧ ❧ ❧

CHAPTER 10

Customer Service

LIFETIME VALUE OF A CUSTOMER

Many business owners miss the boat when it comes to understanding the value of each and every customer. They celebrate when they sell one product to one customer. True success comes when you have a community of customers who buy repeatedly from you. This loyalty and shared community creates a sustainable and successful business model. For instance, Carol, a local jeweler, sells a piece of jewelry to Joe. If Joe's wife enjoys the jewelry, he will probably return to Carol to buy jewelry for other special occasions, and will turn into a repeat customer for Carol. Rather than a single purchaser, Carol now has a customer who has a much larger sales and profit potential. Carol understands the lifetime value of a customer. Isn't someone much more likely to do business with someone with whom they have a good history rather than a stranger? If you have that good history—goodwill—with people, the word will get around, and soon you will have a solid reputation that will attract new business through referrals.

It is much harder to find a new customer than to keep a satisfied customer coming back. One of the greatest assets of a business is its customer list.

The customer cycle has the following stages:

1. Attract the customer (hardest part).
2. Make a sale.
3. Capture your customers' contact information.
4. Make your customer feel special (thank the customer for his or her purchase).
5. Keep in contact with your customer (send the customer advance announcements of new products, special promotions, or events).
6. Answer customer inquiries in a timely and friendly manner (turn complaining customers into happy customers).

7. Create a community or club for customers to join (give them value for free just for joining).
8. Ask your happy customer to "tell a friend" about your business or product.
9. Make a repeat sale to your customer.
10. Repeat the cycle.

Source: From Before You Quit Your Job: 10 Real-Life Lessons Every Entrepreneur Should Know About Building a Multimillion-Dollar Business *by Robert T. Kiyosaki with Sharon L. Lechter, CPA*

> *The smartest thing I've ever done is to evaluate every decision based upon its impact on the ultimate consumer. If the course of action under consideration will meet the consumer's needs or desires, then you can't go wrong. If it won't, you better pass.*
>
> SOURCE: RON BERGER, CHAIRMAN AND CEO, FIGARO'S ITALIAN PIZZA, INC.

Words of Wisdom

BUILD CUSTOMER LOYALTY

Successful businesses are built on a foundation of loyal customers. But how can you inspire your customers to stick with you when other companies are trying to lure them away?

The first step is to develop a profile of your ideal long-term customer. When you're compatible from the beginning, your chances of a lasting relationship are increased significantly. Next, direct your sales and marketing efforts toward prospective customers who fit your profile. Not only are they more likely to stay with you long-term, but also they are often easier to land in the first place.

Once customers are on board, never—not even for a minute—take them for granted. It's expected that you'll provide a quality product, competitive prices, and strong customer service. In addition, find ways to offer extras not offered by your competitors—products, services, or even attitudes that keep customers coming back. Stay in tune with the level of customer satisfaction by using various measurement tools, such as surveys, feedback from employees who have direct contact with customers, and tracking sales volume. Don't let even the smallest problem slip by. You need to be immediately aware when there is a concern and take the appropriate action.

Remember that customers are much quicker to understand that a problem took place, and much quicker to forgive and remain loyal, if the company will just acknowledge that there was a problem, apologize, and take steps to make it right.

Always make it as easy as possible for customers to do business with you. Consider toll-free telephone numbers, free parking, and convenient access. Show your appreciation for your customers' business with such gestures as thank-you notes, birthday and holiday cards, free newsletters, and volume rewards. If your product is something that is consumed on a periodic basis—such as hair styling or automotive services—set up a system to remind customers when the appropriate time period has passed. Postcards or e-mail reminders are good, but a phone call offering to set an appointment is more effective.

Focus your retention program on the customers who fit your ideal profile of a long-term customer. If you lose a customer who's not ideal, you're probably better off. But if you lose a customer who matches your profile, you need to find out why—and the best way is by asking. You can conduct exit interviews with a telephone call, written survey, or e-mail. Make your questions simple, to the point, and non-accusatory; the primary goal is to find out why a customer has left. That information can help in two ways: First, it gives you an opportunity to win back the customer. Second, when you know why customers are leaving, you have the information you need to fix the problem and prevent others from following.

> *It's not about you. It's about the customer. They purchase your product or service for their reason, not yours.*
>
> —RANDY PENNINGTON, PENNINGTON PERFORMANCE GROUP

𝒲ords of 𝒲isdom

TIPS FOR BUILDING CUSTOMER LOYALTY

- *Find out what your customers want and provide it.* Don't guess; ask them through surveys, focus groups, and at other contact opportunities.
- *Dazzle them with service they'll want to tell their friends about.* Be so remarkable they can't help talking about you.
- *Create a sense of belonging.* Form "customer clubs" that offer special benefits and status.
- *Be responsive.* Don't make your customers wait for service—neither on the phone, nor in line in the store. Take care of their needs immediately.
- *Make customers feel welcome.* Greet people enthusiastically when they walk through the door. When they call, make it clear you're delighted to hear from them.
- *Set yourself apart.* Differentiate your company through the quality of your products and services.
- *Always tell the truth.* Never, ever attempt to deceive your customers in any way—they'll find out, and they'll never come back.
- *Keep your facility sparkling.* How well you care for your store, office, or plant is a sign of how well you care about your customers.
- *Reinforce your customers' buying decisions.* Look for ways to let them know how wise they are for being one of your loyal customers.
- *Reward your customers.* Develop "frequent buyer" programs, offer volume discounts, or provide other incentives that show how much you appreciate each order.
- *If it's wrong, make it right.* When a mistake is made, apologize and correct it right away—whether it's your fault or not.
- *Communicate with your customers.* Newsletters, advertisements, in-store signs, and direct mail are just a few ways you can let your customers know they are valued.
- *Be patient.* Building loyalty takes time, and you've got to be in it for the long-term.
- *Ask for feedback.* Give your customers a chance to tell you what they like—and don't like—about your operation and your products, then use that input to improve.
- *Guarantee your products and services.* Put your guarantee in writing and then honor it without hesitation.

RELATIONSHIP-BUILDING TOOLS

1. *Thank-you notes.* This is a no-brainer, but you'd be surprised how many entrepreneurs neglect to write thank-you notes—especially when they get really busy. Take the time to show your customers that you genuinely appreciate their business. They'll remember your thoughtfulness because most of your competition won't send out thank-you notes.

2. *Postcard mailings.* If you target consumers, send out monthly mailings that make good refrigerator fodder, such as "Quote of the Month," "Recipe of the Month," or useful tips on such topics as time-management, gardening, or anything else that interests the bulk of your customers. Avoid being too promotional here. Just provide the kind of information that customers will want to hang on their fridge. The added benefit to you is that whenever guests visit your customers' homes, they'll see your name, potentially leading to conversations about your business.

3. *E-mail updates.* Think of your e-mail update as a press release that you send to your customers. Providing them with regular product, service, and customer updates via e-mail at least once a month will convey a sense of positive momentum. This keeps customers in the loop and, over time, gets them excited to be involved with you and motivates them to pass on referrals.

4. *Getting together over coffee or lunch.* Try to spend face time in a non-sales environment with your customers. Ask about their family, hobbies, personal goals and so forth. When you show customers that you really care about them on a personal level, they're yours for life.

5. *Birthdays, anniversaries, and other special occasions.* These occasions are very important to your customers and their families and friends. Be among the few who actually remember a customer's special days, and that customer will never forget you!

6. *Follow up on well-being.* For example, if you find that a customer's wife has been sick, call periodically just to find out how she's recovering.

7. *Pass referrals.* One of the most powerful ways to encourage loyalty in customers is to pass them referrals. When you get a chance, scroll through your customer database and think through people you know who might add value to your customers.

8. *Entertaining at your home.* Throw a party for your best customers. You'll be amazed at how much rapport and goodwill you can build with people when you get them in your home environment. Your guests will also find value in your party as a networking opportunity for them.

9. *Post-sale feedback.* Demonstrate that you care about the quality of your service. Call customers and ask them questions like:
   - Are you pleased with the service you received?
   - What did you like most about working with us?
   - What would you like to see improved?

Without this invaluable information, you'll have a hard time improving your products and services. Besides, when you ask customers for feedback and implement their comments, they feel a sense of ownership in what you're doing and thus become more loyal to your products and services.

Source: Sean M. Lyden, "9 Tools for Building Customer Loyalty," Entrepreneur.com

CRM: HOW TECHNOLOGY CAN IMPROVE CUSTOMER SATISFACTION

Customer relationship management technology (CRM) is designed to improve customer satisfaction by enabling a business to better understand its customers, their habits, and their needs. For smaller businesses, CRM technology is usually available as a web-based tool, PC software applications, or software plug-ins that link a CRM program to other applications.

CRM technology is most often used by employees who interface directly with customers, such as sales and customer service reps. Data gathered from CRM tools is also analyzed by business owners to identify levels of customer satisfaction, buying patterns, the success (or lack thereof) of a particular marketing or sales promotion with customers, and more.

A general-purpose CRM software program for small businesses may cost about $200 for one or multiple users. The software may combine a contact management database with tools for tracking all forms of customer contact, such as phone calls, letters, and e-mails; forecasting and tracking sales opportunities; scheduling calls and meetings with customers; generating reports on customer activities.

In addition, there are CRM software programs available that are aimed at particular industries. For instance, there are CRM packages developed specifically for the hospitality industry, to enable small and large hotels alike to track guests' room preferences, among other things. Front desk clerks, the concierge, housekeeping staff, and others can input details into a hotel's CRM database, such as a particular guest's preference for foam (vs. feather) pillows. The information is used to build customer profiles that the hotel staff can tap into in order to give returning guests special attention—and that helps improve loyalty.

Accessing a Customer's Entire History— Before the Second Ring

Many CRM programs include modules that can be linked to standard applications that businesses use daily. Today's CRM software has become highly sophisticated, yet it's still easy to use. For instance, Microsoft Dynamics CRM can now be connected, through software plug-ins, to a small business's IP telephone system. When a call comes in, the IP telephone software plug-in automatically links to the Microsoft Dynamics CRM system. A pop-up window of the customer contact record appears on your employee's IP phone screen, their computer screen, or both. Before the second ring, the employee taking the call has access to information about the customer who's calling, such as orders pending, recent returns, and so on.

By being able to access this information instantly, an employee is able to better answer the customer's questions, while the customer is less likely to feel frustrated by the encounter and more likely to feel appreciated by your company—that goes a long way toward keeping customers happy. In addition to accessing existing information, the employee answering the call can easily add new notes to the customer's record. That information is then uploaded back into the CRM system, and the next time the customer calls, the employee who answers can pick up where the previous employee left off.

Off-site workers, such as sales personnel in the field, can also have access to the same customer data over your company's data network. As a result, interconnected CRM software can help you not only to improve customer satisfaction but also to increase employee productivity and reduce costs as well.

Source: Peter Alexander, "Tech Solutions That Help Keep Customers Satisfied," Entrepreneur.com

JUST SAY NO: SOMETIMES YOU CAN'T DO WHAT YOUR CUSTOMERS WANT

Keeping your customers happy is an important part of keeping your customers, but you can't always do exactly what they want. There are three reasons to say no to a client: when you're too busy to do the job right and on time; when you don't possess the right skills for the job; when there's a conflict of ethics. But if you handle the situation with tact and diplomacy, you should be able to retain the client for future work if you want to.

If you're too busy to meet the client's stated deadline, be honest. Explain your own time constraints and let them know what deadline you can meet. They may be willing to wait, but if they can't, consider referring them to someone else who can handle the project. If you don't have time to do the job right, don't accept it and then either miss the deadline or deliver substandard work.

Honesty is also the best approach when you don't possess the right skills. When possible, make a referral to someone more qualified. You might also consider accepting the project and subcontracting to someone else. But if you do this, remember that you are ultimately responsible for the quality and delivery of the work.

Ethical issues are more delicate. If an ethical question affects only a small part of a large project, you may want to back away from just that portion, but never do anything that makes you feel uncomfortable or that you wouldn't want the world to know about. Be professional and diplomatic, but stand your ground.

Turning down clients may well be one of the hardest things an entrepreneur has to do, but you have to be true to yourself and have the strength to say no when it's appropriate.

Companies think they "save money" by cutting back on employees who serve (help) customers. Big mistake. The only people happy about that are companies who have plenty of people (and make plenty of money) like Home Depot.

—JEFFREY GITOMER, AUTHOR AND SPEAKER

WHEN YOU NEED TO SAY SORRY

In a dispute that may have legal consequences, it is important to convey an apology without accepting liability for the situation, especially before all the facts are determined.

An effective apology should be:

- *Empathetic.* It should express the speaker's *feelings* and address and acknowledge the personal *experience* and *feelings* of the victim. This is not the time to review facts or discuss what happened.

- *Causation neutral.* It must not assume that the speaker's actions were the cause of the victim's experience, at least before all the facts are in.

- *Excuse free.* Resist any urge you may have to cite excuses for your actions.

- *Genuine and sincere in tone.* A remarkable professor of mine, the late Earl Latham of Amherst College, used to say to his students, "Sincerity, you know, is one of the more cosmetic virtues." If your apology is not expressed from genuine feelings of empathy and compassion or if it is insincerely expressed, you will hurt more than help your position. Remember that one of the pillars of conflict resolution is the genuine expression of compassion.

- *Brief and to the point.* This is not the time to ramble on about the situation. Make your point, express your feelings, and then stop talking. Naturally empathetic, talkative people have a tendency to accept more guilt and responsibility than is called for by the situation.
- *Based on listening.* Use your active listening skills. The person complaining often has a strong need to unload his or her feelings or express frustration. It is time for you to patiently listen and acknowledge feelings.
- *An expression of accountability.* I firmly believe that a professional or corporation should always be prepared to articulate its accountability and responsibility for its actions, not as an admission of liability or even responsibility for a given situation, but as a matter of general corporate or personal principles.

Source: Stay Out of Court! The Small Business Guide to Preventing Disputes and Avoiding Lawsuit Hell *by Andrew A. Caffey (Entrepreneur Press, 2005)*

DOING IT RIGHT

Never say no or tell a customer what you can't do—always respond to customer questions and requests by telling them what you can do. For example, if a customer wants 100 widgets delivered by Friday and you don't have enough of them in stock, say, "We'll have 50 widgets on your dock before noon on Friday and the remaining 50 to you by the following Wednesday, and we'll give you the quantity discount for ordering 100." Most customers will be reasonable and work something out with you. Don't plant the seed in their minds that you said no to them.

WHEN IT'S TIME TO FIRE A CUSTOMER

Ever had a customer whose nuisance value exceeded his profit potential? Or who demanded champagne service at beer prices? The fact is that some customers just aren't worth it—but how do you deal with such a situation?

The first step is recognizing that the relationship needs to end. Some of the signs that suggest you may want to take that step include:

- The client doesn't respect or appreciate your work.
- They make excessive demands on your company and staff.
- They are not fair-minded in either their expectations or what they are willing to pay.
- They want work done cheaply and under unrealistic deadlines.
- They don't want you to make a profit.
- They pay bills slowly, or sometimes not at all.
- They push you to the limit in all areas, taking advantage at every turn.
- They see you as a disposable vendor, not a valued partner.

It's always a good idea to try to fix the problem before you simply drop the customer. Put the offending party or parties on notice. Talk to them. Outline what the problems are, what the possible solutions are, and ask for their cooperation to help reach those solutions. Be sure to document these efforts so you can refer to them later, if necessary.

If your attempts to make the relationship mutually productive don't work, it may be time to move on and focus on more profitable or prospective clients. Calculate what you will lose in gross revenue, and decide if your business can stand the financial hit. If it can't, put up with the current problem client until you can replace that client's vital gross revenues with one or more new clients.

Once you're in a position to let the client go, ask for a meeting with the highest ranking people in the company. Calmly and professionally explain the situation, review your efforts to correct the problems, and make it clear that you'll have to terminate the relationship if things don't change. Sometimes those higher-ranking people will see the wisdom of what you've done and will intervene and make a difference so you can continue under a better relationship, but if they don't, be prepared to move forward with the termination. Have a plan in place to make the transition as smooth as possible. That plan might include a recommendation of other companies that might be able to serve the client. Of course, you must remain professional throughout the process, no matter how badly the client behaves.

WHEN A CLIENT SEXUALLY HARASSES YOU

It's not just a boss/employee conflict, or a big company problem: sexual harassment in the workplace occurs in a variety of relationships, including between customers and suppliers. And it doesn't have to be a blatant demand for sex in exchange for business; sexual harassment can take the form of a wide range of inappropriate behavior, including a client who tells dirty jokes, makes repeated sexual innuendos, or just uses language you find offensive.

"As a business owner dealing with a customer, you don't have legal recourse under statutes that govern sexual harassment in the workplace," says Carol Hepburn, a partner in the law firm of Campiche Hepburn McCarty & Bianco, PLLC, in Seattle, Washington. Though you may have other legal remedies, depending on the laws of your state and the creativity of your attorney, Hepburn says, "A lawsuit is no fun. Most people just want the harassment to stop. You're better off if you can have a decent and comfortable working relationship." She offers the following advice for dealing with customers who may be harassing you:

- *Do a cost/benefit analysis.* Consider how much business or profit the customer represents, and how much discomfort and distraction the situation is causing. Determine at what point the harassment will outweigh the benefit of the relationship.

- *Consider the motivation.* If you can, determine the motive behind the inappropriate behavior. Are they deliberately trying to make you uncomfortable? Are they trying to establish a power position? Are they trying to make a personal advance? Or, as is often the case, are they simply clueless to how offensive their behavior is?

- *Set boundaries.* When you are the target of inappropriate behavior, discuss it with the other person in a non-confrontational manner and let them know what you will and won't tolerate.

- *Change the contact environment.* If you have been meeting with the client at your home (if you are home-based) or in your or their private office, consider changing the location to somewhere more public, such as a restaurant or even a more open location at their facility. You might also try to cut back on the actual face-to-face contact and do more on the phone or via e-mail. This reduces the opportunity for offensive behavior and lets you avoid a potentially uncomfortable confrontation.

If you're having trouble developing an effective plan of action, Hepburn suggests one single therapy session with a counselor. "I know lots of professionals who use therapists in this manner," she says. A good therapist can help you understand your feelings and come up with a solution that's comfortable and workable for you.

✢ ✢ ✢

NINE TACTICS FOR DEALING WITH ANGRY CLIENTS

1. *Acknowledge the other person's anger quickly.*
Nothing adds more fuel to someone's fire than having their anger ignored or belittled. The faster you verbally recognize their anger, the better.

2. *Make it clear that you're concerned.*
Tell them you realize just how angry they are. Let them know you're taking the situation seriously. Make notes of every detail they give you.

3. *Don't hurry them.*
Be patient, and let them get it all out. Never try to interrupt or shut them up. In many cases, the best move is simply to listen. They'll wind themselves down eventually. In some cases, they'll realize they blew the situation out of proportion and feel foolish for it. They're then likely to accept nearly any solution you offer.

4. *Keep calm.*
Most angry people say things they don't really mean. Learn to let those things pass and take them up after you've solved the present challenge—only if you feel it's necessary to do so.

5. *Ask questions.*
Your aim is to discover the specific things that you can do to correct the problem. Try to get precise information about the difficulties caused by the problem, rather than a general venting of hot air.

6. *Get them talking about solutions.*
This is where you'll learn just how reasonable this client is. By the time you get to this step, their anger should have cooled enough to discuss the challenge rationally. If it hasn't, tell them you want to schedule a later meeting, even if it's in an hour, to come up with some reasonable solutions. Let them do the rest of their fuming on their time.

7. *Agree on a solution.*
After you know exactly what the challenge is, you're in a position to look for some kind of action that will relieve it. Propose something specific. Start with whatever will bring them the best and quickest relief. Don't get into a controversy over pennies at this point.

8. *Agree on a schedule.*
Once you've agreed on a solution, set up a schedule for its accomplishment. Agree to a realistic timeframe that you know you can handle. The biggest mistake you can make is to agree to something that can't be done. If you do, you'd better be ready to face another bout of this person's anger when you don't come through.

9. *Meet your schedule.*
Give the schedule top priority. You've talked yourself into a second chance with this client, so make sure you don't blow it. Once you've satisfied the client with regard to this situation, you'll have earned another opportunity to serve their needs in the future, and the needs of those they'll tell about how well you handled it.

Source: Tom Hopkins, "Anger Management," Entrepreneur.com

KEEP YOUR CUSTOMERS OUT OF VOICE-MAIL JAIL

Voice mail is one of the most popular modern business conveniences and can be a significant communication tool. Even so, whenever possible, answer your phone yourself—and insist that your employees do likewise. Handle calls as quickly and efficiently as possible.

Some other things to keep in mind: The prices of automated answering systems are dropping so much that even very small businesses can afford them. If you use an automated answering system, be sure to tell callers how to reach a live person. Ideally, that information should come very early in your announcement. For example, your greeting might sound something like this: "Thank you for calling ABC Company. If you know the extension of the person you are calling, you may enter it now. To reach an operator, press zero at any time during this message. To place an order, press two. To check on an existing order, press three. For accounting, press four. To hear this message again, press five."

Whether you're a one-person show or you have a sizable staff, change your individual voice-mail announcements daily. Callers need to know whether you're in the office or out and whether they're likely to hear back from you in five minutes or five hours.

> *My father, Bill Yates, told me: "You can accomplish anything and succeed as long as you put your customers' needs before your own—and never get a big head!"*
>
> —SHARON LECHTER, CO-AUTHOR OF *RICH DAD POOR DAD* AND A FOUNDER OF THE RICH DAD COMPANY

Words of Wisdom

Avoid stating the obvious, such as "I'm either away from my desk or out of the office"—well, of course! If you were at your desk, you'd be answering your phone. And always let callers know how to reach a live person when you are not available. Here is a sample individual voice-mail announcement: "This is Jane Smith, and it's Monday, June first. I'm in the office today but unavailable at the moment. Leave your name, number, and the reason for your call, and I'll get back to you within an hour. If you need to speak with someone immediately, press zero, and ask the operator to connect you with Bob White."

> *If you want to earn at the top of your market niche, you have to have relatively unique and/or demonstrably superior services and/or products to offer.*
>
> —JONATHAN BERNSTEIN, PRESIDENT, BERNSTEIN CRISIS MANAGEMENT, LLC

Words of Wisdom

❧ ❧ ❧

CHAPTER 11

Human Resources: Policies, Procedures, and Great Ideas

"Our people are our greatest asset."

How many times have you heard this cliché? Or said it? And when it comes to you operation, is it real or is it lip service?

Turnover is expensive. So is keeping the wrong people on board. If people really are your greatest asset, or if your goal is to create a team where that's true, you need a staff of strong employees who feel valued, appreciated, challenged, and confident in the company. Go beyond the clichés and learn to walk the talk.

CHARACTERISTICS OF ORGANIZATIONS THAT KEEP EMPLOYEES FEELING CONNECTED

Employees who feel connected to your company are more likely to perform at a higher level and less likely to leave in search of a better opportunity. Companies that have the following qualities usually have a strong connection to their people.

A clear focus and direction exists for the business and the individual.
Specific goals and expectations linked to a common, compelling vision provide a sense of contribution and focus. Commitment to the job is enhanced when a visible link exists between individual performance and organizational success.

People receive the time, tools, and training to accomplish their jobs.
The need to do more with less does not mean "do everything with nothing." Frustration develops when barriers are consistently erected that make success on the job impossible. An investment in tools and training reinforces the idea that you want the business to succeed. Providing adequate time to accom-

plish the task sends the message that quality is important.

Efforts are recognized and appreciated.

The best performers usually maintain excellence without recognition. They are internally motivated and hold themselves to a high standard. Sincere recognition of the stars ensures that they don't look for a better environment in which to utilize their talents. Poor performers can be motivated by the realization that managers are willing to recognize their value rather than only look for the negative. The majority of employees do a good job each day. They view recognition as verification that their performance matters. A one-percent increase in performance from those who simply meet expectations makes a tremendous difference to the bottom line.

Poor performance of others is addressed.

Good employees do not want those who are not meeting expectations to be dealt with unfairly. They do, however, grow weary of shouldering more than their share of the performance load. There is no advantage, and considerable harm, in publicizing your efforts to improve someone's performance. Straightforward, sincere efforts to help people improve will show up through a change in the individuals' behavior.

Honest mistakes are used as a learning opportunity.

Think of the most important lessons you have learned in life. How many of those were the results of an honest mistake? Now think of how honest mistakes are handled in your organization. Environments in which people feel punished for honest mistakes create a culture where mistakes are hidden and lines of communication are closed. Most importantly, the organization loses the opportunity to share valuable knowledge that improves performance and results.

Specific and accurate feedback is provided in a positive manner.

Everyone wants information about how they are doing compared to the expectations for their performance. The best feedback acknowledges effort, points the individual toward success, and encourages personal responsibility.

People have fun.

Environments that promote laughter contribute to higher morale, improved productivity, and lowered on-the-job stress. Having fun is not just playing games or dressing up at Halloween. The ability to be relaxed and enjoy oneself creates passion in the workplace that increases loyalty and creates a bond between team members that decrease the desire to find something better.

Source: Randy Pennington, President, Pennington Performance Group

Each person works to their own time and their own beat. It is not a "one shoe fits all."

—GARY LEV, PRESIDENT AND CEO, LTS LEADERBOARD TOURNAMENT SYSTEMS LTD.

NEED TO KNOW? JUST ASK

You probably think you have a good idea what your employees are thinking and feeling, but you might be missing more than you know. It's easy for management to lose touch with workers and think everything is fine when it's not. If you really want to know what's going on, you need to ask—and the most accurate and efficient way to do that is with a survey.

Two main issues affect employee attitudes. The first is their peer group: the people they work for and with. The second is the larger area of pay and benefits and how management treats people. An effective survey will address both these issues.

Generally, employee surveys fall into two categories. One is an issue-specific survey, which asks employees for their opinions on a particular issue or problem. It may be something as serious as insurance coverage or as light-hearted as what to do for the company holiday party. In addition to asking for an opinion, this type of survey is also useful for asking for specific suggestions that will solve the problem. The other is a general employee attitude survey, which covers a wide range of issues. Consider conducting this type of comprehensive survey on a regular basis, perhaps annually or every two years. The process requires both a time and a financial commitment, which varies depending on the size of your organization. But the results will be worth it.

When surveying employees, certain key points are critical. Set up your survey so participants can remain anonymous if they choose; people are more likely to be open when there is no fear of retribution. Explain why you're conducting the survey and how the results will be used. Without this information, there is no reason to participate. Then develop a plan to correct problems revealed by surveys and communicate that plan to your employees.

Rarely will a one-time survey be sufficient. People are often suspicious of the first survey effort, but when they see results, their participation will increase. Follow-up surveys are a tool to reinforce management's concern and provide a vehicle to accurately measure employee attitudes as the working environment changes.

❧ ❧ ❧

HELP EMPLOYEES DEVELOP STRONG TIES WITH EACH OTHER

Leaders like to think that people have a strong sense of loyalty to their employer but that is rarely the case today. Emphasizing team loyalty is far more realistic. Use these suggestions to build employee commitment through team affiliation:

- Make sure every employee is an active participant in at least one team or group that interacts frequently.
- Keep an eye on how friendly those teams are and make it known that you are happy to move anyone to a new team if they aren't happy with their team. Some personality clashes are going to be far easier to avoid than fix. As a leader, you probably don't want to waste your time trying to make incompatible individuals like each other.
- Give employees plenty of opportunities to have fun or relax with their teams. If they only see each other under the pressure of task-specific meetings, they will probably not develop much of a rapport.
- Give the teams interesting challenges to work on, not just routine boring stuff. (If you can't think of anything else, ask them to examine work processes and try to improve them to cut costs, avoid errors, or better retain customers). A healthy challenge gives teams a purpose and their members a shared sense of accomplishment.

Source: Making Horses Drink: How to Lead and Succeed in Business *by Alex Hiam (Entrepreneur Press, 2002)*

INTERNS:
A GREAT RESOURCE FOR YOU, GREAT EXPERIENCE FOR THEM

Even small companies can supplement their staff with interns. You get enthusiastic, energetic workers at an affordable rate; the interns gain valuable work experience and college credit.

Don't restrict an intern's duties to errand-running and low-level clerical work. Take advantage of the fact that, as current college students, they may possess knowledge and capabilities that your existing employees may not—such as technological skills, the latest academic methodologies, and research abilities. Let interns support your marketing and operational efforts and give them the opportunity to work in your operation as your other full-time employees do—remember that it's not uncommon for companies to hire interns for full-time positions after graduation.

Recruit interns with the same care that you use when hiring regular employees. Consider their background, experience, educational level, skills, and goals, and check references. Have a plan in place to supervise them. You may be asked to complete an evaluation of the student's performance at the end of the internship period; take time to do this fairly, completely, and promptly.

Whether or not you pay interns is usually your choice. Some colleges require it; others do not. But you'll likely get a higher caliber of intern and better performance if you provide fair compensation for their time and effort.

Contact nearby colleges and universities for details on their internship programs. Also, let your friends and colleagues know you are willing to consider interns—you never know who might have a qualified son or daughter attending college in another city who will be looking for a summer job at home.

MANAGEMENT TIP

Instead of just telling your employees what to do, ask them to do something better. Choose something they're already doing and suggest that they find ways to improve. Check back periodically to see how they're doing, and recognize effort as well as results.

RELATING TO YOUNGER EMPLOYEES

To be in business in 2010 and beyond, you need to attract and retain Gen X and Y, as well as Millennial, employees. These younger staffers will work hard, but they want to enjoy themselves while they're doing it and they want greater work-life balance than Baby Boomers. To appeal to this group of workers, consider instituting casual dress polices; be flexible with work schedules whenever possible; encourage multi-tasking; give them plenty of feedback; and create a fun, employee-centered workplace—if you take care of them, they'll take care of your customers.

PAY FOR YOUR EMPLOYEES TO LEARN

Looking for an employee benefit that delivers a big bang for the buck? Consider tuition reimbursement. You'll enhance the quality of your staff, build loyalty, and reduce turnover. Here's what to consider when setting up a tuition reimbursement program:

- *What you'll pay for.* Will you reimburse strictly for college-level degree courses or will you also pay for personal enrichment programs and/or non-credit courses? If you have an employee working toward a degree, will you pay for options that get him or her closer to that goal without actually enrolling in classes, such as skill-level testing?

- *How much you'll pay.* Will you reimburse all or a portion of the tuition? What about books? Is there an annual cap on how much you'll pay for each employee? Consult with your accountant about the tax ramifications for both the company and the employee before making this decision.

- *Who is eligible?* Will you reimburse only for full-time or also for part-time employees? Must they be at your company for a minimum period of time before they can use this benefit?

- *The employee's obligation.* Is the employee required to complete the class with a certain grade level to receive reimbursement? What happens if he or she fails? Are employees required to stay with the company for a specific length of time after they receive the benefits or pay back the money if they leave too soon?

- *Schedule flexibility.* Will you structure working hours to accommodate school schedules?

BEING A FAITH-FRIENDLY COMPANY

The "faith-at-work movement" is in its early stages but is getting serious attention from employers and, in some cases, posing major workplace challenges. Your response could make this issue a legal minefield or a source of competitive advantage.

Like the social issues that helped define earlier generations, the topic of faith at work has crept into U.S. businesses. Proposals to form affinity groups, prayer breakfasts, and the introduction of corporate chaplains are among the common requests. Other more subtle signs include e-mail signoffs that quote scripture, employee intranet postings inviting colleagues to a religious service, and requests for specific foods in the company cafeteria. Many employers are uncertain how to deal with such emotional and potentially divisive topics. In many cases, companies try to avoid the issue entirely, but that's a mistake.

It's important to understand the difference between "faith-based" and "faith-friendly." Faith-based implies privileging one faith over another and is inappropriate for most large organizations, particularly publicly-traded companies. Faith-friendly treats all faith traditions equally and recognizes the centrality of faith in many employees. The goal is to create a culture of respect, diversity, inclusion, and tolerance.

The issue is not one that American companies will be able to ignore. Immigration is creating a more religiously and ethnically diverse workforce that will only grow in importance and number in coming years. Globalization means U.S. firms are coming into contact with cultures in which religion is deeply ingrained in the day-to-day workplace and the American emphasis on separation of church and state is antithetical. Take Islam, for example, which teaches very specific notions and laws that guide business terms and behaviors.

What Can You Do?

A thoughtful and progressive policy can serve as a recruitment and retention tool. A small number of large corporations already formally recognize faith-based groups.

"For individuals, the office has become their community, their hub of life, and they want their faith to be a part of it," notes a report issued by The Conference Board. "Not demanding that one's spiritual side be checked at the office door can provide employees with access to a tool to help deal with their emotional and spiritual needs. Strong moral and worker contentment often translates into higher productivity and more customer-friendly attitudes." The opposite is also true. Job performance can suffer if a worker's emotional well-being is neglected. Caring for both the physical and spiritual health of the workforce is becoming a part of good business practice.

Less than one-third of 550 human resources professionals surveyed in 2001 by the Tanenbaum Center for Interreligious Understanding and the Society for Human Resource Management said they had a written policy on religion in the workplace. Yet the same number said there were more religions represented in their workforce than had been five years earlier. And while 77 percent said their company includes religion in their standard harassment policy, only 16 percent said they offered training on religious accommodation.

Although discussion about religion is still rare in many parts of the U.S. in a work context, it plays an important role in most people's lives. How a company discusses the topic and the language it uses determines how employees will view and ultimately respond to a company's actions and policies.

Whatever your policy, it should be consistent. Consider these issues as you deal with creating a policy addressing faith in the workplace:

- Is the policy exclusionary or inclusionary?
- Will it cause or prevent lawsuits?
- Will it promote intra-group fighting or understanding?
- Is it likely to scare off or attract and retain top talent?
- Does it disempower or empower minority traditions?
- Will emotional or rational dialogue be the outcome?
- Is the language neutral? Language can shut down or open up dialogue.

Source: Faith at Work: What Does It Mean to Be a Faith-Friendly Company?, *Executive Action No. 217, The Conference Board*

TAKE YOUR PARENTS TO WORK

Remember when your parents came to school to see what you did all day? Maybe it's time to invite them to your office so they can—once again—see what you do all day.

Many workers, especially those in high-tech and creative jobs, have a hard time explaining their jobs to their parents. Also, Millennium generation workers are accustomed to parents who have been very involved in their lives. A Parents' Day will let mothers and fathers see their adult children in their working environment.

Depending on your particular operation, you can either make your Parents' Day a special company-wide event, schedule it by department, or just let workers know they are welcome to bring their parents in for a visit. Consider hosting a casual lunch, a tour of the facility, and a presentation that demonstrates what you do. Allow time for parents to see your staff in action. The overall cost will be minimal, and the rewards are tremendous.

SELECTING A TRAINER

One of the biggest challenges of choosing a trainer is identifying the true professionals and weeding out the so-called consultants who really just can't find a job. Before you bring in an outside trainer, consider this advice:

- *Determine exactly what you need before you begin interviewing.* Protect yourself and the trainer from possible misunderstandings by outlining clearly what you expect. This spares both of you from potential unpleasantness or ineffectiveness after the project is underway.

- *Ask for written proposals.* By getting it in writing, you'll be able to determine if the trainer truly understands the scope of the project and if he has the resources to meet your needs.

- *Check references.* If the proposal looks good, contact some of the trainer's current and/or former clients.

- *Ask for work samples.* If you want the trainer to create manuals or other types of training aids, take a look at the items she's produced in the past. If it's not what you have in mind, ask if she has the capability to handle something different. And be sure your contract stipulates who owns any training tools she creates.

- *Develop a project timeline.* The only way to be sure a trainer will meet your deadlines is to put them in writing and make them part of the contract.

Never tell people how to do things. Tell them what to do and they will surprise you with their ingenuity.

Words of Wisdom

—GEN. GEORGE S. PATTON JR.

PAYING WORKERS WHEN THE OFFICE IS CLOSED

Winter snow and ice storms, summer hurricanes, other disasters, and even the occasional special event can mean you need to close your office on a scheduled workday. How will you handle employee pay when such a shutdown is necessary? Your policy must meet the requirements of the Fair Labor Standards Act (FLSA), which dictates employee pay.

Exempt employees must be paid for any day when they were ready, willing, and able to work. Because you have no way to know for sure who would have been working had your business been open, you must assume that all your exempt staff scheduled to work that day were ready, willing, and able, and pay them accordingly. There are exceptions to this rule if the shutdown covers an entire workweek.

You are required to pay nonexempt employees only for the hours worked, so you have no legal obligation to pay them during an office closing, whether unexpected or planned. However, if a nonexempt employee comes to work because he wasn't informed of the closing, you may be required to provide some compensation.

Legalities aside, when setting office closing pay policies, give serious consideration to the impact your decision will have on employee morale and commitment. Not paying employees when you don't have to may make short-term economic sense, but could cost you more in the long run. One option is a middle-ground approach, such as paying a percentage of the employee's regular wages for a designated maximum number of days. Whatever you decide, make sure employees are aware of the policy so they know what to expect when a shutdown occurs. Be sure to apply the policy consistently to every member of your non-exempt workforce and all locations of your operation.

ALL YOUR EMPLOYEES SHOULD . . .

- Know what is expected of them.

- Have the materials needed to do their jobs.

- Know who to go to if they have questions or need help.

Source: Dun & Bradstreet

ASK, DON'T TELL

You often know what employees need to do, so it may feel natural to simply tell them. But to get them more engaged and build their self-sufficiency, it might be wiser to ask them instead. This technique is especially useful in any situation where you wish an employee would take more responsibility and initiative or gain skills instead of relying on yours. Questions can include the following:

- What do you think the options are?
- How do you think you might handle this?
- Have you encountered similar problems before?
- What do you think the best starting point might be?
- What are the root causes?
- Why did this happen?
- What do you think you should do next?

Source: Making Horses Drink: How to Lead and Succeed in Business *by Alex Hiam (Entrepreneur Press, 2002)*

High expectations are the key to everything.
—SAM WALTON, FOUNDER OF WALMART

WHEN YOUR INCENTIVE PROGRAM ISN'T WORKING

Offer workers incentives to motivate them to perform better—an idea that makes sense. But what if you implemented a program and productivity hasn't improved a bit? Or worse, it's actually declined somewhat? What's wrong with your people? Chances are, nothing. If your incentive program isn't producing the results you'd hoped for, more than likely the fault lies with the program, not your people. Here's how to give your incentive program an effectiveness check-up.

- *Clearly define the desired results.* Have you articulated exactly what you're trying to achieve with the incentive program? Are you trying to get people to be more productive, work longer hours, be more creative? Whatever it is, people need to know what you want of them, and it needs to be measurable so they know when they've achieved it.

- *Be sure the incentives you're offering are really incentives to your people.* Ask them what they want. You may find people are more motivated by praise and recognition than by trips or other prizes. It's possible that you need a choice of rewards to make your program work. Whatever you offer, don't depend exclusively on advice from an incentive company; they're trying to promote their own products and services, which may not be what your people want.

- *Review your implementation and management procedures.* Your program may be sound and your rewards effective, but if somebody dropped the ball in the management phase, you won't get the results you want.

- *Confirm that it's been effectively communicated.* Does everyone know about the program, how it works, and what's expected of them? If someone was out sick or on vacation the day you announced the program, did you make sure they got the information when they came back?

If your program examination indicates that you've done everything right but the results weren't there, it's time to talk with people one-on-one. Ask each employee why the program didn't have the impact you were looking for. They may have been trying as hard as they could, but only delivering a marginal performance. It's possible they are battling obstacles you can't see. To find out what's getting in their way, ask them how you can help them improve.

If you're considering implementing a new incentive program, ask your employees what they find motivating. Find out if they want public or private recognition; if they want their family involved; if they want products or cash or perhaps even paid time off perhaps even paid time off; if they want individual or group rewards. Whatever program you choose, be sure your day-to-day management is positive. No matter how much money you spend on incentives, it will be wasted if your management style is one of negative reinforcement.

Finally, be sure you deliver what you promise. Failing to provide the rewards when employees meet their goals will guarantee your next incentive program will flop.

> *The day soldiers stop bringing you their problems is the day you stopped leading them. They have either lost confidence that you can help them or concluded that you do not care. Either case is a failure of leadership.*
>
> —General Colin Powell

Words of Wisdom

WITH NEW POLICIES, HOW YOU IMPLEMENT IS AS IMPORTANT AS WHAT THEY ARE

Does this scenario sound familiar? You've been talking to your insurance agent, and after a great deal of research and consideration, you decide to change your health policy to one that will offer better coverage and more flexibility for your employees. But when you announce this new and improved benefit, all you hear is grumbling.

Or what about this? Your vacation and sick leave policies were fairly rigid and not always sufficient to accommodate employees who needed time off for personal reasons. So you restructured the program to one that is far more liberal and user-friendly. But your employees are annoyed at best, angry at worst, and clearly not at all appreciative of your efforts.

What's the problem? No matter how desirable a change in one of your firm policies might be, your implementation process is critical to acceptance by your employees. It's important that your employees do not feel that something is being done *to* them that they have absolutely no choice about, whether or not that is actually the case. The process you use to develop the new policy and then how you inform your employees and schedule the change has a lot to do with how it will be accepted and embraced. Keep in mind, too, that people tend to be uncomfortable with change, even though it may be to their benefit. You want to implement new policies in a way that will make the change as painless as possible.

Unwelcome change can result in low morale, a decline in productivity, and sometimes even unnecessary turnover. The primary keys to avoiding a negative reaction to change are communication and time. Communicate with every affected employee so they understand what you're doing, why it's being done, and what the impact will be on them personally and on the company overall.

When possible and reasonable, get employees involved with the process of developing the new policies. Even though they won't actually make the final decision, they'll feel a greater sense of ownership if they understand what prompted the need for the policy, the reasoning that went into its creation, and what ideas were accepted and rejected before the new program was finalized. With this foundation, implementation may often be a simple matter of relaying the details.

Using the example of changing your health insurance program, you might begin with some surveys to find out what employees like and dislike about the current policy, and what they'd like to see in a new one. The larger your organization, the more formal the survey process will be; in a smaller office, simple conversations with covered employees will suffice. With this information, begin considering the various insurance products. You may want to form a small committee to review each offering and evaluate it for how well it meets your various criteria. When you've made your selection, let the affected employees know either through face-to-face meetings or written notices. It's a good idea to include a brief explanation of the logic behind your choice, for example, that the coverage you chose came the closest to meeting everyone's preferences while still staying within your budget. Then, arrange with your insurance carrier to provide training sessions so everyone understands the new coverage.

Take a similar approach to other policy changes: Explain that there is a need for a policy change; find out what employees would like to have; put together a package that best meets the needs of both the employees and the firm; communicate openly and completely about what is going to happen, why you made the decisions you did, and how it's going to affect both the company and the employees; then monitor the implementation carefully.

Of course, accept the reality that, no matter how well you prepare, you will have people who will resist something new. Allow enough time for people to get used to whatever is going to be different. During the transition period, encourage them to give you feedback. And be alert to signs of trouble, general attitude shifts, perhaps an increase in absenteeism, or other signals that employees are dissatisfied. When you spot a potential problem, address it quickly, before it festers into a major issue.

IF MILITARY DUTY CALLS

- Employees have the right to use their vacation time or personal days during their service; they may also opt for unpaid leave.
- You are not obligated to pay employees who are absent on account of military duties, unless your company policy says you will.
- If your company does have a paying policy for military service time, you cannot require employees to use their vacation or paid leave time.
- You must extend the same benefits to employees who are absent for military service as you do to employees who are on non-military leaves of absence.
- You may temporarily fill vacancies left by military employees absent for service. However, upon their return, military employees are entitled to the same positions they left.

Source: SCORE

FIVE WAYS TO KEEP GOOD PEOPLE

1. Show the connection.
Ensure that every employee is able to see how their job contributes to the success of team members and the entire operation. Interdependent partnerships create a feeling of ownership that enhances relationships and increases results.

2. Remove a barrier every 30 to 60 days.
Ask your staff to identify and prioritize the obstacles that prevent their good performance. Commit to removing one barrier every 30 to 60 days until the list has been exhausted. Begin with those that can be accomplished quickly and provide visible results. Utilize staff at all levels to design and implement solutions. It might require you to adapt your schedule, but the improved productivity and service will be worth it. When the list is exhausted, create a new one and renew the effort.

3. Make recognition and encouragement a priority.
Providing sincere, honest, and specific recognition should be expected from every manager. There is no need to wait for performance that exceeds expectations. Recognition and encouragement are also effective when others have consistently met expectations over time; improved substantially; or plateaued despite consistent effort.

4. Ensure alignment of systems.
Policies and practices that are not consistent with organizational value statements and credos are a leading cause of distrust. Consider an audit of the key human-resource systems to determine those that are most out of step with the environment you are creating. Use employees on the audit team to gain the perspective of internal customers. Performance appraisal, disciplinary practices, selection, dispute resolution, and incentive systems are a good place to begin.

5. Don't forget the majority.
Your staff can be classified in three basic groups. The stars are at one end of the continuum. Those who need to make substantial improvement or be let go are at the other. The majority lie somewhere in the middle. This last group does a good job every day and provides the foundation for your organization's success. Dramatic results can occur with incrementally small improvements within this middle group—it is the majority of your employees who will determine the ultimate success of your operation.

Source: Randy Pennington, President,
Pennington Performance Group

WHEN TRAGEDY STRIKES ONE OF YOUR EMPLOYEES

People who work together often become very close, and when tragedy strikes one of your employees, it can have a tremendous impact on your business. Regardless of the nature of the incident, the following tips can assist the employee and keep your company on track.

- *Take care of the victim.* Find out what that person needs and make sure it's provided. Such needs could range from simple moral support to assisting with a variety of logistical issues such as transportation, food, and dealing with inquiries from friends and even the media. Remember that, in our transient society, many people do not have local family members to turn to in a crisis.

- *Take care of your other employees.* Give them a chance to talk about what has happened and, if necessary, provide grief counseling to help them cope.

- *Keep your customers and vendors informed.* As with co-workers, a bond that goes beyond "strictly business" usually develops between customers and vendors who have worked together over time. They will likely want to express their concern for the affected employee, and they also need to know how the tragedy will affect your business.

- *Help smooth the victim's return to work.* People don't always know how to treat someone who has suffered a tragedy, so take steps to help the person ease back into the workplace. Consider an off-site meeting with colleagues in a casual, candid atmosphere, if possible, before the affected person resumes their duties.

- *Expect performance variations.* You may see noticeable changes—either positive or negative—in the affected employee's performance for a long time. Also, there may be a variety of tasks that the person has to deal with in the aftermath such as insurance claims and other legal issues. Be as patient and helpful as possible, keeping in mind that you also have a business to run.

GREAT ADVICE

If your company makes charitable donations, consider supporting the organizations in which your employees are involved. It's a way you can show respect for your employees' efforts and concerns. Of course, be sure the groups meet your own corporate giving guidelines.

DOMESTIC VIOLENCE IS EVERYONE'S BUSINESS

Each year, somewhere between 1 million and 4 million American women are assaulted by an intimate partner. That may sound like a personal problem, but domestic violence is clearly a business issue. The impact of that violence spills over into the workplace in the form of increased absenteeism, high insurance costs for medical claims, lower productivity, and the relative risk to other employees if the batterer decides to attack his partner at work. In fact, the Department of Justice reports that husbands and boyfriends commit 13,000 acts of violence against women in the workplace every year, and more than 70 percent of employed victims report that their abusers have harassed them at work. Perpetrators cause over 60 percent of their victims to be either late to and/or absent from work.

What should you do if either suspect or have clear evidence that one of your employees is a victim of

---

CONTROLLING WORKPLACE RUMORS

The spread of misinformation can be more damaging to a company than any real crisis. This is especially important in smaller organizations, where workplace rumors can cause enough concern and insecurity that morale and productivity suffers, and your best employees may decide they'd be better off working elsewhere.

Use the following tips before the rumors start to fly.

- *What employees are not told, they invent—so tell them what's going on before their imaginations take over.*
- *Honesty acts on a rumor like water acts on a fire.* Cut the grapevine back with the truth.
- *Keep the workforce informed at every stage of change to avoid panic and help employees feel like an important part of the process.*
- *Avoid closed doors.* They're a sure sign that secrets are being told.
- *Clear, direct, face-to-face team briefings, where questions can be asked and answered, are the best way to communicate news.* It may be tempting to hide behind memos and e-mails, but these should be used in addition to face-to-face meetings, not in lieu of them.
- *Encourage questions and invite ideas.* When you gather the experience of the group, your staff may identify unforeseen problems and innovative solutions.

---

domestic violence? It may be tempting to simply look the other way or, as many companies have done, terminate the victim's employment because of substandard performance. But that doesn't do anything to help the victim avoid serious injury or death; it also doesn't do anything to preserve your corporate investment in the employee's training and work.

A better strategy is to help. One way is to provide all employees with information about domestic violence. Even if you are unaware of any specific situations, this will let them know you are concerned for their safety and will support them if they have a problem.

Safety planning benefits the victim, your company, and the community. By supporting the victim and developing a plan to make her less vulnerable at work, the entire workplace becomes safer. At the same time, you send a clear message to the abuser and to the community at large that domestic violence will not be tolerated or ignored.

For information on how to educate yourself and your employees on the dynamics of domestic violence and safety planning, and on resources in your area, contact the National Domestic Violence Hotline at (800) 799-7233 or www.ndvh.org.

MANAGEMENT TIP

If possible, let your employees choose when they work. Employees who can set their own schedules appreciate the flexibility and you'll likely see lower turnover as a result.

SETTING POLICIES ON FACIAL JEWELRY AND BODY ART

Not long ago, the only body part that was routinely pierced for jewelry was the ear lobe, generally only women did it, and they usually had only one hole per ear. But things have changed. Today, not only is it quite common to see multiple piercings in each ear, an increasing number of people are piercing their noses, eyebrows, lips, and even tongues. Along the same lines, more and more people are getting tattoos, many of which are in prominent places on their bodies.

Like it or not, exotic adornment is making its way out of the counter-culture and into the mainstream. How far can you, as an employer, go in setting policies on this type of accessorizing?

A company does not have the right to tell a person they can't pierce their body; however, a company does have the right to establish a dress code and dictate the appearance of workers on the job. Dress codes may be based on image requirements, safety issues, or a combination of the two. A manufacturing facility may restrict the type of jewelry that can be worn on the production floor for safety reasons. A financial services firm may prefer that employees project a conservative, professional image to clients. As long as your dress code is not discriminatory, you have the right to establish the policies you prefer.

Make your dress code as specific as possible to reduce the risk of interpretation challenges. Stipulating that jewelry must be "in good taste" leaves you open to a debate on just what "good taste" is. Instead, outline what is and is not acceptable. For example, you might define the maximum size and number of earrings someone can wear, or you might set a policy of no facial jewelry. Restrictions on tattoos can range from a policy of "no visible body art," which means all tattoos must be covered at work, to no limits at all.

Reasonableness is an important part of a dress code. When safety is not the issue, allow employees as much self-expression as possible while still being appropriately attired for your industry and their role in the company.

All new hires should be advised of the dress code as part of their orientation. If you decide to implement or change your dress code, consider ahead of time how you will deal with existing employees whose current dress may not comply with the new rules.

Finally, before implementing a dress code, have an attorney or someone who is familiar with labor law take a look at your written policy to make sure it is not discriminatory and that it does not violate any existing legislation.

JOB DESCRIPTIONS

Job descriptions are the cornerstone for most human resources practices. Specifically, job descriptions have the following uses:

- They are helpful in developing postings or advertisements for open positions.
- They identify skills and experience required of candidates for open positions.
- They provide prospective employees with a clear picture of job responsibilities prior to the first interview to ensure the position is actually of interest to the candidate.
- They identify the primary outcomes an employee is expected to achieve.
- They help to clarify the standards expected of each employee.
- They are the framework around which individual employee development and training programs are developed.

- They are used to evaluate job worth, which is key to creating a sound compensation program.
- They become an invaluable tool for implementing effective disciplinary efforts.

When you prepare a job description, you should consider including the following information:

- The essential functions of the position
- Other duties that might be required
- Percentage of time devoted to each outcome
- Working conditions, including special physical and environmental demands
- Supervisory responsibilities
- Reporting relationships
- Qualifications including education and experience

Once you have written descriptions for each position in your organization, don't forget to update them as the organization changes. A description of a position with duties that no longer exist is worthless.

Writing job descriptions can be a time-consuming process. Keep focused on the fact that once you have them written, you will be glad you made the effort.

Source: D. Allen Miller, Business Advantage International, Inc.

MOTIVATING PART-TIME EMPLOYEES

For many businesses, part-time employees are an essential segment of the workforce, but it's not always easy to keep them motivated. They often do low-level work, may not have much opportunity for advancement within the company, and are frequently ignored by full-timers. Nevertheless, regardless of how many hours someone works each week, an employer is entitled to expect the maximum benefit from the time that person is on the job. Try these tips for keeping part-timers enthused and productive:

- *Introduce new part-timers.* Set the foundation for part-time employees just as you do for full-timers. Give them a tour of the facility, a good explanation of what the company does, what its goals are, and what the vision is. There should be an orientation for part-time employees, just as there is for full-time people.
- *Provide benefits.* Make part-time employees eligible for the same benefit programs full-timers receive, such as insurance, vacation, and even tuition reimbursement. Pro-rate the benefits so that what part-timers receive is comparable to full-timers' benefits based on hours worked.
- *Train.* Everyone needs to be adequately trained in how to do their job, no matter how many hours they work. Beyond basic job knowledge, provide ongoing training to enhance and expand skills, and groom part-timers for eventual full-time positions.
- *Create an inclusive environment.* The atmosphere should make part-time staff feel that they are as worthwhile and productive for the time they're there as is a full-time employee. If you give gifts at holidays or recognize birthdays for full-timers, do so for part-timers as well. Invite part-timers to participate in company social events, sports teams, and incentive programs. Encourage them to participate in safety and quality programs.
- *Develop career paths.* Though many part-time employees choose to work on a temporary basis because it suits their needs, a significant number is looking for advancement opportunities. Take the time to find out what their skills and goals are and, if possible, develop a plan for growth within your company that will let them use their skills and meet their goals. Along these lines, you can also avoid burnout and reduce turnover if you give part-timers a variety of tasks and not limit them to "grunt" work.

SUPPORT EMPLOYEES WHO TRAVEL FOR YOUR COMPANY

Business travel is often viewed as the single biggest intrusion that work makes on some-one's personal life. It's challenging, tiring, and can create a variety of problems at home. But there are things you can do to make it easier for employees who are on the road to maintain their productivity while they balance their work and personal responsibilities.

- *Provide a consultation and referral program.* Employees may need assistance with a variety of service and information needs related to travel and to caring for their families while they're gone. This is especially important for inexperienced travelers and employees who are primary caregivers for children and/or elderly dependents. Such a program can provide daycare or agency-care information at the destination (a growing percentage of business trips now include children), help with finding overnight care at home while the employee is gone, or general information about travel issues.

- *Offer dependent care vouchers.* The cost of child care, elder care, and even pet care can make business travel a serious financial burden for employees. Consider a voucher program that reimburses workers for these extra costs.

- *Give as much notice as possible.* While it may be impossible to totally avoid last-minute trips, the more advance notice you can give an employee about a trip, the easier it will be for them to prepare both professionally and personally.

WHEN AN EMPLOYEE FILES BANKRUPTCY

In spite of bankruptcy law reform, which appears to be reducing the number of personal bankruptcies, if you have employees, at some point you may have one who seeks protection from creditors through the courts. It's important that you understand your responsibilities and obligations as an employer under the federal bankruptcy code.

There are two basic types of consumer bankruptcy: Chapter 7, which is a straight liquidation, and Chapter 13, under which the debtor agrees to a court-supervised repayment plan. It's possible that an employee could file a Chapter 7 and you would never know. But, under a Chapter 13 filing, you'll probably receive a document called a "pay order" from the trustee in your particular federal district. This will direct you to pay a certain portion of the debtor's wages to the trustee, who will then disburse those funds to creditors.

If the employee owes you money, such as through a payroll advance or loan, you become another creditor and will be treated as such in court. In a Chapter 7 case, you'll get money only if there are assets available to distribute to all of the debtor's unsecured creditors, and that's rare. In a Chapter 13 case, you would have to file a proof of claim, and would receive the same percentage that other unsecured creditors will receive over the course of the repayment plan. In either case, you cannot use future wages to secure payment outside the court on a debt to you or your company that has been designated part of a bankruptcy action, and an individual cannot legally conceal any debts or assets from the court.

Beyond the actual financial details, keep in mind that an employee who has filed bankruptcy is likely to be experiencing a high level of stress and, perhaps, shame. If you have an employee assistance program, or if your insurance will pay for counseling, discreetly remind the employee that such resources are available. If the employee's job performance suffers, address that as a performance issue unrelated to the bankruptcy. Keep in mind that it is a violation of federal law to discriminate against any employee for filing bankruptcy. A bankruptcy should not affect an employment relationship. That means you cannot treat an employee differently or terminate employment solely because that individual has filed bankruptcy.

FAST FACT

Offering benefits improves employee retention. When a firm offers benefits, it decreases the probability of an employee's leaving in a given year by 26.2 percent and increases the probability of staying an additional year by 13.9 percent.

Source: U.S. Small Business Administration

ON-THE-JOB CLASSES FOR NON-ENGLISH-SPEAKING WORKERS IMPROVES PRODUCTIVITY, SAFETY, AND RETENTION

Today's tight job market and vibrant economy is creating entry-level jobs often filled by workers whose first language is not English. Savvy employers are tapping into this rich segment of the labor pool, and then strengthening the value of those employees by helping them learn English with classes held at the worksite.

Advantages of having employees with improved language skills include:

- *Increased confidence and ability to interact with others, including co-workers and customers.* As workers learn English, they can do more and can advance in the company, which increases loyalty and reduces turnover.

ALTERNATIVE TO SICK TIME

Businesses lose millions of dollars each year due to unscheduled absenteeism. The most-cited reason for last-minute absences is family issues, followed by personal illness, personal needs, stress, and an entitlement mentality.

When an employee is unexpectedly absent, you have to pay direct costs (the salary or wages paid to absent employees) and indirect costs (overtime pay for other employees, hiring temporary workers, and supervisory time spent rearranging work schedules).

The problem is that traditional sick-leave plans do not address the issues that drive employee absenteeism. The solution is to figure out why your employees are taking unscheduled absences, then develop time-off programs that truly fit the needs of both your workers and your company.

An effective absence-control program is a paid time off (PTO) system, which provides employees with a "bank" of hours to be used for various purposes instead of traditional separate accounts for sick, vacation, and personal time. Other programs that have proven effective in small businesses include job sharing, flexible scheduling, allowing leave for school functions, emergency child care, and a compressed work week.

- *Fewer errors and reduced overtime.* Workers who understand instructions don't make as many mistakes, which means they don't need to spend time correcting their work.
- *Safety issues.* Being able to speak and read English increases the comprehension of safety-related instructions and warnings, which can reduce workplace accidents.

In most communities with non-English-speaking populations, the school systems offer English-as-a-second-language (ESL) classes for adults—often for free or at a nominal charge. But many workers can't take advantage of classes held in schools, so educators are encouraging employers with enough potential students to hold classes at the worksite, either during or after business hours. Most adult-education programs require between 15 and 20 students in each class. Worksite classes may mean assisting employees who carpool with transportation, but that's far better in the long run than continuing to struggle with language-related communication problems.

Check with your local school board or adult education agency for details on programs that may be available in your area. Many workplace ESL programs can be customized to meet the needs of specific industries or particular business goals.

WHEN YOU'VE GOT BAD NEWS

You've got a problem. It might be that you've just lost a big client, or there's a major production breakdown, or a key staffer is leaving, or whatever, but you've got a problem, and you need to tell your employees about it. How can you do it without demoralizing them and hurting the company further?

Most importantly, don't put it off. There is nothing to be gained, and much to be lost, by waiting. Rumors get out, and if you don't tell your people, they're going to find out anyway, or they're going to make things up. If at all possible, make your announcement in a face-to-face situation. If your company is small enough, do it yourself; if that's not practical, have managers gather employees together and share the information. People need the opportunity to react and ask questions, and they can't do that if they receive a memo.

When making your announcement, tell them what you know, and be honest about what you don't know. Once you've made your announcement, open the meeting up to questions. If you don't have an answer to a specific question, commit to finding out by a deadline, and then do it. If answering the question at that time would reveal confidential information that you're not ready to release, or perhaps that you can't release because of legal issues, be honest.

When the bad news includes the possibility or probability of job losses, give people as much notice as possible (or as required by law). If you can afford it, offer retention incentives to encourage people to stay with you as long as you need them, rather than jumping ship at the first opportunity.

While the situation is being resolved, hold regular informational meetings and also talk to everyone informally. Make sure people are asking questions and getting the answers they need. If you have an employee assistance program (EAP) as part of your benefit package and it's appropriate, consider using that as a resource to help employees deal with the situation.

TIPS FOR TRAINING SENIOR WORKERS

Now that 65- to 69-year-olds are able to work as much as they want without losing their Social Security benefits, we are seeing more seniors in the labor market. What do you need to know about training and integrating them into your organization? The following tips will help you gain the maximum benefit from having these older workers on your team.

- *Get rid of your own stereotypes.*
  Older people are not automatically senile, stubborn, and set in their ways—in fact, many actually "get it" faster than their younger counterparts.

- *Don't teach them what they already know.*
  Though many seniors, particularly women, are entering the workplace for the first time, the majority have years of experience. They have a lot of the basic jobs skills, such as getting to work on time, treating customers and others respectfully, trying to do a good job; you don't need to teach them those things.

- *Give them the time they need to learn.*
  Older people may need more time, often up to twice as long, to learn a new task or skill, but with that additional time, they can learn to perform new tasks with fewer mistakes than younger workers. Of course, like all people, mature adults learn at different rates; if possible, implement a self-paced program.

- *Create an effective learning environment.*
  Senses, particularly sight and hearing, tend to dim with age. Be sure your training facility has adequate lighting and good acoustics, and that background noise is kept to a minimum. The trainer should check at the beginning of each session to make sure everyone can hear. Visual aids should have large, easy-to-read print with high contrast colors, and should not be posted above eye level, because many older people wearing bifocals have difficulty looking up to read. Most older workers prefer sitting in groups around a table to a traditional classroom or theater-style setting. Be sure to provide frequent breaks for using rest rooms or just moving around.

- *Don't assume seniors will resist change and technology.*
  Increasing numbers of seniors have personal computers at home and are comfortable using the internet. Also, many older workers appear inflexible when in fact they are lacking in confidence and, with training, will quickly become more adaptable and accepting of new technology.

For assistance with training seniors, or to find seniors who have completed various educational programs, contact your local area agency on aging, your public school system's adult education department, or local senior citizens centers.

❧ ❧ ❧

SHOULD YOU MATCH AN OFFER AN EMPLOYEE GETS FROM ANOTHER COMPANY?

Competition for good employees is strong, so you shouldn't be surprised when your top people get offers from other companies. The question is: should you try to keep them by matching or beating the offer? Only if it's someone who is critical to your operation; otherwise, let them go.

Even though the employee tells you the amount of the offer, there's a strong likelihood that the issue is more than just financial compensation. Before you make a counter offer, make sure the issue is a matter of money and not of other things—if someone would consider leaving for a small salary increase, chances are they're really leaving for other reasons. So, if the offer is less than a 15 to 20 percent increase, it's not the money, it's something else. They may feel like they don't have a future with you, or perhaps they don't like their boss. In that situation, you might be able to hang on to the employee short-term by matching the dollar offer, but you'll lose them eventually. However, if the offer is for an increase of 20 percent or more, it could truly be the money, and a substantial raise could keep the employee.

If other employees find out about your counter offer, they may use the same technique to negotiate raises. Avoid this by making confidentiality a key part of your terms. And if those terms are violated and word gets around, you let the individual go—it won't happen again.

HELP YOUR NEW EXECUTIVES SUCCEED FROM THE START

You hire executive-level people because of their knowledge, experience, and skills, and you expect them to be as successful in your organization as they were in their previous positions. But they can't succeed by themselves, and when they fail, the overall damage to the organization can be significant. The techniques you use to help a new executive succeed are basically the same ones you use for any new hire, but the angle is slightly different. Consider these recommendations:

- *Define expectations clearly.* Be very specific when telling a new executive what you expect; even the most brilliant executives can't read your mind.
- *Explain what is valued in your culture.* Help new executives understand the unspoken values and guiding principles, and just as importantly, tell them what isn't valued. New executives often come in confident of their track record and ready to put their own stamp on the organization, but if they're not functioning within the existing culture, they're going to fail. Compounding the problem is that companies are often overly tolerant, expecting new hires to figure things out on their own, over time, but it doesn't happen. So the very first time you see someone operating contrary to your culture, let him or her know in a casual, simple way.
- *Foster a culture for learning.* Certainly this is important for employees at all levels, but many senior staffers may feel like they were hired because of what they already know and believe they don't need to develop further. Make it clear that everyone is expected to continue learning and improving with time, that you expect them to be good now, and better in three months, six months, or a year.

• *Offer feedback frequently and regularly.* This is a basic management process that often falls through the cracks when it comes to executives. Discuss expectations and performance weekly for the first month or so, then every other week for a few months, then monthly. These sessions don't need to be formal evaluations; they might be just 15-minute conversations to identify how the executive is doing, what kind of progress is being made, and what the organization can to do help.

If you've hired senior level people before, take a look at your track record before you hire again. Figure out who has been successful, what made them successful, who failed, and why. Then design a process to circumvent those reasons for failure.

ABUSIVE CUSTOMERS TAKE A TOLL ON EMPLOYEES

If your employees deal directly with customers, such as in a retail or call-center environment, consider offering counseling related to customer abuse. "Retail rage" gets worse around the holidays, but it can happen at any time during the year. If you have an employee assistance program, talk to your provider about acute-stress counseling opportunities for employees who have had to deal with an abusive customer. You can't control your customers, but you can support your people and help them deal with the stress when customers are out of line.

VERIFY SOCIAL SECURITY NUMBERS

Verifying that your record of employee names and Social Security numbers match Social Security's records before you report year-end wages will help ensure the successful processing of your annual wage reports. It will save you administrative costs by reducing or eliminating the need to send Form W-2cs (Corrected Wage and Tax Statements) to Social Security and allows Social Security to properly credit your employees' earnings record, which will be important information in determining their Social Security benefits in the future.

The Social Security Number Verification Service (SSNVS) is a program offered by the Social Security Administration that allows employers to use the internet to match their records with Social Security records before preparing and submitting W-2 forms. You may verify up to 10 names and SSNs (per screen) online and receive immediate results. This option is ideal for companies with few employees to verify SSNs prior to issuing W-2s, as well as to verify new hires. Or you may upload overnight files of up to 250,000 names and SSNs and usually receive results the next government business day. This option is idea if you want to verify and entire payroll database or if you hire a large number of workers at a time.

For complete instructions on how to use SSNVS, visit www.ssa.gov.

HIRE FOR WHERE
YOU WANT TO BE,
NOT WHERE YOU ARE

If you are committed to growing your company, keep your goals in mind as you're staffing your operation. You may find that people who perform well when you're a $5 million company will be struggling when you hit $25 million and will be drowning when you get to $60 million. When you have people whose jobs have outgrown them, look for ways to retrain them or shift them to a position they can handle. Don't let them stay in a position they can't do, because they'll fail and it won't be their fault.

As you grow, hire smart people who have worked in larger companies and who know what to do to take your company to that level. Remember that these people don't come cheap, so be prepared to compensate them with a substantial salary, bonus plan, and stock options.

Source: Russ Whitney, Founder & CEO, Whitney Information Network, Inc.

✦ ✦ ✦

CHAPTER 12

Hiring and Firing

IS IT THE RIGHT TIME TO HIRE?

Do you know when it's the right time to hire? Ask yourself these questions, and see if you've waited too long:

- Are you turning down assignments because you don't have time to do them?
- Have you missed some deadlines? Are you satisfied with the work you're doing?
- Do you spend more than half your time on clerical tasks?
- Are you consistently working more than 10 hours a day and weekends?
- Are your family and friends complaining about your lack of attention or participation?
- Have you needed to hire a temp worker or subcontract out some assignments?
- Do you often feel stressed, overworked, or overwhelmed? Is your health suffering?
- Have you wondered if your business is worth the effort?

Source: Rieva Lesonsky, 365 Tips to Boost Your Entrepreneurial IQ

FIVE TIPS FOR RECRUITING WORKERS IN A TOUGH LABOR MARKET

1. *Get referrals from employees.* Consider giving bonuses to employees whose referrals are hired.
2. *Ask your suppliers.* They can recommend good salespeople who have called on them, or competent technical people who have serviced their equipment.
3. *Approach retirees and other good people who have worked for you before.*
4. *Post an ad on the internet.* Some small-business owners experience success in recruiting through such employments sites as Career Builder, Monster Board, and Career Mosaic.
5. *Consider unconventional sources.* People with disabilities often make excellent employees. One business owner turned to non-violent first offenders, who were not sent to prison but had graduated from a Marine-style boot-camp program instead.

Source: SCORE

FOUR MUST-ASK INTERVIEW QUESTIONS

You should have a number of questions to ask prospective employees. But here are four basic questions you should ask in every job interview:

- *What's the greatest asset you'll bring to this company?* This question is a great ice-breaker and sets the interviewee at ease.
- *What's your greatest weakness?* Asking this still surprises many and the answer is key to how the candidate thinks on his or her feet.
- *What was your favorite and least favorite job?* Look here for the candidate's ability to objectively evaluate a situation rather than subjectively react to it.
- *And the ever-popular "Where do you see yourself in five years?"* The right answer here should reflect a wish list of increased responsibilities.

Source: Rieva Lesonsky, 365 Tips to Boost Your Entrepreneurial IQ

? ? ?

The smartest thing I've done is hire people who are better at a particular task than I am.

Words of Wisdom

—Jim Evanger, Co-Founder and CEO, Designs of the Interior (DOTI), Inc.

COMMON ILLEGAL QUESTIONS TO AVOID WHEN INTERVIEWING

Equal Employment Opportunity Commission (EEOC) guidelines, as well as federal and state laws, prohibit asking certain questions of a job applicant, either on the application form or during the interview. What questions should you sidestep? Basically, you can't ask anything not directly related to the job, including:

- Age or date of birth (if interviewing a teenager, you can ask if he or she is 16 years old)
- Sex, race, creed, color, religion, or national origin
- Disabilities of any kind
- Date and type of military discharge
- Marital status
- Maiden name (for female applicants)
- If a person is a citizen (however, you can ask if he or she has the legal right to work in the United States)

Other questions you should avoid include:

- How many children do you have? How old are they? Who will care for them while you are at work?
- Have you ever been treated by a psychologist or psychiatrist?
- Have you ever been treated for drug addiction or alcoholism?
- Have you ever been arrested? (You may, however, ask if the person has been convicted if it is accompanied by a statement saying that a conviction will not necessarily disqualify an applicant for employment.)
- How many days were you sick last year?
- Have you ever filed for worker's compensation? Have you ever been injured on the job?

Source: Rieva Lesonsky, Start Your Own Business

WHEN AN APPLICANT PROVIDES TOO MUCH INFORMATION

You know certain questions are taboo when interviewing prospective employees, such as asking about marital status, childbearing plans, or racial or religious issues. But what do you do when a candidate volunteers such information?

Begin with a thorough understanding of hiring ground rules. Remember that you are not allowed to make a decision affecting employment where the basis of that decision is illegal criteria. It's not illegal for the applicant to provide you with such information, but it's illegal for you to improperly use that information. The safest strategy is to avoid asking questions or engaging in any dialogue that may at any point give the impression that you're using illegal criteria as part of your screening process.

So what do you do if an applicant begins telling you about their church or the fact that they are planning to get married in a few months? Maintain control of the discussion and take it back to the job. Try saying something like, "I need to explore with you the job at hand and what it is you would bring to the company and why you feel you have the skills to do this job."

And if they tell you they have a disability that is not otherwise obvious? Simply say, "Are you asking me for any particular accommodation in this interview?" If they say no, then be direct and say, "Let's take the conversation back to the job." Even if an employee has a disability that might legally affect your hiring decision, you can't used medical criteria to screen out people until after you've extended a firm offer of employment. Most candidates who disclose off-limits information are not trying to cause a problem. Sometimes people come to an interview very open and honest, and they simply don't realize that they're telling you things you don't want to or shouldn't know. That's why you need to control the interview, keeping the discussion politely but firmly focused on the job, and make thorough notes immediately after the meeting so you can justify whatever hiring decision you make should that ever be necessary.

DOING IT RIGHT

To help your company make the right employment choices:

- Always ask for and check *all* references.
- Have more than one person interview an applicant.
- Have every employee complete a job application.
- Ask questions that directly relate to the job and that will verify information listed on the application and resume.

The real key is the right people. I was in the lower one-half of my class that made the other half possible, so I needed more intellect around me. I've never been afraid to hire people who are much better and much stronger than me. Some execs and some managers are afraid to do that, but I love bringing people around me that are much more talented than I was. It's fun to watch them develop their skills. And if you help them properly, they'll help you, too, to get where you want to go.

—ROBERT A. FUNK, FOUNDER AND CHAIRMAN,
EXPRESS PERSONNEL SERVICES

RESUME RED FLAGS

The resume looks great, but is it true? Though nothing can replace a thorough background check on prospective employees, there are ways to spot resume information that may not be completely accurate. The following examples of resume entries should alert you to a potential problem:

- Positions that are not supported with qualifications elsewhere on the resume. In most cases, a senior manager will have a foundation of education and experience building up to their position.

- A series of positions held at or references from companies that have gone out of business. Certainly companies do close down, but be suspicious of impressive information that can't be verified.

- Job titles that don't make sense for the organization. You might want to question someone who was "director of personnel" for a five-employee company, or "vice president of production" for a service organization that doesn't manufacture anything.

That a resume includes one of these red flags doesn't necessarily mean the candidate is lying, but it does mean that you should investigate carefully and completely.

> *Hire a fulltime personal assistant. I thought I couldn't afford to, but she freed me up from much of the busy-ness and allowed me to focus on what was most important to grow the business.*
>
> —KIM KIYOSAKI, AUTHOR OF RICH WOMAN, REAL ESTATE INVESTOR, AND A FOUNDER OF THE RICH DAD COMPANY

Words of Wisdom

RE-HIRING DILEMMA

Should you rehire former employees? There are advantages and disadvantages to consider. On the plus side, it's possible to reduce the chance of making a hiring mistake because you know the former employee's skills, abilities, and working style, and he knows your system. If he was successful before, he'll likely be successful again.

However, you need to consider carefully why the individual left, what he's been doing in the meantime, and why he wants to come back. Then be sure those facts are compatible with your staffing needs. Don't be tempted to rehire a marginal employee primarily because you need bodies, and don't forget or minimize an individual's undesirable characteristics. Finally, consider the impact on the morale of other employees before you bring back a former worker.

GREAT ADVICE

These tips will help you conduct successful employment interviews:

- Be courteous and respectful.
- Conduct the interview in a private place away from distractions.
- Begin the interview on schedule.
- If possible, conduct the interview without interruptions.
- Allow sufficient time for the interview.
- Appreciate the candidate's accomplishments.
- Do not patronize the candidate.
- Do not argue with the candidate.
- Thank the candidate for his/her time and interest.

Source: Small Business Administration

AVOID HIRING DRUG AND ALCOHOL ABUSERS

Small companies are at greater risk of hiring and then suffering the consequences of drug and alcohol abusers than larger businesses. The larger the company, the more likely it is that they will have a drug testing program in place. Job applicants who can't pass a drug test will likely look for a job with a company that does not do drug testing.

The results of hiring such an applicant are not always clearly visible. Substance abuse in the workplace is insidious. Unless there's an accident or crisis of some sort, you may not realize the culprit is literally negatively affecting your bottom line. Losses can occur in five areas: productivity; absenteeism and tardiness; medical claims; pilferage; accidents. In addition, it is becoming increasingly common for employers to be held liable in court for the behavior of employees both on and off the job, as long as they are operating within the scope of their employment. For example, if your employee takes a customer out to dinner, has a few drinks and is then involved in an automobile crash on the way home, you could be held responsible.

Establishing a substance-abuse prevention program can reduce both losses and liability. It can also work as a marketing tool because you can promote the fact that your customers can trust your products and services because your company is a drug-free workplace. A growing number of large companies and government agencies are requiring that their suppliers have some sort of drug-free program.

An effective drug-free workplace program includes:

- A written policy that clearly articulates expectations, practices, and consequences.
- Employee education and awareness.
- Supervisory training.
- Drug and alcohol testing as appropriate and necessary.
- Employee assistance plan.

FIVE TIPS ON HIRING IMMIGRANTS

1. *Understand the benefits.* Immigrants are often well-educated, intelligent, loyal, and dedicated.
2. *Follow the law.* Contact your U.S. Citizenship and Immigration Services field office or visit www.uscis.gov for information and required forms.
3. *Keep things simple.* Limit the number of languages spoken by your staff to reduce the need for interpreters.
4. *Expect a community to develop among those who speak the same language.* It's ok; they can help and support each other and assist in interpretation.
5. *Encourage your employees to learn English.* Send them to courses offered locally or provide classes on-site.

Source: SCORE

DON'T PUT NEW EMPLOYEES ON PROBATION

The word "probation" carries a very negative implication—most of the time, a person on probation has done something wrong and is being watched to see if it's going to happen again. That's not a very welcoming attitude to extend to a new employee. Instead, call the initial trial period an employment "introductory" period. Define it as the time when your company and a new employee are being introduced to each other to determine whether or not you want to make your relationship permanent. Reserve "probation" for employees with performance problems.

ABOUT FORM I-9, EMPLOYMENT ELIGIBILITY VERIFICATION

The Immigration Reform and Control Act made all U.S. employers responsible for verifying the employment eligibility and identity of all employees hired to work in the United States after November 6, 1986. To implement the law, employers are required to complete Employment Eligibility Verification forms (Form I-9) for all employees, including U.S. citizens. Furthermore, every U.S. employer must have a Form I-9 in its files for each employee, unless the employee was hired before November 7, 1986, and has been continuously employed by the same employer.

Form I-9 need not be completed for individuals who are:

- providing domestic services in a private household that are sporadic, irregular, or intermittent;
- providing services for the employer as an independent contractor (they are from an independent business, contracted to do a piece of work according to their own means and methods, and are subject to control only as to results—the employer does not set work hours, or provide necessary tools to do the job; nor does the employer have authority to hire and fire them); and
- providing services for the employer, under a contract, subcontract, or exchange entered into after November 6, 1986. (In such cases, the contractor is the employer for I-9 purposes; for example, a temporary employment agency.)

Employers are required to maintain I-9 records in their own files for three years after the date of hire or one year after the date on which the employee's employment is terminated, whichever is later.

A new employee must complete Section 1 of Form I-9 no later than the close of business on his/her first day of work. The employee's signature holds him/her responsible for the accuracy of the information provided.

The employer is responsible for ensuring completion of the entire form. No later than the close of business on the employee's third day of employment services, the employer must complete section 2 of the Form I-9. The employer must review documentation presented by the employee and record document information of the form. Proper documentation establishes that the employee is authorized to work in the U.S. and that the employee who presents the employment authorization document is the person to whom it was issued. The employer should supply the employee with the official list of acceptable documents for establishing identity and work eligibility. The employer may accept any List A document (establishing both identity and work eligibility) or a combination of a List B document (establishing identity) and List C document (establishing work eligibility) that the employee chooses from the official list to present (the presented documentation is not required to substantiate information provided in Section 1). The employer must examine the document(s) and accept them if they appear to be genuine and relate to the employee who presents them. Requesting more or different documentation than the necessary minimum to meet this requirement may constitute an unfair immigration-related employment practice. If the documentation presented by an employee does not appear to be genuine or relate to the employee who presents them, employers must refuse acceptance and ask for other documentation from the list of acceptable documents that meets the requirements. An employer should not continue to employ an employee who cannot present documentation that meets the requirements.

It is not unusual for a U.S. employer to hire a new employee who doesn't physically come to that employer's offices to complete paperwork. In such cases, employers may designate agents to carry out their I-9 responsibilities. Agents may include notaries public, accountant, attorneys, personnel officers, foremen, etc. An employer should choose an agent cautiously, since they will be held responsible for the actions of that agent.

Note: Employers should not carry out I-9 responsibilities by means of documents faxed by a new employee or through identifying numbers appearing on acceptable documents. The employer must review original documents. Likewise, Forms I-9 should not be mailed to a new employee to complete Section 2 him/herself.

Source: U.S. Citizenship and Immigration Services, www.uscis.gov

WORTH KNOWING

If one of your employees harms someone else, you may be held liable for negligent hiring and retention. Reduce the risk with thorough pre-hire background checks. Terminate workers who show a propensity for dangerous behaviors.

I once underestimated my management team. I thought I needed to go outside of the company to hire an 'expert,' and that really offended my existing managers. When the person did not work out, they came to me and asked for a chance. They were superb. I remember this anytime I am going to hire someone and always offer it to my existing employees first.

—MICHAEL JANSMA, PRESIDENT, GEMAFFAIR.COM

HIRING CONVICTED CRIMINALS

Sooner or later, you're going to have an applicant who answers "yes" to the question "Have you ever been convicted of a felony?" Should you automatically reject that candidate? Not necessarily. In these days of high employment, good workers are in great demand, and you may find some excellent employees who have criminal backgrounds. And unless you have a legal reason for doing so, a blanket policy of excluding applicants with criminal records could leave you open to liability.

To develop a policy on hiring convicted criminals, begin with a clear understanding of the applicable legal requirements. Many states have laws prohibiting employers from rejecting an applicant strictly on the grounds of a past conviction. However, a criminal conviction may make an applicant ineligible for a job that requires bonding or special licensing.

Once you understand the legal requirements that apply to your business, you can assess whether the applicant is the right person for the job. This means considering the conviction in the overall context of the applicant's background, skills, and abilities, and your staffing needs. For example, you might not want someone who has been convicted of embezzlement as your bookkeeper. Also, you would probably view a recent armed robbery somewhat differently than you would a 20-year-old conviction for marijuana possession.

One of the most common convictions employers have to consider is driving while intoxicated (or driving under the influence). In that case, some issues you'll want to keep in mind is whether or not the person will be driving a company vehicle or driving their own car on company business, and if he or she is insurable. It's always a good idea to be able to demonstrate a legitimate business reason for your hiring choices.

HUMANE FIRING: MAKE DIGNITY AND COMPASSION PART OF THE TERMINATION PROCESS

Firing someone, regardless of the reason, is one of the most difficult tasks a manager has to do. And if it isn't done right, the consequences can range from mildly inconvenient (an uncomfortable display of emotion by the departing employee) to catastrophic (an expensive wrongful termination lawsuit or even violence resulting in serious injury and possibly death).

Employees who are not performing up to your needs and expectations should be given appropriate counseling and warnings with time limits and a performance improvement plan. Make it clear that failure to meet the plan within a reasonable time will result in termination so there is no surprise if and when things reach that point. When an employee commits an offense you have defined as cause for immediate termination, such as theft, gross insubordination, or workplace violence, you must respond immediately. If you have effectively communicated your policies, the firing will not be a surprise. In any case, it's a good idea to have an attorney who practices employment law take a look at your policies and review the employee's file before you fire the worker.

Always conduct the termination process with dignity, compassion, and in accordance with all applicable laws and your own internal procedures. As obvious as that may sound, it frequently doesn't happen. Nightmarish stories of people being fired during phone conversations and even by e-mail abound. But what's easier for you may well make the experience more painful and humiliating for the employee, and those emotions generate anger and the potential for retaliation.

Doing the Deed

Certainly there is never a "good time" to fire somebody, but early in the week is better than the day before a weekend or holiday. Firing on Friday afternoon gives people the chance to stew and let their anger build over the weekend; firing on Monday morning lets them immediately direct their energies to recovery and re-employment.

Choose a private place where others cannot hear or see the meeting, and do not allow any interruptions. Keep the tone cordial and professional, but get to the point quickly. Focus on a single valid business reason for the termination. Make it clear that you are not counseling or negotiating, that the decision has been made and is irreversible. You want the employee to understand the reason for the termination, but don't gloat, blame, place guilt, or stretch out the process unnecessarily. Then move on to an explanation of your separation procedures, give the employee that same information in writing, and bring the meeting to a close.

If the employee wants to talk, resist the temptation to interrupt or contradict. Listen, thank the employee for sharing their perspective, and gently reiterate your position. Be as non-confrontational as possible. You don't need to be a winner, and you do not want the terminated employee to feel like a loser. Don't let the conversation get personal; stick to the business reason for your decision, avoid emotion and personal attacks, and direct the employee's

> *Hire your best friend if they're available. At least you'll have one employee you can trust.*
>
> *Words of Wisdom*
>
> —MICHAEL CURCIO, CEO AND FOUNDER, PYROGRILL FRANCHISING, INC.

attention to the future without making any promises you won't or can't keep. It's a good idea to have two managers present during the separation meeting. If your operation is so small that this isn't possible, bring in a consultant, or even your attorney. The person doing the actual firing should be the employee's immediate supervisor. The second person serves as a witness and may possess interpersonal skills that are helpful in the situation.

Remember that a major concern of many people who are fired is what will be said about them later, so assure them that you will treat the reasons behind the termination as confidential. The details should not be discussed with other employees except the management team involved and others with a legitimate need to know. This not only benefits the departing employee, but also demonstrates to your remaining staff that you will treat all employees with respect and dignity.

Offer terminated employees the opportunity to collect their personal belongings privately without having to face their coworkers. That may mean scheduling a time for them to return after normal working hours. Whether or not the employee chooses to pack up their belongings immediately following the separation interview or later, it's a good idea to escort them through that process and off the premises. This protects both the company and the employee from acts or accusations of theft and sabotage.

Finally, remember that though they may have been fired, they didn't die. Depending on the tone of the relationship and degree of friendship that may have developed, it may be appropriate for you or others in the organization to send a card or note or even make a phone call from time to time while the former employee works through a difficult transition.

❧ ❧ ❧

EXIT INFORMATION PACKAGE

Don't expect anyone to remember everything you tell them in a termination interview. Put together an exit information package the employee can take to review later. Many states have laws regarding what you are required to provide in writing. At the least, your package should include that information; other suggested items to include are:

- The employee's final pay check.
- Written details on the severance benefits they will receive, including amounts and timing of payments.
- Instructions for the return of any company property they may possess, which is not handled at the time of the separation interview.
- Written details on the continuation of various benefits, such as insurance, and appropriate COBRA forms.
- A copy of your reference policy so they will know what potential employers will be told.
- A list of community resources, including how to file a claim for unemployment compensation, how to register with the state job service office, and information on support groups.

Don't wait too long to get rid of an employee who is not a positive influence on the rest of the company. Address performance and attitude issues early.

Words of Wisdom

—CHRIS MURPHY, PRESIDENT,
MURPHY LIGHTING SYSTEMS, INC.

YOUR SEVERANCE POLICY

When employees leave, whether they resign or are terminated, you are under no legal obligation to provide anything in the way of wages or benefits beyond paying them for the time they actually worked. Even so, you might want to consider offering some sort of compensation, or severance, to departing employees. An attractive severance policy can benefit your company in two key ways.

First, it can aid in hiring and retention. A severance policy that offers, for example, one week's salary for each year of service to employees who leave may be viewed as an attractive benefit. Certainly you can exempt employees whose employment terminated for cause. You may also include other restrictions, such as disqualifying an employee from receiving severance if he goes to work for a competitor or discloses trade secrets or confidential information.

Second, it can be used as a tool to obtain a release or waiver of claim. For example, you may offer a severance payment on condition that the employee agrees not to sue you for any real or alleged employment practices violations. Employees don't have to

sign such an agreement, but if they don't, you don't have to pay the severance.

The concept of severance evolved from negotiations between labor organizations and employers. Today, it's common for executives to include severance (sometimes called a golden parachute) in their employment contract. Severance compensation may include cash (paid in a lump sum or over time), continued benefits, and even stock purchase arrangements.

In putting together a severance policy, begin by taking a look at your marketplace. Are other companies offering severance packages? If so, make yours competitive. If not, consider putting those benefit dollars elsewhere. Then think about what you want to accomplish with your policy: do you want a benefit to attract new employees; a program that promotes longevity; a tool to discourage workers from going to competing companies; or a device that reduces the chance of employment-related litigation?

Your severance policy may be a standard package that every employee receives, or it may be negotiated individually based on specific circumstances. Depending on how it is set up, it may come under ERISA (Employee Retirement Income Security Act), and if so, you'll need to be sure it meets federal requirements. Before you implement any general severance policy or a particular agreement, have an attorney review it to be sure it meets any applicable statutes and is not discriminatory.

DOING IT RIGHT

Certainly if anyone has done something that would call for immediate dismissal according to your company policies—for example, theft or violence—then you must take that action and manage the situation. But when the employee is simply not performing to your needs, or if the job requirements have changed but the employee has not, schedule the termination in a way that does the least amount of disruption to your organization.

If I had thought about it, I wouldn't have done the experiment. The literature was full of examples that said you can't do this.

—SPENCER SILVER, INVENTOR OF POST-IT NOTES

❧ ❧ ❧

CHAPTER 13

The Legal Side of Human Resources

LABOR LAWS THAT APPLY TO YOUR COMPANY

It is essential to understand the laws and regulations that impact business. Failure to comply with these government rules will, sooner or later, result in problems—problems that include costly investigations or audits, fines, and a whole lot of worry.

The following is a list of federal employment laws and the number of employees a company must have on the payroll before the company is obligated to comply.

Employers with at least one employee must comply with:
- Consumer Credit Protection Act
- Employee Polygraph Protection Act
- Employment Retirement Income Security Act (ERISA)
- Equal Pay Act
- Fair Labor Standards Act (FLSA)
- Federal Income Tax Withholding
- Federal Insurance Contribution Act (FICA)

- Immigration Reform & Control Act (IRCA)
- Labor Management Relations Act
- National Labor Relations Act (NLRA)
- Uniform Guidelines for Employment Selection Procedures
- Uniformed Services Employment & Re-employment Rights Act of 1994

Employers with 11 or more employees also need to comply with:
- Occupational Safety & Health Act (OSHA Illness/Injury Recording and Reporting Requirements)

Employers with 15 or more employees also need to comply with:
- Americans with Disabilities Act
- Civil Rights Act of 1964
- Pregnancy Discrimination Act
- Title VII of the Civil Rights Act

Employers with 20 or more employees also need to comply with:

- Age Discrimination in Employment Act
- Consolidated Omnibus Budget Reconciliation Act (COBRA)

Employers with 50 employees or more also need to comply with:

- Family Medical Leave Act (FMLA)

Employers with 100 or more employees must also comply with:

- EEO-1 form to the EEOC (Executive Order 11246, requires federal contractors with 50 or more employees and $50,000 in government contracts to file the EEO-1 report each year).
- Worker Adjustment Retraining Notification Act (WARN)

In addition to these federal regulations, each state has its own set of employment laws. Be sure you understand and comply with those rules if you want to make your business viable.

Source: D. Allen Miller, Business Advantage International

WORTH KNOWING

Call local law firms and ask if they offer free newsletters on employment law or other issues that affect your operation. Most firms will be happy to add you to their mailing lists at no charge.

We could all use a little coaching. When you're playing the game, it's hard to think of everything.

—JIM ROHN, AUTHOR AND SPEAKER

Words of Wisdom

EMPLOYMENT PRACTICES LIABILITY INSURANCE

The statistics should alarm you: Every year, between 77,000 and 81,000 charges are filed against employers under statutes enforced by the Equal Employment Opportunity Commission, and more than half of such claims are brought against companies with fewer than 100 employees—companies rarely prepared to deal with such actions.

No matter how happy you think your workers are, if you have employees, you have a risk, says Jeffrey O'Shaughnessy, assistant vice president of business and new product development with The Hartford Steam Boiler Inspection and Insurance Co. in Hartford, Connecticut. "Even in cases where it's all family, we have seen some very ugly disputes," he says. "And even if the claim isn't valid, you still have to respond to it. About three-quarters of all claims are ultimately found to be groundless or fraudulent, but defense costs [for a single charge] can easily be $50,000."

The solution is Employment Practices Liability Insurance, which, says O'Shaughnessy, "provides coverage for charges or allegations of sexual harassment, wrongful termination, and discrimination when those allegations are brought by an employee against his or her employer." The coverage includes defense costs and payment of settlements and/or judgments up to the policy's limits.

Until recently, this coverage was expensive and cumbersome to buy, putting it out of reach of most small businesses. But now, says O'Shaughnessy, the coverage can be added to a standard business-owners policy for as little as $200 a year—sometimes even less—for a company with just a few employees. Your insurance agent can tell you how to get coverage.

SHOULD YOU CONDUCT SURVEILLANCE ON A DISABILITY CLAIMANT?

One of your employees has filed a disability claim. You have doubts about the veracity of the claim, but your insurance company will check it out and you don't need to do anything, right? Not necessarily. Insurance company claims adjusters may be too overworked to thoroughly investigate each case, and they often work on the telephone rather than in person.

So why should you be concerned if your insurance company is willing to pay out hundreds of thousands of dollars in bogus claims? Because just one or two major claims can mean substantially higher premiums or even a canceled policy.

Reasonable surveillance does not violate an individual's privacy if the investigation is conducted in an ethical and professional manner. Also, when people file claims, there is an expectation that the claim will be investigated.

How do you know when video surveillance might be appropriate? The following red flags should make you suspicious:

- Claimant is never home to answer the phone or is "sleeping and cannot be disturbed."
- Leads from co-workers that claimant is active in sports, other work, etc.
- Rehab report shows claimant is "suntanned, muscular, has calluses on his hands, and grease under his fingernails."
- Claimant receives mail at a post office box and will not divulge residence address.
- Claimant has a history of self-employment or is a tradesman (carpenter, electrician) who might work for cash while feigning disability.
- Claimant has moved out of state or country.
- Excessive demands for compensation.
- Disability beyond that normally associated with claimed injury.
- "Dueling doctors." One says claimant is disabled, another says the opposite.

ALL EMPLOYEES NEED EEOC TRAINING

When large companies get sued for discrimination, the case usually makes the headlines. But small companies can be litigation targets as well. Your best defense is to establish an anti-discrimination policy that meets all applicable federal, state, and local regulations—and make sure everyone in your organization understands and abides by it. Provide all employees with a copy of the policy and have them sign a document stating that they have received it and understand that violations will result in disciplinary action.

All employees, supervisors, and managers should receive necessary training so they know what is appropriate workplace behavior and what is not. For example, the line between "just a joke" and a "hostile work environment" is often drawn by perception, and a bit of misplaced humor can result in a nasty and expensive lawsuit.

Many consultants offer training in this area. You can also get assistance (much of it at no cost) from the U.S. Equal Employment Opportunity Commission.

Words of Wisdom

No man can always be right. So the struggle is to do one's best, to keep the brain and conscience clear, never to be swayed by unworthy motives or inconsequential reasons, but to strive to unearth the basic factors involved, then do one's duty.

—Dwight D. Eisenhower

WHEN EMPLOYEES SUE

You know you can be sued by an employee for discrimination or sexual harassment. Did you know that you could also be sued for negligent evaluation, deprivation of career opportunity, and even wrongful infliction of emotional distress? Or for failure to employ by someone you didn't even hire? And there's always wrongful termination.

Make the employer's legal minefield a little less treacherous with employment practices liability insurance (EPLI), which typically pays for the costs of defending many types of employee lawsuits and for judgments and settlements (but not for punitive damages or civil or criminal fines). EPLI can be purchased as stand-alone coverage or as an endorsement to your general business policy.

Even though you think you're doing a good job in respecting employees' legal rights, this coverage is worth considering. If, despite all your efforts, you fail to resolve an employee problem before that person retains an attorney, you'll appreciate having the insurance to cover your costs.

Of course, insurance is not a replacement for good employment practices. Purchase EPLI in conjunction with the development of sound personnel policies and procedures. Effective hiring and screening programs will help you avoid discrimination in hiring. Posting policies throughout the workplace, placing them in employee handbooks, and communicating them in other ways will make your policies clear to all. Be sure employees know what to do if they believe they are the victims of illegal conduct or other activity that violates company policies. And whenever a problem arises, document everything that occurs, no matter how minor it may seem, so that if necessary you can demonstrate the steps you took to prevent and solve employee disputes.

✣ ✣ ✣

I'm slowly becoming a convert to the principle that you can't motivate people to do things, you can only demotivate them. The primary job of the manager is not to empower but to remove obstacles.

Words of Wisdom

—SCOTT ADAMS, CARTOONIST

⚜ ⚜ ⚜

CHAPTER 14

Family Business

Why do you want to start a business with your family? If it's because you think it will be greatly satisfying to build a business with the people you love and it will allow you to spend more time with them, you're not alone. Many family businesses are started for these reasons. Unfortunately, that's not enough of a foundation on which to build a solid business.

Have you ever lived with a good friend—say, as roommates in college? If so, you know that just because you are great friends does not mean you will get along in close quarters. While it doesn't necessarily doom you to pulling each other's hair out and changing the locks while the other one is at work, you do need to sit down together and sketch out all the details of what it will be like to run a business together. You won't really know whether you get along as business partners until you are actually up and running, of course, but some forethought can go a long way toward eliminating messiness down the road. The key

thing to keep in mind is that family "systems" and business practices do not go hand in hand. The quarrels that father and son have over who drank the last of the milk have no place in a business. (Would you ever argue about milk with your boss?)

Statistically speaking, most family businesses do not fail because of a business reason—it's the family baggage that weighs them down and eventually kills things.

Essentially, each family member must be prepared to behave in his or her role exactly as they would in a traditional office setting. Cold as it may sound, the business must come first if you want to be successful. You can call one another whatever you like as far as titles go, but the important thing is that each role is well-defined and you all respect one another's boundaries. For instance, an employee-daughter should not be asking a CEO-dad to "take care of" this or that because she has a softball game that afternoon, and vice versa.

While there are clearly some possible disadvantages to operating a family business, there can also be advantages. Family members are often fiercely committed to making the business succeed—everyone is a strong link, because everyone has a stake in seeing that the business prospers. In addition, family members are often sensitive to one another's needs. While it's certainly wise to keep personal matters out of the business, this rule doesn't always work. If someone has a major crisis, other family members can respond accordingly, taking on that person's work for the day or just taking time to talk it out. Business comes first, yes, but not at the expense of any family member's well-being.

So, before you start your family business, take the time to work out all the details. Do some brainstorming together to decide what type of business you might like to start together—one that will augment everyone's talents and pool them in such a way that your business can grow for years to come. And make sure all parties are aware of the unique risks and rewards associated with family business.

Source: Karen E. Spaeder, "The Good, the Bad & the Ugly of Family Business," Entrepreneur.com

FIVE COMMON TRAPS IN STARTING A BUSINESS WITH YOUR SPOUSE

Avoid the following five common traps so both your business and marriage can thrive.

1. *Misplacing your priorities.* Your relationship should always come first. Don't let the business become more important than the marriage.
2. *Overworking.* Don't fall into the all-work-and-no-play trap. It proves deadly to both the business and the relationship.
3. *Poor communication.* Couples must talk openly and frequently about both business and personal issues.
4. *Forgetting the big picture.* It's all too easy to get bogged down in daily minutiae, but don't lose sight of your business or personal goals.
5. *Conflicting personalities.* In business, it's actually better to think differently than the same. Consider your differences as opportunities to grow your business.

Source: Rieva Lesonsky, 365 Tips to Boost Your Entrepreneurial IQ

Divorce has financial ramifications in every family business, and emotional ones in every business family. While legal strategies, succession and tax planning can minimize the monetary effects on the business of a marital break-up, anticipating its impact on relationships, morale, and even performance in the workplace is an important consideration, too.

—Jane Adams, Ph.D.

ONLINE RESOURCES FOR FAMILY BUSINESSES

Family Business Experts
www.family-business-experts.com

Family Business Institute
www.familybusinessinstitute.com

Family Business Magazine
www.familybusinessmagazine.com

Family Business Network International
www.fbn-i.org

MANAGE THESE FIVE CRITICAL RESOURCES IN YOUR FAMILY BUSINESS

In "Managing Resources: Linking Unique Resources, Management, and Wealth Creation in Family Firms" (*Entrepreneurship Theory and Practice*, Summer 2003), David Sirmon and Michael Hitt examined the strategies behind successful family businesses. They found that success is tied directly to how well a company manages the five unique resources that every family business possesses.

1. Human capital

The first resource is the family's human capital, or "inner circle." When the skill sets of different family members are coordinated as a complementary cache of knowledge, with a clear division of labor, the likelihood of success improves significantly.

2. Social capital

The family members bring valuable social capital to the business in the form of networking and other external relationships that complement the insiders' skill sets.

3. Patient financial capital

The family firm typically has patient financial capital in the form of both equity and debt financing from family members. The family relationship between the investors and the managers reduces the threat of liquidation.

4. Survivability capital

The family company must manage its survivability capital—family members' willingness to provide free labor or emergency loans so the venture doesn't fail.

5. Lower costs of governance

The family business must manage its ability to hold down the costs of governance. In non-family firms, these include costs for things such as special accounting systems, security systems, policy manuals, legal document, and other mechanisms to reduce theft and monitor employees' work habits. The family firm can minimize or eliminate these costs because employees and managers are related and trust each other.

Clearly delineating these unique family resources and leveraging them into a well-coordinated management strategy greatly improves your business's chances of success compared to non family-owned companies.

Source: David Newton, "Managing Your Critical Operations," Entrepreneur.com

---

DOING IT RIGHT

Family members should take care with their business demeanor. Address each other by name in the workplace—not "Mom," "Dad," "Son," or "Dear." Using familial names sends a signal to employees that they're outsiders and puts the family relationship into play where it doesn't belong.

Words of Wisdom

Separating personal from business is a very difficult thing to do, but it's an absolute must. If you're in business with your spouse, separate your responsibilities so that neither of you reports to the other. If you bring your kids into the company, have them report to someone other than you. And make them earn their way. If you don't, you're setting them up for failure.

—RUSS WHITNEY, FOUNDER & CEO, WHITNEY INFORMATION NETWORK, INC.

WHEN THINGS AREN'T WORKING WELL WITH FAMILY MEMBERS

Working with members of your family has the potential to be a very trying, sticky, and challenging situation. It can bring out the best in you and your relatives—and also the worst in your working relationships. It can cause you to minimize or overlook errors or omissions committed by your relative, or it can make you excessively hypercritical and condescending.

Why does this happen? Working with family members is difficult for any number of reasons:

- You know so much about the other person— you've been privy to intimate information about them.
- You've most likely had arguments or negative conflicts with them.
- You have years of experiences with them, both positive and negative.
- You know the other person's "hot and cold buttons," the thoughts, feelings, and behaviors that reward, cajole, and pacify, or punish, threaten, and dismiss the other person.
- Maybe you don't like your relative or, conversely, you're very close to them, which means you could either be overly critical or overly protective.
- You may provide too much supervision or teamwork—or you may provide too little.

As a result of the knowledge and closeness you have with this other person, you may find it difficult to be rational, logical, accurate, or fair with your thoughts, feelings and behaviors when it comes to interacting with that person. Your relationship with them—both at work and in your personal life—is probably suffering. So how do you begin to correct the situation? Follow these steps:

1. Approach the other person and acknowledge that the current relationship isn't working optimally, that something is either "too right" or "too wrong," too positive or too negative.

2. Discuss the impact your behaviors or attitudes are having on other employees and the company as a whole.

3. Agree to meet together or with an experienced, neutral, fearless, and objective HR manager or external consultant.

4. Agree that you're going to work together to improve and maximize the current relationship for your own sakes as well as the sake of the organization.

5. Agree that you want to work toward making the working atmosphere more professional and less personal. You have to agree not to allow your personal feelings, either positive or negative, to enter the workplace. But be warned: These tactics will only work if you empower someone you trust—including another relative—to step in and stop actions that appear to be based on irrational feelings, either positive and negative (in other words, actions that you're taking that overlook or are overly critical of your relative's behavior).

6. Clarify the specific goals each of you agrees to meet so that behaviors and attitudes are directed toward meeting the company's goals and mission. Ensure that any statement of goals you create is specific, can be measured and assessed, and can be successfully achieved.

7. Make sure that your roles are carefully, objectively, rationally, and completely described to ensure optimal clarity by all individuals for all roles. This is an especially critical step because it's very common that working relationships fall apart when this step has not

been taken. When employees, at any level, are confused about who is responsible for what, conflict and misunderstandings result, and productivity, employee satisfaction, and customer satisfaction all decrease. To avoid this morass, you must spend time working on making each individual's explicit obligations. This facet of working together refers not only to each person's tasks and responsibilities, but also to each person's reporting relationships and source of power and influence, including their time, salary and bonuses, employees and equipment.

8. Clarify the work processes that will be used on a daily basis: the process for making decisions, including who can make what kind of decisions, who is involved in these steps, and how decisions are to be made (by an individual, a pair, or small group). Also, consider how to communicate with others and, in particular, which others. Basically, this aspect refers to just who is included in the communications loop and why. Are all the key players to be kept up to date about occurrences? Are key people being left out of the communications loop for reasons of power or jealousy? Are inappropriate people being brought into the loop for reasons of patronage?

9. Build trust. Start by acknowledging the current situation. You'll be appreciated and valued for discussing a topic that others know about but are reluctant to bring up. Make sure that others can trust what you're saying and doing by backing up your thoughts and actions with clarity and explanations. Then, when you make a commitment to change the status quo, do what you're saying and say what

you're doing. Make sure your actions speak for themselves, and when they don't, offer clear explanations. In addition, act with integrity, honesty, and truthfulness in all that you do.

Above all, make certain that you're competent in all that you do. Ensure that you have the knowledge, skills, and abilities to perform at a high level. If you don't, get some training, find a mentor, or redesign your tasks and responsibilities to align them with what you do best. Nothing destroys trust faster than incompetence. Trust is potentially the strongest element in any relationship; without it, organizations fall apart.

10. Show the positive quality of interpersonal relationships. Just because you're related to someone doesn't mean you need to love them or worship them, especially on the job. Nor does it mean that the company is a playground for working out family problems. What is required is that you demonstrate respect for other people, especially your relatives. You needn't be fawning or ostentatious with your praise or criticism of them, but you do need to be professional and appropriate, whatever the true nature of your feelings and attitudes toward others, especially family.

Source: Adapted from: David G. Javitch, Ph.D., "Ten Tips for Working with Family Members," Entrepreneur.com

---

Effective people are not problem-minded; they're opportunity-minded. They feed opportunities and starve problems.

Words of Wisdom

—STEPHEN COVEY, AUTHOR

✤ ✤ ✤

CHAPTER 15

Choosing, Developing, and Pricing Products and Services

CHOOSING A PRODUCT OR SERVICE TO SELL

Ready to break into a new market? Answering these 29 questions will determine if the product or service you want to sell deserves your commitment.

Fully 80 percent of the products and services being consumed today are different from those that were being consumed five years ago. And five years from today, 80 percent of the products being used will be new and different from those being used today.

There are thousands of products and services available to consumers today. And there are unlimited opportunities for you to enter the marketplace and compete effectively with a new product or service that's better in some way than what's already being offered by your competitors. Remember, your skill at choosing that product or service is critical to your success.

Once you have a product or service in mind, you need to begin with a self-analysis:

- What kinds of products do you like, enjoy, consume, and benefit from?

- Do you like the product or service you're planning to sell?
- Can you see yourself getting excited about this product or service?
- Would you buy it and use it yourself?
- Would you sell it to your mother, your best friend, your next-door neighbor?
- Can you see yourself selling this product or service for the next five to ten years?
- Is this a product or service that you intensely desire to bring to the marketplace?

Analyze the product or service from the customer's point of view:

- What does the product achieve, avoid, or preserve for the customer?
- How does the product improve your customer's life or work?
- To what kind of customers will you be selling the product?
- Do you personally like the customers who'll be buying this product or service?

Imagine that you've hired a management consultant to get advice on introducing this new product or service. They're going to cut right to the chase and ask you these very objective, bottom-line questions:

- Is there a real demand for the product at the price you'll have to charge?
- Is the demand large enough for you to make a profit?
- Is the demand concentrated enough so you can advertise, sell, and deliver the product at a reasonable expense?

Dig even deeper into the potential success of your product or service by determining the answer to the following critical questions:

- What is to be sold, exactly? Describe the product in terms of what it does for the customer.
- To whom is the product going to be sold? Describe your ideal customer.
- What price will you have to charge for the product for it to be profitable?
- Who's going to sell the product?
- How is the product to be sold? What method of sales, or process of promotion, will you use?
- How is the product or service to be manufactured or produced?
- How is the product going to be paid for and by whom?

- How is the product or service going to be delivered to the customer?
- How is it going to be serviced, repaired, guaranteed, or replaced?

And you're not done yet. There are a series of additional questions you need to ask before you make a final decision on a new product or service offering.

- Is there a real need for the product or service in today's market?
- Is your new product or service better than anything else currently available?
- In what three ways is your product superior to its competition?
- Is your product lower priced or of better quality than anything else that is available?
- Do you think you could become the number-one supplier in the market for this product or service?

Source: Brian Tracy, "Choosing a Product or Service to Sell,"
Entrepreneur.com

I have made decisions based on "expert" opinion that, in retrospect, weren't as good as the decisions I would have made using my own instincts.

Words of Wisdom

—JIM EVANGER, CO-FOUNDER AND CEO,
DESIGNS OF THE INTERIOR (DOTI), INC.

PAY ATTENTION TO DEMOGRAPHIC TRENDS

We are seeing some interesting demographic shifts in the U.S. Minority groups are increasing in size and market power, and in many areas, minority groups have become the majority. Also, as the general population ages and lives longer, their preferences are driving a substantial portion of market demand.

As you develop products and marketing strategies, consider demographics including age and ethnicity, as well as other trends, such as food preferences, leisure activities, shopping habits, and other lifestyle changes.

HOW DO YOU KNOW WHEN YOU NEED NEW PRODUCTS?

How do you know when you need new products? Early detection of a problem with existing products is critical. The following eight symptoms of a declining product line will provide clues far enough in advance to help you do something about the problem before it's too late. Not all the symptoms will be evident in every situation, but you can start suspecting your product line when more than just one or two crop up.

1. *You're experiencing slow growth or no growth.* A short-term glitch in product sales can happen any time. If, however, company revenue either flattens or declines over an extended period, you have to look for explanations and solutions. If it isn't the economy or some outside force beyond your control; if your competitors didn't suddenly become more brilliant; if you still have confidence in your sales force; if there are no major problems with suppliers, examine your product line.

2. *Your top customers are giving you less and less business.* It may not be worth your while to determine your exact market share when a rough idea of where you stand will suffice. But knowing how much business you get compared to your competitors is critical. Every piece of business your competitors are getting is business you are not getting—and may never get. If your customers' businesses are growing and the business you get from them isn't, your product may be the culprit. Chances are, someone else is meeting your customers' needs.

3. *You find yourself competing with companies you've never heard of.* If you've never heard of a new competitor or don't know much about

them, watch out! They have found a way to jump into a market with new products and technology that could leave you wondering what hit you. It might not be that your product has a fundamental flaw. It's more often the case that someone has brought innovation to the industry. You earn no points for status quo thinking.

4. *You're under increasing pressure to lower your prices.* No one likes to compete strictly on price, and if your product is clearly superior and offers more value than lower-priced competitors, you don't have to. Everyone understands that great new products eventually run their course and turn into commodities. One day, a customer tells you she can't distinguish the benefits of your widget from those of one or more of your competitors, and now you are in a price squeeze. If you want the business, you have to lower your prices to stay competitive. If that was where it ended, things might stabilize, although at a lower price level. But lower prices usually mean lower profit margins, which usually mean less investment in keeping the product current, which means more price pressure, lower margins—and so it goes.

5. *You're experiencing higher-than-normal turnover in your sales force.* Good salespeople want to win customers so they can make more money. When they have trouble competing, they can't win customers or make money. So they look for new opportunities and challenges that will bring them what they want. You'll always have turnover, but heavy turnover is a symptom of something very wrong. It could be an ill-advised change in the compensation scheme or a new sales manager coming in with a negative attitude. But it could also be that members of your sales team are frustrated because

they're having trouble selling your products. When business owners start to pressure their sales forces to get order levels up, morale drops because the salespeople know there isn't much they can do.

6. *You're getting fewer and fewer inquiries from prospective customers.* We all dread the time when the phone stops ringing and prospects stop coming in. When advertising or other forms of promotion aren't creating the results you want, and you see fewer positive results from the money spent, something could be wrong with the way customers see your company. An obsolete product line positions you as an obsolete company.

7. *Customers are asking for product changes you can't or don't want to make.* This is a not-too-subtle sign that your product may no longer meet market needs. There will be times when you have to decide whether filling a customer's request is in your company's best interests. When customers say "I want it this way," you may want to say no because you doubt you could ever recover the costs of the change, even by raising the selling price. But when the customer says "I want it this way, and it's standard at ABC Widgets," you should suspect that you aren't keeping up with changing customer needs. When your competitors have leapt ahead of you in features and benefits, you must either catch up or leap ahead of them with innovations of your own, or you'll fall so far behind you become a marketplace postscript.

8. *Some of your competitors are leaving the market.* In the short term, this sounds great. Your competitors drop out, and you pick up the business they leave behind. The pie is shrinking, and as it does, business gets better than ever. But beware: this is a classic signal of a declining market. Nobody walks away from a growth business. Vibrant growth markets attract new competitors; they don't discourage them.

Source: Entrepreneur.com

THE TOP SIX MISTAKES INVENTORS MAKE

Mistake #1: Expecting unrealistic results
Inventing is not a get-rich-quick scheme.

Mistake #2: Failing to search the market early on
Don't develop your product in a vacuum; do your research to determine the product is not already on the market.

Mistake #3: Assuming everyone will want your invention
Find out if your product is something that people will actually want, and more importantly: buy.

Mistake #4: Sending your idea—and your money—to an Invention Promotion Company

Companies like these prey on hopeful inventors The legitimate companies don't advertise and won't seek money upfront.

Mistake #5: Sinking all your money into a patent
A patent should rarely be your first step. First discern whether your idea is marketable.

Mistake #6: Lacking business acumen
The "idea" is a small component of the overall process.

Source: Tamara Monosoff, "Top 6 Mistakes Inventors Make," Entrepreneur.com

ANYTHING WORTH DOING IS WORTH DOING POORLY

Have you ever noticed that software—such as Microsoft's Windows—comes in versions such as Windows 2.0 and Windows 3.0? What that means is that they have improved their product and now want you to buy the better version. In other words, the first product they sold you was not perfect. They may have sold it knowing it had flaws, bugs, and needed to be improved.

Many people fail to get to market because they are constantly perfecting their product. Like the person who is waiting for all the lights to be green, some entrepreneurs never get to market because they are looking for, or working on, perfecting their product or writing the perfect business plan. My rich dad often said, "Anything worth doing is worth doing poorly." Henry Ford said, "Thank God for my customers. They buy my products before they are perfected." In other words, entrepreneurs start and continue to improve themselves, their businesses, and their products. Many people will not start unless everything is perfect. That is why many of them never start.

Knowing when to introduce a product into the marketplace is as much an *art* as a *science*. You may not want to wait for a product to be perfect; it may never be perfect. It just has to be "good enough." It merely has to work well enough to be accepted in the marketplace. However, if the product is so flawed that it doesn't work for its intended purpose, or otherwise does not meet marketplace expectations or causes problems, it can be very difficult to reestablish credibility and a reputation for quality.

One of the marks of a successful entrepreneur is being able to assess the expectations of the marketplace and know when to *stop developing and start marketing*. If the product is put on the market a little prematurely, then the entrepreneur can simply improve it, and take steps to maintain the goodwill in the marketplace. On the other hand, delay in introducing a product can mean opportunities irretrievably lost, a window of opportunity missed.

For those of you who remember the early versions of Windows, you'll recall how frequently your computer "crashed." (There were some who said that Windows was so full of bugs that it should have come with a can of insecticide.) If an automobile broke down as frequently as Windows did, it would not have been acceptable in the marketplace. In fact, the automobile would have been a "lemon," and the manufacturer would have been forced to replace it. Windows, however, notwithstanding the bugs—the flaws—was phenomenally successful. Why was that? It filled a need in the marketplace and was not out of line with marketplace expectations. Microsoft recognized a window of opportunity and started marketing. As those of you who use the present version of Windows know, if Microsoft had waited for Windows to be perfect, it still would not be in the marketplace.

Source: Before You Quit Your Job: 10 Real-Life Lessons Every Entrepreneur Should Know About Building a Multimillion-Dollar Business *by Robert T. Kiyosaki with Sharon L. Lechter, C.P.A.*

STAGES OF NEW PRODUCT DEVELOPMENT

New product development can be described as a five-stage process, beginning with generating ideas and progressing to marketing completed products.

Generating ideas

Generating ideas consists of two parts: creating an idea and developing it for commercial sale. There are many good techniques for idea creation, including brainstorming, random association, and even daydreaming. You may want to generate a long list of ideas and then whittle them down to a very few that appear to have commercial appeal.

Evaluating and screening product ideas

Everybody likes their own ideas, but that doesn't mean others will. When you are evaluating ideas for their potential, it's important to get objective opinions. For help with technical issues, many companies take their ideas to testing laboratories, engineering consultants, product development firms, and university and college technical testing services. When it comes to evaluating an idea's commercial potential, many entrepreneurs use the Preliminary Innovation Evaluation System (PIES) technique. This is a formal methodology for assessing the commercial potential of inventions and innovations.

Protecting your ideas

If you think you've come up with a valuable idea for a new product, you should take steps to protect it. Most people who want to protect ideas think first of patents. There are good reasons for this. For one thing, you will find it difficult to license your idea to other companies—should you wish to do so—without patent protection. However, getting a patent is a lengthy, complicated process, and one on which you shouldn't embark without professional help; this makes the process expensive. If you wish to pursue a patent for your ideas, contact a registered patent attorney or patent agent.

Many firms choose to protect ideas using trade secrecy. This is simply a matter of keeping knowledge of your ideas, designs, processes, techniques, or any other unique component of your creation limited to yourself or a small group of people. Most trade secrets are in the areas of chemical formulas, factory equipment, and machines and manufacturing processes. The formula for Coca-Cola is one of the best-recognized and most successful trade secrets.

Finalizing design research and development

Research and development is necessary for refining most designs for new products and services. As the owner of a growing company, you are in a good position when it comes to this stage. Most independent inventors don't have the resources to pay for this costly and often protracted stage of product introduction. Most lenders and investors are trapped by a Catch-22 mentality that makes them reluctant to invest in ideas until after they're proven viable in the marketplace. If you believe in your idea, you can be the first to market.

R&D consists of producing prototypes, testing them for usability and other features, and refining the design until you wind up with something you think you can make and sell for a profit. This may involve test-marketing, beta testing, analysis of marketing plans and sales projections, cost studies, and more. As the last step before you commit to rolling out your product, R&D is perhaps the most important step of all.

Promoting and marketing your product

Now that you have a ready-for-sale product, it's time to promote, market, and distribute it. Many of the rules that apply to existing products also apply to promoting, marketing, and distributing new products. However, new products have some additional wrinkles. For instance, your promotion will probably consist of a larger amount of customer education, since you will be offering something that has never been seen before. Your marketing may have to be broader than the niche efforts you've used in the past because, odds are, you'll be a little unsure about the actual market out there. Finally, you may need to test some completely new distribution channels until you find the right place to sell your product.

Source: Entrepreneur.com

PRIVATE-LABEL FOOD AND BEVERAGE SALES WILL EXCEED $56 BILLION BY 2011

Leaving behind the nondescript packaging and "generic" identity of a decade ago, private-label or store-brand food and beverage sales are soaring, with 2006 sales at more than $48 billion and projections that sales will top $56 billion by 2011. Dairy and grain foods lead the pack. In the beverage category, store-brand bottled water and energy drinks top the list.

Market growth comes as no surprise as retailers and manufacturers have replaced the low-quality "generic" products with high-quality products and packaging that rival national brands. Report findings show that 41 percent of shoppers now identify themselves as frequent buyers of store brands. The current wave of high-visibility private-label products—including organics and other premium fare—has effectively contributed to both the building of brand equity and relationship building with core customers.

Source: Packaged Facts, a division of MarketResearch.com

INVENTING TRENDS

1. *Inventors are becoming more diverse.* For many, the word "inventor" conjures the image of an eccentric guy tinkering in his garage workshop or a lab-coated scientist working on his top-secret formula. If these images were originally based in reality, the reality has changed. Developing a good idea presents an equal-opportunity playing field, and those who were formerly under-represented are exploring those opportunities.

   People of diverse demographics are entering the field. "There are great kid inventors, moms, seniors—inventors of every kind," says Peter Russo, founder and CEO of New Approach Development LLC. Stephen Key, of both Stephen Key Designs and www.inventright.com, agrees, noting that he sees more and more parents who tap into their experiences and create solutions based on everyday challenges.

2. *Inventors are stepping into the limelight.* More than ever, inventors are being featured as spokespeople for their products. TV shows and media have also placed inventors squarely in the spotlight. Last year, for instance, individual inventors were featured and celebrated on the high-profile show American Inventor. And TV shows like Modern Marvels feature an inventor as much as his or her invention. *Good Morning America* has hosted the Mothers of Invention Challenge two years in a row, and QVC regularly invites inventors to appear along with QVC hosts to present their products. After all, who can better explain a product's virtues than its creator?

3. *Inventors' mind-sets are changing.* It used to be all about the idea. Now it's about turning the idea into a thriving business. One day I looked around my office and had a realization: I didn't have a single book or magazine on the subject

of inventing! Instead, my desk and bookshelves were covered with issues of business magazines and countless volumes on branding, marketing, and the other elements critical to growing a successful company.

While Russo, Key, and I agree that there's still a tendency for people to believe they'll hit it big with a single invention, we also think the recent burst in media coverage helps inventors by educating them about the sales and marketing process, and its outcomes. In other words, inventors are realizing that a great idea, even if it's patented, is only worth the paper it's printed on unless someone buys it.

4. *Companies are understanding the possibilities of working with inventors.* Perhaps the most significant development is the shift that is occurring with manufacturers, who are increasingly open to products from outside inventors. More and more, I'm personally asked by manufacturing peers how they can best work with inventors.

"It's a great time to be a product developer/inventor," agrees Key. "I think it's a better time now because of the TV exposure and the retail environment. A lot of the larger retailers are looking for new ideas for their private label programs—and they have the shelf space!"

Russo says there's been a shift in the product development process inside large companies. Companies have begun changing their "invented in-house" attitudes, making direct relationships with inventors more common. "I'm seeing more U.S. companies going back to domestic creation of the concept vs. trying to find or develop the concept in China. Some of this can be attributed to the change in the American retail environment," says Russo. "Historically, initial production runs of 50,000 units weren't unusual. Due to shifts in the American retail landscape, U.S. companies have sought smaller initial production runs. I deal with some billion-dollar companies who want to start their production at 3,000 units. One result is that Chinese factories receiving smaller initial runs can no longer economically provide product-development services such as engineering and tooling."

Evidence of this open attitude to new ideas also includes a preponderance of corporate-sponsored inventing contests from companies ranging from Whirlpool to Staples to Dial Corp. And another offshoot of the increased interest in domestic inventions is the creation of companies and organizations that help facilitate this process.

Source: Tamara Monosoff, "4 Hot Inventing Trends," Entrepreneur.com

---

CUT YOUR R&D COSTS BY WORKING WITH A LOCAL UNIVERSITY

If you're frustrated by the high costs of research and development, consider a collaborative effort with a nearby college or university. It can save you money while you take advantage of state-of-the-art facilities, provide a real-life education experience for students, and get a strong product on the market.

To create such an alliance for your company, begin with a clear picture of your own goals and the benefits to the research institution. Look for universities and other institutions doing research in your field, and network into their system until you find the decision-maker. It can take a while to figure out the best fit and find the right contacts, but it's worth the effort. Put together a well-packaged presentation of your business plan, clearly demonstrating your intentions and the net benefit to the research institution. When researchers see the advantages you're bringing to them, they will be eager to work with you.

SALES OF ETHICAL CONSUMER PRODUCTS EXPECTED TO REACH $57 BILLION BY 2011

"Conscientious Consumerism," the trend towards upscale and premium products with an ethical bent, has taken root across America as consumers increasingly preach their social concerns through their pocketbooks. Sales of organic, hormone-free, eco-friendly, locally-grown, cruelty-free, and other ethical products have skyrocketed. Sales of products containing ethical elements will surpass $57 billion in 2011.

Food and beverages dominate retail sales of ethical products with an 82 percent market share. With organics becoming popular in all retail channels, the awareness of ethical edibles has soared, making hormone-free, pesticide-free, fair-trade, and other ethically-labeled foods and beverages widely popular with consumers from all walks of life.

Major corporations have taken note of ethical products' broad appeal. Manufacturers are creating entirely new "ethical" product lines and corporations are going "green" in an effort to build consumer confidence and get a piece of the ethical pie.

Source: Ethical Consumers and Corporate Responsibility: The Market and Trends for Ethical Products in Food and Beverage, Personal Care and Household Items, *a report from Packaged Facts, a division of MarketResearch.com*

BRANDING TO BOOST PET INDUSTRY SALES TO $52 BILLION BY 2009

Humanization—"functional"—and organic, and licensing of nostalgic pet heroes such as Lassie and Old Yeller are just a few of the brand strategies that are key growth-drivers in the overall U.S. pet industry. Branding will continue to be a critical factor in the market's overall growth, which should surpass $52 billion by 2009. High on the branding list is an ongoing psychographic trend known as "humanization"—pets treated like members of the family. Branding pet food as "organic," "functional," or "natural" means nothing to pets, yet such branding hits home with consumers looking for pet foods boasting human-quality ingredients and targeted health appeals, such as weight maintenance and joint care for senior pets.

Health-related branding alone is benefiting sales across every pet sector—from oral care treats to pet toys—regardless of point of purchase. Yet, as the proliferation of pet products in non-traditional outlets—such as wholesale clubs, dollar stores, and gift shops—continues to increase, health and other branding trends become all the more significant as product appeal takes on decidedly different meanings,

---

You can't wait for inspiration. You have to go after it with a club.

—Jack London

The key to success is making a lot of mistakes and learning the lesson behind every mistake. I used to worry incessantly over mistakes. Today, I almost welcome first-time mistakes because I know there is something to be learned.

—Kim Kiyosaki, author of *Rich Woman*, real estate investor, and a founder of The Rich Dad Company

depending on the venue. While value-priced national brands may have strong appeal in dollar stores and warehouse clubs, they may have no appeal at all in non-pet gift stores and department stores where unique and distinctive product lines—such as clothing for posh pups—often fare better.

Source: Brand Building in the U.S. Market for Pet Products and Services: Manufacturer, Private-Label, Licensed, and Human Brands, *a report from Packaged Facts, a division of MarketResearch.com*

REVIEW YOUR PRICES IF . . .

- You introduce a new product or product line
- Your costs change
- You decide to enter a new market
- Your competitors change their prices
- The economy experiences either inflation or recession
- Your sales strategy changes
- Your customers are making more money because of your product or service

HOW MUCH? THE CHALLENGE OF SETTING PRICES FOR SERVICES

Are you charging enough? Many small and home-based business owners don't, often because they aren't sure what a fair rate is, or don't have enough confidence in the value of their own goods and services. When evaluating and setting your prices, keep the following points in mind.

The Going Rate

Find out what the acceptable rate—both high and low—in your industry is. Ask around among your colleagues, or contact professional or trade organizations that track such information. Then mediate that rate with your own level of experience and expertise.

Exclusivity

If you are considered an expert, or are just one or one of a few who do what you do, you can likely charge more than if your field is crowded with competition.

Never lower your price just to get a new client. The clients who debate fees even before you're hired are always the most time-consuming to work with and then don't want to pay fairly for that time.

Words of Wisdom

—Jonathan Bernstein, President, Bernstein Crisis Management, LLC

I have made the mistake of offering to do a project on a fixed-fee or not-to-exceed ceiling basis and underestimating the time required to get the job done. I'll still offer to work that way in certain circumstances, but if there are clearly conditions that could vary and make the job take longer, I add caveats to the contract language allowing for the possibility of a budget increase.

Words of Wisdom

—Jonathan Bernstein, President, Bernstein Crisis Management, LLC

Capacity

Think about how busy you are and how much work you can actually handle. Raise your rates when you're busy; you may end up pricing yourself out of some business, but the business you keep will be more profitable.

Target Market

Examine your target market to determine if it has any pricing limitations.

Value

Analyze the real value of what you do. If you're providing something your clients can't do without, you can charge more for it.

PRICING A PRODUCT

No matter what type of product you sell, the price you charge your customers or clients will have a direct effect on the success of your business. Though pricing strategies can be complex, the basic rules of pricing are straightforward:

- All prices must cover costs and profits.
- The most effective way to lower prices is to lower costs.
- Review prices frequently to assure that they reflect the dynamics of cost, market demand, response to the competition, and profit objectives.
- Prices must be established to assure sales.

Before setting a price for your product, you have to know the costs of running your business. If the price for your product or service doesn't cover costs, your cash flow will be cumulatively negative, you'll exhaust your financial resources, and your business will ultimately fail.

To determine how much it costs to run your business, include property and/or equipment leases, loan repayments, inventory, utilities, financing costs, and salaries/wages/commissions. Don't forget to add the costs of markdowns, shortages, damaged merchandise, employee discounts, cost of goods sold, and desired profits to your list of operating expenses.

Most important is to add profit in your calculation of costs. Treat profit as a fixed cost, like a loan payment or payroll, since none of us is in business to break even.

Source: Entrepreneur.com

❧ ❧ ❧

CHAPTER 16

Purchasing and Dealing with Suppliers

CREATE A FORMAL PURCHASING PROGRAM

Purchasing Policies

Your purchasing policy should answer the following questions.

- Who has the authority to purchase items for the company? What items can that person purchase? Are there any spending limitations?
- What are the business's requirements for adequate supplier competition and what criteria will be used to select possible vendors?
- What is the company's position on the acceptance of gifts?
- Which types of contracts can the business enter into with successful bidders or vendors?
- What is the company's position on conflict of interest and personal loans from suppliers?
- What kinds of information does the company consider confidential?

- What is the procedure for dealing with legal questions?

The Ordering System

The steps your employees and purchasing manager will follow to request, order, receive, and pay for goods and materials make up your ordering system. A good ordering system will help maintain satisfactory supplier relations, improve cash management, aid in inventory control, and increase the overall profitability of your company.

The Purchase Order

Once the purchasing manager has received a requisition, he or she will need to select a supplier and check the price of the items to be ordered. After agreeing on a price, the purchasing manager will send a purchase order to the supplier. This order is a formal request to the supplier to deliver materials or supplies according to the agreed terms and prices. Purchase orders, like requisition forms, can help small businesses keep track of their purchasing activities. Firms can refer to their purchase orders to see if suppliers have shipped the correct goods in the correct quantity. They can also see if suppliers are delivering goods on time. Furthermore, purchase orders can serve as support in any legal disputes if they arise between you and the supplier.

Purchase orders should include information such as the type of product or service you are ordering, the quantity desired, price, and delivery terms. The orders should also have space for any additional information and should include your company name, address, telephone and fax numbers, and logo. You can simply write in this information, stamp it on with a rubber stamp, or design and print your own purchase order forms. Purchase orders should have at least three parts: a vendor copy, an internal file copy, and an accounting copy.

In addition to the standard purchase order, you might choose to use two other types: blanket purchase orders and annual contracts. If you routinely order fairly inexpensive items from a single vendor, you might want to place a blanket order for those items with the vendor. The blanket order covers specific items to be delivered over a specific period of time, such as six months or one year. This type of purchase order lets you take advantage of quantity discounts and saves you the time and trouble of reordering small items you need often. You will also receive a monthly invoice covering your purchases for a given month, instead of several small invoices covering each individual purchase. Annual contracts cover the purchase of a specific product from a vendor over a 12-month period. An annual contract will usually let you fix the price for buying a specific quantity of a given item over a year. You can also arrange to have goods delivered as needed—monthly, weekly, or on another specific schedule.

Receiving Records

A packing list will accompany orders you receive. Make sure that the items shipped match the items indicated on the packing list. Inspect all of the items carefully, paying special attention to any that appear damaged. Initial the packing list to verify receipt and file it in a folder until you receive the invoice for the shipment. If you receive any damaged items, or items you did not order, let the vendor know as soon as possible—they will tell you the best way to return the items and to receive the ones you actually ordered.

Fill out an internal receiving report and distribute it to those who need to know when shipments come in—such as the person in charge of inventory control, the buyer, the employee requisitioning the items, and the person in charge of accounts payable in accounting.

Source: Entrepeneur.com

WORTH KNOWING

Never rely on a single vendor for critical supplies. Keep in contact with other vendors and watch for new ones. It's a good idea to be on good terms with more than one supplier. If your primary supplier ever fails to ship on time, suspends operations because of a natural disaster, or starts offering poor service, you will already know of and have a relationship with other sources to use as a backup. Don't be secretive about these multiple relationships—letting suppliers know that you have alternatives will keep them on their toes and motivate them to provide you with better service.

DO YOUR SUPPLIERS KNOW HOW YOU OPERATE?

Your suppliers will be able to serve you better if they know as much as possible about how you operate. A savvy salesperson will seek this information, but if that doesn't happen, take the initiative to make sure your suppliers know:

- Your purchasing process—who are the decision-makers and what are the internal steps required to make a buying decision.
- Your internal policies governing relationships with suppliers—for example, are your employees allowed to accept gifts or entertainment from vendors?
- Your payment process—how long it takes you to process invoices and what information (purchase order, proof of delivery, etc.) you need from suppliers to quickly, efficiently, and accurately get them paid.

If suppliers are bugging you by not doing things your way, tell them how they can best work with you and you'll both reap the benefits.

There are many good people in the world willing to help without necessarily charging you a lot of money for advice. There are also a lot of people in the world who will charge you a lot of money to give you something "off the shelf" that isn't necessarily customized for your needs.

Words of Wisdom

—JIM EVANGER, CO-FOUNDER AND CEO, DESIGNS OF THE INTERIOR (DOTI), INC.

LET SALESPEOPLE EDUCATE YOU

It's certainly true that the primary goal of any salesperson is to get you to make a purchase, but in the process they can provide you with a tremendous amount of useful information. Sharp sales reps will be looking for ways to help you solve problems. They also know what their competitors, and possibly even your own competitors, are doing. It's worth taking their calls.

However, you should also set some guidelines to avoid wasting your time or theirs. Insist on appointments or see sales reps during designated hours, such as Tuesdays and Thursdays from 2:00 to 4:00 P.M. When a rep calls, find out if they have something specific to say; refuse to see reps who want to drop by "just to see how you're doing."

Prepare for the meeting by having readily available any information the rep might need. For example, if the rep sells copiers, know what your usage is. If the rep sells equipment you might consider for your plant, know your specifications for that particular item. If the rep will need certain data to put together a proposal, be as forthcoming and accurate as possible. Should it be necessary to release confidential information, ask the rep to sign a nondisclosure agreement.

If you're having a problem with a particular vendor, assemble your documentation so you can discuss it. Most sales reps are happy to intercede with a service or billing issue, especially if it means avoiding the loss of a customer.

Throughout any meeting with a sales rep, ask questions. Don't force the rep to guess what you want to know. Invite the members of your team who will actually be using the product to participate in the meeting; they are the best source of information about your requirements. A good salesperson will appreciate the opportunity to include the ultimate users of the product in the presentation and sales process. If the product or service doesn't meet your needs, say so, and give the rep the opportunity to offer alternatives.

Certainly there are plenty of mediocre and even bad sales reps out there. While you should deal with them politely, don't let them waste your time. But do take advantage of the professional rep who wants to meet your needs by treating him as a partner rather than an adversarial nuisance.

MAILROOM COST-CUTTING

In today's modern office, the mailroom is as likely to be the corner of someone's desk as it is an actual room, but it is no less deserving of your attention when it comes to issues of cost and efficiency. In the average business, mailing and shipping can account for almost 10 percent of expenditures, which means ignoring your mail center can be an expensive mistake.

Reducing costs doesn't have to mean reducing service, nor does streamlining your mail center have to be a time-consuming task. Today's technology and resources are greater than ever. To take advantage of what's available, try this approach:

1. *Appoint someone to be in charge.* Even the smallest of offices should have one person who is responsible for mail. That person can implement and monitor appropriate systems and procedures.

2. *Identify what you're sending out.* You can't organize something unless you know what it is, so figure out exactly what type of mail you send and how you schedule it. Calculate the volume and cost of all categories (including general correspondence, statements and invoices, and marketing messages) as well as all methods (regular mail, bulk mail, expedited services, couriers, fax, and e-mail).

3. *Research your various mailing options.* Consider the relative costs and results based on your goals, service availability, and price.

4. *Invest in the proper equipment to get the job done.* Using the right tools will produce better immediate results and generate long-term savings. Such tools include computer and mailing software, specialized printers, folding and inserting machines, electronic scales, postage meters, and shredders.

5. *Make your decisions based on true need.* Many mailing decisions are based on emotion or even habit rather than what's really required. Consider whether specific services—such as return receipts, tracking, insurance, or registered mail—are really necessary. When using expedited services, remember that a difference of a few hours in delivery can mean a difference of several dollars in price. Don't send it "next morning" when "next day" will do; those extra costs add up.

DOING IT RIGHT

Let the folks who will be using office equipment provide input when you are making your purchasing decision. Find out what features they like and don't like, what will help them be more efficient, what they consider to be drawbacks. Allow them to sit in on product demonstrations and give them a chance to test equipment before you buy it. The result will be a more productive staff.

CONTROL PRINTING COSTS

For most companies, printing is almost like taxes: an unavoidable, ongoing expense. Use the following tips to reduce costs while maintaining quality.

- *Print only what you'll use in a reasonable time.* In the past, companies routinely ordered large quantities of printing to take advantage of price breaks, and then had to find a place to store the materials. With today's technology, smaller runs are becoming more competitively priced. Ordering enough brochures or forms to last for a few months rather than a year or more means less money tied up in printing; it frees up storage space and reduces the risk of the items becoming obsolete because key information changed.

- *Proof, proof, and reproof.* It may seem like a time-consuming nuisance to sign off on a proof each time a change is made, but that's better than having the job come off the press with mistakes. Also, never sign the proof without checking it thoroughly; if a mistake slips through and you've approved it, you'll have to pay the reprinting costs.

- *Evaluate your forms.* Periodically review all your forms to make sure they're as functional and efficient as possible. Are you using a six-part form when a four-part one will do? Could two or three different forms be combined to save printing and paper? Be sure your forms are in sync with your changing business.

- *Ask your printer what you can do to reduce costs.* Sometimes something as simple as providing your artwork in a different format can make a substantial difference in price.

- *Don't make your decision based exclusively on price.* Certainly consider price, but also consider quality, consistency, service, and support.

- *Match your needs to the size and capability of the printer.* Learn about the printer: their equipment and capabilities; the type of work they specialize in; what they don't do. If your projects are varied, you may need more than one printer. Ask if the printer will be running the job in their own facility, or brokering it to another shop. If they're not going to do it themselves, ask for referrals and go direct to the source.

EVALUATING SUPPLIERS

You not only need to evaluate suppliers before you place an order, but you should also evaluate them on an ongoing basis. Consider the following points when you review a supplier's performance:

- Timeliness of deliveries
- Completeness of orders shipped
- Quality of items shipped
- Quality of customer service
- Competitiveness of price
- Previous performance with similar orders
- Strength of financial condition
- Ability to meet design specifications
- Expertise of sales representatives and technical staff

CHOOSING YOUR OFFICE CLEANING/JANITORIAL SERVICE

Your cleaning service will usually be in your facility after hours and unsupervised, so it's important to find one that not only does a good job, but also is trustworthy and reliable. The Building Owners and Managers Association (BOMA) International has these tips for choosing a cleaning service contractor:

Develop a list of specifications
List the areas that need to be cleaned and what you expect the contractor to do (dusting surfaces, emptying trash cans, vacuuming/mopping floors, cleaning glass doors, etc.), along with when and how often. Indicate the minimum qualifications you require, such as experience, references, and insurance. You may want to use this list to develop a questionnaire for initial screening.

Prepare a request for proposal (RFP)
With an RFP, you can obtain bids from contractors that pass your initial screening. Be sure the RFP contains all the necessary information to present a reasonable bid, including square footage, unit counts of fixtures, and other specifications and instructions. Expect the contractor to thoroughly examine the premises before submitting a bid, and consider disqualifying any who fail to do so.

Prepare a request for qualifications (RFQ)
With an RFP, you can ascertain the professional qualifications, background, and experience of the bidder. Ask for client references; financial references; evidence of workers' compensation and liability insurance coverage; details on the company's hiring practices—including how employees are screened; training and supervision methods; and a list of facilities that can be inspected.

Develop a list of criteria and a scoring system to evaluate bidders' proposals
According to a BOMA survey, the three most important criteria in selecting a cleaning contractor are experience, price, and references.

ONLINE SHOPPING

Online shopping can help you find great suppliers as well as save you time and money. Purchasing mangers used to be limited to their local areas for suppliers, but the internet has made it possible for even small companies to shop on a worldwide basis.

To find suppliers, check out sites designed for procurement professionals, such as Thomas Net (www.thomasnet.com), Reed Link (www.reedlink.com), and Kelly Search (www.kellysearch.com). These sites can connect you with literally millions of suppliers around the world. You can also use the internet to purchase through a reverse auction, where you post what you want and companies submit offers.

Source: Online Shopper's Survival Guide by Jacquelyn Lynn (Entrepreneur Press, 2006)

GREAT ADVICE

When purchasing new technology, consider getting training on the software or hardware before you buy. That will let you evaluate the quality of training and support, as well as give you a chance to talk to other users before you commit.

BEFORE YOU BUY A TECHNOLOGY RESOURCE, ASK . . .

1. *Who makes it?* Research the manufacturer and be sure it's a financially strong company on which you can rely.

2. *Who provides support?* Will it be the vendor or another company? Check out their support performance claims before you buy to be sure they really are answering the phone when they say they will.

3. *What is the total cost?* Consider the initial purchase, training, customization, installation, annual maintenance, and support.

4. *Is other technology required?* Find out if you're going to have to buy something else to make the new product work. If it's new software, will it run on your existing computer? If it's new hardware, do you have the necessary software or will you have to buy it?

5. *How complicated is the installation process and how long will it take?* Don't expect to be able to just plug it in and have it work. Find out what's really involved and whether or not you'll need to hire a consultant or other service provider to handle it. Also consider whether the installation will create downtime in your operation.

6. *How long has it been around?* Don't buy the first release of anything—give the manufacturers a chance to work out the bugs.

7. *Who else is using it?* Get references and check them. See what's being said about the technology online.

8. *What will it do for your company?* Be sure it will help increase revenues or decrease costs.

9. *Can you test it yourself?* Don't depend on a vendor demonstration—get the actual product and test it yourself before you buy.

10. *Will it speak to your other systems?* Be sure the new technology can be integrated into your existing systems.

Source: Gene Marks, editor of Streetwise Small Business Book of Lists *(Adams Media, 2006)*

Words of Wisdom

When it comes to purchasing equipment and other business expenditures and investments, do your research, be open-minded, listen to other people's advice, don't procrastinate, and go with your gut.

—PAUL A. CURASI, D.V.M., UNIVERSITY ANIMAL HOSPITAL

WORTH KNOWING

Online auctions such as eBay are great resources for all kinds of business purchases, from office supplies and equipment to industrial machinery. You'll find a tremendous selection of new, used, and factory-recondition items, often with warranties and guarantees. However, just because an item is on an auction site doesn't mean you're getting the best deal—shop around.

WHEN AN EMPLOYEE MAKES AN UNAUTHORIZED PURCHASE

You have a purchase authorization system in place, but an employee has made a purchase without proper approval. You have three issues you need to deal with:

1. *The ethical issue of what is the right thing to do with the vendor—and the ethical and right thing to do is pay the vendor for the product or service.*

   The vendor had no way of knowing that the employee was not following procedures. It is entirely appropriate to check with the vendor to see if there is a return policy, but assuming the purchase was a consumable that could not be returned, you should pay the vendor.

2. *The practical issue of paying for the product or service.*

   Of course, the ethical thing to do can occasionally conflict with the practical thing to do. It is one thing if the purchase is $500 but quite another if it is $50,000 and you can't afford it without putting your company in a difficult situation. The right thing to do is still to pay the vendor, but you may need to seek flexibility on the payable. The important thing is to communicate with the vendor if you need to seek accommodation. Don't sit on the invoice and leave the vendor wondering what is going on. Be open and honest, state your situation, and ask the vendor for the flexibility you need if the amount is too large to pay.

3. *The employee management issue of how to handle the situation with the employee.*

   Andrew Carnegie was said to have called an employee into his office after a $500,000 mistake. The employee assumed he would be fired. Carnegie gave him more responsibility since he had just invested $500,000 in the employee's education. Certainly every employee who makes a mistake should not be automatically promoted, but it's important for you to separate facts from feelings. Your first emotional response will probably be to fire the employee. After all, you now have to pay for something you would not have purchased. However, take the time to think about your response. If this is a situation where the employee knew your guidelines and chose not to follow them, it may be appropriate to terminate the individual's employment. But, it might make sense to keep the employee if this is an honest mistake made in an honest attempt to helping the business. You need employees who are engaged and committed to help your business succeed. You don't want to send the message that risk taking is not allowed or encouraged.

   Source: Randy Pennington, President,
   Pennington Performance Group

✤ ✤ ✤

CHAPTER 17

About the Money

BUSINESS BORROWING

In the U.S., business borrowing reached an all-time high of $606 billion in 2005, up from $429 billion in 2004. Most of the increase was the result of increased borrowing by the non-financial corporate sector. The increase in capital expenditures was supported by a large increase in internal sources of funds.

Net business borrowing by non-financial corporations continued to increase in 2005, soaring by 66 percent to an annual rate of $289 billion from $175 billion in 2004. Nevertheless, corporate borrowing remained below the high levels reached in the late 1990s.

Net borrowing by non-farm, non-corporate businesses increased to a record high, accounting for 50 percent of total business borrowing in 2005. Borrowing by this sector has, until the recent past, been at lower levels and less volatile than corporate borrowing; however, it increased significantly in 2004 and 2005. High levels of borrowing in commercial mortgages over this period contributed to the large increases.

Source: U.S. Small Business Administration

FUNDING A BUSINESS

If you have good credit (generally considered a credit score of 700 or above), you should be able to establish a business credit line with a commercial bank if you personally guarantee the loan. Make sure the bank you are dealing with is a Small Business Administration (SBA) preferred lender so that you have a relationship established if you opt for an SBA loan later on.

If you have credit challenges, consider collateralizing the business credit line by depositing money with the bank. It may seem nonsensical to tie up money that you need for your business just to borrow it back and pay interest, but the interest is tax deductible and the expense is a cost of establishing your business credit. Pay your loan on time, or better yet, a bit early. Sit down with your banker at least once a year and negotiate a larger credit line, more favorable terms, or a release from the requirement to secure the loan on deposits. Most importantly, inquire if you qualify for an SBA loan.

Using Your Home Equity

If you are not able to establish a true business line of credit but you own your home, a home equity line of credit (HELOC) may be an option. The interest rates on HELOCs are usually favorable, but they come with certain drawbacks. There are potential tax consequences to using a HELOC to finance your business—especially if the amount borrowed exceeds $100,000. Additionally, another type of income tax called alternative minimum tax could apply, limiting the tax deductibility of HELOC interest if the funds borrowed are not used primarily to improve your home. The biggest drawback of all is that borrowing on your HELOC doesn't improve your business credit position.

Using Your Retirement Plan Fund

Proceed with caution if you are thinking about using retirement savings to fund your business. Many fledgling entrepreneurs withdraw monies from qualified retirement plans they established with former employers to begin their business. This is a very expensive funding alternative because you will have to pay income tax plus an additional 10 – 25 percent penalty on the withdrawal.

As an alternative, you may be able to establish a qualified plan [401(k)] for your new company and roll the funds from your previous employer's qualified plan into your new plan. If established correctly, you may have the option to borrow up to 50 percent of your plan funds without the income tax

and penalty hit. You then repay yourself with interest.

The rules for establishing a 401(k) for your new company can be complex, so speak with your CPA or a knowledgeable financial planner before you try this.

Source: Brian M. Lewis, CPA

FINDING MONEY TO FUND YOUR BUSINESS START-UP OR EXPANSION

Consider these sources when looking for capital:

- Personal savings
- Personal assets
- Friends and relatives
- Credit cards
- 401(k) financing
- Loans on life insurance
- IRAs
- Banks and credit unions
- Angel investors
- Venture capital firms
- Customer financing
- Employee stock ownership (ESOP)
- Factoring accounts receivable
- Equipment leasing
- Home equity loans
- Mergers and acquisitions
- Purchase order financing
- State-specific economic development programs
- Microloans

TYPES OF SBA LOANS

The Small Business Administration offers numerous loan programs to assist small businesses. It is important to note, however, that the SBA is primarily a guarantor of loans made by private and other institutions and does not offer loans to small businesses.

Basic 7(a) Loan Guaranty

This loan serves as the SBA's primary business-loan program to help qualified small businesses obtain financing when they might not be eligible for business loans through normal lending channels. It is also the agency's most flexible business-loan program since financing under this program can be guaranteed for a variety of general business purposes, including start-ups and to meet various short- and long-term needs of existing businesses. Loan proceeds can be used for most sound business purposes including working capital, machinery and equipment, furniture and fixtures, land and building (including purchase, renovation and new construction), leasehold improvements, and debt refinancing (under special conditions). Loan maturity is up to 10 years for working capital and generally up to 25 years for fixed assets.

Certified Development Company (CDC), 504 Loan Program

This loan provides long-term, fixed-rate financing to small businesses looking to acquire real estate or machinery or equipment for expansion or modernization. Typically a 504 project includes a loan secured from a private-sector lender with a senior lien, a loan secured from a CDC (funded by a 100 percent SBA-guaranteed debenture) with a junior lien covering up to 40 percent of the total cost, and a contribution of at least 10 percent equity from the borrower.

Microloan, a 7(m) Loan Program

This provides short-term loans of up to $35,000 to small businesses and not-for-profit child-care centers for working capital or the purchase of inventory, supplies, furniture, fixtures, machinery, and/or equipment. Proceeds cannot be used to pay existing debts or to purchase real estate. The SBA makes or guarantees a loan to an intermediary, who in turn, makes the microloan to the applicant. These organizations also provide management and technical assistance. The loans are not guaranteed by the SBA. The microloan program is available in selected locations in most states.

Loan Prequalification

This allows a business to have their loan applications for $250,000, or less, analyzed and potentially sanctioned by the SBA before they are taken to lenders for consideration. The program focuses on the applicant's character, credit, experience, and reliability rather than assets. An SBA-designated intermediary works with the business owner to review and strengthen the loan application. The review is based on key financial ratios, credit and business history, and the loan-request terms. The program is administered by the SBA's Office of Field Operations and SBA district offices.

WORTH KNOWING

Commercial banks are the largest suppliers of debt capital to small firms, supplying more than 80 percent of lending in the credit line market and, with the exception in leasing, more than 50 percent in other markets, such as commercial mortgages and vehicle, equipment, and other loans. Very large banks with assets of at least $10 billion are making a significant percentage of small loans of less than $100,000.

Source: Small Business Administration

THE CLOUT OF COMPENSATING BALANCES

Compensating balance is a fancy phrase for "cash flow." It's not the amount of money you have, but the amount of cash you control—if you control significant amounts of cash, you can have significant clout with a bank.

Let's say you started a property management company and picked up five contracts. The buildings have fifty units each with average rents of $800 a month. That means every month you collect $40,000 from each building, or $200,000, to be deposited in the bank. In a year, that's $2.4 million—and that makes you a million-dollar player. Even though it's not your money, you get credit as the person who places those funds in the institution. If you control where it goes, it doesn't matter if it's your money or not. Of course, you're going to be paying out $170,000 to $180,000 every month to the property owners, but there will be a lag time between the deposits, when you write your check, and when that check is cleared. That lag time is called float, and it's a time when banks can use that money to make more money for the bank. Anytime money is in a bank more than twenty-four hours, the bank is earning money on it. So, while those deposits may be little more than a bookkeeping chore to you, they are valuable to the banker. Even though electronic banking has reduced the float, it's still important to the bank.

Remember, deposits are the lifeblood of a bank. Deposits make the banker look good, and a million-dollar account makes a banker look very good, indeed. When you have a large compensating balance, you have clout.

Property management is not the only business with the potential for significant compensating balances. A typical fast-food franchise unit, for example, may net only $150,000 a year, but it may gross $1.5 or even $2 million, and that money has to be cycled through a bank.

You don't necessarily have to have money of your own if you have compensating balances. You just have to realize how much clout you have and use it to your advantage. Keep your eyes open to opportunities to control where other people put their money, and let the banker know when you do have that control.

Source: Building Wealth: Achieving Personal and Financial Success in Real Estate and Business without Money, Credit, or Luck by Russ Whitney (Simon & Schuster, 2006)

THE THREE TS OF A GOOD BANKING RELATIONSHIP

Talk

For a relationship to thrive, the business owner needs to talk—communicate—regularly with the banker. The talk must be frank and open, even when reporting a negative development.

Time

A relationship takes time to grow. Don't rush it, and don't expect it to bear fruit immediately. Like friendships, a good banker relationship will age well over the course of its duration.

Trust

With honest, frequent communication and time, trust develops, which is the foundation of the relationship. When trust exists on both sides, the relationship has the crucial component to make it a lasting one.

Source: Small Business Administration

VENTURE CAPITAL FUNDS AND ANGEL INVESTMENTS

Funds invested by venture capitalists totaled roughly $22 billion in 2005, about the same amount as in 2004. However, the number of deals in 2005 totaled 2,939, up from 2,399 in 2004. The venture-capital industry continued a shift toward later-stage investing, a trend that has been in place since the late 1990s. As a result, funding for early-stage companies dipped slightly to $4.1 billion in 2005 from $4.4 billion the previous year. Later-stage funding rose by 22 percent from $8 billion in 2004 to $9.7 billion in 2005 and accounted for 952 deals. Funds raised by venture capital firms increased to $25.2 billion.

The angel investor market grew modestly in 2005, by 2.7 percent from the previous year, with total investments of $23.1 billion. A total of 49,500 entrepreneurial ventures received angel funding in 2005, up 3.1 percent from 2004. Active investors numbered 227,000, with an average of four or five joining forces to fund an entrepreneurial startup in 2005. Angels are the largest source of seed and startup capital in 2005; they provided $12.7 billion—55 percent of their total investment—to seed and startup companies.

Source: U.S. Small Business Administration

TIPS ON FINDING ANGEL INVESTORS AND VENTURE CAPITALISTS

1. *Do some research.* Identify the most likely candidates by asking your accountant, banker, and lawyer.
2. *Keep an open mind—potential investors may be anywhere.* According to *Success* magazine, one entrepreneur found an angel investor among the motorcyclists he rides with on weekends.
3. *Surf the web.* A good place to start is www.nvca.org, the site of the National Venture Capital Association.
4. *Make presentations at venture capital forums or fairs.* Your local university business school of Small Business Administration office should have information on such events.
5. *Check your library or the web for such references as* Pratt's Guide to Venture Capital Sources *and* The Directory of Buyout Financing Sources.

Source: SCORE

Successful entrepreneurs are those who analyze and minimize risk in the pursuit of profit.

—BRIAN TRACY

Words of Wisdom

If somebody says you can't do something, sometimes you're going to have to prove them wrong.

—ROBERT A. FUNK, FOUNDER AND CHAIRMAN, EXPRESS PERSONNEL SERVICES

Words of Wisdom

FAQS ABOUT VENTURE CAPITAL

What Kind of Investors are Venture Capitalists?

Venture capitalists are professional investors who specialize in funding and building young, innovative enterprises. Venture capitalists are long-term investors who take a hands-on approach with all their investments and actively work with entrepreneurial management teams in order to build great companies.

Where do Venture Capitalists Get Their Money?

Most venture capital firms raise their funds from institutional investors, such as pension funds, insurance companies, endowments, foundations, and high-net-worth individuals. Those investors who invest in venture capital funds are referred to as limited partners. Venture capitalists, who manage the fund, are referred to as general partners. The general partners have a fiduciary responsibility to their limited partners.

In What Types of Companies and Industries do Venture Capitalists Invest?

Venture capitalists invest in young and innovative companies that have great potential for growth. Venture capitalists were instrumental in developing industries, such as the computer, biotechnology, and communications industries. Today, the majority of venture capital is invested in high technology companies. However, venture capitalists invest in all types of companies in many industry sectors.

How are Venture Capitalists Different from Other Investors?

Venture capitalists are long-term investors who take a very active role in their portfolio companies. When a venture capitalist makes an investment he/she does not expect a return on that investment for five-to-seven years, on average. The initial investment is just the beginning of a long relationship between the venture capitalist and entrepreneur. Venture capitalists provide great value by providing capital and management expertise. Venture capitalists are often invaluable in building strong management teams, managing rapid growth, and facilitating strategic partnerships.

How do Venture Capitalists Realize a Return on Their Investment?

Most companies in which venture capitalists invest are private enterprises. Accordingly, the venture capitalist only realizes a return on their investment if the company goes public (IPO) or is merged or purchased by another company (M&A).

How does Angel Investing Differ from Venture Capital?

Venture capital firms are professional investors who dedicate 100 percent of their time to investing and building innovative companies. Most venture capitalists have a fiduciary responsibility to their investors. The angel investment community is an informal network of investors who invest in companies for their own interests. Typically, angel investors invest less than $1 million in any particular company, whereas venture capitalists usually invest more than $1 million per company.

What's the Difference Between Venture Capital and Private Equity?

Venture capital is a subset of the larger private equity asset class. The private equity asset class includes venture capital, buyouts, and mezzanine investment activity. Venture capital focuses on investing in private, young, fast-growing companies. Buyout and mezzanine investing focuses on investing in mature companies.

Source: National Venture Capital Association, www.nvca.org

THE LIES ENTREPRENEURS TELL VENTURE CAPITALISTS

1. *"Our projections are conservative."* An entrepreneur's projections are never conservative. If they were, they would be $0. I have never seen an entrepreneur achieve even their most conservative projections. As a rule of thumb, when I see a projection, I add one year to delivery time and multiply by 0.1.

2. *"[Big-name research firm] says our market will be $50 billion in 2010."* Even if the product is bar-mitzvah-planning software, every entrepreneur claims the market potential is tens of billions. Do yourself a favor: remove any reference to market size estimates.

3. *"[Big-name company] is going to sign our purchase order next week."* Only play this card after the purchase order is signed, because no investor will fall for it.

4. *"Key employees are set to join us as soon as we get funded."* When a venture capitalist calls these key employees, he usually gets the following response: "I recall meeting him, but I certainly didn't say I would leave my $250,000-a-year job to join his company." If key employees are ready to rock 'n' roll, have them call the venture capitalist and confirm it.

5. *"No one else is doing what we're doing."* Well, either there's no market for it, or you're so clueless that you can't use Google to figure out you have competition. Neither a lack of a market nor cluelessness is conducive to securing an investment.

6. *"No one else can do what we're doing."* The only thing worse than cluelessness and the lack of a market is arrogance.

7. *"Hurry, because several other VC firms are interested."* There are maybe 100 entrepreneurs in the world who can make this claim. The fact that you're reading this article means you're not one of them.

8. *"Oracle is too big/dumb/slow to be a threat to us."* There's a reason Larry Ellison is where he is, and it's not that he's big, dumb or slow. Entrepreneurs who utter this lie look naive at best, stupid at worst.

9. *"We have a proven management team."* If you were that proven, you wouldn't be asking for money. A better strategy: state that you have relevant experience, you'll do whatever it takes to succeed, you'll surround yourself with proven advisors and you'll step aside whenever it becomes necessary.

10. *"All we have to do is get 1 percent of the market."* First, no venture capitalist is interested in a company that wants just 1 percent of a market. Second, it's not easy to get even 1 percent, so you look silly pretending it is. Instead, show an appreciation of the difficulty of building a successful company.

Source: Guy Kawasaki, "10 Lies VCs Know You're Telling," Entrepreneur.com

---

WORTH KNOWING

Though venture capital has made it possible for many companies to start and grow, it's not a panacea. It's not always easy to get, and agreements tend to favor the funding source. Be sure you understand what you're getting—and giving up.

VENTURE CAPITAL ORGANIZATIONS

Regional Venture Capital Organizations in the United States

The Atlanta Venture Forum
www.atlantaventureforum.org

Colorado Venture Capital Association (CVCA)
www.coloradovca.org

The Collaborative, Minnesota
www.collaborative.net

Connecticut Venture Group
www.ct-venture.org

Council for Entrepreneurial Development, North Carolina
www.cednc.org

Dallas/Ft. Worth Private Equity Forum
For more information about the DFW Private Equity Forum, contact Pam Jackson at pamela.jackson@ey.com.

Evergreen Venture Capital Association, Washington State
www.evca.net

Florida Venture Forum
www.floridaventureforum.org

Illinois Venture Capital Association
www.illinoisvc.org

Long Island Capital Alliance
www.licapital.org

Michigan Venture Capital Association
www.michiganvca.org

Mid-America Healthcare Investor Network (MHIN)
For more information, contact Dan Broderick at dbroderick@masonwells.com

Mid-Atlantic Capital Alliance (MAC), Greater Philadelphia area
www.macalliance.com

The Mid-Atlantic Venture Association (MAVA), Greater Washington, DC, area
www.mava.org

Minnesota Venture Capital Association (MVCA)
www.mnvca.org

Missouri Venture Forum
www.missouriventureforum.org

The New England Venture Capital Association (NEVCA)
www.newenglandvc.org

New Jersey Tech Council
www.njtc.org

New Mexico Venture Capital Association
www.nmvca.org

OCTANe, Orange County, CA
www.octaneoc.org

Pittsburgh Venture Capital Association
www.thepvca.org

San Diego Venture Group
www.sdvg.org

Texas Venture Capital Association
www.txvca.org

Upstate Venture Association of New York (UVANY)
www.uvany.com

Venture Club of Indiana
www.ventureclub.org

VENTURE CAPITAL ORGANIZATIONS, continued

Venture Club of Louisville
www.ventureclub-louisville.org

Venture Investors Association of New York
www.viany.org

The Western Association of Venture Capitalists (WAVC)
www.wavc.net

Young Venture Capital Organizations

New England Venture Network
www.nevnweb.com

New York Private Equity Network
www.nypen.net

Young Venture Capital Association
www.yvca.net

Young Venture Capital Society
www.yvcs.org

Venture Capital Organizations Outside the United States

African Venture Capital Association
www.avcanet.com

Association Française des Investisseurs en Capital
www.afic.asso.fr

Australian Private Equity and Venture Capital Association
www.avcal.com.au

Belgian Venturing Association
www.bvassociation.org

Brazilian Private Equity and Venture Capital Association
www.abcr-venture.com.br

British Venture Capital Association
www.bvca.co.uk

Canada's Private Equity and Venture Capital Association
www.cvca.ca

China Venture Capital Association
www.cvca.com.hk/index.asp

Czech Venture Capital and Private Equity Association
www.cvca.cz

European Venture Capital Association
www.evca.com

Finnish Venture Capital Association
www.fvca.fi

German Private Equity and Venture Capital Association
www.bvk-ev.de

Gulf Venture Capital Association
www.gulfvca.org

Hong Kong Venture Capital & Private Equity Association
www.hkvca.com.hk

Hungarian Venture Capital Association
www.hvca.hu

Indian Venture Capital Association
www.indiavca.org

Irish Venture Capital Association
www.ivca.ie

Israel Venture Association
www.iva.co.il

VENTURE CAPITAL ORGANIZATIONS, continued

Japan Venture Capital Association
www.jvca.jp/en

Latin American Venture Capital Association
www.lavca.org

Netherlands Venture Capital Association
www.nvp.nl

*Russian Private Equity & Venture Capital
   Association*
www.rvca.ru

*Singapore Venture Capital and Private Equity
   Association*
www.svca.org.sg

Spanish Venture Capital Association
www.ascri.org

Swedish Venture Capital Association
www.svca.se

*Swiss Private Equity & Corporate Finance
   Association*
www.seca.ch

Thai Venture Capital Association
www.venturecapital.or.th

Source: National Venture Capital Association, www.nvca.org

❧ ❧ ❧

CHAPTER 18

Growing Your Business

STRATEGIES FOR BUSINESS GROWTH

1. Open another location.

This might not be your best choice for business expansion, but it's listed first here because that's what often comes to mind first for many entrepreneurs considering expansion. Before opening another location, make sure you're maintaining a consistent bottom-line profit and that you've shown steady growth over the past few years. Look at the trends—both economic and consumer—for indications on your company's staying power. Make sure your administrative systems and management team are extraordinary—you'll need them to get a new location up and running. Prepare a complete business plan for a new location. Determine where and how you'll obtain financing. Choose your location based on what's best for your business, not your wallet.

2. Offer your business as a franchise or business opportunity.

If someone else could take your business model and run with it, consider franchising. Start by networking within the franchise community. Become a member of the International Franchise Association and find a good franchise attorney as well as a mentor who's been through the franchise process.

3. License your product.

This can be an effective, low-cost growth medium, particularly if you have a service product or branded product. Licensing also minimizes your risk and is low-cost in comparison to the price of starting your own company to produce and sell your brand or product. To find a licensing partner, start by researching companies that provide products or services similar to yours. But before you set up a meeting or contact any company, find a competent attorney who specializes in intellectual property rights.

4. Form an alliance.

Aligning yourself with a similar type of business can be a powerful way to expand quickly.

5. Diversify.

Consider selling complementary products or services; teach adult education or other types of classes; import or export yours or others' products; become a paid speaker or columnist.

6. Target other markets.

Your current market is serving you well. Are there others? You bet. Think about who else might be able to use what you offer, then take your product to the markets that need it.

7. Win a government contract.

"The best way for a small business to grow is to have the federal government as a customer," wrote Rep. Nydia M. Velázquez, ranking Democratic member of the House Small Business Committee, in August 2003. "The U.S. government is the largest buyer of goods and services in the world, with total procurement dollars reaching approximately $235 billion in 2002 alone."

8. Merge with or acquire another business.

Grow your customer base and other resources through a merger or acquisition.

9. Expand globally.

It's easier than ever to sell products and services internationally.

10. Expand to the internet.

Create a web site and make it work for you.

Source: Karen E. Spaeder, "10 Ways to Grow Your Business,"
Entrepreneur.com

PARTNERING TO INCREASE PROFIT

Even with the aid of technology, there are limits to what a small business can accomplish by itself. You may understand that, but what if you still want to do more? A workable solution is partnering. Though it takes many shapes, the core of the partnering concept is that two or more businesses team up to achieve something together that they can't do alone.

Partnering with other businesses can help you provide a broader product or service package to a particular market segment; it can give you the resources to handle a single major project for a client; or it can organize the resources you need to meet certain components of your customers' needs. In all of these scenarios, partnering creates the opportunity to present your clients with the same vision of seamless capacity that large corporations do—while working from your home or small office in a relationship with other similar-sized businesses.

There are no fixed rules for individual partnering agreements. The concept is rapidly evolving, with some partnering associations looking like a stand-alone business that is separate from the partners' primary companies, and others more closely resembling outsourcing or subcontracting. Some business owners partner only under carefully drawn contracts; others do it on a handshake. What's important is that you develop an arrangement for work performed and compensation received that satisfies everyone involved.

Growth happens when you learn something and duplicate the process.

—Robert A. Funk, Founder
and Chairman, Express
Personnel Services

Partnering allows very niche-oriented businesses to serve clients who have complex needs, and lets them compete against large firms that have all the necessary staff in-house. For example, a homebased human resources consultant could team up with a small law firm, an accountant, a management consultant, and a marketing person to provide a broad scope of client services that are marketed under one name but delivered independently or through a cooperative effort.

Partnering can also give you the resources to handle a large one-time project without increasing your overhead or actually hiring new employees. Another advantage of partnering is that it is a way for a homebased business to grow substantially without having to move to a commercial location.

Tips for Effective Partnering

- *Choose partners carefully*—be sure they have the skills and abilities you need, and share your level of commitment.
- *Define the scope of partnership*—are you working on an equal basis, or will one of you function as the managing partner? What roles will each partner play? How will the compensation be calculated and distributed?
- *Put it in writing.* A detailed, well-crafted partnership agreement will prevent misunderstandings, memory lapses, and future conflicts.
- *Develop and stick to an operations plan.* How will the work actually happen? How and when will the partners interact?

- *Plan for the unexpected.* How will you handle problems and resolve conflicts? If one partner wants to dissolve the agreement, who ends up with what?
- *Set a minimum "no exit" time period.* New ventures take time to become productive. Make a mutual commitment to stick with the partnership long enough to give it a chance to prove itself.

GREAT ADVICE

Be sure you are getting the maximum amount of business from each customer. Tell your existing customers about additional products and services you offer that they may not be aware of. Be sure you are talking to everyone at the client company who has the need for your product and the authority to buy it. Ask your current contacts for names of others you should be talking to.

THE THREE WAYS TO GROW A BUSINESS

1. Increase the number of customers
2. Increase the average transaction value
3. Increase the frequency of repurchase

Words of Wisdom

From our perspective, we're one-quarter of the way up the mountain. We're not looking down the mountain; we're looking up. We don't want to take away from what we accomplished, but we don't have the time to sit back and pat ourselves on the back. We need to be focused on the three-quarters of the mountain we have to climb. It's going to be a lot of work and we know that.

—JIM EVANGER, CO-FOUNDER AND CEO, DESIGNS OF THE INTERIOR (DOTI), INC.

BARTERING:
CASH-FREE TRANSACTIONS
ARE GROWTH TOOLS

Long before banks, credit cards, and even cash, people bartered for goods and services. And though it's unlikely that your local supermarket will accept a few hours of your labor in return for a week's worth of groceries, there are still plenty of opportunities for cash-free trading in today's marketplace. The total value of goods and services exchanged by businesses through reciprocal means in 2004 was estimated at $8.25 billion, and about 75 percent of that occurs through commercial barter exchanges.

Barter exchanges function almost like a cash-less bank for their members—they tracked barter credits and take a small commission on each transaction. According to the International Reciprocal Trade Association (IRTA), bartering is a business strategy that can be used to open new markets, win new customers, reduce inventories, drive revenues, and increase profitability.

Keep in mind that not all barter exchanges are the same. If you're considering joining one, IRTA offers these tips:

- Treat your barter credits with the same respect you give "real" money; don't buy things on barter that you wouldn't buy with cash.
- Be sure you can get what you need for your business from the exchange you join. Prepare a list of your needs and wants, and find out if the exchange can provide them.
- Ask for and check referrals.
- Find out how many clients are currently trading, and how many are on standby or reserve, which means they are unwilling to take more barter business until they have spent the trade dollars they have accumulated.
- Check the barter prices to see if products and services are priced fairly and competitively.

- Check the geographic coverage of the exchange's client base, and the proximity of suppliers of goods and services you want.
- Ask if the company provides consulting service on the use of barter, in addition to brokerage and management services.
- Compare the barter contracts, costs, and services of several exchanges in order evaluate the best deal for you.
- Remember that barter sales are taxable income; don't do business with anyone who promotes barter as a tax dodge.
- Make the usual business reference checks on the barter exchange with, for example, the Better Business Bureau and Chamber of Commerce. Also find out what professional associations—such as IRTA—the exchange belongs to.

Of course, it's entirely possible and practical to barter for goods and services outside of an exchange. Be sure your transaction is clearly defined in writing so there are no misunderstandings. You agreement should clearly state who is going to do what, by when, and what the non-performance consequences are. Check with your accountant to find out how to document the deal for record-keeping and tax purposes.

Just because it starts out good does not mean you will succeed. Most new businesses experience a rush at first and then the newness wears off and you have to start working. Be prepared.

Words of Wisdom

—MICHAEL JANSMA, PRESIDENT,
GEMAFFAIR.COM

OPENING A SECOND LOCATION

How do you know when it's time to expand your business to a second location? Take this five-point test.

1. *Do you have the desire to make the effort, take the risk, and own a business that you don't personally operate?* Owning and operating a business is very different from owning a business someone else operates for you—which will likely be the case for your second location.

2. *Is your business performing well financially?* If your first location isn't doing well, chances are a second one won't, either.

3. *Do you have the know-how to own a business you don't operate?* It's a different thing, and requires a different set of skills.

4. *Is your existing business running smoothly?* Consider how much time your business requires; be sure you can realistically take the time and energy away from it to focus on a second location.

5. *Do you have the money?* Opening a second location takes initial capital as well as operating funds. Have sufficient cash resources to get you through a worst-case scenario.

GROW THROUGH STRATEGIC ALLIANCES

You can accelerate growth, add new products and services, and enter new markets by forming strategic alliances. Choose your alliance partners carefully; be sure your agreements are thorough, mutually beneficial, and include necessary exit plans.

Hang on to the dream of what you want to accomplish and why. It will sustain you on the dark days when you believe the assistant manager job at the fast food outlet looks appealing. But never assume that the dream alone will get you where you want to go. Focused execution is critical.

—RANDY PENNINGTON,
PENNINGTON PERFORMANCE GROUP

EXPAND YOUR BUSINESS THROUGH PRIVATE LABELING

Looking for ways to reach new markets? Consider private labeling, which is when you manufacture a product that is sold under another company's label.

As a market opportunity, private labeling is significant. For example, the majority of the store-brand products sold today are manufactured under private label agreements. And most private-label orders are large, which makes them attractive to manufacturers.

If you're going to pursue private labeling, it's a good idea to start small. Get comfortable with the process before moving on to larger customers. In the early stages, stay as close to your own niche as you can. Private labeling is a good way to get into markets you're not serving, but start with areas you're familiar. You can broaden later on.

Be sure you have enough space to accommodate the process. You'll probably need to store a certain amount of product, as well as the required labeling and packaging.

Work closely with your customers on the actual label. Make a checklist of everything that must be on the product—contents, warnings, UPC codes, weights, etc.—and provide that to your customer so they can design their label. If there's a potential for the product to be exported, work with your customer to be sure the labeling meets the destination country's requirements.

Keep in mind that private labeling may put you in competition with yourself at the retail level. But most companies that purchase products to sell under their own label are going to do it anyway, and private labeling gives you access to a market share you would probably not otherwise have.

Private labeling marketing is done discreetly, mostly through word of mouth and direct contact with companies that use private labeling sources. Expect your private label customers to demand a high degree of confidentiality—and a comparable degree of quality. Don't cut corners on your private label products. They need to have the same quality as the products you market under your own label.

FOCUS ON THE FUTURE

It's easy to get wrapped up in day-to-day operations, but growing a business requires long-term strategic planning. Set aside time every week to think about where your company will be in three to five years and how it's going to get there. Talk with your team and get them thinking the same way. Don't let new technologies or industry changes sneak up on you; research and plan so that you stay ahead of market shifts and customer demands.

IDENTIFY AND DEVELOP THE NEXT GENERATION OF LEADERS FOR YOUR COMPANY

One area of planning many entrepreneurs often overlook is grooming the next generation of leaders and managers for their organization. Designate your successor long before your own departure—whether you're looking at retirement or starting another venture. The person you select should have both the ability and the willingness to do the job, and then you need to prepare him to take over. The best way to do that is by providing the experience with a hands-on, planned rotation through the key areas of the company in order to build the necessary and appropriate skills. It also helps to let others in the company, as well as your customers, know what you're doing.

It should be clear that this person is your heir-apparent. Other employees and even customers will usually be enthusiastic about helping the up-and-coming leader, contributing to a seamless transition when the time comes. Also, when an individual knows he or she is the next in line, his or her loyalty to the organization is strengthened.

Five years or less is a good timeframe for designating and developing a new leader. If you plan for more than five years, the enthusiasm for the new role will wear off. Also, there's an excellent chance the person will

---

Assume you will have great success and set goals to plan for your exit strategy.

Words of Wisdom

—SHARON LECHTER, CO-AUTHOR OF *RICH DAD POOR DAD* AND A FOUNDER OF THE RICH DAD COMPANY

Be creative. Use unconventional thinking. And have the guts to carry it out.

Words of Wisdom

—LEE IACOCCA

PREPARE FOR THE RETIREMENT OF YOUR KEY EMPLOYEES

Say "retirement planning," and most of us think about savings and pensions. But there's another very important angle to this issue, and that's the impact on your company when a key person retires. Regardless of how formal you make the process, the continuity of your company's performance depends on preparing for the retirement of key personnel, says Tom Saporito, president of RHR International in Philadelphia. The firm is a pioneer in the area of corporate psychology. Saporito suggests the following approach.

- Have a clear understanding with key managers about when retirement is likely to take place. "You need to create an environment where retirement is a continual part of the dialog, where you recognize that it is a natural occurrence, and where you can have discussions that are frank and in the best interests of the company as well as of the individual," Saporito says.

- Identify potential successors. Know who, within your organization, has the potential to fill the retiring person's position.
- Evaluate whether or not the job will change, and if so, why and how. Consider industry trends, your own growth strategy, and other issues that may affect the job and how it is performed. With that in mind, Saporito says, you can develop a plan to prepare potential successors to be ready to take over the job when the time comes.

"When you have a clear understanding with key managers about their retirement plans, you've got time to prepare your company," Saporito says. You should be talking about this at least two or three years in advance of the target retirement date. "It's an important, prudent step in being a well-managed company."

⚜ ⚜ ⚜

be recruited away from you. Most people aren't patient enough to wait more than five years to take over.

Don't confuse grooming your company's next leader with developing managers. Leaders set the tone, the vision, the direction for the organization. They're the people who are out front leading the charge, and usually, in a small organization, there's only one of them. You may have several managers; they are the ones who manage outcomes of individual activities, and they need to be developed and trained so they are prepared for the future.

> *The more I face the things I fear, the more uncomfortable situations I face and break through, the greater my growth and success. Life is not about being comfortable.*
>
> *Words of Wisdom*
>
> —KIM KIYOSAKI, AUTHOR OF *RICH WOMAN*, REAL ESTATE INVESTOR, AND A FOUNDER OF THE RICH DAD COMPANY

GETTING READY
FOR A SALE OR MERGER

Whether you are merging your company or preparing for an outright sale, there are steps you will have to take to ensure that the deal you are making is the best possible for you and your company.

1. *Know what you are selling.* There are several ways a business is valued. You should understand the basics so that you can set a reasonable price for your business and evaluate any offers you may receive.

2. *Clean up any mess.* If you were putting your house up for sale, you would make sure that it was clean and fixed up to appeal to any potential buyer. You need to do the same with any business you intend to sell. A cleanup of the business premises is a good idea. Sell off inventory that is just taking up space. Pay down debt. Look at your income statement and make sure your margins are as good as you can get them. Show your potential buyer how profitable your company can really be.

3. *What about a business broker?* A broker may help you evaluate the company and set a price; can attract potential buyers who would otherwise not know of your company; should prequalify all potential buyers to make sure you only spend time with serious inquiries, and will handle much of the paperwork.

4. *Sign confidentiality agreements.* Before you begin to turn over any sensitive information, always have a potential buyer sign an agreement about nondisclosure.

5. *Make the deal.* It is often best to allow others to handle the negotiations. You are too close to the situation and any criticism from the other party may make you defensive. So, while you may do the "dog-and-pony show," let an advisor hammer out the specific terms. Once you have begun to talk price and terms, it is time to call in the professionals.

6. *Enter the due diligence process.* There is a period between the acceptance of the sale and the closing. This is the time for the buyer to look over all the details of the financials and make sure everything is exactly as it was represented. Deals are often specified to be contingent upon the resolution of the due diligence process. Once you have made the sale, you may be less resistant to the pressure of a buyer who tries to lower the price based on everything he or she checks. Make sure the sales agreement covers as much as possible and watch out for this technique.

7. *Make sure you get paid.* One of the most critical elements of your sale is how and when you will see your money. A very experienced buyer will try to buy your business using its own cash flow. You, on the other hand, will want to get as much up front as you can. In the end, you will likely get a little of each. The best deal is one that pays a high proportion of the sale price up front and has a short-term payout of the balance.

Source: Suzanne Caplan, Second Wind: Turnaround Strategies for Business Revival

---

The best advice came from Walt Disney when he said, "Get a good idea and stay with it. Dog it, and work at it until it's done right." The real key to success is perseverance, not the best product or the best price. Those we read about today were successful because of perseverance.

—GARY LEV, PRESIDENT AND CEO, LTS LEADERBOARD TOURNAMENT SYSTEMS LTD.

Words of Wisdom

❖ ❖ ❖

CHAPTER 19

Taking Your Business International

STEPS TO GOING GLOBAL

When you're ready to expand into the international marketplace, these steps will guide you in making the right decisions and developing the best strategies.

1. Assess your export possibilities.
Do a general assessment of your company's products to see if they are suitable for, and competitive in, the international market. Consider issues such as shipping; installation; shelf life; after-sale maintenance and repair; the need to translate labels and instructions into another language; government import/export restrictions.

2. Identify potential international customers.
Gauge your product's viability in the international market and identify those countries with the most potential.

3. Select the best country for your product.
Assess your product's marketability in the countries identified in the second step and develop a market entry strategy for each country.

4. Prepare to visit your target country.
Once you have selected a target country (or countries), plan to make a marketing visit.

5. Select a marketing agent.
Some kind of business arrangement with a local representative or agent is necessary to successfully market your product in almost any country in the world. The agent will help you work in what is often a very different business environment than that to which you are accustomed. The type of agent or business relationship you select will depend on your products, the country, and the way you want to do business.

6. Determine your promotion and pricing.
Consider all of the issues related to promoting a product in a foreign market and pricing it, including the difficult and delicate subject of

payoffs, which are often required in international marketing.

7. Be prepared for the sales challenges.
Set up solid payment methods and be aware of potential political issues, technological issues, corrupt officials, industrial espionage, and even sabotage.

Source: Take Your Business Global: How to Develop International Markets *by Gerhard Kautz* *(Entrepreneur Press, 2004)*

Words of Wisdom

One can choose to go back toward safety or forward toward growth. Growth must be chosen again and again; fear must be overcome again and again.

—ABRAHAM MASLOW, PSYCHOLOGIST

BEFORE YOU SEND EMPLOYEES OVERSEAS

Do your plans for international expansion include opening an overseas office? Your chances of success and profits will be greater if you develop a comprehensive expatriate program before you transfer any employees to a foreign office. Sending someone overseas to live, even temporarily, is far more complex than sending someone on a short-term business trip.

- Decide in advance if the position you're creating will always be filled by someone from headquarters, or if your intent is to have the person you are now sending overseas identify, hire, and train local personnel to staff the facility.

- Get country-specific tax advice before you spend any money. Consult an accounting firm that specializes in international tax issues.

- Provide cross-cultural training for the employee and his or her family. This lets everyone know what to expect in the foreign country, and ideally should include an advance trip to the location before they actually move. Language training for the entire family—both in advance and after the employee moves— should be part of this package.

- Arrange for destination services, which include having someone meet the employee and family on their arrival, help them get settled and acclimated, and identify some local resources for them.

- Be sure you have all the logistics in place beforehand, such as visas; medical exams; inoculations; clarifying whether or not your medical insurance will cover the employee in a foreign country; school for the children; storage of personal property they won't be taking; how they will deal with their home if they own one, etc.

- Set policies on annual home leave and perhaps paid R&R trips if appropriate.

- Your expatriate plan should also include a repatriation plan. Most companies simply guarantee the employee a job when they return from overseas, but don't consider what that job might be. Think about how you're going to use the skills the person has gained, how you're going to get a return on your investment. It's very expensive to send someone to work in another country. If you don't have a meaningful plan for when the employee comes back, he or she may leave the company and you'll lose that investment.

For information and resources in developing your expatriate program, contact the U.S. State Department and ask for the appropriate country desk, that country's embassy in the U.S., and the U.S. embassy in the foreign country.

NETWORKING IN OTHER COUNTRIES

We now live in a fully global society, where it's imperative to have an awareness of cultural differences as they relate to networking etiquette. We often notice differences within our own states, and certainly between regions of the nation. But what about businesses networking with businesses in other parts of the world?

Differences in culture can become stumbling blocks to developing a strong relationship—which is, after all, the ultimate goal of networking. It becomes very easy for a "them" vs. "us" situation to develop, and to focus on the differences as problems that'll hinder working together. It's important to find things that bring you together—things that are similar for us all. For example, we all speak the language of referrals, and we all want to do business based on trust. This transcends many cultural differences. That said, we should be aware and pre-

---

We all speak the language of referrals, and we all want to do business based on trust.

WHY GO GLOBAL?

International expansion is not necessarily the best way to grow your company. The U.S. market is big enough for most small businesses to expand almost indefinitely. But entering the international arena can protect you against the risk of decline in domestic markets and, most important, significantly improve your overall growth potential.

pared for some of these particular cultural differences that can affect the way we network with other cultures. These can be as simple as the way we hand out a business card, to as complex as how close we stand to one another, and the usage of specific idioms.

Networking in today's market takes finesse and knowledge of the culture in which you're networking. Below are three areas where cultural differences require a closer look at networking etiquette.

Business Card Etiquette

Exchanging business cards is an essential part of most cultures. In most Asian countries, after a person has introduced him or herself and bowed, the business card ceremony begins. In Japan, this is called meishi. The card is presented to the other person with the front side facing upwards toward the recipient. Offering the card with both hands holding the top corners of the card demonstrates respect for the other person.

The business card means much more in the Asian culture than it does here in America; it's truly an extension of the individual and is treated with respect. Things like tucking it into a pocket after receiving it, writing on it, bending or folding it in any way, or even looking at it again after you've first accepted it and looked at it are not considered polite and can insult your Asian networker.

Consideration of "Personal Space"

When networking and meeting others with whom you wish to pursue word-of-mouth marketing, it's crucial to understand the subtle, unspoken dynamics of personal space in every culture. Someone might not even be able to put a finger on what it is that sours the business relationship, when in reality, it's nothing more than discomfort from having his or her "bubble" encroached upon. Some cultural dynamics are fine with close, personal interaction, while others demand a bigger bubble. This is not a point to underestimate.

There are three basic separations to consider when taking personal space into account. For Americans, they typically are: public space (ranges from 12 to 25 feet), social space (ranges from 4 to 10 feet), personal space (ranges from 2 to 4 feet), and intimate space (ranges out to 1 foot). In Saudi Arabia, social space equates to our intimate space, and you might find yourself recoiling while your business associate may get the impression that you're stand-offish. In the Netherlands, this might be reversed due to the fact that their personal space equates to our social space. Do your homework and be sensitive to cultural differences in this area. You may find it interesting to take a look at how this pertains to dealing with businesspeople at home as we mix more and more with professionals from other cultures in our everyday dealings.

Use of Slang

When using slang in a business environment, you might want to keep in mind that what means one thing to us might have no meaning, or a very different meaning, to a businessperson from another culture. I have some personal experiences in this area, some humorous, others quite embarrassing! One of my business associates and I were talking with his business partner from South Africa. Even though we were all speaking English, one of the phrases we used caused his partner to go completely silent. We had both reassured him that we would keep him in

---

In his dialect, we had told him that we would keep him pregnant!

---

the loop regarding some aspect of the business. It wasn't until two weeks later that he re-established contact with us and shared that he finally understood what we really had meant. You see, in his dialect, we had told him that we would keep him pregnant! Not at all what we had intended, I can assure you.

In another case, we learned that some European countries don't have a direct translation for "word of mouth," so they translate it to "mouth-to-mouth." I had to explain that this has a totally different connotation in the United States. There were a lot of people over here getting quite excited about this "mouth to mouth" marketing taking place in Europe!

Another example is that it took me a few minutes to figure out what my Australian associates were saying when, upon meeting me, they all said (incredibly fast): "g'daymight." I finally had to ask and was told: "Oh, for our American friend here—we are saying 'good day mate.'"

It was invaluable to me to be able to have my Israeli Director in BNI, Sam Schwartz, coach me regarding the Orthodox Jewish custom of not shaking hands with someone from the opposite gender. He and his associates effectively coached me on how to recognize when a businesswoman was an Orthodox Jew by noting if she was wearing any type of head covering (a normal hat would not have been recognized by me as this type of indicator, had he

---

DOING IT RIGHT

Don't assume that if it works in America, it will work anywhere. Tailor your sales and marketing efforts to each country. Don't ignore the cultural differences that shape the marketplace. The same goes for pricing, shipping, payment terms, and packaging.

*Do your homework ahead of time
so you won't make an inappropriate
gesture, remark, or other offensive behavior.*

not coached me in), or a knee-length skirt with opaque tights worn underneath so that no skin was visible. Again, I wouldn't have even noticed that this was any type of indication, but he was able to clue me in.

If you have the opportunity to network with others from different cultures and countries, don't hesitate because you're not sure how your actions will be interpreted. Just do your homework ahead of time so you *won't* make an inappropriate gesture, remark, or other offensive behavior. Networking basics are universal. With some care for taking into account the cultural nuances that'll give you a leg up, you can be assured that your networking etiquette will be appreciated here at home, and as your business takes you into other countries.

Source: Dr. Ivan Misner, "Networking Etiquette Around the World," Entrepreneur.com

---

RESOURCES FOR DOING BUSINESS ABROAD

U.S. Department of State
www.state.gov

Export.gov
www.export.gov

U.S. Trade Development Agency
www.tda.gov

A Basic Guide to Exporting
www.unzco.com/basicguide/index.html

International Trade Administration
http://trade.gov/cs/

U.S. Department of Agriculture
www.usda.gov

Stat-USA
www.stat-usa.gov

❖ ❖ ❖

MARKETING, ADVERTISING, SALES, AND PUBLIC RELATIONS

"If a man can write a better book, preach a better sermon, or make a better mousetrap than his neighbor, though he build his house in the woods, the world will make a beaten path to his door." These words, attributed to Ralph Waldo Emerson, sound great and many business owners wish they were true—but they're not. Customers will not trip over themselves getting to you. You must reach out to them. Even the wildly popular products for which people stand in long lines and pay exorbitant prices are popular because of the marketing behind them. In this section, we'll look at strategies for marketing, advertising, sales, and public relations that will drive customers to make a beaten path to your door.

⚜ ⚜ ⚜

CHAPTER 20

Marketing

WHAT MARKETING IS *NOT*

The American Marketing Association defines marketing as "the process of planning and executing the conception, pricing, promotion, and distribution of ideas, goods, and services to create exchanges that satisfy individual and organizational goals."

In addition to knowing what marketing *is*, knowing specifically what it is *not* may help you formulate your plan. Marketing is *not*:

Selling
Selling is the process of exchanging goods or services for payment—a result of marketing, but not marketing.

Management-driven
Look to the customer—not to management—for answers and ideas involving marketing.

Industry-driven
Just because the rest of the industry does something a particular way doesn't mean you have to follow suit in your marketing plan.

A single solution
There is no one marketing technique that works all the time, in every situation.

THE KEY TO SUCCESSFUL MARKETING IS YOUR SERVICE

Several years ago British Rail—the company that operates much of Britain's rail service—discovered that its ridership had gone into a steep decline. Like many large companies with too much money and not enough creative thinking, British Rail executives turned to their marketing department for a quick and easy solution. The answer: "We need a new ad agency, a new ad campaign."

They decided they needed a marketing blitz that would lure their customers back to the ticket windows. In the process of shopping for a new agency, the British Rail executives trooped off to the offices of a prominent London ad agency to discuss their needs. As they entered, they were met by a very rude receptionist who told them to sit and wait.

They waited.

They waited some more.

After an insulting length of time, an unkempt staff member of the agency led them to a disheveled conference room featuring a tabled covered with partially read newspapers, stained coffee cups, and plates of stale, half-eaten food.

Again, the executives were left to wait. Finally, a few of the agency people, carelessly dressed and ill-groomed, began drifting in and out of the room, ignoring the British Rail executives.

When the understandably annoyed executives asked what was going on, they got a curt brush-off and a shrug of the shoulders. The agency people acted as if they didn't care.

Finally, the British Rail people had had enough. The head of the delegation vented his outrage—whereupon one of the ad agency executives smiled, approached him, and said: "Gentlemen, your treatment here at this agency is not typical of the way we treat our customers. In fact, we've gone out of our way to stage this meeting for you. We behaved this way to demonstrate what it's like to be a customer of British Rail. The real problem at British Rail isn't in your advertising. It's your people, your customer service. We suggest that you let us help you fix your employee attitude problem first, before we attempt to fix your advertising."

The British Rail executives were shocked at first, but the agency won the account. It stood out. It proved it was remarkable. The ad people had the courage to point out to British Rail that the answer to their problem was right inside the four walls of their operation.

And so is yours.

Source: The 10-Minute Marketer's Secret Formula: A Shortcut to Extraordinary Profits Using Neighborhood Marketing *by Tom Feltenstein (Entrepreneur Press, 2005)*

WRITING YOUR MARKETING PLAN

It doesn't have to ever make the best-seller list, but it does have to be written well enough that you have a clearly-drawn map to guide the marketing side of your business. Your marketing plan is an integral part of your overall business plan, an essential component to taking your company from a "good idea" to a profitable operation, and evidence to funding sources—both lenders and investors—that you have thought through how you will ultimately sell your product or service and make money doing it.

No two marketing plans are exactly alike, but the ones that work all contain the same fundamental elements. Follow this basic structure:

Define your product

You need to know precisely what your product or service is and what it will do for your customers. Be very specific. Successful marketing requires a solid understanding of the features and benefits of every aspect of your product.

Identify your customers

Who will buy your product and why? Again, be specific. Where do these people live and work? How

Never stop rainmaking, developing new business.

—JONATHAN BERNSTEIN, PRESIDENT, BERNSTEIN CRISIS MANAGEMENT, LLC

much money do they make? How often will they buy? Understand various buying sensitivities, such as the importance of brand, location, guarantee, and price.

Identify your competition

Know your competition as well as you know yourself. Who else sells what you sell? Where are they? How do they market? How similar are their products? What are the comparative advantages and disadvantages between what they do and what you plan to do? What is their pricing structure? What do their customers like and dislike about them? What would make their customers buy from you instead?

You may believe you don't have any direct competition—that is, no one else in your market is doing exactly what you do. But if that's the case, how do you know there's a need for your business? And how are your prospective customers getting that need met currently?

Set your prices

How much you charge affects both your profitability and your position in the market. Understand what your costs are, what competitors are charging, and how your price relates to your overall marketing strategy.

Explain how you will interact with your customers.

This includes the general promotion of your business as well as the actual sales process. How will prospective customers learn about you? What will drive them to you? Will you advertise? Make personal calls? Put up clever signs? Use the internet? Will you have a retail store front, be in an office complex or industrial park, or are you going to be home based? Once a potential customer becomes aware of what you have to offer, how will you convert them from prospect to buyer? How will they actually receive the product— will they come to you, or will you deliver?

Develop a very specific plan and plot it out at least one year in advance. Incorporate what you'll do for holidays and other special dated events, such as trade shows. Consider necessary lead time; for example, if a Yellow Page ad is important to your overall marketing plan, what is the deadline for placing the ad and when will the new directory be distributed?

Along with what you're going to do, calculate what it will cost, and what you expect the outcome to be. Though you can't always accurately predict results, you should have a sound rationale for spending money before you do. The cost of marketing will vary by industry, but a general average is five percent of sales. Regardless of how much you spend, spend it on the methods that will give you the biggest return on your marketing investment.

As you develop your plans, keep in mind that this is not a linear process. For example, you may begin with a particular product, then as you study the demographics of your market, realize that you can capture a greater share of that market with a few product adjustments. It's possible that what you learn by studying your competition may prompt you to make changes in your plans for interacting with your market. You need to also incorporate your production capacity into your marketing plan—do you have the capability to produce a sufficient amount of product to meet your sales projections?

This is why you should give yourself a lot of physical room as you develop your marketing plan. Even if you're using a business plan program on your computer, make notes on large sheets of paper and paste them up on the wall so you can easily see how each portion of the marketing plan interacts with the other. Though these software products vary in depth and quality—many are excellent—the basic physical limitations of a computer monitor force you to focus on one element at a time and don't allow you to see the overall picture without printing out your plan.

> A great resource for information on your market is your competition. Go to their web sites and sign up for all their newsletters, white papers, technical papers, industry surveys, and conference reports. Get on their e-mail lists.
>
> —FROM *MADSCAM: KICK-ASS ADVERTISING WITHOUT THE MADISON AVENUE PRICE TAG* BY GEORGE PARKER

Words of Wisdom

RESEARCHING YOUR MARKET

Whether you're just starting out or you've been in business for years, you should always stay up-to-date with your market information. Here are the best methods for finding your data.

The purpose of market research is to provide relevant data that will help solve marketing problems. This is absolutely necessary in the start-up phase. Conducting thorough market surveys is the foundation of any successful business. In fact, strategies such as market segmentation (identifying specific segments within a market) and product differentiation (creating an identity for your product or service that separates it from your competitors) would be impossible to develop without market research.

Whether you're conducting market research using the historical, experimental, observational, or survey method, you'll be gathering two types of data. The first will be primary information that you will compile yourself or hire someone to gather. Most information, however, will be secondary, or already compiled and organized for you. Reports and studies done by government agencies, trade associations, or other businesses within your industry are examples of the latter. Search for them, and take advantage of them.

Primary Research

When conducting primary research using your own resources, there are basically two types of information that can be gathered: exploratory and specific. Exploratory research is open-ended in nature; helps you define a specific problem; and usually involves detailed, unstructured interviews in which lengthy answers are solicited from a small group of respondents. Specific research is broader in scope and used to solve a problem that exploratory research has identified. Interviews are structured and formal in approach. Of the two, specific research is more expensive.

When conducting primary research using your own resources, you must first decide how you will question your target group of individuals. There are basically three avenues you can take: direct mail, telemarketing, or personal interviews.

Direct mail

If you choose a direct-mail questionnaire, be sure to do the following in order to increase your response rate:

- Make sure your questions are short and to the point.
- Make sure questionnaires are addressed to specific individuals and are of interest to the respondent.
- Limit the questionnaire's length to two pages.
- Enclose a professionally prepared cover letter that adequately explains what you need.
- Send a reminder about two weeks after the initial mailing. Include a postage-paid self-addressed envelope.

Unfortunately, even if you employ the above tactics, response to direct mail is always low, and is sometimes less than five percent.

Phone surveys

Phone surveys are generally the most cost-effective, considering overall response rates; they cost about one-third as much as personal interviews, which have, on average, a response rate that is only 10 percent. Following are some phone survey guidelines:

- At the beginning of the conversation, your interviewer should confirm the name of the respondent if calling a home, or give the appropriate name to the switchboard operator if calling a business.
- Pauses should be avoided, as respondent interest can quickly drop.
- Make sure that a follow-up call is possible if additional information is required.
- Make sure that interviewers don't divulge details about the poll until the respondent is reached.

As mentioned, phone interviews are cost-effective but speed is another big advantage. Some of the more experienced interviewers can get through up to 10 interviewers an hour (however, speed for speed's sake is not the goal of any of these surveys), but five to six per hour is more typical. Phone interviews also allow you to cover a wide geographical range relatively inexpensively. Phone costs can be reduced by taking advantage of cheaper rates during certain hours.

Personal interviews

There are two main types of personal interviews:

The group interview. Used mostly by big business, group interviews can be useful as brainstorming tools resulting in product modifications and new product ideas. They also give you insight into buying preferences and purchasing decisions among certain populations.

The depth interview. One-on-one interviews where the interviewer is guided by a small checklist and basic common sense. Depth interviews are either focused or nondirective. Nondirective interviews encourage respondents to address certain topics with minimal questioning. The respondent, in essence, leads the interview. The focused interview, on the other hand, is based on a pre-set checklist. The choice and timing of questions, however, is left to the interviewer, depending on how the interview goes.

When considering which type of survey to use, keep the following cost factors in mind:

- *Mail.* Most of the costs concern the printing of questionnaires, envelopes, postage, the cover letter, time taken in the analysis and presentation, the cost of researcher time, and any incentives used.
- *Telephone.* The main costs are the interviewer's fee, phone charges, preparation of the questionnaire, cost of researcher time, and the analysis and presentation of the results of the questioning.

- *Personal interviews.* Costs include the printing of questionnaires and prompt cards if needed, the incentives used, the interviewer's fee and expenses, cost of researcher time, and analysis and presentation.
- *Group discussions.* Main costs are the interviewer's fees and expenses in recruiting and assembling the groups, renting the conference room or other facility, researcher time, any incentives used, analysis and presentation, and the cost of recording media such as tapes, if any are used.

Secondary Data

Secondary data is outside information assembled by government agencies, industry and trade associations, labor unions, media sources, chambers of commerce, etc., and is found in the form of pamphlets, newsletters, trade and other magazines, newspapers, and so on. It's termed secondary data because the information has been gathered by another, or secondary, source. The benefits of this are obvious—time and money are saved because you don't have to develop survey methods or do the interviewing.

Secondary sources are divided into three main categories:

Public

Public sources are the most economical, as they're usually free, and can offer a lot of good information. These sources are most typically governmental departments, business departments of public libraries, etc.

Commercial

Commercial sources are equally valuable, but usually involve costs such as subscription and association fees. However, you spend far less than you would if you hired a research team to collect the data firsthand. Commercial sources typically consist of research and trade associations, organizations like SCORE and Dun & Bradstreet, banks and other financial institutions, publicly traded corporations, etc.

Educational

Educational institutions are frequently overlooked as viable information sources, yet there is more research conducted in colleges, universities, and polytechnic institutes than virtually any sector of the business community.

Government statistics are among the most plentiful and wide-ranging public sources of information. Start with the Census Bureau's helpful *Hidden Treasures—Census Bureau Data and Where to Find It!* In seconds, you'll find out where to find federal and state information. Other government publications that are helpful include:

- *Statistical and Metropolitan Area Data Book.* Offers statistics for metropolitan areas, central cities, and counties.
- *Statistical Abstract of the United States.* Data books with statistics from numerous sources, government to private.
- *U.S. Global Outlook.* Traces the growth of 200 industries and gives five-year forecasts for each.

Don't neglect to contact specific government agencies such as the Small Business Administration (SBA). They sponsor several helpful programs such as SCORE and Small Business Development Centers

> *Nothing will ever be attempted if all possible objections must first be overcome.*
>
> —SAMUEL JOHNSON, AUTHOR

Words of Wisdom

(SBDCs) that can provide you with free counseling and a wealth of business information. The Department of Commerce not only publishes helpful books like the *U.S. Global Outlook*, it also produces an array of products with information regarding both domestic industries and foreign markets through its International Trade Administration (ITA) branch. All the above items are available from the U.S. Government Printing Office.

One of the best public sources is the business section of public libraries. The services provided vary from city to city but usually include a wide range of government and market statistics, a large collection of directories including information on domestic and foreign businesses, as well as a wide selection of magazines, newspapers, and newsletters.

Almost every county government publishes population density and distribution figures in accessible census tracts. These will show you the number of people living in specific areas, such as precincts, water districts, or even 10-block neighborhoods. Other public sources include city chambers of commerce or business development departments, which encourage new businesses in their communities. They will supply you (usually for free) with information on population trends, community income characteristics, payrolls, industrial development, and so on.

Among the best commercial sources of information are research and trade associations. Information gathered by trade associations is usually confined to a certain industry and available only to association members, with a membership fee frequently required. However, the research gathered by the larger associations is usually thorough, accurate and worth the cost of membership. Two excellent resources to help you locate a trade association that reports on the business you're researching are *Encyclopedia of Associations* (Gale Research) and *Business Information Sources* (University of

California Press) both can usually be found at your local library.

Research associations are often independent but sometimes affiliated with trade associations. They often limit their activities to conducting and applying research in industrial development, but some have become full-service information sources with a wide range of supplementary publications such as directories.

Educational institutions are very good sources of research. The data ranges from faculty-based projects, often published under professors' bylines, to student projects, theses, and assignments. Copies of student research projects may be available for free with faculty permission. Consulting services are available either for free or at a cost negotiated with the appropriate faculty members. This can be an excellent way to generate research at little or no cost, using students who welcome the professional experience either as interns or for special credit. Contact the university administration departments and marketing/management studies departments for further information. University libraries are additional sources of research.

Source: The Small Business Encyclopedia
and Knock-Out Marketing

DOING IT RIGHT

"Too often new entrepreneurs assume that competitors will just keep on operating the way they always have even if they lose market share to the new entrepreneur. Unfortunately, competitors do respond, sometimes decisively, when a new entrepreneur takes business. Businesses need a feature that gives them a sustainable advantage, one that competitors can't easily duplicate, in order to succeed."

Source: Don Debelak, author of Business Models Made Easy

People who have good relationships at home are more effective in the marketplace.

—ZIG ZIGLAR

MARKET RESEARCH RESOURCES

Click Z Network
www.clickz.com
Interactive marketing news, information, commentary, advice, opinion, research, and reference.

Neilson/NetRatings
www.netratings.com
Internet media and market research.

Jupiter Research
www.jupiterresearch.com
Research, analysis and advice, backed by proprietary data.

MarketResearch.com
www.marketresearch.com
Large and continuously updated collection of market research.

Free Demographics
www.freedemographics.com
Demographic market analysis.

ResearchInfo
www.researchinfo.com
Marketing research industry resources.

Trends Research Institute
www.trendsresearch.com
Projects future trends and their impact on business and industry.

NEGATIVE OPTION MARKETING

In a traditional sales transaction, the seller makes his presentation and the prospective customer says either yes or no, and that's pretty much the end of it. But negative option marketing turns things around.

Early book and record clubs were the pioneers of negative option marketing. Customers "joined" the clubs and received books or records either free or at a heavily discounted price, then agreed to purchase a certain number of products at the regular price over a period of time. Customers who failed to decline the book or record of the month received it automatically.

Negative option marketing (also called advance consent marketing) has become more prevalent and is being used in a variety of industries. The central characteristic of a negative option offer is that the seller interprets the consumer's silence or failure to take an affirmative action to reject goods or services, or to cancel the sales agreement, as acceptance of the offer. Typically, the offer is often presented as a "free trial" and charges will begin after a specified time if the customer fails to cancel.

Proponents say that continuous service and automatic renewals benefit consumers, but the potential for abuse is significant. The Federal Trade Commission logs hundreds of thousands of complaints on this issue every year. Some states are implementing legislation restricting—and in some cases, banning—the use of negative option marketing.

Businesses that choose to use negative option marketing should take care that the offer meets all applicable regulations, that salespeople are trained to provide complete details, and that complaints are dealt with promptly and fairly.

Some online marketers are using the negative option technique to build e-mail lists. The marketer sends an e-mail stating its intention to send future messages and if the recipient doesn't reply, permission is assumed and a list is quickly built. The marketer then begins sending e-mails to that list and renting or selling the list to others.

Studies show that opt-in e-mail lists have a better response than those built through negative option tactics. If you're renting a list, find out how it was created and avoid those produced through a negative option opt-out campaign. Successful marketing depends on trust, not tricks.

BUYING POWER OF U.S. GAYS AND LESBIANS WILL EXCEED $835 BILLION BY 2011

The buying power of gays and lesbians is expected to exceed $835 billion by 2011, as the U.S. gay and lesbian population reaches 16.3 million the same year. Such phenomenal growth and consumer power has not gone unnoticed by major national marketers. LOGO, the new gay and lesbian cable TV outlet, has more than 80 major brands as sponsors, and advertisers are increasingly targeting gays in mainstream media—particularly online, as gays tend to have a higher proclivity towards digital entertainment than their heterosexual counterparts.

Source: The Gay and Lesbian Market in the U.S., *a report from Packaged Facts, a division of MarketResearch.com*

Be sure to have a written strategic lead generation plan. Then be sure you have the sales process down perfectly. No sales = no customers = no business.

—Thomas Fenig, Founder and CEO, Outdoor Lighting Perspectives

---

CAUSE MARKETING: BUILD YOUR BUSINESS WITH GOOD DEEDS

Can you do good works while promoting your company's products and services? Definitely. It's known as cause marketing, and essentially involves choosing a nonprofit organization and supporting it with direct financial assistance, in-kind donations, and/or volunteer time.

Getting the company involved builds community goodwill, customer loyalty, and a stronger bond among your own employees. Done correctly, cause marketing creates a win/win situation—but it has its pitfalls. Keep the following points in mind.

- *Choose the cause carefully.* Avoid controversial issues; instead, support a mainstream cause that is likely to offend no one. It should have some relevance to and be compatible with your business. If you feel strongly about a divisive cause, support it on your own time.
- *Check out the agency.* Be sure the organization you're supporting is legitimate, well-run, and demonstrates a strong degree of accountability.
- *Be totally committed.* Embrace the cause completely, and follow through on your promises. If you're not sincere, it will show.
- *Get your employees on board.* Enthusiasm is contagious, so lead by example.
- *Promote and publicize your efforts.* Make customers and the public aware of what you're doing with discreet but visible mentions in your promotional materials.
- *Keep good records.* In addition to being important from a tax and general business perspective, you want to be ready in case someone wants to see evidence that you're keeping your word.

BILLING: A HIDDEN MARKETING OPPORTUNITY

If you send out invoices or monthly statements, make them a marketing opportunity. You can usually include a brochure or flyer without increasing the weight of the envelope enough to require additional postage. Use these invoice stuffers to announce special promotions, alert customers to changes in your location or hours, or remind them of particular products or services. If appropriate, incorporate a coupon or other reply vehicle. It's ok to send the same stuffer more than once; repetition is the key to successful advertising. Consider developing a series of pieces that is rotated on a regular basis—just be sure the series is coordinated with your overall marketing strategy.

DOING IT RIGHT

Because it's easier and more profitable to retain an existing customer than find a new one, remember to thank your customers for their business. Make your expression of gratitude genuine, perhaps with a handwritten note or a telephone call with no other purpose. Consider having the thanks come from behind-the-scenes; for example, a production worker or delivery driver could thank a customer for a particular order.

Talent is cheaper than table salt. What separates the talented individual from the successful one is a lot of hard work.

Words of Wisdom

—STEPHEN KING, AUTHOR

PUT YOUR INVOICES TO WORK IN THE MARKETING DEPARTMENT

Your invoices and statements can do more than simply collect your money; they can actually help grow your business. You're sending out invoices anyway, so since you have the cost involved, you may as well make them a marketing communications tool. That way, you're not only billing your customers, you're giving them important information about how they can more effectively do business with you.

Plan your invoice messages several months in advance. Decide which events and programs to promote in each billing cycle. Remember that computer-generated invoices can be programmed to automatically include messages about upcoming events, new products and services, specials, and seasonal information.

Printing directly on the invoice means your message won't be discarded, as most envelope stuffers are. While a stuffer may get tossed, the invoice won't. Also, because most invoices pass through several hands for approval before they are paid, you can be assured that your invoice message will be read by top-level decision-makers.

LOW-COST MARKETING IDEAS

The most effective marketing programs work not because the companies spent huge sums implementing them, but because they were carefully researched and planned, targeted to an identified market, monitored for results, and adjusted when necessary for maximum effect.

Ideas for Low-Cost Marketing

Strategic partnerships

Team with non-competing businesses that share your market to offer mutually-beneficial promotions. By partnering, companies can share marketing costs and reach a greater number of potential customers for less money. Partnering opportunities are limited only by your imagination; take a look at your customers and think about what else they purchase—it doesn't necessarily have to be directly related to your business. A house painter could team up with a fence company; a pest control service could partner with a security service (keeping all types of nasty intruders away); a bookkeeping service and a virtual assistant service will likely find some common clients; a restaurant located near a automotive service center could offer a free beverage to customers waiting for their cars to be repaired.

Though high-profile partners have a strong appeal, it's not essential that your partner be a household name. At the same time, don't be afraid to approach a large corporation with a partnering proposal; big companies are always on the lookout for low-cost ways to increase business, just as you are. Finally, you don't need to limit yourself to just one partner; wisely-selected multiple partners can further reduce your costs and increase your results. Remember, it's important to make sure that the program is indeed a partnership, with all parties investing and benefiting with relative fairness, and all operating with complete integrity.

Target marketing

One of the simplest ways to control marketing costs is to target your program so you are not wasting your efforts attempting to reach people who are not prospective customers or sending a message that is meaningless to a particular market segment. Target marketing also helps in developing partnership agreements.

Take the time to study the various segments of your particular market, and develop focused campaigns to reach each one. Don't try to use the same ad to reach senior citizens that you use for young families; it won't work, and your money will be wasted.

Special/seasonal promotions

Tying promotions to seasons and special events allows you to use general public awareness to build your own company. If appropriate, such promotions can also add an element of fun and overall appeal that may be more difficult to create without the seasonal link. Be sure that your promotion calendar synchronizes your sales goals with your customers' buying patterns.

Consistent image

Establish and follow systems and procedures to make sure your image is consistent and your brand name and logo are linked in your customers' minds with a dependable level of product and service performance.

The customers have two choices: they can go to somebody else, or they can come to you. You've got to understand what is going to make them come to you.

Words of Wisdom

—IMRAN AZHAR, CO-FOUNDER, AZHAR THERAPY & FITNESS, OKLAHOMA CITY, OK

YEAR-ROUND HOLIDAY MARKETING

If you think holiday marketing begins just after Halloween and ends on New Year's Day, think again. For most small businesses, holidays from Father's Day to Administrative Professionals' Day provide terrific hooks on which to hang marketing promotions.

To get you thinking outside the gift box, here are 12 months of holidays to consider—plus creative ideas for using less traditional holidays to grab your customers' attention.

February

Valentine's Day is a bonanza for restaurateurs and jewelers, but other entrepreneurs also can use the day to tell customers they're appreciated. Show your company's love by sending letters with special rewards—such as money off a purchase—to your best customers or clients. Rewards at this holiday, rather than just at the more traditional times of year, will grab attention and be appreciated.

Also in February are Groundhog Day, Mardi Gras, and Presidents' Day. Want to be inventive? A professional services firm could enhance its client relations (and loosen an otherwise stiff image) by throwing a Mardi Gras-themed party, while an air-conditioning and heating contractor could send a direct mail piece using Groundhog Day as a hook, offering customers a special discount on heating maintenance services to help them get through six more weeks of winter.

March

The two biggest holidays on my calendar in March are St. Patrick's Day and my birthday. Granted, my birthday may not be of any interest to your customers, but they'll definitely enjoy being appreciated on their own

birthdays. Include a field in your customer database for birth dates, and depending on your type of business, send a gift, card, or reward.

As for St. Patrick's Day, there are many fun tie-ins—from the color green to the luck of the Irish—you can develop into marketing hooks. And the first day of spring is March 21. Traditionally, this is the kick-off for major spring retail promotions.

April

Ah, April Fools' Day. Businesses large and small have used this day as an opportunity to draw public attention. In one well-publicized April Fools' hoax, Taco Bell placed ads in major newspapers announcing it had purchased the Liberty Bell to help reduce the federal deficit and was planning to move it to Irvine, California. Americans were furious. There were more than 400 TV mentions and thousands of newspaper and radio mentions worth millions in media coverage, even though Taco Bell sent out a news release revealing the hoax just a few hours later. The smart promotional gambit resulted in a $500,000 sales increase for the company on April 1 and a $600,000 increase on April 2.

Earth Day is on April 22, and you don't have to be a green company to take on an environmentally friendly promotion, such as planting trees and letting your customers know about it. And let's not overlook Administrative Professionals' Day (formerly known as Secretaries' Day) on April 25. This holiday is prompting small businesses to take action: the Vermont Teddy Bear Co., for instance, has added a page to its website to sell gifts for the occasion.

May

The two biggest holidays in May are Mother's Day and Memorial Day. Small businesses in the hospitality, consumer services, and retail categories typically realize the greatest gains from Mother's Day promotions. Husbands and daughters make the bulk of all Mother's Day purchases, and consumers spend more on this holiday than most others, including Father's Day. The most popular service given as a Mother's Day gift is a half-day spa treatment. To promote your Mother's Day offerings this year, consider using e-mail as a low-cost, high-return tactic to promote everything from jewelry to flowers.

June through September

While not the big spending holiday Mother's Day has become, Father's Day is still a terrific hook for small businesses looking for an early summer boost. Since women make the most purchases for fathers and husbands, create promotions that appeal to their desire for convenient, easy shopping and cost savings.

Summer officially begins on June 21, but long before that, the season can provide a wonderful hook for specials or promotions that tie in to warm-weather vacations and fun. Campground owners, for example, can ramp up marketing campaigns that target families with RVs looking for affordable vacations.

Since the Fourth of July is a major retail marketing holiday, smaller businesses may want to stay out of the fray and concentrate promotional dollars on less-crowded holidays. If you offer products related to back-to-school promotions, August is your month. And retailers should plan a marketing push for Labor Day sales on September 3.

October

Trick or treat! Halloween is more popular than ever, with many adults attending costume parties and even sales of pet costumes seeing a dramatic upswing. For small nonprofits and fundraising organizations, Halloween provides a wonderful marketing opportunity. You can create a haunted event,

get other local businesses involved as sponsors or partners, and sell tickets in multiple locations.

Halloween is also a smart hook for businesses promoting child safety products and services. You can win media coverage, including newspaper and radio interviews, by producing a fact sheet with safety tips along with a pitch letter to send to targeted editors and journalists.

November through January

November 1 officially marks the start of the holiday selling season, so why not put a new spin on Thanksgiving promotions? Instead of focusing on holiday decorations or falling retail prices, make an effort to help others while enhancing your company's image in the process. You can sponsor meals for the homeless. Or you and your staff can engage in a visible community improvement project. Work to enlist other businesses in your area, and share your story with the local media. Then you can proceed with your company's traditional winter sales promotions with a strong PR lift and community goodwill. And retailers can keep the momentum rolling into January with New Year's Day sales, followed by special promotions tied to the chilly weather.

Source: Kim T. Gordon, "12 Months of Holiday Promotions," Entrepreneur.com

---

Prospects don't care about you. They care about themselves and anything they have to read or listen to that is not related to them is of little or no interest.

Words of Wisdom

—Jay Conrad Levinson and Al Lautenslager, *Guerrilla Marketing in 30 Days*

BUSINESS GIFT-GIVING MADE EASY

Whether it's for Christmas, birthdays, anniversaries, or other occasions, choosing gifts for those key clients and business associates can be a challenge. So how do you choose a gift that is useful (otherwise, what's the point?), ethical, politically correct, reasonably priced (so it won't look like you're trying to "buy" business), has no potential for liability (a primary reason alcohol has lost popularity as a holiday gift), and won't offend anyone?

First, decide who will be on your gift list. All your clients? Or only certain ones? What about other business associates?

Next, determine the recipients' policies on accepting gifts. Many organizations limit gifts to a certain dollar value; others refuse them outright; still others allow employees to accept just about anything. Check with the company's personnel department or discreetly ask your contact. You'll also want to get a feel for the individual's attitude about gifts beyond the formal policies.

Now, set your budget and select the gifts. Gift-giving to business contacts is certainly a part of your marketing efforts, but keep the cost in proportion to the benefits received.

Some ideas to consider:

- *Plants*. Plants are a very neutral gift with an environmental flavor; choose one that is known for cleaning indoor air. Be sure to include a tag with care instructions.
- *Memorabilia*. If you have a news clipping of your client being mentioned in a positive way, or if you have a photograph of your client at a happy event, have it framed. It will likely hang on the wall and be a reminder of your thoughtfulness for years to come.
- *Books*. Books are always a good choice in business or personal gift-giving. Be sure the bookstore has a liberal return policy, avoid controversial subjects, and don't buy anything dated that may be hard to exchange.
- *Charitable donations*. You can approach this from two directions: Either give a specific donation in a particular customer's name to a charity you know they support, or give a single large donation to a charity of your choice and send out a letter to everyone saying that's what you've done in lieu of individual gifts. In either case, you don't have to indicate the amount you gave. Choose a neutral organization that enjoys popular support.
- *No gift at all*. This is a perfectly acceptable alternative to the gift-giving dilemma. If you decide not to give gifts, don't make a big deal about it. Unless you have a reputation for splashy presents, chances are no one will notice.

Whatever you decide to do about giving gifts, always acknowledge the ones you receive. A hand-written thank-you note is your best choice.

LET THE MARKET PULL YOUR BUSINESS

Pay attention to what the market is telling you, and you may discover an unexpected and profitable direction for your business. That's what happened to Julian Gordon, founder and president of American Ramp Systems®, a division of Gordon Industries, Inc.

Gordon is an aeronautical engineer who formed Gordon Industries in 1970 as a manufacturer of metal products (doors, railings, stairs, etc.). His market was primarily contractors and architects.

"In the late 1990s, people started asking us if we could build ramps," Gordon says. "We thought we would sell the ramps primarily to our existing construction market, but when we advertised, we got calls from individuals who needed ramps on a short-term basis. At first, we just said we couldn't help them. But they kept calling. Finally, we did some research, determined that the market was viable, and developed our patented ramp system."

Gordon created the American Ramp Systems division of his company in 1998 and began franchising in 2002. The product is a patented steel wheelchair ramp system assembled from modular components designed for both interior and exterior use and is available for both purchase and rental. The ramps are easy to install and can be removed without damaging the building. The key segments of the company's market are: home healthcare; aging or disabled individuals wishing to remain at home; ADA compliance for existing public buildings; and short-term rentals.

"The aging population is going to contribute significantly to the ongoing and increasing need for our products," Gordon says. "The healthcare industry is constantly looking for ways to reduce costs and maximize their resources, and a ramp is a tool that allows people to stay in their homes and still have access to the services they need."

American Ramp Systems is growing at an impressive pace because Gordon listened when the market expressed a need and then took steps to meet that need.

Marketing strategies are not one-size-fits-all and they don't come with a guarantee. What is wildly successful for one company may be a total failure for another.

If you're doing your own admin work to save money when you're not 100 percent booked, you are stealing time you would probably be better off spending on new business development activities.

Words of Wisdom

—JONATHAN BERNSTEIN, PRESIDENT, BERNSTEIN CRISIS MANAGEMENT, LLC

MARKETING IDEAS TO CONSIDER

- Contests
- Newsletters
- Search engine optimization
- Product demonstrations
- Seminars and speeches
- Premiums (advertising specialty items)
- Articles and books
- Bonuses (a free this if you buy that)
- Coupons
- Donations
- Samples and free trials
- Special benefits or rates
- Press releases
- Networking and referrals
- Referrals

TEST YOUR MARKETING STRATEGIES

- Even with the greatest idea and thorough planning, concept and reality can be two different things. Before you roll out any marketing campaign, test it to be sure it will have the results you want.
- The easiest way to test a marketing strategy is to implement it on a small scale before committing to a large-scale effort. It's also a good idea to do some comparison testing. Run two different ads and see which one pulls better. Mail two different pieces and see which one draws the higher response. Compare the cost and results generated by various strategies and go with the ones that produce the best results for you.
- Be careful not to extend the conclusion of your test beyond the test itself. Don't assume that a different set of circumstances will produce the same results; instead, test every possible angle. For example, let's say you tested a free printed newsletter and the test indicated you wouldn't get enough of a response to justify the cost of the newsletter. You should probably decide against a print newsletter—but don't assume that an online newsletter will produce the same poor results. Test the online newsletter as well.
- Remember that if the test tells you something won't work, the test itself was not a failure, it was a tremendous success—and it saved you a lot of time, money, and energy pursuing a strategy that would have failed.

THINK SMALL: FOCUS YOUR MARKETING

- *Pinpoint and attack your competitors' weaknesses.* Maybe they aren't open during the hours customers want them to be. Maybe their product selection or availability is limited. Maybe their premises are dirty. Maybe they don't offer extra services like delivery or on-site service. By analyzing what they're doing and doing it better, you can turn their head start into your advantage.
- *Don't try to reach everyone with a "one-size-fits-all" ad campaign.* Instead, identify your primary customer group and start marketing aggressively to them alone.
- *Use low-cost, highly targeted vehicles to deliver your message.* Put up fliers in churches, supermarkets, and other places where your customers go. Advertise only in the publications you know they read. You'll make more money by tight focus than by a scattered approach.
- *Communicate with your customers one-on-one.* Shop where they shop, attend the events they attend, and get to know them. You'll learn just as much as you ever will by spending tens of thousands of dollars on expensive focus groups and market research.

⚜ ⚜ ⚜

CHAPTER 21

Advertising

ADVERTISING TRENDS

Do you suspect that DVRs are keeping most people from seeing your ads on TV? Are you convinced that radio is losing its listeners to satellite radio and the iPod? Do you wonder if the newspaper readers of yesterday are getting their news from the internet today? It's no secret that advertising isn't working as well as it once did. But media fragmentation isn't the problem.

In truth, only 11.7 percent of U.S. households are equipped with a DVR, but response to TV ads is off by far more than 11.7 percent. Broadcast radio has only lost about 4 percent of its audience over the past three years, and even the most aggressive doomsayers are predicting that radio will lose no more than 11 percent of its audience by the year 2010. But response to radio ads is off by far more than that. Newspaper readership peaked in 1984, and today's number is only about 16 percent below that banner year. But the response to newspaper ads isn't nearly what it was back then.

What's Going On?

We've entered the age of stimuli bombardment, visual saturation, sound bites, and microscopic attention spans. The number of images and voices shouting for our attention has accelerated beyond critical mass, and the resulting explosion has fragmented the public mind. In a nutshell, we've developed mental filters to guard against hypercommunication.

I'm paid according to how much my clients' sales grow, so I needed to figure out what the problem was—and then fix it. Here's what I discovered, tested, and proved.

Internet browsing has trained the public to more quickly disregard empty words.

Message relevance has become more important than repetition. (Keep in mind that I did not say repetition no longer matters.)

Bottom line: Meaningful messages are working better than ever, especially when the fundamental premise of your ad is clearly stated in the opening line. Ads full of unsupported claims and overworked "image building" phrases are rejected quicker today than ever before.

You and I spend about a minute a day sorting the mail, right? Up until a few years ago, these six minutes each week were our only exercise in high-speed content evaluation. Now we're spending at least six hours a week scanning search engine results, web pages, and e-mail for relevant, meaningful information. These hours of practice are teaching us—and our customers—to more quickly recognize and disregard empty words.

The buying public is still out there. What's gone is the willingness to pay attention to drivel.

Ads that would have produced good results just a few years ago are failing today. Others are working far better than expected. Fortunately, there's a pattern—and things you can do to ensure your ads get noticed. To see the kind of results that advertising can still deliver, you're going to have to:

- Talk about things your customer actually finds interesting.
- Write your ads in a style that rings true.
- Avoid heroic chest thumping, such as "We are the number-one . . ."
- Close the loopholes in your ads—ambiguous claims make you seem dishonest.
- Use specifics. They're more believable than generalities.
- Remember that substance is more important than style.
- Relate to the customers on their own terms.

If your ad delivers a meaningful message that rings true from the moment of contact, you'll find that it works regardless of which media you choose. The new rule is to say what you've got to say, and say it clean. The opening line of your ad is its most important element, so open big. I'm not talking about hype—something of the "Save up to 75 percent this week only at blah blah blah" variety. I'm talking about making a statement that's fundamentally more interesting than what had been in your customer's mind.

Source: Roy Williams, "Advertising Trends: Pushing Past Media Overload," Entrepreneur.com

WHAT IS THE NEW MEDIA AND HOW IS IT DIFFERENT?

The catch-all phrase "New Media" primarily covers electronic-based methods of connecting with customers. Since the launch of the internet, these have grown tremendously and include web sites, e-mail, blogs, e-retailing, e-commerce, e-banking, and just about anything else you can stick an "e" in front of to make it trendy. New Media is a series of options that go beyond the traditional ones of print, direct mail, billboards, TV, and radio—options that enable advertisers to communicate with existing and prospective customers through a series of interactive computing vehicles, often across sophisticated, multimedia platforms.

What it all means in plain English is that you can now talk to your customers through computers, cell phones, VoIP phones, PDAs, games, set-top-box TV devices, even interactive supermarket trolleys. And you can do it in a way that encourages them to talk back to you, take advantage of immediate offers, let you track what their preferences are, and find out why they like some of the things you have to offer and why they dislike others. It's a rapidly changing world.

Source: MadScam: Kick-Ass Advertising Without the Madison Avenue Price Tag by George Parker

CONSIDER CAMEL MAIL

No, we're not talking about an alternative to the postal service; we're talking about the design of your direct mail pieces. Camel mail is an envelope with a hump that indicates there's something unusual inside. The hump sparks curiosity and most people won't be able to resist opening the envelope.

You can use a variety of items to create the hump—a small promotional item (key chains, pins, small pads, etc.), a gift, or paper (perhaps an article or other information) folded in a way that creates a bulky lump in the envelope. Ideally, the item should relate to your offer and/or reinforce your message.

Of course, camel mail alone won't guarantee a successful direct mail campaign. The hump will increase your chances of getting your envelope opened, but your message must be strong enough to capture the reader's attention and generate action.

ADVERTISING ADVICE

Perhaps the greatest obstacle to good advertising is excess. Don't cram in so much copy that the ad is unreadable or over-design so that the sales message is lost. Good ads are attractive, eye-catching, and sell the product or service by emphasizing solutions instead of problems.

Source: Small Business Administration

MOST-COMMON ADVERTISING BLUNDERS

The quest for instant gratification

The ad that creates enough urgency to cause people to respond immediately is the ad most likely to be forgotten immediately once the offer expires. It is of little use in establishing the advertiser's identity in the mind of the consumer.

Trying to reach more people than the budget will allow

For a media mix to be effective, each element must have enough repetition to establish retention in the mind of the prospect. Too often, however, the result of a media mix is too much reach and not enough frequency. Will you reach 100 percent of the people and persuade them 10 percent of the way? Or will you reach 10 percent of the people and persuade them 100 percent of the way? The cost is the same.

Assuming the business owner knows best

The business owner is uniquely unqualified to see his company or product objectively. Too much product knowledge leads him to answer questions no one is asking. He's on the inside looking out, trying to describe himself to a person on the outside looking in. It's hard to read the label when you're inside the bottle.

Unsubstantiated claims

Advertisers often claim to have what the customer wants, such as "highest quality at the lowest price," but fail to offer any evidence. An unsubstantiated claim is nothing more than a cliché the prospect is tired of hearing. You must prove what you say in every ad. Do your ads give the prospect new information? Do they provide a new perspective? If not, prepare to be disappointed with the results.

Improper use of passive media

Nonintrusive media, such as newspapers and Yellow Pages, tend to reach only buyers who are looking for the product. They are poor at reaching prospects before their need arises, so they're not good at creating a predisposition toward your company. The patient, consistent use of intrusive media, such as radio and TV, will win the hearts of relational customers long before they're in the market for your product.

Creating ads instead of campaigns

It is foolish to believe a single ad can ever tell the entire story. The most effective, persuasive, and memorable ads are those most like a rhinoceros: they make a single point, powerfully. An advertiser with 17 different things to say should commit to a campaign of at least 17 different ads, repeating each ad enough to stick in the prospect's mind.

Obedience to unwritten rules

For some insane reason, advertisers want their ads to look and sound like ads. Why?

Late-week schedules

Advertisers justify their obsession with Thursday and Friday advertising by saying, "We need to reach the customer just before she goes shopping." Why do these advertisers choose to compete for the customer's attention each Thursday and Friday when they could have a nice, quiet chat all alone with her on Sunday, Monday, and Tuesday?

Overconfidence in qualitative targeting

Many advertisers and media professionals grossly overestimate the importance of audience quality. In reality, saying the wrong thing has killed far more ad campaigns than reaching the wrong people. It's amazing how many people become "the right people" when you're saying the right thing.

Event-driven marketing

A special event should be judged only by its ability to help you more clearly define your market position and substantiate your claims. If one percent of the people who hear your ad for a special event choose to come, you will be in desperate need of a traffic cop and a bus to shuttle people from distant parking lots. Yet your real investment will be in the 99 percent who did not come! What did your ad say to them?

Great production without great copy

Too many ads today are creative without being persuasive. Slick, clever, funny, creative, and different are poor substitutes for informative, believable, memorable, and persuasive.

Confusing response with results

The goal of advertising is to create a clear awareness of your company and its unique selling proposition. Unfortunately, most advertisers evaluate their ads by the comments they hear from the people around them. The slickest, cleverest, funniest, most creative, and most distinctive ads are the ones most likely to generate these comments. See the problem? When we confuse response with results, we create attention-getting ads that say absolutely nothing.

Source: Roy H. Williams, "Top Advertising Blunders,"
Entrepeneur.com

! ! !

FINDING THE RIGHT ADVERTISING AGENCY FOR YOUR COMPANY

Here's how to find the right advertising agency for your organization, regardless of where and how you intend to advertise.

- Make a list of ads you have seen recently that impressed you—ads that have caught your attention.
- Analyze what it is about those ads that made an impression.
- Call the companies featured in the ad and ask to speak with the person who manages the advertising. Make it clear that you're not trying to sell anything; you just want to know who their agency is. Most ad directors will be happy to tell you and even give you some additional information about the agency and how it works.
- Make a list of three or four agencies that you think have done good work for their clients and contact them.
- Meet with each agency to get a feel for how it will work with you.
- Choose the one you like best and set up a three-month trial period.
- At the end of the trial, decide if you want to stick with that agency or go to your second choice.

SETTING AN ADVERTISING BUDGET

Consider the following issues when setting your advertising budget.

1. Industry average spent as a percentage of sales/revenues.
2. Your last year's sales.
3. This year's forecast sales.
4. Total overall number of customers last year.
5. Number of new customers gained last year.
6. Total number of customers forecast this year.
7. Deciding whether to spend above or below the industry average.
8. Going with the entrepreneurial gut that got you where you are today.

If you feel the money you intend to spend on a well-thought-out and well-constructed advertising program is going to help you grow your business, then it's imperative that you fund it properly, continue to work on improving it, and give it sufficient time to do the job.

Source: MadScam: Kick-Ass Advertising Without the Madison Avenue Price Tag *by George Parker*

THINK LIKE YOUR CUSTOMER

To decide if a particular advertising option is right for you, think the way your customers (and prospects) do. What channels are they watching, what radio stations are they listening to, and what publications are they reading? That's where you need to be putting your advertising. Just because a medium reaches a million people doesn't mean you should advertise in it—if those million people are not your potential customers, you'll be wasting your money.

MOST POPULAR PROMOTIONAL PRODUCTS

1. Shirts (T-shirts, polos, button-downs, etc.)
2. Writing instruments
3. Desk/office/business accessories
4. Glassware/ceramics (including mugs)
5. Caps/headwear
6. Other wearables (jackets, slacks, ties, etc.)
7. Calendars
8. Magnets
9. Recognition awards/trophies
10. Heath and safety products

Source: Advertising & Specialty Institute, 2005 survey

DON'T FEEL PRESSURED BY YOUR COMPETITION

Often, everyone in a market or industry gets on the same bandwagon at about the same time. As a leader, it can be hard to go against conventional wisdom. As a result, you may often find your so-called vision is simply to do what everyone else thinks companies like yours should be doing right now. Margaret Whitman, CEO of eBay, showed a laudable independence of mind when she held back and refused to join the throng of dotcom companies spending huge amounts on prime-time advertising before they were profitable. For instance, in 1999 her competitors went for multimillion-dollar Super Bowl ads, but she held back and waited another year before launching her first big ad campaign. In hindsight, her prudence was warranted. eBay has survived and thrived while those early big spenders have mostly left the stage.

Source: Making Horses Drink: How to Lead and Succeed in Business by Alex Hiam (Entrepreneur Press, 2002)

DIRECT RESPONSE TV: THE INFOMERCIAL HAS MATURED

Direct response television (DRTV) advertising has come a long way since the strategy made its debut with the Veg-O-Matic—one of the first food processing appliances to gain widespread use. The greatest advantage of DRTV is that can be monitored minute-by-minute, which allows the sponsor to quickly determine demographic desires, best time slots, and the strengths and weaknesses in program content.

DRTV advertising is a science and not a "copycat" medium. It is not a "one-size-fits-all" form of marketing. Because many producers of winning conventional advertising attempt to use the same techniques when producing DRTV, only one in twenty-five campaigns is successful. Each product or service to be considered for DRTV must be carefully analyzed to determine the best use of ad dollars.

In 1984, when the FCC started allowing commercials in excess of one minute, late-night television time could be bought very inexpensively, and the 30-minute infomercial was born. In the years since, television stations, networks, and cable providers have seen an increasing demand for these time slots. As a result, a half-hour that could be purchased in 1984 for $100 now sells for $5,000 or more. This increase has prompted those who might have considered advertising an item through DRTV with a sale price of say $39.95 to look at items selling for $99.00 or more. Advertisers have also developed what's known as the short-form—a one or two-minute infomercial (the 30-minute show is referred to as long-form).

An infomercial is not "destination TV." A specific program title for an infomercial is not printed in newspaper or TV guides, so it isn't likely that any viewer will check local listings and tune in.

Infomercials are most often referred to as "Paid Programming." Because of this, infomercials get their viewers through "channel surfing." Back in the days of 13-channel TV, it was almost guaranteed that, while surfing, a viewer would see at least part of an infomercial. Today, with 500+ channels in our homes and with on-screen TV guides, surfing has almost become extinct, greatly decreasing the visibility of the infomercial. As more and more channels are added, the DRTV producer will be looking for outside sources to advertise their programs. Today, many are using newspaper ads and the internet to direct the viewer's attention to their TV program.

As the quality of online video streaming is perfected, many infomercial marketers will start to bypass TV altogether and simply run their programs on the web. While this allows for extremely targeted marketing, it also means that you're likely to miss the accidental viewer who might turn into a customer.

Even though DRTV continues to stand on its own as one of the best marketing vehicles available, how successful it will be for your product will depend on capturing an audience. Be sure your infomercial producer knows the industry. One of the best ways to find an infomercial producer is to look at the companies that are successfully using DRTV and find out who created the shows and bought the air time.

Source: Don Abbott, President, Abbott Video Productions, Inc.

NUMBERS TO KNOW — To launch a product infomercial through the testing stage will cost from $300,000 to $800,000. Then you'll need to spend more money on the actual roll-out.

Source: Don Abbott, President, Abbott Video Productions, Inc.

WHY CONSIDER OUTDOOR ADVERTISING?

You might think of outdoor advertising as colorful billboards along streets and highways. Included in the outdoor classification, however, are benches, posters, signs, and transit advertising (the advertising on buses, subways, taxicabs, and trains). Outdoor advertising reaches its audience as an element of the environment. Unlike newspaper, radio, or TV, it doesn't need to be invited into the home, and it doesn't provide entertainment to sustain its audience. Here are some reasons why you may want to include outdoor advertising in your media mix:

- Since it is in the public domain, outdoor advertising assuredly reaches its audience.

- People can't switch it off or throw it out. People are exposed to it whether they like it or not.

- Its messages work on the advertising principle of frequency. Since most messages stay in the same place for a period of a month or more, passers-by see the same message a number of times.

- Particular locations can be acquired for certain purposes. A billboard located a block in front of your business can direct people to your showroom, or you can reach rural areas efficiently by placing a billboard in each small town.

Source: Small Business Administration

❧ ❧ ❧

CHAPTER 22

Sales

THE TEN LAWS OF SALES SUCCESS

Bill Brooks of the Brooks Group estimates that more than 85 percent of customers have a negative view of all salespeople. But it doesn't have to be that way. You can prove the masses wrong, and learn to develop the skills that will have people thinking differently about the selling process. In fact, selling can be one of the most rewarding tasks you'll undertake as a business owner—but only if you follow these ten tactics:

Law #1: Keep your mouth shut and your ears open
This is crucial in the first few minutes of any sales interaction. Remember:

1. Don't talk about yourself.
2. Don't talk about your products.
3. Don't talk about your services.
4. And, above all, don't recite your sales pitch!

Obviously, you want to introduce yourself. You want to tell your prospect your name and the purpose of your visit (or phone call), but what you don't want to do is ramble on about your product or service. After all, at this point, what could you possibly talk about? You have no idea if what you're offering is of any use to your prospect.

Law #2: Sell with questions, not answers
Remember this: nobody cares how great you are until they understand how great you think they are. Forget about trying to "sell" your product or service and focus instead on why your prospect wants to buy. To do this, you need to get fascinated with your prospect; you need to ask questions (lots and lots of them) with no hidden agenda or ulterior motives.

Many years ago, I was selling CDs at a music festival. It didn't take me long to figure out that it wasn't my job to sell the CDs—it was my job to get the earphones on every person who walked by my booth! I noticed right away that whenever people sensed I was attempting to "sell" them a CD, their walls of defense immediately went up and they did everything in their power to get as far away from me as they could. So instead, I made it my job to introduce new music to anyone who wanted to put on the earphones. Once they heard the music, they either liked it or they didn't. I didn't do any "selling," and I made more money that week than any other CD hawkers at the festival. Back then, I didn't know anything about sales, but I knew enough about human nature to understand that sales resistance is an oxymoron: The act of selling creates the resistance! Which leads us to the next principle:

Law #3: Pretend you're on a first date with your prospect

Get curious about them. Ask about the products and services they're already using. Are they happy? Is what they're using now too expensive, not reliable enough, too slow? Find out what they really want. Remember, you're not conducting an impersonal survey here, so don't ask questions just for the sake of asking them. Instead, ask questions that will provide you with information about what your customers really need. When you learn what your customers need and you stop trying to convince or persuade them to do something they may not want to do, you'll find them trusting you as a valued advisor and wanting to do more business with you as a result.

Law #4: Speak to your prospect just as you speak to your family or friends

There's never any time that you should switch into "sales mode" with ham-handed persuasion clichés and tag lines. Affected speech patterns, exaggerated tones, and slow, hypnotic sounding "sales inductions" are never acceptable in today's professional selling environments. Speak normally, (and of course, appropriately) just as you would when you're around your friends and loved ones.

Law #5: Pay close attention to what your prospect isn't saying

Is your prospect rushed? Does he or she seem agitated or upset? If so, ask "Is this a good time to talk? If it's not, perhaps we can meet another day." Most salespeople are so concerned with what they're going to say next that they forget there's another human being involved in the conversation.

Law #6: If you're asked a question, answer it briefly and then move on

Remember, this isn't about you; it's about whether you're right for them.

Law #7: Only after you've correctly assessed the needs of your prospect do you mention anything about what you're offering

I knew a guy who delivered a sales pitch to a mannequin (I'm not kidding)! He was so stuck in his own automated, habitual mode, he never bothered to notice that his prospect wasn't breathing. Don't get caught in this trap. Know with whom you're speaking before figuring out what it is you want to say.

Law #8: Refrain from delivering a three-hour product seminar.

Don't ramble on and on about things that have no bearing on anything your prospect has said. Pick a handful of things you think could help with your prospect's particular situation, and tell him or her about it. (And if possible, reiterate the benefits in his own words, not yours.)

Law #9: Ask the prospect if there are any barriers to them taking the next logical step.

After having gone through the first eight steps, you should have a good understanding of your prospect's needs in relation to your product or service. Knowing this, and having established a mutual feeling of trust and rapport, you're now ready to bridge the gap between your prospect's needs and what it is you're offering. You're now ready for:

Law #10: Invite your prospect to take some kind of action

This principle obliterates the need for any "closing techniques" because the ball is in the prospect's court. A sales close keeps the ball in your court and all the focus on you, the salesperson. But you don't want the focus on you. You don't want the prospect to be reminded that he or she is dealing with a "salesperson." You're not a salesperson, you're a human being offering a particular product or service. If you can get your prospect to understand that, you're well on your way to becoming an outstanding salesperson.

Source: Len Foley, "The 10 Laws of Sales Success," Entrepreneur.com

---

Words of Wisdom

We clearly recognize that what we offer is not a necessity. It's a postponable, discretionary purchase. And because of that, we have worked hard on refining our sales process. People have said that we overemphasize sales, but I don't think so. When you own your business, you wear a lot of hats. You are ultimately responsible for everything—sales, installation, service, accounting, etc. But I look at it this way: If you don't sell anything, you don't have to worry about service or installation or accounting.

—Thomas Fenig, Founder and CEO, Outdoor Lighting Perspectives

---

SALES CHARACTERISTICS TO LOOK FOR

Stellar sellers and entrepreneurs share many personality traits. Entrepreneurs will excel because they have such enthusiasm for their services, and their ebullience is embraced by prospects accustomed to the same old hackneyed pitches. Great closers possess an aura of competence and zeal that never fails to take them to the top of the board each month. To understand the valuable qualities in selling, we asked experts and business owners to identify the characteristics that allow a salesperson to transcend the trite:

- *Creativity.* Having an appreciation for the nonobvious solution is a must if a sales pro is going to outpace the pack.
- *Passion.* Genuine love for a product gets salespeople through the inevitable dark times, and makes their offers all the more irresistible to their clients. Passion, like creativity, cannot be faked, so it has great weight with customers.
- *Integrity.* Integrity tops the list of qualities salespeople need. Feeling good about a purchase is a hallmark of buying from a salesperson with integrity.
- *Tenacity.* Shelving feelings of rejection to keep plugging away is another essential requirement for sales success.
- *Commitment.* The sales cycle for any big deal can typically take months, even years. Keeping an eye on the prize, as well as continuing to sell to other prospects simultaneously, takes commitment.

On the flip side, there are certain traits that will surely doom any salesperson to the also-ran heap: lack of integrity, for instance, and not being prepared when trying to make a sale. And of course, there's the ultimate vice: dishonesty.

Source: Kimberly L. McCall, "Character Sketch," Entrepreneur.com

QUALITIES OF TOP SALESPEOPLE

1. *Are entrepreneurial.* They see themselves running their own business within a business. They're highly motivated, focused, and organized.
2. *Have developed a process.*
3. *Think about clients, not quotas.* The best salespeople focus on the customer.
4. *Sell solutions.* Great salespeople see themselves selling more than just widgets; they sell solutions. They tailor their sales pitches to offer a clear solution that solves the customer's problem.
5. *Get customers thinking.* Great salespeople can make customers see value early on so they're selling themselves on the solution.
6. *Aren't afraid to get creative.*
7. *Are on the move.* The really great salespeople are going out and seeing customers and prospects.
8. *Know when to move on.* Great salespeople don't waste time on dead ends. They're experts at targeting their resources.
9. *Stay current.* They keep up with products, clients, trends, and what the competition is doing.
10. *Love what they do.* Top-grade salespeople are passionate about their work.

Source: Chris Penttila, "Have You Got It?", Entrepreneur.com

The entrepreneur has to be the best salesperson in the company. A company suffers if you have people who can't sell running it. Entrepreneurs are constantly selling—to customers, to investors, to employees.

—ROBERT KIYOSAKI, AUTHOR OF *RICH DAD POOR DAD* AND FOUNDER OF THE RICH DAD COMPANY

The difference between the impossible and the possible lies in a man's determination.

—TOMMY LASORDA

CHOOSING THE RIGHT SALES MANAGER

In assembling an ace sales team, you promoted your finest salesperson to sales manager. She's smart and assertive, and unfailingly gets clients to sign on the dotted line. Fast forward several months: That employee is threatening to quit, morale is hovering around zilch, and you're dazed from the fallout. What went wrong?

"It's rare that a superstar salesperson makes a good sales manager," says Herb Greenberg, co-author of *How to Hire and Develop Your Next Top Performer: The Five Qualities That Make Salespeople Great* (McGraw-Hill 2003). The "blood running down their chin" drive of top sales performers isn't what makes a great leader, he adds. "Think of the biggest sports stars. How many have gone on to become great coaches? Not many." That's because the skill sets for each role are different. Super closers are motivated by their egos, which help them deal with rejection while simultaneously pushing forward. They also enjoy the thrill of the chase and the high of closing a big deal, and a restlessness that keeps them in motion, not sitting around cubicles. But put those people behind desks, reading reports and delegating closes to others, and they become ineffectual mopes. "I see salespeople get promoted to positions of authority because they were star performers," notes Jennifer White, author of *Drive Your People Wild Without Driving Them Crazy* (Capstone/Wiley & Sons 2001). "They really liked being the superstar, but the natural progression is to climb the corporate ladder. So they do, and they're miserable because of it."

Your ideal sales manager may not be a current employee. "It's better to look outside the company for new talent," says Stephan Schiffman, president of D.E.I. Management Group, a sales training company in New York City that has worked with more than 500,000 sales professionals since 1979. "Outside hires bring fresh ideas to an organization. In the highly competitive world of sales, this is key."

When you search for new sales manager talent, look for the following indicators of future failure or success.

- *Enormous egos need not apply.* The sales manager's job is to motivate, not overwhelm. "Never hire a sales manager with a big ego," says White, "because it'll bite you every time."
- *Experience counts.* Find someone who can get up to speed right away. "Don't hire someone thinking you'll train them," White says. "You won't. You don't have time for it."
- *Look for leadership and mentoring skills.* "A good manager has lots of patience and follow-through ability," counsels Greenberg.
- *Company fit.* Seek out a manager who is comfortable in an entrepreneurial environment.

> *Internalize the Golden Rule of sales that says, 'All things being equal, people will do business with, and refer business to, those people they know, like, and trust.'*
>
> —BOB BURG, TRAINER AND MOTIVATIONAL SPEAKER

> *Don't celebrate closing a sale, celebrate opening a relationship.*
>
> —PATRICIA FRIPP

White suggests asking prospects how they handle chaos and a fast-moving organization.

- *Details, details.* Managers are responsible for running reports and knowing how to analyze outcomes. Says White, "Hire someone who understands the numbers and can drive the right results."
- *Ability to delay gratification.* Sales is about the immediate "yes." Sales management is about mentoring, supporting, and cajoling until you get it.

Source: Kimberly L. McCall, "Star Search," Entrepreneur.com

GREAT ADVICE

Don't let your expectations rule your actions. About a year ago, I had an unsuccessful sales meeting about a product I was marketing. Recently, I set up another meeting with the same people to show them some new developments and new products. It was hard to get excited about the meeting, but I went anyway. As soon as I got there, I realized I had almost made a huge mistake. My product had changed and so had their business. They were now in a better position to receive what I had to offer, and the meeting went exceptionally well. If I had let my expectations rule my actions, I never would have gone to the meeting!

Source: Barry Farber, author of Superstar Sales Secrets and The 12 Clichés of Selling

DON'T LET YOUR SALESPEOPLE SELL YOU OUT OF BUSINESS

If your salespeople don't understand the financial aspects of your business, they might be making sales that don't generate profits for you company. Salespeople often don't understand the bottom-line impact of the deals they make with customers.

Salespeople can poison sales by offering discounts without realizing how much additional volume they need to make up for the loss in gross profits. Salespeople also inadvertently generate losses instead of profits by offering extended terms when the cost of carrying the accounts receivable is more than the profit on the transaction, or by spending too much on marketing without calculating the amount of sales necessary to support the campaign.

The solution is to build a strong alliance between your accounting department and your sales department. Invite your accounting staff into your sales meetings so they can participate in helping the salespeople understand the numbers and cost accounting procedures. Let your salespeople know that making *profitable* sales is far more important than simply making sales; teach them to focus their efforts on the more profitable portions of your product line. Salespeople also need to understand the impact of the cost of the sales process—travel, entertainment, etc.—on the profitability of the transaction. When they clearly comprehend issues such as the time value of money, they'll be able to better negotiate terms; for example, they may agree to a discount, but only if the customer pays cash.

Understanding the profitability issues of their own company will give your salespeople the skills to understand the same issues as they relate to their customers, and will enhance their overall selling abilities.

WHEN OUT-OF-TOWNERS VISIT

In today's global marketplace, chances are excellent that at some point you'll host a visit by an existing or prospective customer from out of town. The impression you make will be indelible, but whether it's good or bad will depend on how well you plan.

Whether or not you're paying for the accommodations, check out their hotel carefully. Be sure it offers all the necessary and appropriate amenities—including shuttle service to the airport and other locations—and, if possible, negotiate a discounted rate.

Be prepared to play the role of host for the entire time your visitors are in town—not just when they're in your office. To find out what they want and expect from you in terms of after-hours entertainment, the best approach is to ask simply. Be prepared to make some suggestions and include information about local attractions or events, if possible. Though business travelers occasionally bring along spouses and family members, it's unlikely they'll expect you to provide entertainment for them as well—but if they bring it up, be prepared to deal with the situation graciously.

SEVEN MOST COMMON BUSINESS GIFT-GIVING MISTAKES

1. Giving gifts that hint of a need of change or self-improvement.
2. Spending too much or too little effort, money, or creativity.
3. Taking clues from retailers rather than the recipient.
4. Waiting until the last minute to shop.
5. Giving gifts with strings attached.
6. Giving gifts without taking into consideration the preferences of the recipient.
7. Giving gifts only when they are expected.

Source: Creatively Corporate, www.creativelycorporate.com

TURN OLD EMPLOYERS INTO NEW CUSTOMERS

If you started your own business after a stint in the corporate world, you may find your former employer a prime prospective customer. You have significant advantages selling to your former employer. You know the system, the company way. But that knowledge will only get you in the door. There may be a honeymoon for a while, but at some point, you're going to be expected to perform as well or better than anybody else out there.

It's critical to recognize that your relationship with the company has changed. As a supplier, you may be dealing with different people, perhaps higher up on the corporate ladder, than you did before. Some of your former co-workers may see you as a threat to their own job security. Also, their bosses may not be entirely comfortable if you have overt personal relationships with company employees, so you many need to stop socializing with former co-workers.

If, on the other hand, those former co-workers see you as an ally, they can be very helpful—but it's help you shouldn't count on. Don't expect to be told company secrets, or to be able to neglect the account and continue to retain it. You go into the relationship with an edge, but that just gets you your first assignment. The future depends on the quality of product or service you provide.

Any fool can paint a picture, but it takes a wise man to be able to sell it.
—Samuel Butler

GIVE CUSTOMERS ALTERNATE WAYS TO BUY

Consider the likelihood of this scenario: A customer comes into your store, sees an item that would make a great gift but isn't sure about size or color preferences, so she puts it down and leaves. Or a customer stops in on his lunch break, picks up a couple of items, but the line at your register is long enough that he's concerned about getting back to work on time. So he puts the merchandise down and leaves. Will either of these customers come back? Maybe, but maybe not.

You can increase the chances of a sale if you provide phone and online ordering and make that information clearly available in your store. Post "visit our website" signs and place brochures by the cash register and in racks by the door so customers can conveniently purchase even if they are unable to come back in person.

HOW TO SELL BY SOCIAL NETWORKING

Social networking enables you to find and target niche markets easily, quickly and absolutely free. Start an active dialog—just never lie about who you are. Your honesty and integrity add real value to your business.

–Jennifer Kushell co-founder, YSN.com (Your Success Network)

Nothing will kill a sale faster than lack of enthusiasm.
—Brian Tracy, Chairman and CEO of Brian Tracy International

DO YOU WANT FRIES WITH THAT?

Fast food restaurants have thoroughly mastered the art of upselling. No matter what you order, you'll always be asked if you want something more. Your employees should do the same with every sale, regardless of your product.

Upselling is when you help someone who has already made the decision to buy from you, and is in the process of making a purchase, decide to buy a little more. If you sell clothing, suggest a shirt to go with that suit or a belt to go with that dress. For shoes, recommend polish or cleaner. If you sell cars, suggest a service or protection package. If you sell computers, suggest an enhanced screen or other accessories. If your products are battery-operated, offer extra batteries. Assume the customer will want the item and begin your suggestion with the benefits of having it. Say something like, "That's a beautiful

---

THE THREE BIGGEST MISTAKES IN UPSELLING

1. No attempt is made to upsell.
2. The salesperson comes across as being pushy.
3. The upselling is made in an unconvincing manner so the customer generally refuses.

Source: Jeff Mowatt, JC Mowatt Seminars Inc.

---

dress. We have a belt that's just perfect with it. Would you like to see it?"

Most upselling can be done quickly, usually in just a few minutes, and there is absolutely no customer acquisition cost involved for the additional sale. When handled properly, upselling is a simple way to tell your customers you want to be sure they're satisfied while increasing your own profits.

TO SELL IT, GIVE IT AWAY

For many products, one of the most effective ways to sell is to give them away first. Especially if your product is subject to repeat purchases, providing consumers with a free sample may be exactly what it takes to turn them into loyal—and paying—customers.

Food products are a great example. How often have you been in a grocery store and made an unplanned purchase because you were given a sample? Cosmetics, cleaning supplies, paper goods (both for the home and office), office supplies, and more can all be effectively sold through a sample program.

Samples can make customers more comfortable with their purchase decision, particularly when you have a premium-priced product. Use these tips to develop and measure a sample program:

- Calculate your cost per contact and cost per sale.
- Send an adequate supply.
- Be sure prospective customers know what to do with your product.
- If you're providing samples to a retailer, include suggestions for displaying and demonstrating the product.
- Combine samples with other marketing techniques, such as coupons.

❧ ❧ ❧

CHAPTER 23

Public Relations, Media Relations, and Publicity

WHAT IS PR?

According to Wikipedia, "Public relations (PR) is the business, organizational, philanthropic, or social function of managing communication between an organization and its audiences. There are many goals to be achieved by the practice of public relations, including education, correcting a mistruth, or building or improving an image."

Within public relations, you also have media relations—that is, your relationship with the media—and publicity, which is often the result of your public relations efforts. Understanding these terms will aid you in developing an effective PR plan for your company.

> *The goal of PR is top-of-mind awareness.*
>
> —JAY CONRAD LEVINSON AND AL LAUTENSLAGER, *GUERRILLA MARKETING IN 30 DAYS*

Words of Wisdom

WAYS TO SPREAD THE WORD ABOUT YOUR BUSINESS FOR FREE

In the spirit of guerrilla marketing, here are five types of free marketing using PR.

Writing articles

Writing about how to do something is always something of value to readers. Writing articles gives you instant credibility. Submitting online, as well as offline, provides another good chance to get your name in print at no cost. Not a writer? Write down ten questions you think your prospects might have about a particular area of your expertise and write out the answers to those questions. This can be an article. Lists are great articles and can be top ten lists, checklists, mistakes made, and so on.

Free reports

Offering a free report online is a good way to get an e-mail from prospects so you may market to them later. You can do the same thing offline to get contact information. Offering the report offline is a good way to get a prospect to call or contact you. The information gained from the exchange can then be used for subsequent marketing over and over again.

Online forums

Participating in online newsgroups and forums is another way to get your name in front of a prospective buyer. Participating by answering and asking questions will position you as an expert and a resource for others. Many online forums will let you put an e-mail signature with a link to your website or an affiliate web site.

Letters to the editor

A little-known secret that's a good follow-up to a press release is a letter to an editor. This is free PR. Many times, a letter to the editor has a better chance of getting published than the actual press release. You'd be surprised how many people read this column in publications. You can even write a letter to the editor about someone else's PR. Don't ignore this one.

Hosting an event

Hosting an event for your business or at your business can be the equivalent to getting an article published in a targeted publication. The event can take the form of an open house or a ribbon-cutting ceremony. Publicizing the event is news in the eyes of an editor, a producer or a target market member. Not only can you publicize the announcement of the event, but you can also invite the media and publicize the event itself. Another kind of event is a seminar or presentation of some type. Again, the same PR leverages can occur.

These are just some of the many free PR avenues that can increase the top-of-mind awareness with your target customers and prospects. You don't need a huge budget for any of these tactics. In fact, most can be done with no cost involved at all.

Source: Al Lautenslager, "Free PR Tactics," Entrepreneur.com

THE TRUTH ABOUT COMMON PR MYTHS

Myth #1: It's important to put a positive spin on everything
Not every situation is positive. In order to be truthful, you can't always put a bullish slant on the circumstances.

Myth #2: If you don't want to answer a reporter's question, change the subject
A popular media training technique is called "the bridge," and it works like this: If a reporter asks you a question you don't want to answer, you say something like, "That's a great question, but I think the more important point is . . ." That kind of question dodging is one of the quickest ways to earn a reporter's ire. Use the bridge to make your point, but answer the question.

Myth #3: You should participate in every interview that's requested of you
No way. Before you get on the phone or in front of the microphone and start talking, you need to know the context of the story. Get some background on the topic and decide if there's a good business reason for doing it. For instance, it might be a good idea to participate in a profile of your company in an industry trade publication. However, if a reporter is doing a general story that isn't really relevant to your business or your key audience, and which could position your business in a negative way, you may want to pass on participating.

Myth #4: Reciting how many other media interviews you've done impresses journalists, producers, and editors.
Most reporters are looking for fresh voices and ideas and prefer to avoid "overexposed" sources. It's preferable to say that you're an experienced interviewee to let the journalist know you're familiar with

the interview process. That will likely make him or her more comfortable with you as a source. If you're asked for particular outlets in which you've been featured, then provide them.

Myth #5: A good news release is the best way to get media attention for your company

A generic, "one-size-fits-all" news release is likely to have "one-size-fits-nobody" result. Create customized pitch letters and talking points for interviews. Find out which topics are of interest to the media and put that information in the easiest format for journalists to use.

Myth #6: Mention your company, product, or book as often as possible

It's annoying and distracting when the expert mentions the name of the book in almost every sentence. Mention your book or product when it's appropriate, trying for two or three mentions in a broadcast or one credit in a print piece.

Myth #7: Whenever you don't want something printed or broadcast, just say it's "off the record"

Saying something is "off the record"—usually used when a source gives background information to put something in context and doesn't want it to be attributed—is risky because a journalist doesn't have to abide by it.

Myth #8: Answer every question so that you look like the expert

It's ok to say that you don't know something—and far better to say that you'll get the answer than to bluff or lie.

Myth #9: If you advertise in a medium, they'll give you better coverage

One of the fastest ways to alienate journalists is to suggest that they are influenced by advertising.

Myth #10: The bigger the words, the smarter you sound

Jargon and overblown language can get you jettisoned as a source. Using obscure industry terminology or overly complex language increases the chance that the journalist will misunderstand the information and wrongly report it. Simple language is almost always best.

Myth #11: Never show emotion

It's important to appear sincere and believable, whether the news is good or bad. Don't fall to pieces in front of the camera, but showing an appropriate level of emotion can make your message more believable.

Myth #12: Media training is what you need most to be successful in media relations

Media training is not a stand-alone component. Have a process that includes a solid plan for dealing with the media and developing relationships.

Source: Gwen Moran, "12 PR Myths—Busted!",
Entrepreneur.com

SPREAD YOUR MESSAGE THROUGH A RADIO TOUR

By conducting your own PR radio tour, you can win the publicity you need, generate millions of gross impressions to promote your business and even establish yourself as an expert in your field. If you or someone on your staff is skilled at making sales calls, you'll find that securing bookings for radio appearances isn't much different.

Source: Kim T. Gordon, "Riding the Airwaves," Entrepreneur.com

PR TOOLS AND TACTICS

- Establish a news release calendar to plan out the releases you intend to issue throughout the year. You may need to revise this calendar as the year progresses, but it'll give you some initial structure and help you stay focused on generating news.
- Media outreach in the form of pitching reporters and placing articles is still the essence of PR, and the foundation for any PR program is a solid media list. Before engaging in any PR activities, take the time to carefully research and build a database of key reporters. Your list should contain the contact details of the publications and journalists that pertain to your industry and be organized according to how valuable each is in terms of reaching your target audience. Once you've created a list, schedule time on your calendar for media outreach. Contact each reporter individually to introduce yourself and to arrange informal meetings where you can discuss the outlook for your company and industry.
- Publications' editorial calendars offer an excellent vehicle for planning media exposure.

Researching them will enable you to identify opportunities to offer yourself as an expert source, contribute an article or even suggest a feature on your company. Once you've set your list of targets, begin contacting them as soon as possible. Most editorial outlets have deadlines several months ahead of their publication dates. Pay careful attention to the closing dates, or you'll risk losing out on the opportunity.

- Contributed or bylined articles can be an excellent way to generate exposure and establish yourself as an industry expert. Research magazines, newspapers, and web sites to find those outlets that are open to such articles, then contact the editor to propose a topic. Remember to make sure the focus of the media outlet is in sync with your business objectives and the article contains your key messages.
- Case studies are very attractive to the media because they offer a tangible, real-world example of the benefits of your product or service. The challenge with developing case studies is they require active customer participation. So

FIVE EASY WAYS . . .

To Prevent Crises

1. Implement no major operational decision without asking a PR-savvy person to help you anticipate the response from all stakeholders, internal and external.
2. Sit down and think, really think, about what failure to prepare for crises could mean to all the people with whom you work, to those your organization serves, and on a very personal

basis. Then let your conscience, not merely business instinct, guide your actions.

3. Ensure that at least two members of your leadership team are extremely internet-savvy.
4. When negatively criticized, say, with all sincerity, "You could be right." Then smile and break off the conversation.
5. When finding yourself caught up in a disagreement in which you're attempting to "fix" things, ask yourself, "How important is it?"

PR TOOLS AND TACTICS, continued

talk to your clients and ask them if you can report on their successes. While this will require your customers to share their "war stories," it offers them—and you—a chance to shine.

- Speaking opportunities offer another avenue for generating exposure. When planning your PR activities for the year, research conferences, trade shows, and "webinars" for opportunities to nominate yourself as a keynote speaker or a member of a panel discussion. The value in securing such engagements can be tremendous, especially for a growing business; however, they also require vigilant planning because most speaking opportunities are finalized several months in advance.

- Blogs and social media have grown in popularity as communications tools because they offer a way to have an active discussion with a motivated audience. When considering PR tactics, don't forget to research the blogs that relate to your industry and get to know the styles and personalities of their authors. Technorati, the leading blog search engine, is a great place to start. A presence in the blogosphere can add to your company's perception as a thought leader. But remember, all material published on a blog is open to a wide audience and can initiate a line of discussion that may not always jive with your point of view. If you want to launch your own blog, there are free tools, such as Blogger and Blog.com, that enable you to do this easily. When it's all set up, make sure it gets listed on Technorati.

- Crisis planning is an essential part of your business's PR plan. It should include all possible negative scenarios and the appropriate responses to them. Ensure that other members of your business are aware of crisis procedures, and take time to do a test run to help iron out any inconsistencies or holes in your plan.

Source: Rachel Meranus, "Developing a PR Plan,"
Entrepreneur.com

To Cause Crises

1. Underestimate the power of a single angry consumer with a computer.

2. Have critical policies for which personnel receive little or no training and/or refresher training.

3. Use lawyers as a default response to detractors.

4. Fail to consider and plan for the impact of losing a key contractor or vendor.

5. Hire senior-level executives from other organizations without conducting thorough background checks.

Source: Jonathan Bernstein, Bernstein Crisis Management, LLC

People begin to become successful the minute they decide to be.

—HARVEY MACKAY

Words of Wisdom

DEALING WITH FALLOUT

When something bad happens in your industry, but not directly to your company, your first response may be one of relief. But don't take too much time thanking your lucky stars; you're likely to be in the path of some negative fallout, and you need to address it. For example, when a plane crashes, all airlines are concerned about reassuring the traveling public. Your own business may not be subject to so dramatic a risk, but unless you have a monopoly, you could be affected by someone else's misfortune.

You can approach a problem on three levels: national, local, and as an individual. If you have a national association, look to it for guidance and an action plan. Associations know how to mobilize immediately. They have the media contacts and information-distribution processes already in place. Your local association or professional organization may also be a resource. Or you may choose to handle the situation on your own. Whatever you do, take an educational approach.

Educating the public is a very big part of the recovery process for the industry that's been injured. Offer tips to help people avoid a repeat of whatever happened, or to make them feel more comfortable and to reestablish trust. If people have suffered, express sympathy and offer support—even to the point of holding a fundraiser for victims. The key is to take action quickly, using a strategy that is tasteful and appropriate for the circumstances and will put your company in a positive position.

A GIVING PLAN

You know how important it is to have a plan for your business. It is equally important to have a plan for your philanthropies. The more you give, the more you will be asked to give. Without a plan and purpose, your contributions may not be as effective as you'd like. Your plan should cover more than just how much money you're going to throw at a problem. Yes, financial contributions are important—but they're not enough. Effective community involvement goes way beyond writing checks and includes giving your time and influence, and perhaps even some in-kind donations (noncash gifts).

I have never been one to talk a lot about the donations I make, but the fact is that publicizing what you do for the community can be very beneficial to the people and organizations you want to help. Certainly it's good publicity for the company, but more importantly, it's great exposure for the charity and another chance for it to get in the spotlight and gain support. Whenever I make a donation, I encourage others to follow my example.

If you have the resources—whether it's a celebrity name, or money, time, or expertise, etc.—to bring attention to a cause you support, you should do it.

Source: The Millionaire Real Estate Mindset by Russ Whitney (Doubleday, 2005)

CAPITALIZE ON PUBLICITY

1. Put a link to the story on your web site.
2. Include media coverage in your printed marketing materials.
3. Frame your great media coverage for others to see.
4. Mention it to others.
5. Send it to your local newspaper.
6. Send it to your alumni magazine.

Source: Margie Fisher, "7 Ways to Milk Your Media Coverage," Entrepreneur.com

DON'T WRITE PRESS RELEASES ONLY FOR JOURNALISTS

Gone are the days when you wrote a press release, sent it to the media, called reporters to see if they received it, then crossed your fingers and hoped they'd print it. Thanks to the internet, those days are gone forever. Now, the world is your audience. Start writing press releases directed at people anywhere who need what you are offering, not just journalists. The internet makes it possible for you to post press releases to your web site and to send them to press-release-distribution services, which will send them all over the internet.

When someone is looking for information on a certain topic and uses a search engine to find it—even if they don't know you—they'll stumble across your press release if it includes the keywords they used during their search. Let's say you live in Boston and you sell antique doorknobs. You can write a press release about your products, being careful to insert the phrase "antique doorknobs" and other relevant keywords throughout your release. Then you post the press release to your web site and to press-release-distribution services. A woman in New Zealand who needs antique doorknobs for a house she is refinishing does a Google search for "antique doorknobs." Google finds those keywords in your press release online and includes it in the search results. The woman in New Zealand reads your release, visits your web site, sees your catalog, and buys the doorknobs she needs—all before a journalist has even seen your press release. If reporters write about your doorknobs, that's great. But even if they don't, you've already made a sale. Now isn't that a lot easier than trying to get your release printed in a newspaper in New Zealand?

Adapted from "89 Ways to Write Powerful Press Releases" by Joan Stewart, The Publicity Hound, www.publicityhound.com

PARTS OF A PRESS RELEASE

1. Contact information
In some cases, you'll want to include more than one contact person. You should include the contact information for the publicist—who journalists can call for more information—as well as contact info for other people in your company such as sales reps, whom someone can contact if they want to ask a question about what you're selling. Contact information should include name, shipping address (why make people hunt for it?), phone, e-mail address, and web site URL. Notice that the e-mail address and web site URL links are live.

2. Headline and sub-head
A well-written headline catches the reader's attention. A well-written sub-head makes the reader stay and keep reading.

3. Dateline
The dateline offers perspective for the reader because it shows where the press release originated and the date it was written. Datelines should include a city and state since press releases are now posted online, and people in other countries might not be familiar with all the states and provinces in countries other than their own.

4. Body copy

The body copy might constitute up to 90 percent of your entire press release. This is where you include not only key facts about products and services, but also benefits. At the end of the release, include the word "END" set off with dashes.

5. Call to action

The call to action is part of the body copy. This is where you lead readers by the hand and tell them exactly what you want them to do. Do you want them to click on a link to visit your web site? Or click on a link that takes them to an order page? Or click on a link that leads them to a sign-up page at your web site where they can read a free special report or download an e-book, in exchange for their e-mail address? Or make a donation? Or buy tickets to an event? Or call their congressman? Include a call to action in virtually every press release you distribute.

6. Hyperlinks (or links)

The hyperlinks, or links, can be scattered throughout the press release. Links take people where you want them to go. You can link to things like your bio, product pages at your web site, free articles at your web site, or any other place that includes information that's too long or in-depth to include in the press release. Links can also bring people directly into your sales funnel. Include no more than a half-dozen links in each press release—you don't want your readers to get sidetracked and miss the call to action. Also, be sure every link opens in a new window so your readers are able to return to the press release and continue reading each time they click on a link.

7. The optional part of the press release and the Safe Harbor Statement

The optional part for everybody is right at the end where you can write a note to the media about extra little things you can offer such as photos, graphics, illustrations, other sources for stories they are writing, etc. Or write a note for readers about anything else you want to tell them. This note is like a postscript.

Publicly-held companies must include a Safe Harbor Statement in their press releases. It goes at the end of a public company press release in which the information could be considered "forward-looking," because it will have an impact on the future performance of the company. Safe Harbor language was required as part of the Private Securities Litigation Reform Act of 1995 and is supposed to be a protection for investors and companies, letting investors know when content in a press release could have an impact on future performance such as stock price. It's also protection for the public company (hence the title "safe harbor provision")—if you let the public know that your release includes "forward-looking statements," you reduce your liability from shareholder actions, especially lawsuits.

Source: Adapted from "89 Ways to Write Powerful Press Releases" by Joan Stewart, The Publicity Hound, www.publicityhound.com

CREATE A BUZZ–HONESTLY!

In buzz marketing, honesty is key. "If you overplay it, people will know that it's not real," says Peter Shankman, president of The Geek Factory, a New York City PR firm that creates buzz marketing campaigns. "If, all of a sudden, someone gets a couple of recommendations about a company from people they trust, that's interesting. If they get many recommendations from people they don't know, that's probably not going to ring true." So don't encourage people to say things they don't mean or pummel your target with messages that aren't genuine.

Source: Gwen Moran, "Harmful Hype? Successful strategies for buzz marketing," Entrepreneur.com

MEDIA RELATIONS RULES TO LIVE BY

1. *Respond promptly.* "Remember that these people are usually on tight deadlines," says Barbara Laskin, president of Laskin Media Inc., a New York City media training firm. Even if you're unable to do the interview, say so in a timely manner.

2. *Never say "no comment."* If you cannot answer a question, provide a reasonable explanation instead, says David Margulies, founder of Margulies Communications Group, a strategic PR and crisis communications firm in Dallas.

3. *Never lie or speculate.* "Aside from the fact that lying is wrong and unethical, it will come back to haunt you," says Karen Friedman, founder of Karen Friedman Enterprises Inc., a media training firm in Blue Bell, Pennsylvania. It's always better to tell the truth and explain why you did what you did, even if your explanation is shaky.

4. *Know the medium's audience.* Every media outlet is different, says Margulies. "Every audience wants you to address WIIFM—what's in it for me."

5. *Stick to what you know.* Do not try to be an expert or comment on an issue about which you are not fully informed, says Margulies.

Source: Gwen Moran, "12 PR Myths—Busted!", Entrepreneur.com

Words of Wisdom

Regardless of how you feel inside, always try to look like a winner. Even if you are behind, a sustained look of control and confidence can give you a mental edge that results in victory.

—ARTHUR ASHE, PROFESSIONAL TENNIS PLAYER

BEYOND PRESS RELEASES

There are many ways to communicate your message in addition to press releases.

Events

These can be open houses, celebrity visits, clearance sales, "meet the owners," or other events that give you a reason to invite customers and prospects to your place of business. The most important invitee of all for effective PR is the media. This includes newspaper officials and reporters, editors, management, and similar titles from radio and TV stations. Meeting people from the media also gives you a reason to follow up later, which helps you establish good relationships with those that control the news and features. Related to an event is the press conference. These are usually held to introduce a new product or person, provide a response to a situation, or handle anything else that's extremely newsworthy.

Fact sheets, newsletters, and brochures for customers and prospects.

This almost sounds more like part of the marketing plan than the PR plan, but these marketing vehicles can be tailored to support PR and one-time situations and enhance media relations. Add members of the media to the distribution list for these.

A PR firm

You can make your company seem more newsworthy and media-friendly by hiring a PR agency. This doesn't have to be done on an ongoing basis. There are PR professionals who will work with you, event by event, or project by project. This should only be done if it's part of your overall plan and the budget is in line with your company financials.

FAQ development

Radio and TV people, believe it or not, sometimes have trouble selecting topics to fill their air time and finding good people to interview. A radio or TV interview opportunity might arise in the near future, so take some time now to prepare yourself. Compile a list of answers to anticipated questions or questions that make your point. These FAQs can also be included in your media kits, posted on your web site, and distributed when meeting with customers and prospects.

Speaking engagements

Nothing gets the word out more than the spoken word. When you speak to a group, you are the center of attention, competing with no one for share of mind. You're also in a situation where you can best communicate your marketing message. Speaking is a great form of PR. Many times the speaking engagement is publicized ahead of time, and sometimes the media will show up at such events. This increases the likelihood of post-event PR. This is all synergized when you are an expert on a particular subject.

Source: Al Lautenslager, "PR Is More Than Just Press Releases," Entrepreneur.com

---

GREAT ADVICE

Position yourself as an expert in your industry or profession with the local media. Let them know you are an easily accessible source whenever they need a comment on any aspect of your business, particularly if they are looking for a local angle to a national story. Don't try to sell your product or service; you're promoting your expertise, and the media will include your title and company with the interview. Speak candidly about the issue, be clear and concise, and—most importantly—be available on short notice.

CHOOSING AND WORKING WITH A PR FIRM

- *Be sure the PR firm you select is familiar with your industry.* For example, we specialize in franchising, so we understand the legalities and all the nuances involved in helping our clients achieve their goals. To be effective, a PR firm needs to understand your company and industry.
- *Define your PR goals.* You need specific goals for your PR program. You might want to sell more product; improve the company's image; or gain positive exposure with consumers, investors, and other groups. Whatever your goals, be sure your PR firm understands your objectives and has the means and a plan to reach them.
- *Let the PR firm do its job.* Once you've selected a firm and established your goals, let the experts determine which media strategy will help reach your objectives. Don't try to direct the PR firm or insist on sending out press releases against the firm's advice. A good PR firm knows what is an appropriate news item and when to send it out in press release form.

Source: Rhonda Sanderson, President and Founder, Sanderson & Associates

---

WORTH KNOWING

Don't expect a PR firm to provide a complete written plan before you sign the contract and pay a fee. That's part of their product and there's no reason for them to give it to you before you agree to hire them.

THE NEW RULES OF MEDIA RELATIONS

- Non-targeted, broadcast pitches are spam.
- News releases sent to reporters in subject areas they do not cover are spam.
- Reporters who don't know you yet are looking for organizations like yours and products like yours. Make sure they will find you on sites such as Google and Technorati.
- If you blog, reporters who cover the space will find you.
- Pitch bloggers, because being covered in important blogs will get you noticed by mainstream media.
- When was the last news release you sent? Make sure your organization is "busy."
- Journalists want a great online media room!
- Some (but not all) reporters love RSS feeds.
- Personal relationships with reporters are important.
- Don't tell journalists what your product does. Tell them how you solve customer problems.
- Does the reporter have a blog? Read it. Comment on it. Track back to it.
- Before you pitch, read (or listen to or watch) the publication (or radio program or TV show) you'll be pitching to!
- Once you know what interests a particular reporter, send her an individualized pitch crafted especially for her needs.

Source: David Meerman Scott, author of The New Rules of Marketing and PR: How to use news releases, blogs, podcasts, viral marketing and online media to reach your buyers directly *(Wiley, 2007)*

FIVE TIPS ON HIRING A PUBLIC RELATIONS FIRM

1. Be clear on what you want from a public relations effort. Some things a PR firm can do for you are to get you positive exposure in the media, create and conduct special events, and help you build and maintain a solid reputation.
2. Be realistic about what a PR firm can't do. It can't whitewash an unethical business or cover up fraud or other illegal activities.
3. Interview a number of firms. Get their ideas on how they can help you and seriously consider those with the best ideas.
4. If you're looking for only local publicity, hire a local firm. But if you want a national program, your PR firm can be anywhere.
5. Once you've hired a company, keep your account executive fully informed about your business. Treat him or her as part of your strategic team.

Source: SCORE

Business is like war in one respect. If its grand strategy is correct, any number of tactical errors can be made and yet the enterprise proves successful.

Words of Wisdom

–GEN. ROBERT E. WOOD

✧ ✧ ✧

THE ROLE OF THE INTERNET IN YOUR BUSINESS

Whether you're on the cutting edge of technology or struggling to keep up, the internet is a critical component of your operation. You don't have to understand how it works to know how to make it work for you.

❧ ❧ ❧

CHAPTER 24

Online Sales and Marketing

BEFORE YOU LAUNCH A WEB SITE: EIGHT BIZ WEB SITE MYTHS

If you're feeling pressure to create a web site for your company, you're not alone. Even if you don't want to sell your products or services directly over the internet, simply maintaining a professional-looking, well-functioning site can make a new company appear more established. (Conversely, having an unappealing, poorly functioning site can hurt business.) However, before you get started developing the online component to your business, consider the following common misconceptions:

1. "If I build it, they will come."

Marketing your site may not be as easy as it seems. You'll need economical ways to direct traffic to your site on a national—or international—level. Perhaps the most obvious way is to advertise on search engines like Google and Overture, but this can get expensive.

Unfortunately, it can take months or even years for your URL to turn up near the top of organic searches. Investigate other ways to get eyes to your site, like affiliate programs, e-mail newsletters, and partnering.

2. The more you offer, the more you'll sell.

Trying to be all things to all people rarely works. It may seem logical that the more things you have for sale online, the more people you'll attract. But even if you attract them, will they buy? The "general" aspect of your offering will communicate that the value of your product or service is equal to that of others—so price becomes the only issue, and branding becomes more difficult. In today's marketplace, there's a powerful demand for specialized products and services. The point is to differentiate your company from your competitors, so determine your niche and stick to it.

3. The best way to generate sales is to copy the competition.

It can be tempting to copy your competitors in everything from marketing strategies and positioning to sales offers and design choices. Remember the adage that imitation is the sincerest form of flattery? This means that when you imitate, you're not just reminding your audience about your competition—you're suggesting they're better! Certainly you can learn things from what your competition does, but blaze your own trail if you're serious about branding your company.

4. Your home page should explain everything about your business, or you'll lose visitors.

You've got about three seconds to hook visitors—do not bore them with visually overwhelming text. Grab their attention by being concise, clear, and compelling.

5. Once I get my site up and running, sales will skyrocket.

Yes, your potential customer pool has grown exponentially—but so has that of your competition's. How will you stand out? How will you locate the people most likely to buy your product or service, and get them to visit your site?

6. Web sites should be slick, with lots of bells and whistles.

On the internet, functionality is king. High-tech gimmicks may look great, but they load slowly. It's best to find a good balance between form and function.

7. Building a web site is easy—I'll just buy a how-to book.

Whether you can do it yourself depends on the type of site you want and your own experience and skills. For example, will you require shopping cart functionality or database programming? Building a web site is deceptively complex and requires a variety of skill sets, from being HTML savvy to good having artistic taste. You might want to think about hiring a web design pro.

8. Everybody else has a site, so I should, too.

Determining the real purpose of your site is crucial. Is it to sell your product? Increase awareness of your business? Provide information to drive local sales? Add credibility? Despite what some critics say, creating an "online brochure" is a legitimate reason to build a site. However, that's very different from selling directly over the internet. Clarifying your purpose for wanting a web site is a perfect starting point.

Source: John Williams, "Eight Biz Web Site Myths,"
Entrepreneur.com

NUMBERS TO KNOW
More than 1 billion people worldwide use the internet.
Source: Internet World Stats

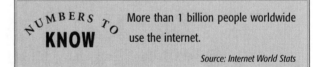

Not having a web site is akin to being in business and not having company stationery, a telephone, lawyer, accountant . . .
Not having a web site makes you look like a nebbish and is inexcusable.

—FROM *MADSCAM: KICK-ASS ADVERTISING WITHOUT THE MADISON AVENUE PRICE TAG* BY GEORGE PARKER

NUMBERS TO KNOW
An estimated 2.4 billion people worldwide use e-mail, and that number is expected to increase to 3.2 billion by 2011.
Source: Radicati Group

GUIDELINES FOR EFFECTIVE WEB SITE DESIGN

Your web site should be user friendly and have the ability to keep visitors at the site to see the information you want them to see.

Web sites . . .

- Need to be well organized, clear, and concise.
- Need to be easy or viewers won't come back.
- Can't confuse or frustrate the viewer.
- Need good design. It determines the navigation.
- Need to be consistent from page to page.
- Need to be updated regularly.

Navigation Tips

- Remember that viewers make all the decisions about where they want to go and what buttons to push.
- Visitors need to be able to find their way around your site.
- You need to tell visitors exactly where they are and how to get back to where they were.
- The navigation bar and tools should be the same on every page.
- Have as few pages as possible.
- Take site architecture seriously.

Site Design Tips

- Keep it simple.
- Put content on every page.
- Have a site map.
- Don't use a lot of text. Most people won't read the text, they'll skim it.
- Make everything easy to read. Use clear fonts; upper and lower case (all caps is hard to read); and no tiny type.
- Use only one or two typefaces.
- Remember that visitors are in a hurry and want information fast.

- Provide alternate text for all your major images.
- Do not use page counters.
- Do not use blinking or flashing text.
- Do not use busy backgrounds that distract from the text.
- Do not use background music.
- Do not use automatic pop-up windows.
- Maintain a theme but make pages different so they don't look exactly the same; use combinations of pictures and text to maintain visual interest.
- Keep pages short so the visitor does not have to scroll.
- Keep the size of graphic files small so viewers do not have to wait for them to open.
- Identify PDF files—nobody wants to click on a link and be surprised when it's not a web page.
- Don't force visitors to download a new browser or a special plug-in.
- Have links open in a new window.
- Check all your text for correct spelling, punctuation, and grammar.
- Give each page a title and be sure the titles make sense.
- Make sure the first thing visitors see is a compelling headline that describes the most important service or product you offer.
- Flash intros should be super-quick or have a "skip intro" option.
- Do not have any "under construction" pages—launch only when ready.
- Use testimonials.
- Have an "About Us" page to help visitors learn about you and feel comfortable with you.
- Contact information (e-mail, phone, fax, physical address) is essential.

Source: Elizabeth Jowaisas, Jowaisas Design

GIVE YOUR ONLINE CUSTOMERS PAYMENT AND PURCHASE ALTERNATIVES

Some people don't like to make purchases online, although they'll use shopping web sites for consumer research. Others like to shop online but prefer not to give their credit card information over the internet. To meet the needs of these customers, give them payment and purchase alternatives.

Set up your online shopping cart to accept all major credit cards plus alternatives such as PayPal or Google Checkout. Provide a telephone number so customers can call in their orders; this can be handled in-house or through a fulfillment service. Also provide a printable order form for customers who would prefer to fax or mail their orders. Of course, if you sell to other businesses, consider opening accounts for creditworthy customers and issuing monthly invoices.

WEB SITE TRENDS

- Marketing will continue to move online—the public expects a web site as part of the overall presentation.
- Aim for higher rankings in the top search engines. Most searchers click on a link within the first page of results. Have your site optimized with keywords and metatags, and invest in a paid search campaign.
- Most viewers will do online research, so make sure you have a strong web site with informative content.
- Developing richer customer relationships will be more important for sales. Web sites are becoming similar, so knowing what your customers want will make all the difference.
- RSS (really simple syndication) information feeds for e-retailers will become more popular. Getting your web shoppers to sign up for your RSS feed shows (and proves) an interest in your business.
- Online video will become more of a force with online retailers.
- YouTube will be used more to create buzz marketing.

Source: Elizabeth Jowaisas, Jowaisas Design

With market maturation comes opportunity for the retailers that can harness the power of the internet to influence off-line sales.

The key for retailers is to create clear, simple, and convenient links to the off-line channels that persuade shoppers to stay with them as they cross channels.

—David Schatsky, President, JupiterKagan

FOUR RULES FOR WEB SITE MARKETING COPY

1. Emphasize benefits, not features.
2. Write to a targeted audience.
3. Include a call to action.
4. Pay attention to layout.

Source: Entrepreneur.com

WEB SITE DESIGN: A TEN-STEP DEVELOPMENT PROCESS

Good web sites are no accident. They follow a logical process.

1. Meet and list concerns, preferences, likes, dislikes. Make a list of what will be done and by whom. Discuss the decision-making process and designate a primary contact.
2. Develop a detailed site map.
3. Refine/revisions of the site map.
4. Develop trial pages to determine creative direction.
5. Prototype key pages to refine the design.
6. Design the site.
7. Refine/revisions of the site.
8. Program the site.
9. Refine/revisions of the programming.
10. Launch!

Source: Elizabeth Jowaisas, Jowaisas Design

SEND YOUR E-NEWSLETTER BY AN OUTSIDE SERVICE PROVIDER

Advantages of using an outside service provider over sending out your own e-news are:

- It is much less labor intensive.
- You won't be accused of spamming by your ISP.
- Distribution is fast and won't hog your computer's resources.
- You get reports on bounces and user response.

Before you start searching for the right provider, you need to define what you're looking for. Common features you'll want to include are the ability to easily move your database of e-mails and names in and out; opt-in set-up; reader tracking information; bounce management; ability to segment your list personalization. You'll also need to estimate the number of recipients and distribution frequency to have an idea of a service provider's fees. Here are a few tips:

1. Solicit recommendations on e-newsletter service providers from colleagues, based on your own parameters.
2. Research other providers and get additional input on those recommended.
3. Focus on these critical factors:
   - *Ease of use.* It should be straightforward and fairly quick to import your mailing database, manage your list online, create and send e-newsletters, and review results.
   - *Deliverability.* Ask prospective providers what they do to ensure the highest probability of e-news receipt. Ideally, they will maintain a strict anti-spam policy, build relationships and feedback loops with major ISP's, and get on white lists (lists of approved e-mail addresses) to ensure your e-news is delivered. Ask what kind of information you get on bounces and how bounces are handled. You'll want to know which e-mail addresses are hard bounces (the address no longer exists) and which are soft bounces (undeliverable at the present time).
   - *Reliability.* Make sure your provider has a track record of reliable service. Ask for references or statistics to prove it. Your organization has too much to lose if something happens—your e-mail list gets copied or your newsletter goes out looking very different from the way you previewed it.
   - *Flexibility.* You may want to switch from text to HTML format at some point, to send both for different purposes or to segment your e-mail addresses by state or title.

UNINTENTIONALLY BAD COMPANY URLS

Y ou need a web site and your web site needs a URL (an address). Before finalizing your domain name, look at it as others might see it, not just as you think it looks. Consider the companies and organizations below—not one gave enough thought to their domain names.

Company/organization name and site description	URL
Who Represents?, a site where you can find the name of the agent that represents a celebrity.	www.whorepresents.com
Experts Exchange, a resource and information site	www.expertsexchange.com
Pen Island, custom made pens	www.penisland.com
Therapist Finder, helps you find a mental health professional in California	www.therapistfinder.com
IP Anywhere, a companion software product for Symantec's pcAnywhere®	www.ipanywhere.com
Art designers	www.speedofart.com
The Deans of Art, a fine art gallery presenting the work of Terri and Adam Dean	www.deansofart.com
Lake Tahoe vacation information	www.gotahoe.com
Kids Exchange, a consignment site for used children's clothes	www.kidsexchange.com
MacHome, a magazine for Mac users	www.machome.com
F.A. Gray, Inc., paint and wallpaper	www.fagray.com
Northern Kentucky, a site promoting the area	www.staynky.com

• *Tracking.* One of the greatest benefits of e-newsletters is the generation of quantifiable results. Make sure your e-newsletter provider tracks how many people (and who) get it, open it, and/or click through to your web site.

• *Pricing.* Usually a monthly fee based on the size of your list and/or number of e-mails sent. Some providers also charge a modest one-time set-up fee.

Source: Nancy E. Schwartz, "Selecting the Best E-News Service Provider," www.nancyschwartz.com

E-NEWSLETTER SERVICE PROVIDERS

Accucast
www.accucast.com

Bronto
www.bronto.com

Campaigner
www.campaigner.com

Constant Contact
www.constantcontact.com

CoolerEmail
www.coolere-mail.com

ExactTarget
www.exacttarget.com

iMakeNews
www.imakenews.com

Intellicontact
www.intellicontact.com

internetViz
www.internetvis.com

(Note: this is not a complete list.)

MINIMIZING ONLINE CHARGEBACKS

Credit card chargebacks are a challenge for any merchant, but especially for online sellers. It's not unusual for people who would remember a brick-and-mortar purchase to forget the details of an online transaction. If a customer disputes a charge from an online sale, the credit card company can deduct that amount from your account, even though you delivered the merchandise and the customer was satisfied.

To reduce the number of chargebacks for your online sales, your order confirmation messages (both the page that shows the final transaction on your web site as well as a follow-up e-mail sent later) should remind customers to print the receipt and save it for their records. If you're selling to a business, the reminder should include notifying the accounting department of the purchase. Also, if there is any difference at all in the public name of your company and the name on your merchant account, be sure to say, "Your credit card statement will reflect a charge of $145.35 from XYZ Company."

MARKET ON CRAIGSLIST

From e-commerce websites to furniture wholesalers, small businesses both online and off are realizing the marketing power of Craigslist.org, which gets an estimated 10 million unique visitors per day. For the most part, posting on the site is free.

From services like tutoring, car repair and real estate to products such as wholesale furniture, consignment goods and retail e-commerce, Craigslist is the ultimate destination for online marketers. If you manufacture goods, provide services directly or sell products regionally, Craigslist is a marketing tool you should consider. You can also easily promote an eBay store, a franchise operation or a referral partner. And it's a bourgeoning business opportunity for affiliates and webmasters looking for new ways to find customers.

Source: Shanon Lewis, author of The Unofficial Craigslist Book,
www.craigslist-book.com

WHY YOU SHOULD CONSIDER BLOGGING

- A blog can generate new sales leads.
- A blog allows your business to engage with current and potential customers in a direct, informal, no-pressure way. You can communicate the strengths of your product or service, the expertise of your top executives, and the breadth of your company's experience in ways that traditional marketing and advertising don't allow. This can help engender a better understanding of your company as well as inspire customer loyalty.
- Because of its collaborative nature, a blog can help you gain insight into customers' needs and interests. You can then use this information to develop new products or services or fine-tune existing ones.
- A blog can make your company appear more "alive" and approachable. A web site promoting your products or services is an essential marketing tool. But a blog, in effect, gives your company a personal voice, which can also help boost customer loyalty.
- Blogs cost little, if any, money. Some public blogging sites are free; others charge only nominal fees. Also, blogs are often extremely easy to set up and update, with virtually no training required.

Source: Peter Alexander, "Should You Start a Business Blog?," Entrepreneur.com

You may be disappointed if you fail, but you are doomed if you don't try.
—BEVERLY SILLS, OPERA SINGER

Words of Wisdom

ASSESSING YOUR BLOGGING READINESS

1. What problem does blogging solve?
It solves the "transparency and authenticity" issue bedeviling corporate America—gives you an instant publishing channel to use any way you want.

2. What's the business case for blogging?
Although the ROB (return on blog) is soft, blogs are the perfect expression of FREE and fast. They give you a zero-transaction-cost way to connect with and learn from your customers (or employees). A public blog gives you high search engine rankings at little cost.

3. Why do we need to pay attention to the blogosphere?
You can ignore the blogviators. But listen to the influential blogs, interact with them, and you'll be part of the new global conversation that's happening alongside MSM's [mainstream media] version of events.

4. What about credibility in the blogosphere?
Valid question. Beware. Unfortunately, half-truths spread quickly. Credible blogs will bubble up—make your own a trusted resource.

5. How do we know if blogging is right for our organization?
Consider the willingness to be open; whether you can add value with what you have to say; whether your company is in the eye of the media; whether you trust your employees to talk about your company; whether there is a need for trust in your brand; how a blog would mesh with other online content you are creating.

Source: from The Corporate Blogging Book by Debbie Weil

HOW TO BE A SUCCESSFUL BLOGGER

Start by setting goals, policies, and tone

Decide what you want to accomplish with your blog and let those goals influence your content. For example, you may want to establish yourself as a "thought leader" in your industry, boost your site's status in search engine results, or differentiate your business from the competition. Also, if your blog will have multiple in-house authors, decide on basic ground rules, such as never trashing the competition. If possible, make a staff member the blog editor to check entries before they're posted for grammar, typos, tone, and consistency.

Keep it relevant and personal

Blog readers want to know what you—or others in your company—think about the trends relevant to your industry. If you run a local real estate firm, your readers would likely want to know your thoughts on buying and selling trends in your area. Make your entries personal by speaking directly to readers. Tell them a story. Use an authoritative yet conversational and informal voice.

Make it useful

When you offer helpful tips and links to other resources on the web, your readers will be more inclined to tell others about your blog. For instance, have you read a new book that's relevant to your readers' interests? If so, write a short review of it in your blog. If your blog is an information resource for your industry, other bloggers and web site owners will want to link to it—the more sites that link to your blog, the more likely it will show up near the top of search engine results.

Use relevant keywords throughout your blog.

This is another way to boost your blog's chances of showing up at or near the top of search engine results.

Keep readers hungry.

If your blog entries are clear, concise, and compelling, readers will want to return again and again.

Use a soft sell.

Don't use your blog to re-purpose press releases, brochures, or other content originally created for marketing, PR or advertising. Readers can smell a blatant pitch a mile away.

Update often.

Readers expect blogs to be refreshed regularly. If you update your blog once a month or less, you may not develop a devoted readership. Shorter, more frequent updates are preferable to longer, infrequent ones.

Consider sharing the duties.

Blogging requires a time commitment. Sharing the blogging duties with others in your company can take the pressure off. Plus, multiple voices can make a blog more interesting.

Stick to it.

If you decide to start a blog, make a commitment to keep it going. An abandoned blog won't give readers a favorable impression of your company.

Be prepared to evangelize.

Because blogging is still relatively new, some stakeholders in your company may be unconvinced of its potential return on investment. Explain how a blog might help your business. Provide examples of blogs you admire and, if possible, how those blogs translated into sales leads, better customer relations, or other benefits.

Consult with trusted advisers.

Before embarking on any new marketing initiative, it's always a good idea to consult with those whose opinion you trust. Do you know a business owner with a business-oriented blog? If so, ask what impact the blog has had on their business. Also ask your in-house or contract-marketing expert for input on your blog's goals, content, or tone. Finally, talk to your webmaster, site designer, or other web-savvy adviser. Should you add a blog to your small-business web site or create one on a separate, public site? What keywords would they recommend using?

Source: Peter Alexander, "Should You Start a Business Blog?", Entrepreneur.com

---

TOP TEN TIPS FOR WRITING A SUCCESSFUL CORPORATE BLOG

1. Choose the right topic (be sure it's specific).
2. Find your voice.
3. Invite a conversation.
4. Package what you write (ten tips, five rules, seven ways).
5. Always, always link.
6. Write for web readers.
7. Write for Google searchers.
8. Publish consistently.
9. Take risks.
10. Have fun (the "dancing" part).

Source: from The Corporate Blogging Book *by Debbie Weil*

IMPROVING YOUR SEARCH ADVERTISING RESULTS

1. Know your business.

The point of a search advertising campaign is precision: reaching the right users at the right time. And the first step toward achieving this is to know your business. What products and services are you selling? What's your precise market niche? What selling strengths do you want to play to? Do your homework up front so your campaign planning will be as effective as possible.

2. Identify your goals and organize around them.

Once you have a clear sense of your business, stay focused on it as you establish the goals for your ad campaign.

3. Choose the right keywords.

Choosing keywords is both an art and a science. Start by brainstorming a list that's as wide as possible. Once you have a good list, you'll want to sort it (many advertisers put them into a spreadsheet to make this easier). Finally, you should refine your list by cutting irrelevant keywords that don't really relate to your business, and then organize the remaining keywords into themed groups.

4. Write ads that get people clicking.

Now that you've set up your keywords and grouped them in ad groups, your next step is to write the ads that users will see in their search results when they search on those keywords. You have three lines with which to grab that potential customer's attention. Here are a few tips for getting it right:

- Get to the point quickly.
- Include your keywords in your headline.
- Write copy that encourages users to click through to your site.

5. Target the right users.

Who are you trying to reach? Once you know your potential customers' key demographics, you can target individual campaigns by language and region. For instance, some keyword advertising programs allow you to reach potential customers in more than 40 languages and you can also target on a regional, city, or customized level, such as a 20-mile radius around your business.

6. Track your results.

Measuring your results will tell you which keywords bring you the most customers, which ads bring in the most business and, ultimately, how much return you're getting on your investment (ROI). Then you can adjust your campaign settings based on those results. Stay alert for creative ways to track offline conversions as well. Your keyword campaigns are just a piece in your overall sales puzzle; even purchases or signups that happen offline—such as by phone or at your place of business—might have been driven by your web site and your keyword advertising program. The best way to measure your offline results is by tracking customers to a conversion, such as with a coupon or an order form, or simply by asking customers how they found you.

7. Control your spending.

Keeping regular tabs on your account statistics means knowing which ads and keywords bring you results, not bidding more than you can afford to spend, and always focusing on relevance, that is, never letting yourself pay for keywords and ad text that aren't goal-focused and producing results.

8. Test, test, test.

Search advertising means never resting on your laurels. Take a moment to review what you've set up, one campaign at a time. Successful advertisers are constantly revising their campaigns, just as searchers are constantly searching for different things. To flourish in this ever-changing environment, you should continue to test and refine your keywords and ads, build on ones that work, and delete others that don't.

9. Stay relevant.

Don't just change your campaign based on test results; also stay responsive to product, seasonal, industry, and competitor changes.

10. Utilize all the available features.

Many programs provide "help center" resources that are easily available online and are up to date in order to help you learn everything you need to know to boost your campaign performance.

Source: Sheryl Sandberg, "Improving Your Search Advertising Results," Entrepreneur.com

---

TOP TEN SEARCH PROVIDERS

Google

Yahoo!

Windows Live Search

AOL Search

My Way

Ask.com

EarthLink Search

Dogpile

Comcast Search

NexTag Search

Source: Nielsen/NetRatings, 2007; data for December 2006

STRENGTH IN NUMBERS

The power of groups, the clout that crowds can exercise to get what they want, is nothing new. What is new, however, is the dizzying ease with which likeminded, action-ready citizens and consumers can now go online and connect, group, and ultimately exert influence on a global scale. Call it group power, call it CROWD CLOUT: "Online grouping of citizens/consumers for a specific cause, be it political, civic, or commercial, aimed at everything from bringing down politicians to forcing suppliers to fork over discounts."

Source: Trendwatching.com

GET VISITORS TO SAY YES WITH THESE OPT-IN OFFERS

These days, consumers know that their personal information is gold, and they won't give it to you unless you give them a really compelling reason to opt in to your list. Your opt-in incentive should: offer specific benefits; relate to the reason people are visiting your site in the first place; and give visitors a reason to look forward to your e-mails or keep returning to your site. Consider these ideas:

1. Offer a free course.
2. Offer a free e-book.
3. Offer downloadable articles.
4. Offer other "downloadables."
5. Offer a regular contest, puzzle or game.
6. Take a survey.
7. Offer a members-only forum or discussion board.
8. Offer members-only specials.

Source: Derek Gehl, "8 Opt-In Offers Your Visitors Can't Refuse," Entrepreneur.com

GOOGLE ADWORDS: THE KEY TO DYNAMIC ONLINE ADVERTISING

The following interview was conducted with Perry Marshall and Bryan Todd, Google AdWords experts and co-authors of *Ultimate Guide to Google AdWords* (Entrepreneur Press, 2007).

What kinds of companies can benefit the most from Google AdWords?

If you've got someone, anyone, looking for you on Google—or on any site that Google serves—you stand to benefit. You just have to find where they are and how they're asking about you, and then put yourself in front of them, and do what it takes to get noticed. And Google makes that easier and faster—and less risky—than any time before in the history of buying and selling.

If an entrepreneur wants to get started on AdWords today, what knowledge do they need?

You need to know who it is you can help best, and find out whether he or she is actually looking for you on Google. If so, you're set. Your job, then, is getting your customer to talk to you and honing your Google ads, your web site, and your whole message based on what he or she tells you.

So many advertisers think they're going to rake in a bundle by being all things to all people. But it's the opposite on Google. It's all about finding a niche—a kind of person whose need only you can meet—and giving him something he can't find anyplace else.

Will AdWords be expensive? How does it compare to other advertising methods?

Google AdWords has probably got the lowest barrier to entry of any advertising method out there. You don't have to pull together eight digits' worth of venture capital. You don't have to go massively into debt. You don't have to buy property or hire an agency. And you certainly don't have to pour $2 million bucks into a Super Bowl commercial with some talking sock.

But "cheap" or "expensive" advertising can be misleading. Don't get caught thinking in terms of a "budget." Your goal is to spend a dollar and make a return. If you could guarantee that, by taking our advice, for every dollar you spend you get $1.25 or $2.00 or $5.00 in return, wouldn't you be eager to spend more rather than less?

How do you recommend choosing keywords?
Well, you certainly can't do Google long-term without good keywords and lots of them. But the advice in our book is a little contrarian: Every keyword represents a particular person who's in a particular mindset at the moment. So make the job easier on yourself by starting with one person, and getting your message and your sales process tuned to him or her first, then go after other keywords later on. One market at a time, in other words.

DOING IT RIGHT

Pay-per-click ads are an excellent form of very targeted marketing, but a key to their success is to drive prospects to the right page. Shoppers want to be able to quickly find what they're looking for, so when someone clicks on your pay-per-click link, take them to the page with the item they want. For example, if someone is searching for outdoor widgets, and you happen to sell them, the link should take them to a page on your site showing those outdoor widgets with ordering information—not just to your home page. If they land on your home page and realize they have to do further searching to find the product, they're likely to just click the back button and try someone else's link. So point your pay-per-click ads to specific pages and make it easy for people to buy from you.

And there are some great tools out there—Wordtracker, software tools like AdWord Analyzer, and Google's own keyword tool gives you a helpful angle on things, too.

What are the three most important things to consider when using AdWords?
1. Who exactly is your customer?
2. How can you get him to tell you what he really wants?
3. How can you do a better job of echoing the conversation inside his head?

That's the major stuff. Everything else is a secondary matter of tweaking dollars and numbers.

Are there any businesses that should not advertise this way?
Well, I'd never tell a person, "Do not advertise on Google!" The real question is, is your customer looking for you there? In many cases, he just plain isn't; or there are too few of him there to merit the effort. The key is, we teach you how to figure out if this is for you, without spending an arm and a leg. It's direct marketing at Mach Two speed. You're dealing with real, live customers, and testing and tweaking to find ways to get them to respond and buy. And when you follow the right principles, it works!

⚜ ⚜ ⚜

NUMBERS TO **KNOW** Seventy-seven percent of online shoppers use consumer-generated product reviews/ratings, and those who find them useful are more loyal to stores with reviews/ratings featured.

Source: Jupiter Research

AUTOMATIC MARKETING WITH AUTORESPONDERS

It's been said that customers need to hear your name at least seven times before they buy from you. Autoresponders make it easy to ensure that they do.

Essentially, an autoresponder is a computer program that automatically answers e-mail messages sent to it with one—or several—responses. For example, if your web site is mycompany.com, you could set up your autoresponder to reply to e-mail messages sent to special e-mail addresses, such as subscribe@mycompany.com, info@mycompany.com, or newsletter@mycompany.com. Most web hosts include autoresponder-type packages with their services; however, in these days of overwhelming spam, it's often more effective to use a professional autoresponder service, such as Aweber.com or GetResponse.com. This improves your ability to ensure delivery, to manage large lists of e-mail addresses, and to avoid accusations of spam.

Use autoresponders to send out automatic responses to support queries; to send out price lists; for e-mail newsletters; for marketing follow-up; for online courses…an autoresponder's uses are limited only by your needs.

Options for obtaining leads for your autoresponders include opt-in forms on your web site and advertising. You could also use mailing lists you currently have, adding all the leads to a particular autoresponder. However, be careful with this approach. Make sure that the people on your lists have requested information from you. If they haven't asked for the information you're sending them, you may be accused of sending spam.

Spam accusations can have serious consequences. Your messages may be blocked by large internet service providers like AOL and EarthLink, and even more seriously, you may find that your web hosting company removes your site from the web. You also run the risk of customers filing law suits.

An easy way to avoid spam accusations with an autoresponder is to use a process called "double opt-in." This means prospective customers have to sign up for your information—which gives you proof via the IP address of the computer they're using—as well as respond to a verification message, confirming that they're willing to receive information. This provides you with the defense you need should you be accused of spamming.

To be sure your autoresponder messages get opened, make your subject lines compelling (but avoid words that trigger spam filters). If you're sending a newsletter, your subject line should clearly state the name of the newsletter so the recipient can

The two smartest things I've done are learning how to optimize a web site, starting with my own, and launching and continuing a regular, free e-mail newsletter for anyone who would care to subscribe.

Words of Wisdom

—Jonathan Bernstein, President, Bernstein Crisis Management, LLC

SUBJECT LINE WORDS THAT TRIGGER SPAM FILTERS

To keep your e-mails from being blocked by spam filters, avoid using trigger words in your subject line. This is not a complete list because spam filters can be customized and the number of terms continues to increase as spammers figure out how to exploit the filters. There are also body-text words and phrases that will trigger spam filters.

Some of the offending words are easy to spot; others are commonly used business words. Using quotation marks, dollar signs, exclamation points, all capital letters, and even toll-free telephone numbers in subject lines will frequently trigger mail filters. It's difficult to guess what spam filters will consider to be junk e-mail and there is no easy or guaranteed solution. It's a good idea to work with a knowledgeable e-marketing consultant and track your results closely.

50% off!	Collect	Give it away	Opportunity
Accept credit cards	Collect child support	Giving it away	Order now
Act now!	Compare	Great offer	Please read
Additional income	Compare rates	Guarantee	Promise you
All natural	Congratulations	Guaranteed	Removes
All new	Consolidate debt and	Hidden	Removes wrinkles
Amazing	credit	Hidden assets	Reverses aging
Amazing stuff	Consolidate your debt	In accordance with	Satisfaction guaranteed
Apply online	Copy DVDs	[some spam law]	Save up to
As seen on	Credit	Information you	Search engine listings
Auto e-mail removal	Credit bureaus	requested	Serious cash
Avoid bankruptcy	Credit card offers	Join millions	Special promotion
Be amazed	Cures baldness	Loans	Stock disclaimer statement
Be your own boss	Dig up dirt on friends	Lose weight	Stop
Big bucks	Discount!	Meet singles	Stop snoring
Billion dollars	Don't delete	Million dollars	Stops
Brand new pager	Double your income	MLM	Subscribe
Bulk e-mail	Drastically reduced	Multi level marketing	Time limited
Buy direct	Earn $	No cost, no fees	University diplomas
Buying judgments	Earn per week	No fees, gimmicks, medical	Unsecured debt or credit
Cable converter	Easy terms	exams, questions, etc.	Vacation
Call now!	Eliminate debt	No investment	Viagra
Calling creditors	Free!	No obligation	Visit our web site
Cash	Free grant money	No purchase necessary	While supplies last
Cash bonus	Free installation	Offer	Why pay more?
Casino	Free investment	Offshore	Winner
Cell phone cancer scam	Free leads	One time	Work at home
Cents on the dollar	Free preview	Online marketing	You're a winner!
Check or money order	Get paid	Online pharmacy	You've been selected

easily identify it. Commercial autoresponder packages allow you to track clicks on hyperlinks in your messages so you can measure response rates.

Autoresponders are an excellent marketing tool, because they can work for you 24/7/365, with little expense. They can extend your marketing reach, and used with care, they build your company's brand and bottom line.

Source: Charlene Davis, business writer and co-author of Make Big Profits on eBay *(Entrepreneur Press)*

NUMBERS TO KNOW

Online retail sales are expected to reach $171 billion in 2011 and will be 10 to 15 percent of total U.S. retail sales. Web influenced off-line sales will grow at a slightly faster pace than online sales. Offline retail sales influenced by online research will reach $1 trillion by 2011.

Source: Jupiter Research

TURN YOUR ERROR PAGE INTO A MARKETING MESSAGE

At some point, some of your site visitors will likely land on a "404 error" page. Perhaps your server can't find the web page they're trying to reach because it's been moved, deleted or renamed. That URL no longer works, but unfortunately, it still shows up on sites, blogs and search engine results pages. Don't panic. There's a simple solution to turn a mishap into marketing: Customize your 404 page.

Start by making your error page design mimic your home page design. By incorporating your site's look and feel, as well as site navigation, visitors are quickly reassured that they've got the right company. Just let them know they've got the wrong page. State that the page they are looking for can't be found, but don't stop there.

Invite lost visitors to click around; any site navigation you've included will show them where they can go. Also, link to your site's search tool, if you have one. That can help them quickly locate the information they're trying to find. Most important, provide links to helpful resources on your site. This is powerful.

You can direct them to your online newsletter, or any opt-in offer, to get them on your e-mail list. And you can recommend your products and services so they'll take a step closer to doing business with you.

Watch your words, however. When transforming your error message into a marketing opportunity, avoid the hard sales pitch. After all, you can't be certain what these visitors want. So phrases such as "buy now" or "order today" could scare them off. Instead, offer suggestions, recommendations and resources. These types of informational words point people to particular pages without any pressure to buy.

And feel free to have fun with your 404 page. An entertaining error page isn't a new concept. But now, in addition to amusing visitors about your page's disappearing act, you can leverage today's user-driven communities such as blogs and social networks to publicize it. This could turn your concealed page into a communication and marketing gem.

Source: Catherine Seda, "Use Site Error Pages as a Marketing Tool," Entrepreneur.com

✢ ✢ ✢

CHAPTER 25

E-Commerce

WHAT IS E-COMMERCE?

The basic definition of e-commerce is business done on and through the web. In simplest terms, it's the selling of products online. Via your own web site or an online marketplace like eBay, you can promote and sell products online, taking orders and accepting payment—all without stepping foot behind a storefront or ever seeing your customers face-to-face.

The most amazing aspect of e-commerce is its ability to impact sales and marketing efforts immediately. By going online, suddenly a neighborhood bakery or a homebased consulting service expands its reach to a national or even international base of potential customers. Web-based sales know no international boundaries. Forrester Research, which analyzes online trends and statistics, projects the online retail market for U.S. businesses will be $230 billion by 2008. That's a full 10 percent of anticipated total U.S. retail sales.

Not only is the internet increasing the number of potential customers that a company can reach, but also it's driving profitability, according to research from Ipsos, commissioned by PayPal. The survey discovered that, far from being an extra "expense," internet operations boosted businesses' bottom lines. Of small businesses that sell online, 64 percent said the internet has increased their revenues or sales, 48 percent felt the internet helped to expand their geographic reach in the United States, and 73 percent saved money by decreasing administrative costs.

Cash flow is of significant importance to a new business—online or brick and mortar. The Ipsos study found that small-business owners who conduct business online feel it allows them to receive payments faster and conduct business more easily. When entrepreneurs move online, they establish themselves on a par with larger competitors. On the internet, even the smallest online retailer can be as attractive and functional as the largest big box store—without the need for a physical presence on every street corner. Often, small shops project a "boutique" feel that attracts shoppers, who perceive smaller businesses as more distinctive than larger stores.

Source: Entrepreneur.com

THE DOS AND DON'TS OF SEARCH ENGINE OPTIMIZATION

The Dos

1. *Ask relevant sites to link to your site.* In the past, scoring a high ranking with a search engine was all about positioning your keywords in "prime real estate" positions in your text and site coding. All that has changed, however, because these days, search engines place a huge amount of importance on the number of sites that link to yours. But it's not just the quantity of links that matter, it's also the quality. Search engines look at how relevant the links are, i.e., how much the content of the linking site has in common with the content on your site.

2. *Pay attention to keyword inclusion and placement.* Keywords may no longer be the sole determining factor of a site's ranking, but they're still pretty important. The most useful places to include them are:
   - In your domain name—only make sure your keywords are in the root of your URL,

---

SEVEN WAYS TO TURN A PROFIT ONLINE

No matter what your business is, you should always be thinking about ways to diversify your revenue streams to boost your profits. Here's a list of seven ways you can earn income on the web:

1. *Sell your own products.* The main advantage to selling your own products is that you ultimately control how much profit you make on every sale and therefore have the potential for the biggest profit margin. You know exactly what each product costs, and you can try out different price points to see what works best. People appreciate good value, and removing the middleman is a great way to provide your customers with competitive prices that keep them coming back for more.

2. *Sell your own services.* It's easy to get started selling a service online, but your revenue potential, in most cases, is limited. When you sell a service, you're essentially selling a relationship with yourself. And this requires that you spend more time and effort establishing your credibility and developing rapport with your visitors than is typically required on a site selling a physical product.

3. *Drop ship products.* Drop shipping lets you sell quality, brand-name products on your site for a hefty profit, while the drop shipper takes care of fulfilling the order. They warehouse the stock, pack the orders, and ship them out to your customers.

4. *Recommend affiliate products.* As one of the company's "affiliates" or promotion partners, you earn a commission each time someone you've referred to their site makes a purchase. To adver-

---

not the stem. For example, if your main keyword phrase is "cell phones," try to get a domain name such as "www.cell-phones.com" instead of "www.mobileusa.com/cell-phones." Some search engines will actually penalize sites for including key words in the stem of a URL.

- In the title tags in your source code.
- In the meta description of your site. This is much less important than it used to be, but it can't hurt.
- In your meta keyword tags.

3. *Create content-rich information pages to direct traffic to your site.* An easy way to boost the number of pages that link to your site is to create some pages yourself. Be sure the information relates to the content on your site and has your keywords placed in advantageous positions. This will boost the ranking of your pages with the search engines and ensure they get lots of traffic—which they can then redirect to your site.

4. *Submit your site to online directories.* Be sure to submit your site to important directories such as Yahoo!, the Open Directory Project, and About.com, as well as smaller directories. Your listing on these directories will help your ranking with the major search engines.

5. *Multiply and conquer.* Create a community of related sites that link to each other. Why stop at only one information page? The more content-rich sites that point to your site, the better. You can also boost the number of links that

---

SEVEN WAYS TO TURN A PROFIT ONLINE, continued

tise their wares, you might post a banner on your site that links to the affiliate program's site, or you might publish an article about the company and their products in your newsletter.

5. *Sell ad space.* Once your site has lots of highly targeted traffic, or a large, targeted opt-in list, you may be able to sell advertising. Advertisers are willing to buy ads when they're being directed at large numbers of their target market. Selling ad space can be a great additional profit stream, but it's unlikely to keep your business afloat on its own.

6. *Create a joint venture with like-minded businesses.* Joint ventures are all about related businesses teaming up and combining skills, products, services, and resources to create new streams of income and profit. One great way to profit through joint ventures is to seek out products or services that would benefit your visitors, and then approach the companies that provide those products or services.

7. *Start an affiliate program.* With your own affiliate program, you can recruit an army of people (your affiliates) who will recommend your product on their web site for a percentage of any sale they refer. You have the power to exponentially increase your income as more and more affiliates sign up and you continue to teach your existing affiliates how to increase their commission checks (and your income).

Source: Corey Rudl, "7 Ways to Turn a Profit Online," Entrepreneur.com

point to your site by dividing it into several separate sites that all link to each other. This works especially well if you sell a number of different products or services. If you build a different site to focus on each of your products and services, then you can also concentrate the use of specific keyword phrases on each site. It's another great way to boost your search-engine ranking.

The Don'ts

1. *Beware of irrelevant links.* Yes, it's a good idea to get a lot of different links pointing to your site, but the search engines only like relevant links. If they find sites that have nothing in common with the content on your site linked to your web site, they'll lower your relevancy rating.

2. *Beware of irrelevant keywords.* Search engines hate finding irrelevant keywords on your site—especially in your meta tags. If they catch you using keywords that have nothing to do with the actual content of your site, they'll penalize you for it.

3. *Don't "keyword stuff" your meta tags.* In the past, people used to repeat their keywords in their meta tags over and over again. This used to get them a high ranking with the search engines—but not any more. Search engines are on to this trick and will punish you for it by dropping your ranking.

4. *Don't create "link farms."* Link farms are the evil cousins of the information pages we discussed above. In the past, some spammers used to build multiple "doorway" sites that existed only to multiply the number of links pointing to their sites. Unlike content-rich information pages, these doorway pages would usually only include a string of keyword terms that would earn them a high ranking with the

search engines. The search engines have caught on to this tactic, however, and will drop you from their listings if they find you using it.

5. *Avoid "free-for-all" link pages.* Don't bother placing links to your site on pages where everyone and their cousin is invited to put up a link. Such sites have extremely low relevancy ratings and will cost you points with the search engines.

Source: Corey Rudl, "The Dos and Don'ts of Search Engine Optimization," Entrepreneur.com

THE ABCS OF WEB SITE LAW

Age

The age of your users impacts the web site. According to Federal Trade Commission (FTC) regulations through the Children's Online Privacy Protection Act (COPPA), a web site must get a parent's permission for children under 13 to disclose information. Also, remember that children under 18 should not be permitted to view information that is adult in nature. In addition, children under 18 may not be able to agree to contracts such as your web site user agreement and purchase contracts. Finally, the FTC also regulates advertising and other content directed at children.

Bulletin Boards, Chat Rooms, Etc.

Any posting ability by users should be subject to site submission rules and a user agreement. The rules should obtain users' consent not to post pornographic, defamatory, or infringing materials and, through your user agreement, consent to your company not being liable for other users taking such actions.

Copyright

The footer of your site should display a copyright notice for the content of the site. The notice should read "© [date] [copyright owner name] All rights reserved." You should also deposit a copy of the site with the Copyright Office to record ownership of the site's content, look, and feel. Finally, under the Digital Millennium Copyright Act, depending on the purpose and the users' activities on the site, your company may be eligible to register for limited liability offered by the act. You should consult your attorney for review of the act and how to register.

Domain Name

When building your web site, domain names are an important part. Often they are directly tied to your business name, your logo, and your brand. Picking a domain name should involve the same careful thought as naming other products or services. Choosing a domain name should include analysis of trademark law in relationship to the name. Under current law, domain names may be awarded to trademark holders over others through arbitration or litigation. This means that having trademark registration in the same name as your domain name may ensure that you retain ownership of the name.

Export

If people from other countries use your site, then you are exporting. If you sell to such people, you are exporting the item you sell and entering into contracts with people of other countries. If you use encryption on the site, then you are exporting technology regulated by the Departments of Commerce and Defense. Various government departments regulate the countries with which U.S. companies may do business and when a company needs an export license to transmit items, technology, or information abroad. Doing business with certain countries, such as Iraq, Iran, Cuba, North Korea, Syria, Yugoslavia, and others, is severely restricted. Depending on the information on your site, what

kind of business you do, the technology and information involved, your site may be subject to regulations, and you should consult with your attorney.

Framing

It is important to be careful how your web site frames to other sites. There have been trademark cases regarding consumer confusion over which site is which, and which site is the source of the content and data. Also, be careful, because some sites' "terms and conditions" and/or "user agreements" prohibit collecting and reprinting data displayed on the site—even if such data is factual, such as times and places for events.

Giveaways

Sweepstakes, contests, lotteries, and giveaways are governed by state and national laws as to how they must be conducted. Florida and New York require registration with the state if the prizes are over $5,000 in value. Most importantly, you should have rules outlining the terms and conditions of the giveaway. The rules are an offer from the sponsor that the participant accepts by entering. The offer, plus the acceptance, make a binding contract covering the giveaway.

Home Page

On the footer of the home page of the site, you should have a link to your privacy policy, your user agreement or terms and conditions, and your copyright notice.

Insurance

Be sure that your business insurance covers web site activities. Often web site activities are excluded from errors and omissions and other business insurance. Lloyds of London and a few other companies have insurance specifically covering materials and sales via web sites, including security of credit card numbers and other important data.

Jurisdiction

One of the primary reasons for having a user agreement is to better address the issues of jurisdiction. Under current law, web site owners may be subject to jurisdiction and law in any state or country where its users are located. Being subject to the law of so many different locations makes trying to comply with the law and trying to assess your risk tricky. An attorney can help you consider which markets are your highest risk and how to lower your risks through consultation with local counsel or blocking users from those regions. Additionally, you should consider that many foreign jurisdictions do not offer protections for intellectual property that are comparable to those in the United States. Therefore, if a user in such a region steals content or software from your site, you may have little legal recourse, and a hard battle to fight on foreign soil and in a foreign language.

Linking

When linking to other sites, you should consider two factors. First, what is the word or image you are using for the link and is it a trademark of another site or company. If so, you need the trademark owner's permission to post the trademark on your site. Second, you should always link to the home page of a web site since there have been "deep linking" cases claiming loss of advertising revenue that would have been gained if the users had been directed through the home page.

Metatags

Courts have not permitted use of another company's trademarks as metatags on competitors' sites. These cases arose when company A used company B's trademarked term in the metatagging of company A's site so that when a user looked for company B, company A would come up in the listing. For example, it would not be permitted for Coca-Cola™ to use the metatag "Pepsi" on the Coca-Cola™ web site.

Notification

The Digital Millennium Copyright Act (DMCA) established procedures for advising a web site that its contents may infringe on another person's copyright. If the Digital Millennium Copyright Act applies, these procedures should be outlined in a notification policy on the site.

Obscenity

Materials considered "obscene" by state or federal law are not permitted on the internet and, especially, may not be viewed by children. What is obscene is based on the local standards of the viewing community. This makes prior determinations of what is acceptable somewhat complex. If you have questions about your site and its content, you should review them with your attorney.

Privacy Policy

If you collect any information from users of your site—using cookies or otherwise—the FTC requires you to have a privacy policy. The privacy policy should contain an explanation of how you collect the users' information, how and where the information is stored, how the user can delete or change the information, and to whom the information is disclosed and for what purpose. The European Union also has similar and strict regulations on collection of information via web sites.

Rules for Mail Order

The FTC and some states have guidelines for selling items by mail, which have been extended to cover internet sales. These guidelines cover return policies, customer contact, and other information about how to inform your customers about your products, shipping, and sales procedures.

SEC

The Securities and Exchange Commission (SEC) considers a web site to be a means of disclosing information to the public about a company. Therefore any information disclosed on your web site should be given the same review and consideration that your company gives all public disclosures with regard to "forward-looking statements" and "material" information.

Trademark

Trademarking the name of your company, logo, mottos, and domain name is an important part of your business development and should be reflected on your web site. Your nationally registered marks should display an ® and unregistered marks should display a ™ or ℠.

User Agreement

Having a user agreement or "terms and conditions" may be the most important part of a web site. A user agreement requires each user to agree to be bound by a contract governing his or her use of the site by clicking "I agree" before being permitted to use the site. Be aware that simply posting your legal agreement without forcing the user to click "I agree" prior to use is unlikely to bind your users to the terms. The user must take an active step through which she agrees to the terms and must not be allowed to proceed to use the site without such step.

View Source

The ability for users to view the source code of nearly all web sites by using the "view source" command in browsers means that the source code for your web site is not protectable by trade secret law. For something to be protected by trade secret law, it must not be publicly known, the owner must take some effort to keep the information secret, and the information must have monetary value to the owner. If the information is publicly available on the web through "view source," the information is not a trade secret.

Warranties

Statements on your web site about your products and services are express warranties to customers. It is important to carefully review all web site text to be sure that what your company promises is true and corresponds with its other policies and advertising.

When you review, look for statements that are absolute statements, which may be hard to prove or verify if the FTC were to request that you do so.

XXX

If your site contains adult materials, be sure to consult your attorney regarding special legal requirements regarding notice prior to entering the site, notice requirements under federal regulations, and other laws applicable to the adult entertainment industry.

Your Risk

The law is all about risk. The more time and money you spend following laws and regulations governing your business, the lower your risk of fines or successful claims by government or third parties.

Zero

The amount your company may have left after ignoring all the laws, regulations, and risks.

Source: Judith Silver, "A to Z of Legal Issues (web site)," Entrepreneur.com

A user agreement allows a company to:

- dictate how the site may be used (for example, for reading and printing materials)
- dictate how the site may not be used (for example, reverse engineering the coding tricks, copying content, for illegal purposes)
- dictate who may use the site (for example, persons over 18, U.S. citizens)
- dictate procedures or policies for the site (for example, return policies, complaint policies, notification of copyright infringement policies)
- dictate your company's waiver of implied legal warranties (for example, implied warranties of noninfringement, fitness for particular purposes, etc.)
- dictate the limit of your company's liability for the site, other users postings on your site, sites you link to, etc.
- dictate jurisdiction for any disputes relating to the site

Source: Judith Silver, "A to Z of Legal Issues (web site)," Entrepreneur.com

GREAT ADVICE

Review your web site to be sure that the text matches your regular business contracts. For example, your web site should not promise a 60-day money-back guarantee if your contract states only a 30-day warranty.

Source: Judith A. Silver, CEO and founder of Silver Law Inc.

DON'T GET ACCUSED OF SPAMMING

The internet can be a powerful vehicle for your marketing messages—but it only works if those messages are actually getting to the intended recipients and not being routed to a spam folder or, worse, blocked totally. If you get labeled as a spammer, you can be quickly blacklisted by ISPs and that will prevent your legitimate e-mail from getting through.

Keep the following points in mind:

- *Respect and process "unsubscribe" requests promptly.* If someone doesn't want to be on your list, take them off. Periodically check your unsubscribe link to be sure it's working.
- *Only send subscribers what they actually signed up for.* If they agreed to receive your e-newsletter and other marketing messages, that's all you should send them. If you develop a new e-newsletter, don't just automatically send it out—send a message offering the opportunity to subscribe. If you expand your product line, don't assume all your customers will be interested in information about the new items—ask them first.
- *Don't sell or rent your list unless you have received permission from the people on it.*
- *Create a clear, easy-to-understand privacy policy and make it easy for users to opt-out.* Better yet, develop an opt-in procedure so that customers must ask to be included on your lists.
- *Keep track of all your computers, servers, and other computing resources* so that you know where your legitimate e-mail is being sent from and can quickly identify bogus addresses or a system that may be infected with a virus that is sending out spam.
- *Be sure all your databases and address lists are current.* Synchronize multiple lists to keep them clean so that you don't remove a cus-

tomer from one database but leave him on another.

- *Limit the number of e-mail addresses from your organization that are published online.* E-mail addresses that are available via the internet usually receive substantial amounts of spam and can be used by spammers as spoofed addresses. By limiting those published outside your organization, you make it easier to filter for incoming spam and monitor for misuse.

- *Use only legitimate, reputable third-party mailers* if you're outsourcing newsletters and other electronic messages.

If I had known how quickly the online commerce would grow, I would have invested much more cash, time, and effort in the beginning and been able to capitalize on that rapid growth better.

—MICHAEL JANSMA, PRESIDENT, GEMAFFAIR.COM

ONLINE PRODUCT REVIEWS–LET YOUR CUSTOMERS TELL OTHERS WHAT THEY THINK

What do customers think of your products? Let them tell other shoppers by posting their comments on your web site. As plenty of e-tailers have discovered, online reviews by happy customers carry more weight with other buyers than most forms of marketing communication.

"The more clutter we get in traditional media, the more consumers are talking to each other," says Peter Kim, a senior analyst at Forrester Research in Cambridge, Massachusetts. Online reviews are an increasingly popular way for consumers to communicate with one another.

Tom Cox of Golfballs.com is a believer. "There [are] lots of great reasons to have reviews," says the co-founder and CEO of the $7.5 million business. "People who are shopping love to leave reviews. They provide relevant content for both readers and search engines." The Lafayette, Louisiana, online

retailer of golf equipment decided to add reviews to its site last year. So far, giving customers the opportunity to speak their minds has paid off. "Customers who have left reviews have purchased 58 percent more golf equipment than customers who haven't," says Cox. What's more, customers who leave reviews have a higher average transaction size and a greater lifetime value than nonreviewers.

Managing all those comments can get tricky at times. "Our customer service folks usually catch [inappropriate reviews] and clean [them] up," says Cox. "But if someone leaves a legitimate review, even if it's bad, we leave it."

A number of companies offer tools to help you get started: PowerReviews (www.powerreviews.com) offers a free outsourced solution. Bazaarvoice (www.bazaarvoice.com) offers a hosted and managed solution, which starts at $2,000 a month,

---

ONLINE PRODUCT REVIEWS—LET YOUR CUSTOMERS TELL OTHERS WHAT THEY THINK, continued

monitors reviews, and updates them regularly. The Prospero CommunityCM (www.prospero.com) platform lets you manage online reviews yourself for about $395 a month.

Sam Decker, vice president of marketing and products at Bazaarvoice, has these tips for making reviews work.

1. *Encourage customers to talk.* "A simple gift certificate offered to customers [if they] share new opinions can increase review volume 500 percent to 800 percent in a matter of weeks," says Decker.

2. *Have them log in.* "This best practice ensures that reviewers are invested in sharing their opinions [and] increases the credibility of the community," says Decker. "It also makes it easier to moderate and analyze the community."

3. *Use customer comments in your marketing.* Decker suggests you use average rating icons in ads and catalogs, or repurpose review text as copy for marketing collateral.

Source: Melissa Campanelli, "Why You Should Encourage Online Product Reviews," Entrepreneur.com

---

CREATE USER-FRIENDLY ONLINE FORMS

You've worked hard to lead prospects to your web site. But you're not done yet. Test-drive your online forms—they could be blocking the business opportunities your marketing campaigns are bringing in.

An online form allows prospects to take a variety of actions: contact you, subscribe to your e-zine, request information, and of course, order something. A form is a communication tool for them and a marketing tool for you. You need an online form to collect contact information and to get permission to communicate with prospects. Otherwise, once they leave your site, they could be gone forever. In itself, an online form is not effective marketing, however. In fact, if you're committing the following mistakes, yours could be costing you customers.

Requiring unnecessary information

Do you really need prospects to provide personal information such as a company title, phone number, mailing address, and registration of a login name and password? If not, remove these fields or label them as optional.

Restricting open fields

Ever type so many characters that a field ended before you finished? Expand the length of your fields to account for long names, e-mail addresses, and other information you require.

Forcing repeat work

If your forms are not completed correctly, are prospects forced to start over? They won't. Be sure to retain the information already entered while pointing out the area that needs attention.

Don't just fix your forms; optimize them. Try the following time-tested tips to make your forms better marketing tools:

- *Include your contact information.* Give prospects the option to call you instead of, or in addition to, completing your online form.

- *Offer your e-zine.* While they're already contacting you, invite them to subscribe to your newsletter.
- *Ask how they found your site.* This optional question could give you insightful marketing information without putting off prospects.

Your online forms get prospects to make initial contact with you. Make this process painless—your online forms won't get a second chance to make a first impression.

Source: Catherine Seda, "Making Online Forms User-Friendly," Entrepreneur.com

---

THE SOCIAL SHOPPING TREND CAN HELP GET PEOPLE TALKING ABOUT YOUR PRODUCTS

With the vast majority of Americans researching products on the internet before they purchase them in stores or on the web, it's no surprise that a whole new form of shopping is emerging. "Social shopping" is the intriguing offspring of social networking and online shopping, and it can offer your growing business just the marketing leg up it needs.

Unlike the many retail sites that display products for sale, many increasingly popular social shopping sites (some still in beta testing stages) consist of product listings from site users who recommend their favorites, often with a strong emphasis on what's hot, new and exciting. And insiders know that listing their own products on the right social shopping sites can build buzz that leads to sales.

This accessible form of word-of-mouth marketing offers a wealth of opportunities for entrepreneurs with limited budgets. To help you navigate these new waters, let's take a look at why and how social shopping works.

1. *Online research leads to sales.* Almost 90 percent of respondents to a BIGresearch "Consumer Intentions and Actions" survey conducted in June 2006 said they occasionally or regularly research products online before buying them in a store. When it comes to online purchasing, a study released by Yahoo! and OMD found that nearly three-quarters of the people surveyed use trusted, familiar websites when purchasing online, and the majority (54 percent) say the internet is their most trusted shopping information source. So no matter whether you sell exclusively online, through a brick-and-mortar store or both, influencing online shoppers can have a profound effect on sales.

2. *Peer-to-peer recommendations deliver credibility.* Social shopping websites allow for word-of-mouth marketing at its best. The internet empowers consumers and accelerates the flow of information. Product recommendations that come from peers may be more trusted, so site visitors may return more often and be more likely to spread the good word and purchase the products they learn about on the sites. Social shopping sites reflect users' personal tastes and allow for online conversation. Visitors can learn what's popular, get shopping ideas and follow links to products they wouldn't necessarily find on their own.

3. *Sites have distinct personalities.* Here's a sampling of the hottest social shopping sites.

THE SOCIAL SHOPPING TREND CAN HELP GET PEOPLE
TALKING ABOUT YOUR PRODUCTS, CONTINUED

- ThisNext.com: Users can browse recommended products, add them to their wish lists, recommend or find out where to buy them, and create themed lists of their own.
- Crowdstorm.com: This site measures the buzz around products based on user recommendations. Popular items go to the top of the list.
- Kaboodle.com: Users create wish lists with photos and links to products for sale online. It's easy to post a summary of anything found on the internet.
- Stylehive.com: This is the hot site for women's fashions and interests.
- Wists.com: Users tend to focus on interesting new products and share links to the ones they want to buy.

4. *Social shopping sites are an open door for entrepreneurs.* Right now, any business owner can use them to build positive word-of-mouth that leads to sales. But you'd better move quickly. Some sites are testing free-use models as they build traffic and will likely adopt paid structures as they reach critical mass, perhaps through revenue generated by marketing agreements with vendors and retailers or by selling the trend information generated by users.

As with any marketing campaign, your first step is to get to know the media. Bookmark your favorite social shopping sites and learn how they work. Test the waters by posting one or two products with their URLs, taking special care to send your click-throughs to specialized landing pages so you can measure your results. Then have fun and stay active—and keep your postings interesting by sharing products others will want to buz about.

Source: Kim T. Gordon, author of Maximum Marketing:
Minimum Dollars: The Top 50 Ways to Grow Your Small Business
and Big Marketing Ideas for Small Budgets

❖ ❖ ❖

CHAPTER 26

The Internet and Your Employees

YOUR INTERNET POLICY

To ensure that your organization does not become a victim of employee internet abuse, it is essential that you not only develop a policy, but that you communicate clearly and frequently what is and is not appropriate internet and e-mail use. You policy and employee communications should cover the following points.

- All messages created, sent, or retrieved over the internet are the property of the company, and should be considered public information.
- The company reserves the right to access and monitor all messages and files on the computer system.
- Employees who access the internet or use company e-mail are representing the company. All communication should be for professional purposes and conducted in an ethical and lawful manner.

- The company internet access point should not be used for personal gain or advancement or to promote personal beliefs or agendas.
- Use of the internet should not interfere with the employee's work or productivity.
- Information published on the internet should not violate or infringe upon the rights of others. No abusive, profane, or offensive language should be transmitted through the system.
- Employees should not be allowed to access or transmit material of a sexual nature including jokes, stories, cartoons, and photographs.
- Harassment of any kind should be prohibited. No messages with derogatory or inflammatory remarks about an individuals or groups race, religion, national origin, or physical disability should be permitted.

- To prevent computer viruses from being transmitted through the system, there should be no unauthorized downloading of any software.
- Violations of any of the above guidelines will result in disciplinary action up to and including discharge.

A written copy of the policy should be given to each employee who should sign an acknowledgment that he or she has read and understands it. This signed acknowledgment should be placed in the employee's personnel file.

Source: D. Allen Miller, Business Advantage International, Inc.

FIVE WAYS TO KEEP EMPLOYEES IN LINE WHILE THEY'RE ONLINE

1. Establish a written internet policy that prohibits employees from using company computer assets to visit inappropriate sites, or upload or download objectionable material from the internet.
2. Clearly communicate the fact that the organization's computer resources are not to be wasted, and are to be used strictly for approved business purposes.
3. Enforce cyberlanguage and content guidelines designed to keep net copy clean and clear.
4. Don't leave compliance to chance. Back up your internet policy with monitoring and filtering software.
5. Don't expect your employees to train themselves. Reinforce your internet policy with on-going employee education.

Excerpted from The ePolicy Handbook ©2001, *Nancy Flynn, Executive Director, The ePolicy Institute.*

E-MAIL CAN BE EVIDENCE

If you thought the "e" in e-mail stood for "electronic," wise up. Nowadays, good old e-mail is likely to be "evidence" if you, your company, or any of your employees is the target of a legal attack.

That's the lesson being hammered home across the country over the past few years, beginning with Bill Gates's televised failures to recall embarrassing e-mail dredged up during Microsoft's antitrust hearings. Gates and Microsoft escaped that incident without serious damage, but the costs of failure to police e-mail are going up. In 2003, for instance, a manager at a Wall Street investment firm was sentenced to one to three years in jail, fined $400,000, and barred from the securities industry for life for destroying e-mail sought by prosecutors in a trading scandal.

Your chances of being caught in a similar trap are going up, too. In a 2001 survey conducted by the ePolicy Institute—an education and research organization—9 percent of U.S. companies reported being ordered by a court or regulator to cough up e-mail. In 2003, the same survey found the number had risen to 14 percent. "E-mail has become a real target of almost every type of business litigation," says Michael R. Overly, an attorney with Foley & Lardner in Los Angeles and author of *E-Policy: How to Develop Computer, E-mail, and Internet Guidelines to Protect Your Company and Its Assets* (AMACOM).

Unfortunately, e-mail presents a daunting challenge for entrepreneurs. The problem starts with its image. Many people treat e-mail as if it were casual and informal, when it is anything but. It may not carry a company letterhead or a signature, but e-mail has the same legal weight as any memo, letter, report, or other written document your company prepares. "It's when people forget that they have the same responsibilities as when they were negotiating a contract that they run into trouble," says Stephen Northcutt, director of training and certification for The SANS Institute, a Bethesda, Maryland, computer security organization.

E-mail also seems less permanent than other written communication, but it may be more permanent than printed documents, warns Rick Edvalson, president of IntegriNet Solutions LLC, a Boise, Idaho, computer services firm. Copies of e-mail are created on your computer and recipients' computers as well as on any mail-server computers that relay the mail. Some copies will be backed up to tape and stored indefinitely. "They acquire an eternal life of their own," says Edvalson.

Any of those e-mail messages could become key evidence in civil or criminal litigation involving your firm. What to do? Experts recommend three steps:

1. *Have a written e-mail policy.* It should govern what can be said in e-mail as well as how long e-mail is to be kept. SANS Institute guidelines suggest keeping e-mail on administrative and financial matters for four years and general correspondence for one year. "Ephemeral correspondence," such as personal messages and status reports, can be destroyed after reading. See a sample policy at www.sans.org.

2. *Train employees in the use of the policy.* For instance, teach them to categorize e-mail as administrative, financial, or other with a line at the top of the message, making it easier to sort and dispose of e-mail as appropriate. Explain the purpose of the policy as well as penalties for failure to follow it.

3. *Enforce those penalties.* Twenty-two percent of companies surveyed by the ePolicy Institute said they had fired people for failing to follow company e-mail policy. Such enforcement may convince a judge or jury that you tried to control your e-mail in good faith, and save you embarrassment or worse.

Whatever you do, don't forget that e-mail can be evidence. "E-mail is a document like any other," says Edvalson. "These files are not benign and innocuous. They carry meaning and importance that can affect the well-being of the company."

Source: Mark Henricks, "Watch Your Back," Entrepreneur.com

⚜ ⚜ ⚜

MANAGEMENT TIP

Stress to your employees that e-mail is not a private form of communication. It's more like a postcard that anyone can read than a letter in a sealed envelope.

MAKE SURE YOUR E-MAIL IS READ AND RETAINED, NOT IGNORED AND DELETED

Are your electronic sales letters doing a good job of opening prospects' doors and closing sales? Or is your e-mail being ignored (or worse yet deleted) before it is read?

The experts at The ePolicy Institute (www.ePolicy Institute.com) offer tips for business writers eager to produce super-effective electronic sales letters.

Write a subject line with OOMPH.
A small but powerful weapon in the battle to capture reader attention, the subject line should reveal what the e-message is about before it's opened. "Attracting and Retaining Top Performers," for example, says more than "Employee Benefits."

Never begin with thank you.
You only have a few seconds to grab the reader's attention. Start strong. Make your point in the first few words of your e-mail, then repeat, rephrase, and reiterate.

Write as though mom were reading
Don't write anything you wouldn't feel comfortable saying in an elevator crowded with customers, colleagues, and competitors. An inaccurate keystroke or the recipient's decision to forward your message could land it on thousands of unintended readers' screens.

Obey the rules of e-etiquette.
No shouting. No flaming. No spamming. Translation: Don't write in capital letters. Don't send hostile messages. Don't forward electronic junk mail.

Remain gender neutral.
Your intended reader may be male, but the ultimate decision-maker could be a woman. Avoid masculine pronouns and other "turn-off" language.

TIPS FOR DEALING WITH JUNK E-MAIL

Spam—the electronic equivalent of junk mail—is more than a nuisance. Sorting through it can reduce productivity and cost you time; some spam messages carry malicious programs that can damage your computer or allow hackers to access your system; if you get too much spam, you might miss legitimate e-mail, such as customer correspondence.

Some tips for dealing with spam:

- *Don't just delete it.* That sounds easy enough, but it's better to use filtering tools to block spam before it ever gets into your inbox. Most e-mail programs have spam filters and you can supplement those with additional spam-blocking programs.

- *Instruct employees on how to use anti-spam software and set guidelines for when they can use their company e-mail addresses to buy products or register for services online.* Remind them to report surges in spam to a designated person.

- *Use disposable addresses.* Create an account in an e-mail program that will allow you to forward mail to your permanent address. Use that address when signing up for various online offers. When the volume of spam to the disposable address gets too heavy, delete it and create a new one. Only use your permanent address for mail from individuals and companies you know and trust.

- Avoid posting your address publicly. If you must, you can fool address-mining software by writing it this way: yourname(at)domain.com and telling people to replace the (at) with @.

Inquire about attachments.

Some companies prohibit the opening of attachments. Always ask if the recipient would prefer receiving material as an attachment or as part of the e-letter itself.

Resist the urge to CAPITALIZE!!!

The eye is accustomed to reading a mix of upper and lowercase letters, so stick with standard style. Don't slap exclamation points on the end of sentences!!! Instead, pump up your writing with descriptive language and well-crafted sentences.

Don't use e-mail to deliver bad news.

Without the benefit of body language, facial expressions, or intonation, e-mail is no way to deliver bad news. Meet or use the phone to notify a customer of production delays, reject a prospect's credit application, or fire an employee.

Acknowledge e-mail's limitations.

E-mail is the best way to deliver news fast, but it's not the best route to a quick reply. Your reader is under no obligation to check in-coming messages regularly, if at all. For an immediate reply to a pressing issue, opt for a phone call or meeting.

CONSIDER ALLOWING PERSONAL INTERNET USE AT WORK

Certainly you don't want employees spending all day doing personal online shopping, playing games, and exploring social network sites, but consider that an employee who spends 20 or 30 minutes handling personal business on the office computer may not need to take time off during the business day to deal with those chores out of the office or on the phone. Let your policies reflect reality.

DEALING WITH INFORMATION OVERLOAD

The information age has spawned its own problem: information overload. Try the following tips for managing today's information flood.

- *Schedule appointments with yourself to deal with incoming information.* Set aside time in the morning and the afternoon to deal with your paper mail, e-mail, and voice messages. You know how long it typically takes you to handle what comes in, so split that time in half, and physically schedule two appointments with yourself each day on your calendar to manage the information.

- *Read while you hold.* Spending time on hold when trying to complete telephone calls is a big time-waster, but you can turn it into a productivity tool if you keep a pile of articles you've been "meaning to read" nearby. Five minutes per day equals 2.5 reading days per year.

- *Schedule your mail handling.* Establish a time each day to deal with incoming mail—don't drop everything when the mail arrives. Don't let low-priority mail interfere with high-priority tasks; instead, save the mail for a quiet time in the afternoon when your energy and productivity levels are down.

- *Purge your flow of inbound information.* For one month, track every report, subscription, and memo distribution list you're on. At the end of the month, go through the list and decide what you need to continue receiving, what should be discontinued, and what should be routed to someone else.

- *Travelers' tip:* Make an appointment with yourself the day after returning from a trip. Give yourself three to four hours to go through accumulated mail and messages and "deal with your desk."

- *Keep your files thin.* Don't retain copies of minutes, reports, and correspondence if someone in the office also has a copy filed. Note a throw-out date on all paperwork before filing so it can be readily tossed when you purge your files. And file documents digitally whenever possible.

- *Set up a central location for information and maintain reports and other research there.* It's not necessary for everyone to have a personal copy of everything.

- *Use voice mail effectively.* Leave detailed messages so the person you are calling can gather necessary information for an accurate response when returning your call.

- *Set policies to control information-generation.* Instruct employees to only send material to the appropriate people and to avoid generating unnecessary correspondence. Resist duplicating communications unless absolutely necessary. Finally, be concise and purposeful; keep your communications brief and to-the-point, and be sure everyone in your organization follows your example.

DEALING WITH E-MAIL HARASSMENT

The overwhelming majority of cases of e-mail harassment occur due to a breakdown in a personal relationship between the parties. In many cases, senders will identify themselves and clearly state the reason behind the activity, which may include threats.

If an employee becomes the target of e-mail harassment, it should be reported to a manager so the situation can be evaluated. If you have any reason to suspect that the safety of your employees or any other person is at risk, contact your local law enforcement agency immediately.

BRAINSTORMING VIA E-MAIL

Many years before e-mail was invented, Dr. C.C. Crawford came up with a clever way to generate good ideas on a topic. He had one person write an idea down, then hand the paper to another person, who added an idea of their own and passed it along. No talking was permitted because that tended to inhibit people's creativity. As a slip of paper circulated in a room, each person's idea inspired new ideas in the others until a large volume of interesting ideas was generated. While effective, this joint brainstorming method is rarely used because it can be a hassle to get a group of people together and have them all sit silently around a conference table jotting ideas on slips of paper and then passing them along. Most employees grumble when subjected to the rules of this method.

Enter modern e-mail. E-mail systems naturally make the Crawford process possible without any extra effort or hassle. All you have to do is to send an e-mail saying, "I need some ideas about X. Please jot down any ideas that occur to you, regardless of their quality, since one idea can lead to another. Then forward this to the next person on the list. When they have added their thoughts, they can forward it to the next person, and so on until it comes back to me. Thanks for your help." Add a list of all the people you want to include in your virtual thinking session and the e-mail will zip electronically through the list and eventually come back to you, having accumulated comments and ideas from everyone. If need be, you can circulate it another time for more ideas.

When you adapt Dr. Crawford's method to e-mail it becomes so quick and easy to solicit ideas and pass them along that there is no reason you can't do it any time you need a little creative input.

Source: Making Horses Drink: How to Lead and Succeed in Business *by Alex Hiam (Entrepreneur Press, 2002)*

WHEN YOU'RE THE TARGET OF AN ANTI-EMPLOYER WEB SITE

Just about everything is available on the internet these days—including web sites that criticize companies, promote litigation against employers, or support union organization attempts. So what should you do when an anti-employer web site is targeting your company?

First, don't panic. There is a natural tendency—because of the newness of the internet—to overreact to the situation and believe such a web site will be more problematic than it actually is. Stop and assess the situation calmly. Take a thorough tour of the site. Study the information presented; consider how it's presented; check to see what other sites are linked to this site; try to identify the individual or organization behind the site. For example, the site may be sponsored by a union that is trying to organize your workers. It may be the work of a consumer or environmental group that doesn't like something your company is doing. Or it may be the product of a disgruntled employee (either former or current) trying to incite further discontent.

Once you've completely examined the site, you can make a determination of what its impact might be and how—or even if—you want to respond. You may decide that the site is not going to affect your company from either an employee or customer perspective. When you come to that conclusion, you might very well decide that there are better uses of your time than reacting.

If you do decide some action is necessary, keep the following in mind.

- *You don't need to respond via the same medium.* For example, if the web site is targeting your employees with anti-company messages, you can communicate with them in any number of ways, such as personal meetings (either one-on-one or group) and correspondence (letters, newsletters, bulletin board announcements). Similarly, you can probably also reach your customer and supplier bases much more quickly and more efficiently using other communication tools.

- *Be cautious about contacting the web site operator.* Anything you send to the web site may well end up posted on that site, so don't provide additional fuel for their position.

- *Remember the First Amendment.* The content of most anti-company web sites is protected as free speech, unless it includes defamation, false advertising, or trademark or copyright infringement. If you think you may have a legitimate legal claim, consult an attorney before taking any action on your own.

You may be tempted to try to get the web site shut down, but that's usually not the best idea. It indicates that you have something to hide. You're better off dealing with the issues the site raises.

On the positive side, such sites give you a tremendous amount of information on what your adversaries are doing, what they consider to be key issues, and the arguments they are advancing. So whether or not you decide to take action, it's a good idea to monitor such sites regularly.

⚜ ⚜ ⚜

PROTECTING YOUR BUSINESS

There are times when it feels like, as a business owner, you have a target on your back and everyone is aiming at it. The key to protecting your business, your people, your property, and yourself is to be proactive. Understand what your risks are and take steps to manage them.

❧ ❧ ❧

CHAPTER 27

Risk Management, Insurance, and Disaster Preparedness

YOU CAN'T ELIMINATE RISK, SO MANAGE IT

Recognizing the risks in all areas of your business—management, marketing, contracts, personnel, and the particular ramifications of your product or service on customers and the market—is the first step in effective risk management. Follow the steps outlined below before talking to an insurance representative about the type of coverage you need for your business:

- Make a list of the risks your business faces.
- Evaluate your liabilities from your customers' point of view.
- Chart the customers' path as they come into contact with your shop—across the sidewalk, through the door, under the ceiling fan, up to your counter, and so on.

After identifying the risks, estimate the probability of financial loss in the various situations that could go wrong. Develop a worst-case scenario and put a price tag on it: shop damage,

employee injuries, harm to a customer because of your product or service. Next, determine the most economical way to handle the possible losses, considering the following avenues:

Assumption means assuming the risk and the accompanying financial burdens.

Sometimes absorbing a risk is prudent. If you're a one-person graphic-design business, no employees are going to be injured on the job. Nor are you likely to be sued for personal injury if clients infrequently visit your office. However, if you own a bakery that employs 30 people, you'd best not assume any risks pertaining to employees getting injured on the job or a customer tossing their cookies because of eating one of yours.

Avoidance means removing the cause of risk

If a caustic material is making employees hesitant and fearful, replace it with a nonhazardous substance. The cost is small compared to what you'd pay if an accident happened. An organized company-safety program that implements suggestions from employees and insurance safety representatives can also help eliminate potentially dangerous situations in your business.

Loss reduction is the transfer of the risk to another party altogether

When your own delivery service has problems—tardiness, damaged goods, mechanical breakdowns, and employee hassles—consider contracting a delivery service to take all the headaches away. Similar circumstances include contracting for maintenance, electrical, plumbing, carpentry, bookkeeping, landscaping, and security. To contract out these responsibilities is to buy a form of insurance—you have shifted the risk and responsibility to another party for a negotiated fee.

However, shifting the risk and responsibility doesn't necessarily shift the liability. When the new landscaping crew improperly installs a sprinkler head causing water damage to the inside of a nearby Jaguar, you can hold the landscaping firm liable, but the man who falls into the cactus plant by your front office and injures himself will hold you liable for planting it there. Know what your potential liabilities are and make sure you're covered.

Self-insurance entails setting aside a specified amount of money each year to cover any losses incurred. The owner holds the cash in a reserve fund, rather than paying premiums to an insurance company. In practice, this is risky for small firms that could experience a large loss. If the reserve fund is not large enough to cover the loss, the company will be sunk. A growing business with several geographically diverse units is more suited for self-insurance, as are big nonprofit organizations like school systems.

All of the above can be used to offset some of the risks a business faces. However, some areas of risk require the transfer of that risk through insurance, to make sure your business is protected and not overly exposed. Sound insurance planning requires attention on all fronts. The usual, plain-vanilla insurance packages need to be complemented by additional special coverages relevant to your business. Cover your largest loss exposure first: the lives and health of you and your employees—the most valuable assets your company has.

Source: Entrepreneur.com

CAN YOU AFFORD TO REPLACE IT?1

What will it cost to replace your building, equipment, and furnishings if you experience a covered loss—and will your insurance company pay for all of it? Probably, but check your policy to be sure.

Most commercial policies pay replacement cost coverage, which means the cost to replace the property without a deduction for depreciation, up to the policy limits and, of course, subject to the policy's deductible. The key is to be sure the limits on the policy reflect the current replacement value. Know the extent of your inventory as well as the value of all your furniture, fixtures, and equipment and what it would cost to replace those items in today's dollars.

RISK MANAGEMENT WORKSHEET

While insurance is a must, you can also control your exposure to risk by instituting programs to minimize it. Use the following checklist to get started.

Protecting Proprietary Information

❏ Make sure everyone who sees your secret information is aware that it's secret. Notify partners, customers, suppliers, and employees exposed to proprietary secrets that the material is confidential. Get them to agree not to use it against you or disclose it to anyone without your written permission. Get this in writing; have all parties sign nondisclosure agreements. Stamp documents "Confidential."

❏ Enforce physical security. Put up "No Trespassing" signs, erect fences, lock entrances and exits, hire security guards. Lock your secrets up.

❏ Use employee and visitor identification badges to control access to your business. Establish rules requiring people to sign sensitive documents in and out.

❏ Set up passwords. Use them to access computers, copiers, fax machines, and other machines that could be used to copy or transmit secrets.

❏ When employees leave, take measures to ensure that secrets don't leave with them. Collect sensitive materials from the offices of terminated employees before allowing them to return to their desks. Before they go, remind them of the nondisclosure documents they signed.

General Crime Prevention

❏ Be wary of people who don't appear to belong in or around your business. Ask them questions. If their answers are vague, unconvincing, or suspicious, call the police.

❏ Encourage employees to keep their personal possessions in sight at all times. Don't leave purses of briefcases unattended in public areas or unlocked offices. Things can disappear in a matter of seconds.

❏ Instruct everyone to lock office doors when they step out, even for just a minute.

❏ Install deadbolt locks on external doors. Burglars typically spend no more than a few minutes or even seconds attempting to break into a building. Sturdy, properly installed, deadbolt locks on all external doors are a must.

❏ Have a trustworthy locksmith rekey locks on all new facilities as soon as you move into them.

❏ Install outdoor floodlights to eliminate dark areas where criminals might hide. Make sure parking areas are well-lit.

❏ Never leave the keys in company cars or other vehicles. Have a sign-in board where they can only be picked up by authorized employee. Never leave car doors unlocked.

❏ Join business community groups that have the mission of fighting crime. When companies join together to fight crime, they can make a significant difference.

RISK MANAGEMENT WORKSHEET, continued

Giving Your Business an Insurance Checkup

The following is a list of the common business assets you should consider protecting against damage and loss.

- ❏ Automobiles, trucks, construction equipment, and other mobile property.
- ❏ Buildings you own or lease.
- ❏ Cash and securities.
- ❏ Computer equipment and data storage media.
- ❏ Furniture, equipment, and supplies.
- ❏ Improvements to the premises.
- ❏ Intangibles such as trademarks and good will.
- ❏ Inventory.
- ❏ Leased equipment.
- ❏ Machinery.
- ❏ Outdoor property not attached to a building, such as signs and fences.
- ❏ Records and papers, including accounts receivable, books, and other documents.

Source: Entrepreneur.com

BASIC TYPES OF BUSINESS INSURANCE

Good insurance decisions begin with an understanding of business insurance and what it covers. The basic types include:

General liability and property

If someone is injured using your product or service, or while on your property, your liability coverage pays the damages and funds your legal defense. Property insurance covers your physical assets, such as your building, equipment, furnishings, fixtures, and inventory.

Umbrella policy

These policies provide additional liability coverage after the limits of the underlying policy are reached; essentially, they act as an "umbrella" over your basic policies.

Commercial vehicle

These policies cover the vehicles your business owns and operates. If you or your employees use personal vehicles for business purposes, appropriate coverage may be available through a personal automobile policy, but check with your agent to be sure.

Professional liability

If you provide a professional service, this insurance protects you for negligence and/or errors and omissions that injure your clients.

Directors and officers

Popularly known as D&O, this coverage protects corporate directors and officers for wrongful acts typically described as bad business judgment.

Key man

This insurance pays cash to the company on the death of a key person—usually an owner or senior executive—to help the business deal with the financial impact of the loss and replace those services.

Business interruption

If you are unable to operate due to a covered peril, business-interruption insurance replaces lost income and pays ongoing expenses and is involved in setting up in a temporary facility.

Employment practices

This is a relatively new type of insurance that provides coverage for an employer against claims made by employees, former employees, or potential employees for such actions as discrimination, wrongful termination, sexual harassment, and other employment-related allegations.

Destroyed or damaged records

If your business records—such as accounts receivable—are destroyed or damaged, this coverage compensates you for your inability to collect income as well as the cost of reproducing the records.

Workers' compensation

This is insurance that pays for medical care and physical rehabilitation of injured workers and helps to replace lost wages while they are unable to work. State laws, which vary significantly, govern the amount of benefits paid and other compensation provisions.

It's unlikely that you'll have separate policies for each type of coverage. Most insurers offer a range of package policies designed to cover a range of standard small-business risks. Such packages can save you money—but may also provide coverage you don't need or *not* provide a specific coverage that you do need—read the policy carefully and be sure you know exactly what it does and doesn't cover.

SPECIALTY INSURANCE

Beyond traditional business coverage there is a wide range of specialty products that you may want to consider. You can buy coverage to compensate you for losses due to weather; to cover against damages by flood and earthquake (typically not included in standard property policies); to provide liability for foreign-made products; to cover intellectual property claims; to pay for losses due to internet security failures or damage caused by computer viruses and malicious code.

If you operate internationally, consider foreign accident and health insurance for those employees and their family members traveling outside the United States; political risk insurance; commercial property and marine cargo insurance; kidnap and ransom/extortion insurance; and foreign commercial general liability. If you're not already in the international market but plan to be, start shopping now for international coverage. It's part of building the capacity to go overseas. Keep in mind that while many domestic policies indicate worldwide coverage, it's only worldwide if the suit is brought back to the United States and more and more claims are not being brought back to the U.S. Don't put your business at risk when you enter the global market.

IS YOUR HOMEBASED OPERATION COVERED?

An estimated one in ten U.S. households operates some type of full or part-time homebased business, but nearly 60 percent of them do not have proper business insurance. If you think your homeowner's policy covers your business, think again.

Homeowner's insurance is not designed to cover business exposures. Some policies include limited coverage for business equipment, but do not provide liability or business interruption coverage. That means your homeowner's insurance won't pay if a customer is injured on your property or if theft, accidental damage, or other type of disaster forces you to shut down for a period of time, your income is not protected. Also, you may have other business insurance needs, such as workers' compensation or product liability, which you need to address. To be sure your homebased business is covered, start by checking your homeowner's (or renter's) policy. Ask your insurance agent if endorsements to add business coverage are available.

Homebased businesses have a number of additional insurance options, including a business owner's package policy (BOP), an in-home business owner's policy, or traditional commercial coverage. Your agent can help you analyze your operation and risks, and decide what is most appropriate for you.

WORTH KNOWING

Property insurance policies typically do not cover damage from floods, earthquakes, and acts of terrorism. Talk to your agent about purchasing these coverages separately.

THE DIFFERENCE BETWEEN CANCELLATION AND NONRENEWAL

Canceling an insurance policy means that, at some point during the term of the policy, the insurer terminates your coverage. Once a policy has been in force for 60 days, an insurer can only cancel it if you fail to pay the premium or if you have committed fraud (such as filing a false claim or making misrepresentations on your application).

Nonrenewal means that when the term of the policy expires, it is not renewed. That's a decision either you or the insurer can make. Specific laws vary by state, but in general, insurance companies must give you a certain amount of notice and a reason for nonrenewal.

WHEN TO USE A PUBLIC ADJUSTER

When you buy insurance, the claims process sounds so simple: you suffer a loss, you file a claim, you get your money. The reality can often be more complicated, and it may be to your advantage to hire someone familiar with the claims process to help you—that someone would be a public adjuster.

By definition, a public adjuster represents the policyholder and interacts with the insurance company to assist the policyholder in presenting their claim for insurance benefits. Because claims for business losses are often complex, entrepreneurs may find it worthwhile to delegate the task of handling them, but it's important to have the right public adjuster—one who is experienced with commercial claims, who has handled claims similar to yours, and who has a reputation for honesty and integrity. Be wary of an adjuster who promises more than you are entitled to—the insurance company will likely scrutinize his work more closely, and an inflated claim could lead to charges of insurance fraud.

Public adjusters are listed in the Yellow Pages under "adjusters," but your best bet is to find one through referrals. Ask the insurance company's adjuster who they like to work with. Also ask other business owners for recommendations. Find out how long the adjuster has been in the business, what their claims-handling background is (you want one with substantial claims experience from both the insurance-company side and the policyholder side), and get references. Fees are negotiable and typically based on the amount recovered. They range from 8 to 15 percent, with most being in the 10 to 12 percent range.

Finally, once you've hired an adjuster, don't abdicate all responsibility for the claim. Insist that the adjuster provide you with regular status reports and copies of correspondence, and consults with you as significant events occur.

Do you always need a public adjuster? No. If the claim is simple and straightforward, you'll save money by handling it yourself.

MORE COMPANIES ARE BUYING TERRORISM INSURANCE

Nearly 60 percent of large- and mid-sized U.S. businesses obtained insurance to cover property terrorism risks in 2005—up from 50 percent in 2004 and 27 percent in 2003. Smaller companies (those with total insured values under $100 million) were less likely to purchase this coverage, although nearly half of them did so in 2005. The cost of property terrorism insurance averages 25 percent lower in 2005 than in 2004.

Source: Marsh, Inc.

MAKE YOUR SUPPLIERS' INSURANCE YOUR BUSINESS

If you think insurance is a business decision best made by the company's owner, you're right—to a point. But when that company is your supplier, you just might want to have some input into what type of coverage they have. Generally, you'll be concerned with property insurance (which covers your interest in tangible property) and liability coverage (which protects you in case of a lawsuit). You can use your position as a customer to insist that your suppliers provide you with additional peace of mind through certain types of insurance coverage.

When you are in business, you want to consider the other party's insurance as additional protection. Who buys the insurance is a matter of bargaining power, custom, and practicality. For example, if you buy your product components from a variety of different sources as part of your purchase terms you may want to insist that your suppliers carry liability coverage to protect you should a claim be made based on a product failure due to a specific component. Or if your period of exposure to potential liability or property damage is of limited duration—perhaps because your business is seasonal or event-driven—it may be more practical and customary for the supplier to provide coverage than for you to do so.

Once you've determined that it's appropriate to require your supplier to have specific coverage, there are a number of ways to make sure what you ask for is actually enforced. One is to get a certificate of

---

Once you've determined that it's appropriate to require your supplier to have specific coverage, there are a number of ways to make sure what you ask for is actually enforced.

insurance, which is a document that typically describes the type of coverage a company has. What is actually included on a certificate of insurance can vary by state and carrier. For the most part, all a certificate does is state the coverage that was in force when the certificate was issued, and does not give you any assurance that the coverage will continue in the future, or that the policy will actually pay a claim to your benefit. However, in many cases, your situation will be such that it's appropriate to accept a certificate of insurance. Examine the document for genuineness. It will usually be on a form; check for current dates, a signature, the policy number, duration, and limits. Do you recognize the carrier? Is there any limiting language that might be constricting? Can you verify the information?

A safer approach is to ask your vendors to name you as an additional insured on their policy. In this case, you not only get the benefits of the policy, but you'll be notified if the policy is canceled for any reason. The cost to name someone as an additional insured is nominal and sometimes even free.

BE SURE YOUR TELECOMMUTERS ARE PROPERLY INSURED

More and more employees are heading home to work. If you've decided to reap the benefits of the telecommuting trend, you need also to make sure you're covered from an insurance standpoint. It's possible your existing coverage is sufficient, but you might need to make some changes to be adequately protected. Consider these issues:

- *Workers' compensation.* An employee who sustains an injury while working or during working hours, even though they are in their home, is protected by workers' comp. Develop a system that clearly defines when the employee is considered to be "at work" and when he's not.

- *General liability.* This coverage primarily deals with the issue of people on the premises. Will your telecommuters meet with customers or other business associates in their homes? If so, add their residences as additional locations to your business liability policy.

- *Equipment.* If you have equipment or other business property in the employee's home, you need to make sure it is listed on your business property policy, or that you are willing to accept the risk if it is not insured. You should also have a clear understanding with the employee of what you will and won't be responsible for. For example, you may want to hold the telecommuting employee responsible for damage to equipment that resulted from negligence (such as if a child pours juice on a computer keyboard) but not for events beyond their control (such as a lightning strike or fire).

- *Customer property.* If your employees ever take property belonging to customers to their homes, be sure your insurance agent knows and has provided for that coverage in your policy.

In most telecommuting situations, making sure the employee is properly covered will either not affect your premiums at all, or at worst mean only a small increase.

IN CASE OF EMERGENCY

Many entrepreneurs believe that preparing for disaster is too expensive or time-consuming. But that's not necessarily true, say crisis-management experts. The most important steps for surviving a crisis cost little or nothing. Being unprepared, however, can be the costliest strategy of all.

People First

Every effective disaster-recovery program begins with a simple step, explains John Laye, an adjunct instructor at FEMA's Emergency Management Institute. Companies should hold seminars for employees on how to prepare themselves and their families for potential disasters, and to set up emergency response teams of four or five employees—at least one team for every floor of the building the company occupies—trained in CPR, first aid, basic firefighting, and evacuation procedures. Much of this information and training is available for free from the American Red Cross and local fire departments, Laye adds.

While the fire department is training your personnel in CPR, ask them to visit your office and assess potential hazards and evacuation routes. Then invite the police to come by and evaluate your company's physical security. This has two added benefits: If you ever have a real emergency, firefighters and police will be familiar with the layout of your building; they'll also know the team leaders to contact when they need briefing.

Laye recommends running practice drills twice a year—more often if your business has a high turnover rate—to improve your emergency response teams' ability to go it alone if you are caught in a natural disaster. "In an earthquake or tornado, this practice really pays off because the fire department isn't coming," says Laye.

Business Second

"Gather your managers in some quiet place and say 'OK, you come to work one morning and, for whatever reason, the building is wrapped in yellow caution tape and you can't get in,'" says Laye. "Ask them 'Who are your key people, and what do they need to keep the business running?'" Laye adds that key employees aren't always the top executives—at insurance companies, for example, some of the most important people work in the mailroom. The next step? Ask your managers to predict what could go wrong and how the company should respond in each case.

After the initial meetings, establish a crisis-management team, selecting members with expertise in all areas of the company. Unlike the emergency response teams, which serve to ensure employee safety, the crisis team deals with the aftermath of the event—how to keep the business going and back to normal as quickly as possible.

Communication, Always

After a disaster strikes, the crisis team's first job is communication—especially spreading the word to employees about the event and how the company plans to deal with it. This can be as simple as a pre-recorded message on a toll-free number that tells people not to show up that day, or as complex as an automated system that calls members of a facility's emergency crew and asks a series of questions to evaluate their fitness for duty.

At least one-fourth of all businesses that close because of a disaster never reopen.

Source: Institute for Business and Home Safety

FAST FACT

Businesses also need to assure customers, suppliers, shareholders, and the local community that the company is intact and the situation is in hand.

The most important part of surviving any kind of disaster is to make it a "rehearsed event," says Laye.

Create a plan, then practice it until you have your response down cold.

Source: Daniel Tynan, "In Case of Emergency," Enterpreneur.com

---

EMERGENCY RESOURCE CENTERS

American Red Cross
www.redcross.org
The American Red Cross offers domestic disaster relief and services in five areas: community services that help the needy; support and comfort for military members and their families; the collection, processing, and distribution of life-saving blood and blood products; education programs that promote health and safety; and international relief and development programs.

DisasterHelp
www.disasterhelp.gov
This web site is part of the President's Disaster Management Egov Initiative–a larger initiative aimed at greatly enhancing Disaster Management on an interagency and intergovernmental basis.

Emergency Preparedness Information Exchange (EPIX)
epix.hazard.net
The purpose of EPIX is to facilitate the exchange of ideas and information among Canadian and international public and private sector organizations about the prevention of, preparation for, recovery from, and/or mitigation of risk associated with natural and socio-technological disasters.

Federal Emergency Management Agency (FEMA)
www.fema.gov
FEMA is tasked with responding to, planning for, recovering from, and mitigating against disasters.

Institute for Business & Home Safety (IBHS)
www.ibhs.org/business_protection
IBHS is a nonprofit association that engages in communication, education, engineering, and research. Its mission is to reduce deaths, injuries, property damage, economic losses, and human suffering caused by natural disasters.

Ready.gov
www.ready.gov
Ready.gov is a commonsense framework designed to launch a process of learning about citizen preparedness. The site includes information for businesses, individuals, and youngsters.

U.S. Department of Housing and Urban Development (HUD)
www.hud.gov
HUD can provide critical housing and community development resources to aid disaster recovery. HUD's disaster recovery teams are located in offices throughout the country.

❧ ❧ ❧

CHAPTER 28

Lawsuits, Litigation, and Other Legal Issues

KEEP YOUR COMPANY IN COMPLIANCE

If you're in business, you're expected to comply with various government requirements. And being subject to regulation means you're also subject to periodic compliance inspections by the appropriate agency.

"Obviously, it's better to be in compliance before a government audit," says Jon Miller, a labor and employment law attorney with Berger, Kahn, Shafton, Moss, Figler, Simon & Gladstone in Irvine, California. "Some government-agency audits may uncover minor violations, which simply lead to a formal order or informal request for modifications. Others may uncover substantial violations, which can threaten the very existence of a business with [corporate] fines and, in some instances, may even involve a threat of [individual] fines or jail time for managers and owners."

Depending on your specific industry, you may need to comply with certain safety regulations, record-keeping requirements, environmental-protection procedures, professional-certification requirements and other operational practices. If you have even one employee, there are a variety of state and federal employment regulations you must follow. The more employees you have, the greater the number of regulations that apply. So the very first step in setting up your own internal compliance audit program is to thoroughly understand all of the various regulations applying to your business.

Join local and national trade and professional organizations related to your industry. They'll help you stay up-to-date on changes, provide education, and be a vehicle for you to network with other individuals who do what you do. You should also contact the regulatory agencies that have jurisdiction over your operation for guidance on compliance issues.

The process is more complicated when it comes to employment regulations. Many states have a clearinghouse for employment-related information; start with your state's department of labor. Also, federal regulations aren't in one place, and that makes getting and staying in compliance a challenge. Take the time to do the research yourself, retain a consultant or labor attorney to do it for you, or hire a staff person to manage compliance issues.

Once you figure out what you need to do, conduct an internal audit to see where you're complying and where you're not, then put together a plan to correct any shortcomings. Your audit should also verify whether you're complying with your own internal policies—just because you made the rules, doesn't mean you can disregard them whenever you feel like it. For example, if your policy requires you to follow a particular protocol before firing an employee, yet you fail to do that, you're setting yourself up for a wrongful-termination lawsuit—even though you may not have violated state or federal laws.

In developing your compliance program, keep in mind that you probably won't be able to correct everything immediately. Set realistic priorities and make incremental corrections. Create a checklist and periodically review it. Make sure it covers the important issues in each regulatory category. How often you need to conduct audits depends on the size of your company, how quickly it's growing, and your industry's regulatory requirements.

Finally, keep in mind that compliance audits can be more than protective devices; they can also double as marketing and recruiting tools. They send a positive message to customers, prospective employees, and the general public by reminding them that you not only know what you're supposed to do, you actually do it.

STAY ON THE RIGHT SIDE OF CONSUMER PROTECTION LAWS

There are several legal issues that small-business owners should consider addressing when it comes to customer interaction. These include advertising, retail pricing and return policies, warranties, and consumer protection laws. Here's a brief rundown:

Advertising

The Federal Trade Commission (FTC) is the national agency that governs compliance with the laws of advertising. Generally the FTC may take action in cases of false or deceptive advertising. State and local governments, individual consumers and competitors may also take action against a business that violates advertising laws.

Action by government agencies against violators usually begins with an attempt to persuade the business found to be in violation to take voluntary action. If that attempt is unsuccessful, the government can issue a cease-and-desist order, bring a civil lawsuit, seek a court injunction to stop a questionable ad, and even require the violator to run corrective ads that admit an earlier ad was deceptive. Some states even have laws that provide for criminal penalties such as fines and jail terms for violators, but the latter is a rare occurrence.

Advertising Compliance

Stay out of trouble by following some basic rules:

- Don't promise more than a product will deliver. If a product will remove some but not all types of stains, list only those on which your product will work.
- Be sure the visual image you show in your ad truly reflects what you're selling.
- If you're using someone's picture or written endorsement or quoting from someone's copyrighted work, be sure you get his or her permission in writing.

- Don't knock your competitors.
- Have sufficient quantities of advertised items in stock or state that "Quantities are limited."
- Be careful about advertising something as "free."
- If you advertise credit terms, you should provide all details such as down payment amount, terms of repayment, annual interest rate, and so on.

Product Pricing and Return Policies

- Using vocabulary such as "regular" or "reduced" prices is fine if you can prove that you offered the merchandise at a particular price for a specified period of time before "reducing" it.
- If you offer merchandise for sale at a price that's higher than $25 at a location other than your normal place of business—such as at a flea market or a business expo—you should give customers a written receipt or copy of the sales contract and a notice of their right to cancel the sale within three days.
- Other than the "three-day rule," the law does not require you to give any refunds on sales, but you may want to do so anyway to promote good customer relations. If you have a refund policy, you should post the written policy conspicuously in your location.
- If you do business by mail order, you need to become familiar with the FTC's mail order rule.

Warranties

There are two basic types of warranty: express and implied. Both federal and state laws may enforce warranties. Services as well as products can be warranted.

- Express warranties are statements or promises about a product or about a promise to correct defects or malfunctions in a product, and can be either oral or in writing. Of course, merely giving an opinion or praising a product is not a warranty. For example, "You look good in that," or "I think you're really going to be satisfied with this shampoo" aren't warranties.
- Written warranties don't need to be called a warranty or be part of a formal written contract to be legally treated as one. Any statements in product literature or in advertisements may be considered a warranty.
- Implied warranties don't stem from anything said either orally or in writing or anything done by the seller. They're automatically assumed whenever a product is sold—for example, it's assumed a lawnmower will cut grass that's four inches tall or less.

These implied warranties automatically guarantee that the product is fit for ordinary use and any special uses of which the seller is aware.

Breach of Warranty

Who's liable if a customer buys a product from you and the product fails to live up to the warranty? Sometimes the manufacturer, sometimes the retailer, sometimes both. Who's liable is in part determined by who made the warranty to begin with and how much the retailer was involved in helping the customer to select the product. This is a complicated legal area and requires competent legal advice.

Consumer Protection Statutes

Remember that consumers have a great deal of clout these days and they can sue not only to recover the cost of actual loss but also, in some cases, to recover additional punitive damages even if the violation isn't proved to be intentional on the seller's part.

A wise retailer will conduct an audit of potential and actual practices and now pay for competent legal advice to prevent having to pay for legal advice after someone files suit.

Source: Carlotta Roberts, "What You Need to Know About Consumer Protection Laws," Entrepreneur.com

YOUR CONTRACTS CAN KEEP YOU OUT OF COURT

The civil lawsuit industry is costing individuals, professionals, and businesses in the United States billions of dollars every year. The fear of being sued has invaded every aspect of our lives. For more than half a century, the courts have consistently agreed that parties to a contract can decide the process by which any disputes under the contract are to be resolved. Resolving disagreements can be built right into the terms of agreement at the beginning of the relationship, long before any dispute arises. On the other hand, any contract that is silent on dispute resolution invites the parties to sue one another in court.

It works like a champ. If you place a provision in your contracts that requires the parties to arbitrate any dispute under the contract, there is a 99.5 percent chance that the dispute will never see the inside of a courtroom. Federal and state courts have consistently upheld this principle.

The dispute resolution advantages available through simple contract provisions are truly extraordinary. There is no more powerful tool available for avoiding the courthouse, and it is surprisingly underused by most businesses and professionals.

Many of my own clients have found success with a three-tiered provision that first requires the parties to negotiate in good faith. Then, if they cannot resolve the dispute, it will be submitted to nonbinding mediation with a professional mediator acceptable to both sides. If it still cannot be resolved, it will be submitted to binding arbitration with an arbitrator selected mutually by both parties.

Source: Stay Out of Court! The Small Business Guide to Preventing Disputes and Avoiding Lawsuit Hell *by Andrew A. Caffey (Entrepreneur Press, 2005)*

PRESIDENTS IN A BOTTLE

One Baltimore lawyer is well known for a unique contract provision that offers an unusual insight into the value—and the means—of avoiding litigation. If a dispute arises under the contract, she requires the two presidents of the contracting parties to spend not less than two hours in a face-to-face meeting discussing nothing other than the dispute. After that time together, if the dispute still exists, either party is free to file a court action. Not only does this provision immediately stop the early and mindless shovel pass to the lawyers, but it keeps the parties-in-interest involved in the decision making for as long as possible. And what president is going to have the patience and passion to discuss a dispute for two hours with another businessperson and not find mutually acceptable grounds for settlement? She hasn't yet seen her clients in court.

Source: Stay Out of Court! The Small Business Guide to Preventing Disputes and Avoiding Lawsuit Hell *by Andrew A. Caffey (Entrepreneur Press, 2005)*

ALTERNATIVE DISPUTE RESOLUTION ORGANIZATIONS

American Arbitration Association
800-778-7879
www.adr.org

International Institute for Conflict Prevention and Resolution
212-949-6490
www.cpradr.org

JAMS, The Resolution Experts
800-352-5267
www.jamsadr.com

YOU CAN FIRE YOUR ATTORNEY

Remember that you are the boss when it comes to your attorney. You can fire your attorney at any time. If you are not satisfied with the work your attorney is doing for you, you are entitled to terminate his or her services; however, you must pay for services rendered up to the date of termination.

It's common for problems between attorneys and clients to be due to poor communications. Let your attorney know if you are not pleased and try to reach a solution before taking further action. If your attorney has appeared in court on your behalf and the case is pending, a judge may have to approve the decision to remove the attorney from the case.

DEVELOP AN ACCOUNTABILITY MINDSET TO AVOID AND RESOLVE DISPUTES

- *Evaluate your organization to determine where you may be vulnerable to disputes that can lead to litigation.* Involve your board of directors and your employees in the review, and be prepared to take responsive action when weaknesses are identified.
- *Take steps* today *to address your conflict management and negotiation skills.* Is your level of training where it should be? If not, line up training to improve your organization's skill levels, and set a high standard to be met by all staff.
- *Take the time to create a conflict resolution program that everyone in the organization will buy into.* Adopt an internal ombuds program or other informal procedure so that employees have somewhere to turn besides the courts. Identify organizations to which you will turn when you need ADR (alternative dispute resolution) assistance. Find a mediator who knows your business *before* you need the service.
- *Review your contracts.* Do you require disputes under the contract to be negotiated, mediated, and arbitrated before anyone can go to court? Are there other provisions that protect not only your legal rights but also your exposure to lawsuits?
- *Do you teach and promote accountability as part of your personal approach to your profession and/or business?*

Source: Stay Out of Court! The Small Business Guide to Preventing Disputes and Avoiding Lawsuit Hell *by Andrew A. Caffey (Entrepreneur Press, 2005)*

INCLUDE A VENUE PROVISION IN YOUR CONTRACTS

When there's a dispute over a contract, it's not uncommon for the parties to land in court—the question is, which court? If you're doing business with customers and suppliers outside your local area, you could find yourself involved in a courtroom battle being waged hundreds or even thousands of miles away. Most states have basic venue statutes, which provide that, in the absence of a contract stipulating otherwise, lawsuits be filed in one of three places: the county in which the contract was entered into, where the defendant resides, or where the cause of action (the breach of contract) occurred. But these statutes may not always work to your advantage. Also, though you may be able to change the venue after a legal proceeding has begun, that process will only delay getting the real dispute settled. That's why it's a good idea to address the issue of venue in your contract, long before a problem arises.

In addition to selecting the location of a possible lawsuit, you also need to specify what court—state or federal—will have jurisdiction. Generally, state court is less expensive, faster, and more user-friendly than federal court.

Another important provision is choice of law. This means you should decide in advance which state's laws will apply, keeping in mind that laws regarding various aspects of commerce can vary significantly by state. Typically, the choice of law matches the venue.

Your venue clause does not have to be lengthy or complex; it should simply state the location (county), jurisdiction (court), and state law that will apply in the event of a dispute or breach of contract. If the other party objects to your venue clause, of if you are asked to sign a contract and you object to the venue clause, work toward a resolution in your negotiation process, get legal counsel, and make your final decision based on what is best for your company.

GREAT ADVICE

Instead of the traditional holiday party, avoid the potential for liability with an alternative celebration. Consider giving employees a half-day off to shop (with or without a store gift card) or a restaurant gift card.

TIPS TO AVOID HOLIDAY LAWSUITS

- *Double-check the legalities of your company's sexual harassment policy.* Anytime a company pays for an event, whether it's on or off site, it's considered a company-sponsored event and is covered by the company's harassment policy. This includes lunches, cocktail hours, and other forms of entertainment that can be paid for with the company credit card. Even if the company isn't covering the expenses, the event can still fall under the umbrella of scrutiny if business is being discussed. Make sure your policy clearly defines harassment behavior and covers any outside events.

- *Make sure the insurance policy covers employee injuries at events.* This is especially true if employees are required to attend. Employers are responsible for any injuries that occur at a company-sponsored event.

- *Assign someone to be responsible for monitoring inappropriate behavior.* A manager or other responsible employee can watch for signs of inappropriate behavior and prevent uncomfortable situations before they happen or get out of control. Having an appointed person can also take the pressure away from other employees who may not want to get involved in a sticky situation.

- *Extend the employee party to include spouses and children.* Changing an event from a drinking and partying atmosphere to a family-oriented one creates an environment where inappropriate behavior rarely occurs.

- *Limit alcohol consumption.* Alcohol consumption clearly gives rise to all kinds of incidences. Ways to prevent over-intoxication include serving beer over hard liquor whenever possible; providing drink tickets to limit employees to a maximum number of alcoholic beverages (generally two or three); and have professionals serve the alcohol.

- *Provide a car service to ensure all employees get home safely.* Anything that happens to an employee between the time they leave your event until they reach home can create liability for you. Provide a car service regardless of what an employee has consumed so that everyone is comfortable using it.

STAND UP AGAINST SHAKEDOWNS

A growing wave of shakedown lawsuits hitting small businesses nationwide are costing a cumulative $88 billion per year in settlements and attorney fees. In some cases, businesses have been forced to lay off employees and even close their doors as litigation continues to spiral out of control, rivaling baseball as America's favorite pastime.

Although dealing with a frivolous lawsuit can be pricey for entrepreneurs in terms of both time and money, the bigger problem arising from the many shakedown lawsuits that have hit the courts in greater numbers recently is that these affect all small-business owners in the form of higher insurance rates, which increases the cost of goods and services.

As an increasing number of small businesses fall prey to predatory law suits, more and more are getting wise and looking to partner with lawsuit abuse and reform organizations throughout the country. But what else can be done to help stop the problem before it affects your small business? Here are a few tips:

- Make sure you're adequately covered with the right type and amount of insurance.
- Post any necessary warnings about safety issues.
- Stay on top of all necessary business codes and regulations.

- Attorneys and groups fighting frivolous lawsuits suggest voting for politicians who advocate tort reform.

- If you are sued, don't panic or make any hasty decisions—plaintiffs and their attorneys are often seeking a quick buck and may simply move on to someone else if you don't respond immediately.

- Research the law firm suing you to find out if they have a history of similar frivolous lawsuits. If they do, contact the office of the attorney general in your state.

- Create, print, and distribute an employee manual that includes all company rules, guidelines, and regulations for your employees. Make sure you include sections on what constitutes grounds for dismissal as well as what's considered inappropriate behavior. Have each employee sign a form acknowledging that he or she has received the employee manual.

Do what you can to protect your business, but remember that someone who's determined to sue will do so simply because they can.

Source: Rich Mintzer, "Standing Strong Against Business Shakedowns," Entrepreneur.com

COMMON SMALL BUSINESS LEGAL MISTAKES

- Not using good written contracts
- Ignorance of the law
- Failing to maintain good business records
- Not providing employees with clear expectations and policies
- Getting involved in avoidable litigation
- Ignoring intellectual property rights and issues
- Not retaining an experienced lawyer when needed

PROTECT YOURSELF AGAINST PROFESSIONAL VICTIMS

Some scam artists make a career out of faking injuries and trying to get a settlement. These people typically target businesses with high customer traffic and inexperienced employees, such as grocery stores, fast-food restaurants, convenience stores, theaters, and pet shops. Some cruise from business to business, looking for an extension cord stretched across an aisle, a top-heavy stack of boxes, or a wet floor with no warning sign. Others create a hazard, spilling soap on a restroom floor or grapes in the produce aisle. Then, just like a stunt double who knows how not to get hurt, they fake a fall or pull boxes down on top of themselves. After employees come to the rescue, the person's next move is probably a letter to your insurance company demanding compensation. According to the National Insurance Crime Bureau, 10 percent of all insurance claims are fraudulent. After reviewing medical documentation of the "head injury" or "sciatic nerve damage"—typically soft tissue injuries that a good scammer knows how to fake—the insurance company is likely to offer a settlement. That costs you in higher premiums.

If a customer appears hurt, be sympathetic and helpful because it might be real. But keep a single-use camera handy to take pictures of the scene. Call both an ambulance and the police, who will ask for identification. Ask if anyone else saw what happened, but beware of "witnesses" who seem too eager. Report any suspicions to your insurance adjuster.

Source: Steven C. Bahls and Jane Easter Bahls, "Professional Victims," Entrepreneur.com

⚜ ⚜ ⚜

CHAPTER 29

Asset Protection and Fraud Prevention

ASSET PROTECTION:
KEEPING WHAT YOU'VE WORKED SO HARD FOR

It's easy to overlook simple things that can protect your business from excessive taxes and lawsuits. The following will help you keep the business you've worked so hard to build and protect your personal assets from your business liabilities.

1. Do not do business as a sole proprietor.
Operating as a sole proprietor provides absolutely no asset protection because there is no way to insulate you personally from your business activity. If the business encounters liability, you will be sued personally, putting your personal as well as your business assets at risk. In addition, the income of sole proprietorships is subject to self-employment tax at a rate of 15.3 percent. Finally, you do not have the ability to diversify your income.

2. Set up a formal business as a corporation, limited liability company (LLC), or possibly a limited

partnership (LP), and file with your Secretary of State (or other appropriate state agency).
Choose the legal structure that is most appropriate for your type of business (see page 57 for more about this).

3. Once you have filed with the state, maintain the proper business documents to preserve your asset and liability protection.
Don't make the common mistake of assuming that all you need to do is the initial filing. Corporations require bylaws, annual meetings, and resolutions. LLCs require proper operating agreements and LPs require partnership agreements. Find out what your state requires and make all the necessary annual filings on time.

4. Keep the business name separate and distinct from your own name.
Naming the business after yourself has the potential to create confusion in the eyes of

vendors, partners, or consumers. Don't put yourself in a position where a potential plaintiff can claim he was under the impression that he was dealing with you personally and not the business.

5. Always present yourself as an officer or manager of the company.
This puts people on notice that you are not acting in a personal capacity but on behalf of the business.

6. Obtain all the appropriate licenses as required by your state, city, or county.

7. Keep business and personal assets separate.
One of the most common mistakes small business owners make is commingling business and personal funds. When you commingle funds and do things like write a check for a personal expense out of your business account, you give a potential plaintiff grounds to successfully argue that your business is nothing more than your alter ego and should be disregarded in a lawsuit, making you personally liable in a suit against your business.

8. Have insurance that is adequate and appropriate for your operation.

9. Be sure your attorney and accountant are both skilled in the areas of business law and business taxation.

10. Create a formal asset protection plan that you review and update annually.

Source: Greg Boots, Anderson Business Advisors, PLLC

A man without money needs no more fear a crowd of lawyers than a crowd of pickpockets.

Words of Wisdom

—WILLIAM WYCHERLEY, *THE PLAIN DEALER* (1677)

INTERNAL CONTROLS

Set up a system of internal checks and balances to so that financial duties are handled by two or more employees. To avoid the possibility of a single employee embezzling funds undetected, the same employee should not authorize, process, and record financial transactions. Review credit card statements carefully and require two signatures on checks.

- Conduct periodic internal audits, both scheduled and unscheduled. Have an external source audit your finances at least once a year.
- Make vacations mandatory. Employees who never take time off may be afraid that irregularities will be discovered in their absence.
- Set up a system so employees can report fraud anonymously, without fear of retaliation.

DOING IT RIGHT

An asset protection plan will almost never save you money on taxes. Asset protection and tax planning are two completely separate issues. If someone promises you that an asset protection plan—particularly one that includes offshore trusts and other entities—can reduce your taxes, you should get everything in writing and verify it with a trusted and knowledgeable independent resource—chances are you are in the early stages of a scam. Don't let greed overcome your common sense. Asset protection means protecting your assets from predators. Tax planning means taking advantage of legal and ethical ways to reduce your tax liability.

COMMON BUSINESS SCAMS

Scam artists are getting more and more adept at exploiting the weaknesses of small businesses. While some scams are golden oldies, they're still putting money into scammer's pockets—and taking it out of the pockets of small business owners. The best defense against scams is to be aware and vigilant. Here are five of the most common small business scams and how to avoid them.

1. Advance Fee Loan Scams.

Whether it's offered in a newspaper ad, on the internet, or by e-mail, this scam offers money at reasonable rates—if you send money. They may say they need the money for insurance purposes or to get the money across the border. Whatever the reason, you'll never see that money again—nor will you see the money they were supposedly going to loan your business.

How to avoid this scam
Be aware that it is illegal in both Canada and the U.S. to ask for money up front in exchange for a loan. If you're asked to pay anything before you've received an agreed-on loan, walk away.

Related scam: bogus equipment leasing deals
Your company gets a letter saying that you're pre-approved for leasing. All you have to do is send in your first (or your first and last) month's payment. The scam is that you never receive the equipment you were expecting to lease.

2. Fraudulent Billing Scams

Your business receives an invoice for goods or services that you haven't ordered. The hope of the scammers is that your business will just pay up. Easy money for them; easy loss for you.

How to avoid this scam
Examine your invoices carefully. Educate your staff about phony invoices. Set up your payables system so that at least two people must authorize any payments.

Related scam: the surprise check
Your business receives a check for a small amount. The catch is that the check is actually a "promotional incentive." If you cash it, the company will claim that you've agreed to whatever terms are printed on the back of the check, and start the billing process immediately.

3. Business Identity Theft

Identity theft is the fastest growing fraud in North America, according to the Better Business Bureau, and business identity theft is growing apace. Just as someone can steal your personal identity, so they can steal your business's identity. Once stolen, the thieves can use your business name and financial information to open a bank account and run up expenses.

How to avoid this scam
Take steps to protect your business data. Shred all your discarded paper, including anything that has your business name on it. Be careful when responding to e-mail asking you to do such things as verify your account. Be wary about information you give out over the phone.

Related scam: phishing
Internet "come-ons" that trick consumers and small businesses into providing bank or other financial information.

4. Work-at-Home Scams

Preying on people who want to have home-based businesses, these scams offer the opportunity to "make big bucks" working at home. Sometimes the ads say all you have to do is own a computer. Other times, the work-at-home scam involves stuffing envelopes or assembly work. The scam is simple: you pay for the information or the materials you supposedly need. Rather than being the key to making money, what you get is useless.

How to avoid this scam
Don't bite. These are not profitable opportunities; the only ones who make money from them are the scammers. If it seems too good to be true, it is. You never have to send money to get information about legitimate business opportunities.

5. Credit Card Scams

Fraudulent use of credit cards is also on the rise. In the standard credit card scam, someone will call and place an order, offering to pay with fraudulently obtained credit card information. The business fills the order, but later is informed that the credit card was stolen and the amount of the transaction will be charged back to the business's account.

How to avoid this scam
Always use due diligence to ensure that orders are legitimate. Be particularly leery of overseas callers, new callers placing large orders, and/or callers requesting rush shipping. If you are suspicious, ask the customer for the name of the credit card's issuing bank and its toll-free customer service number, which is printed on the back of all credit cards. Tell the customer you will check with the bank and call him back.

Sick scam twist
Overseas credit card thieves are using the TTY phone service for the deaf and posing as hearing-impaired callers. These scammers use the TTY relay operator to place an order for multiple high-end items.

Source: Susan Ward, "The 5 Most Common Business Scams and How to Avoid Them," sbinfocanada.about.com/od/scams/a/commonscams.htm

---

RULES FOR PROTECTING YOUR COMPANY AGAINST OFFICE SUPPLY SCAMS

1. *Know and insist on your rights.* If you receive merchandise you didn't order, you may keep it as a gift. Telemarketers are required to provide you with certain information when they call, including the fact that it is a sales call, who is doing the selling, and the total cost of the goods or services.
2. *Document orders.* Keep records on who ordered what, and limit the number of people who have the authority to purchase items.
3. *Don't pay any bill unless it matches your documentation.* Have a system in place that allows you to confirm that deliveries match invoices.
4. *Train employees.* Educate all employees who answer the phone about telemarketing scams and establish a procedure for routing sales calls to the appropriate buyer.
5. *Do not pay for—or return—unordered merchandise.* If the seller cannot produce evidence that you ordered the product and you do not believe they made an honest mistake, you may keep the merchandise. You should, however, report the incident to the proper authorities.

Source: Federal Trade Commission

As I grow older, I pay less attention to what men say. I just watch what they do.

—ANDREW CARNEGIE

Words of Wisdom

DEALING
WITH EXTORTION

It's the stuff movies are made of: bomb threats, product tampering, sabotage, and kidnapping. You might think it will never happen to you because you're a small, relatively obscure company, but that could actually be what makes you an attractive target to an extortionist.

Being a victim of extortion or threats is not a factor of size, and it's not always connected to a perception of wealth. You can fall victim for many reasons. A small company might be an easier target than a large multinational, which many times is perceived as having a very significant security force in place. And while a large company might be able to weather the costs of a kidnapping or product recall and negative press campaign, for a smaller company the damage could be irreparable.

The first step in protecting your company from various forms of corporate terrorism is to understand that it can, indeed, happen to you. The source will likely be one of five types of perpetrators: disgruntled employees—either current or former—or someone else with a personal grudge against you or the company; criminals who are looking primarily for financial gain; psychotic or mentally ill individuals; terrorists; and "hoaksters." Possible scenarios include an unhappy employee who threatens to release company secrets or plant a virus in your computer; threats from a stranger or a fanatic to injure people or damage property if a ransom is not paid; product tampering; and threats to generate negative publicity if the company fails to take specific actions.

The next step is to develop a crisis management plan. Though you certainly can't plan for all contingencies, think in advance about what steps you will take so you can react calmly and with a sense of purpose to resolve a situation. Decide who will be in charge of what, and plan for communicating with law enforcement, the media, your customers, and your employees. It's a good idea to meet with a crisis management consultant before anything happens; establishing such a relationship in advance may cost a small amount of time and money, but it will be invaluable if a real need arises.

Consider, too, how you will handle the costs associated with an incident. Some of the expenses may be covered under your regular business insurance, or you may want to investigate special policies. For example, some insurance companies offer kidnap and extortion and product tampering insurance.

PREVENTING "OFF-BOOK"
CASH THEFT

For many companies, especially cash businesses, employee theft is considered just another cost of doing business. Particularly hard to spot are "off-book" thefts, which involve stealing the money before it ever gets into your bookkeeping system. The most common off-book schemes include skimming, where a portion of the cash received is pocketed before the sale is rung into the register; fraudulent voids, where sales are voided and made to look like the sale was canceled, a mistake was made, or the customer returned the merchandise; and swapping non-cash for cash, where checks or credit card receipts are not entered in the register and a similar amount of cash is removed.

Typically, business owners don't realize such thefts are occurring until so long after the fact that identifying the perpetrator is impossible. The awareness often comes about when financial reports indicate reduced profits. When the thief is not greedy and is stealing very small amounts, it may be virtually impossible to detect.

Here's how you can detect and prevent off-book theft:

- *Be sure customers can see the cash register display.* This lets customers see for themselves that they aren't being over-charged and that the amount they are asked to pay is the amount that was rung into the register.
- *Always give receipts.* Make it a policy to give receipts with every sale, and consider offering customers some sort of a reward—such as a gift certificate or discount off a future purchase—if they are not given a receipt.
- *Review your transactions daily.* Look at cash register tapes and credit card charge slips for any unusual patterns, excessive voids, or other suspicious activity. The benefits of this routine go beyond identifying theft; if, for example, you have an employee who voids a lot of sales, they may be stealing, or they may just need some training on how to properly operate the equipment.
- *Require a supervisor's approval on voided sales.* Such scrutiny makes it harder for an employee to pocket cash unseen.
- *Consider various visual monitoring methods.* Mystery shoppers and plain clothes security may spot employee theft. Or you might want to install surveillance cameras.
- *Use controls that will help you take action.* It's not enough to quantify a loss; you also want to be able to identify who was responsible. Your theft control measures should pinpoint the source as well as the amount of the loss.

If you need help to develop loss-control measures, start with your accountant, who should be able to help you with various record-keeping techniques that will identify where and how losses are occurring. Or you may want to contact a risk management or security consultant with expertise in your particular industry.

❧ ❧ ❧

AFFINITY FRAUD: AVOID INVESTMENT SCAMS THAT TARGET GROUPS

Affinity fraud refers to investment scams that prey upon members of identifiable groups, including religious, elderly, ethnic, and professional groups. The fraudsters who promote affinity scams are group members, claim to be members of the group, or enlist respected leaders within a group to spread the word about an investment deal. In addition, fraudsters increasingly use the internet to target groups with e-mail spams. These scams exploit the trust and friendship that exist among groups of people who have something in common. Because of the tight-knit structure of many groups, it is usually more difficult for regulators or law-enforcement officials to detect an affinity scam. Victims of such scams often fail to notify authorities or pursue their legal remedies, but are more likely to try to work things out within the group.

Avoid Being a Victim

To avoid affinity and other scams, you should:

- *Check out everything—no matter how trustworthy the person who brings the investment opportunity to your attention.* Never make an investment based solely on the recommendation of a member of an organization, or religious or ethnic group to which you belong. Investigate the investment thoroughly and check the truth of every statement you are told about it. Be aware that the person telling you about the investment may have been fooled into believing that it is legitimate when it is not.
- *Do not fall for investments that promise spectacular profits or "guaranteed" returns.* If an investment seems too good to be true, then it probably is. Similarly, be extremely leery of any investment that is represented to have no risks; very few investments are risk-free. Generally, the

greater the potential return an investment offers, the greater the risks of losing money on it.

- *Be skeptical of any investment that is not fully documented in writing.* Fraudsters often avoid putting things in writing, but legitimate investments are usually in writing. Avoid an investment if you are told they do "not have the time to reduce to writing" the particulars. You should also be suspicious if you are told to keep the investment opportunity confidential.

- *Don't be pressured or rushed into buying an investment before you have a chance to think about—or investigate—the "opportunity."* Just because someone you know made money, or claims to have made money, doesn't mean you will, too. Also, watch out for investments that are pitched as "once-in-a-lifetime" opportunities, especially when the promoter bases the recommendation on "inside" or confidential information.

Source: U. S. Securities and Exchange Commission

PROTECT YOUR BUSINESS FROM ESPIONAGE

The FBI estimates that every year billions of U.S. dollars are lost to foreign competitors who deliberately target economic intelligence in flourishing U.S. industries and technologies. Protect your business by recognizing that the threat is real, putting together a plan to protect your trade secrets and other intellectual property, and providing ongoing security training for employees. If you believe you have been the victim of economic espionage, contact your local FBI office immediately.

Source: Federal Bureau of Investigation

WEB SITE ANTI-FRAUD MEASURES

1. *Create metrics for your business.* Keep track of how much fraud you are having, what your chargeback rate is, and what your review rate is.

2. *Aim for a low fraud rate*–less than 0.2 percent, based on chargebacks.

3. *Optimize your fraud-screening tools.* In general, when merchants accept an order, they run it through their screening tools to determine if it's suspicious and if they need to review it manually.

4. *Use a variety of fraud-prevention tools.* The top three are address verification services, customer follow-up when the order looks suspicious, and the use of card verification codes.

5. *Stay one step ahead.* Some fraudsters will get 100 different credit card numbers, but use the same e-mail address and order from the same computer. A velocity check across multiple fields is a hot new anti-fraud technology that allows online merchants to track how often they see different credit card numbers with the same e-mail or IP address.

Source: Melissa Campanelli, "Anti-Fraud Measures for Your Site," Entrepreneur.com

❧ ❧ ❧

CHAPTER 30

Intellectual Property

UNDERSTANDING INTELLECTUAL PROPERTY

Intellectual property (IP) is the ownership of ideas. Unlike tangible assets such as computers or your office, intellectual property is a collection of ideas and concepts.

There are only three ways to protect intellectual property in the United States: through the use of patents, trademarks, or copyrights. A patent applies to a specific product design; a trademark to a name, phrase, or symbol; and a copyright to a written document. All three methods have limitations—there's no one perfect way to protect an idea.

HOW BIG OF A PROBLEM IS IP THEFT AMONG SMALL BUSINESSES?

While it is difficult to determine the exact scope and extent of the problem, every indication is that copyright piracy, trademark counterfeiting, and patent infringement have become significant problems in the business community in general, including small businesses. Certainly any small business that exports its IP protected products abroad or sources its products or parts overseas must take into account the potential for rampant IP theft in many countries.

Small businesses in the United States are at a particular disadvantage, however, because they may lack the knowledge, expertise, or resources necessary to prevent the theft of their ideas and products. In fact, research conducted by the USPTO (United States Patent and Trademark Office) this year found that only 15 percent of small businesses operating overseas know that they need to file for IP protection abroad.

Many small businesses also may not have personnel overseas, so they lack the "eyes and ears" needed to be vigilant globally, and the theft of their IP can often go undetected. In addition, small businesses generally do not have the level of access or the resources, such as specialized legal counsel, that may be available to larger companies.

Source: U.S. Patent and Trademark Office

YOUR COMPANY AND PRODUCT NAMES ARE VALUABLE ASSETS

When it comes to trademark infringement, there are two critical times you need to worry about: when you do it to someone else, and when someone else does it to you, says Stephen Elias, an attorney and co-author with Kate McGrath of *Trademark: Legal Care for Your Business & Product Name* (Nolo Press). Elias defines trademarks as the business and product names, logos, sounds, shapes, smells, colors, packaging, and other unique characteristics that distinguish particular products and services from those offered by a competitor.

If you infringe on someone else's trademark, at the least you could be ordered to cease and desist, which means the costly process of changing your company or product name (that could include new signage, stationery, marketing materials, etc.). At the most, you could be sued for and be forced to pay statutory and actual damages, as well as attorney's fees. If you are concerned that you might be infringing on someone else's trademark, see an attorney who specializes in patent and trademark law for advice.

If someone infringes on your trademark, you risk losing business (if customers are unable to distinguish between you and the other company) and your reputation could be tarnished. Even small, homebased businesses need to be concerned about trademarks, especially, Elias says, if you are doing business on the internet, because that puts you in a worldwide marketplace. He offers the following tips for protecting your company and product names:

- *Choose a distinctive name.* The more distinctive a name, the easier it is to protect.
- Conduct a trademark search to confirm that the name—or a name so close that yours would confuse the public—is not already in use.
- Register the name with your state's trademark office (usually the Department of Commerce or Secretary of State's office) and with the United States Patent and Trademark Office in Washington, DC.
- If your mark is federally registered, use the trademark registration ® symbol to let others know you are serious about protecting your mark.
- File all appropriate and necessary documents to maintain your state and federal registration, and renew those registrations as necessary.
- Use your mark. If you fail to use your mark for two years or more, it may be considered abandoned and others can use it.
- Maintain control of your mark. Be sure your mark is always properly used, and take immediate action whenever you become aware of an infringement.

Your business may not be in the same league as Disney, IBM, Xerox, Apple Computer, or McDonald's—yet, anyway—but that doesn't mean you shouldn't protect your name with the same zeal these corporate giants do.

> ### WORTH KNOWING
>
> The term "counterfeit" describes fake goods. The term "piracy" describes the act of reproducing movies, music, books, or other copyrighted works without permission from the copyright owner.

PROTECT YOUR INTELLECTUAL PROPERTY

Be Vigilant

Much of today's intellectual property theft occurs on-line, so monitor the internet for potential counterfeiting in addition to your marketplace monitoring. You may also wish to monitor trade journals to learn about foreign markets or industry sectors being exploited by intellectual property thieves.

Learn More

To learn more about protecting your intellectual property rights, visit:

- *www.stopfakes.gov/smallbusiness.* The U.S. government site dedicated to small businesses.
- *www.uspto.gov.* The U.S. Patent and Trademark Office site, a comprehensive go-to source for intellectual property information.
- *www.copyright.gov.* The U.S. Copyright Office site with comprehensive information on copyright.
- *www.cbp.gov.* The U.S. Customs and Border Protection (CBP) site, with information on the recording of registered U.S. trademarks and copyrighted works with the CBP.
- *1-866-999-HALT* to report IP theft.
- *www.wipo.int.* The web site of the World Intellectual Property Organization (WIPO), with information on the Patent Cooperation Treaty and the Madrid Protocol.

Source: U.S. Patent and Trademark Office

THREE TYPES OF PATENTS

1. Utility patents may be granted to anyone who invents or discovers any new and useful process, machine, article of manufacture, or composition of matter, or any new and useful improvement thereof.
2. Design patents may be granted to anyone who creates a new, original, and ornamental design for an article of manufacture.
3. Plant patents may be granted to anyone who creates or discovers and asexually reproduces any distinct and new variety of plant.

Source: U.S. Patent and Trademark Office

KEEP TRESPASSERS OFF YOUR INTELLECTUAL PROPERTY

To an entrepreneur, nothing is more valuable than an original idea, be it a new business plan, a product design or even the look of a web site. And like any other precious object, these ideas must be protected lest they somehow find their way into the clutches of unscrupulous competitors who would like nothing better than to call the fruits of your labor their own. Enter firstuse.com, an online registry for intellectual properties and other important documents.

In business since last October, the company's unique authentication process allows users to document text, graphic, video or audio files in any spoken or computer language without requiring them to divulge the actual contents of the files themselves. To register a document with firstuse.com, the user uploads a copy of the file to the web site, which creates a 'digital fingerprint,' a binary code representation of the file, which firstuse.com encrypts and saves on its database. Then, the company creates a time- and date-stamped digital registration certificate that can be viewed at firstuse.com by anyone seeking to validate the ownership of the file. Document registration can be done 24 hours a day, from any computer in the world with access to the internet.

While the registration certificate is not a legally binding document, it has already been successfully used in U.S. courts as supplemental documentation of the ownership of intellectual property.

Obviously, there are other ways for you to legally document your intellectual property, ranging from filling out a copyright application to simply sending the document to yourself via registered mail, but firstuse.com contends that there is no other method as timely or as tamper-proof as an online registry. Even data that is stored on a private computer can be easily altered, says Craig Honick, co-founder of firstuse.com.

"Digital files can be backdated or manipulated in other ways," Honick says. "So when you bring them into court or [as evidence in] a dispute of some kind over documentation, someone can easily say 'You could have done that last night and dated it two years ago.'"

Registering proprietary information with firstuse.com, which starts at $15 per transaction, may also serve to discourage lawsuits over intellectual property in the first place, contends Honick. "If [competitors] know that you have documentation registered with firstuse, they'll be less likely to challenge your ownership of an idea. It just won't be worth their time or money to try the case."

Honick believes the logo of firstuse.com stamped on documentation of intellectual properties will eventually have the same force as the copyright symbol does today.

Source: David Doran, "Top Secrets," Entrepreneur.com

❧ ❧ ❧

CHAPTER 31

Physical Property

Regardless of the physical location and size of your business, you have probably made an investment in physical property that deserves protection on a day-to-day basis. And in protecting your physical property, you are also protecting yourself, your employees, and your customers.

PROPERTY CHECKLIST
The following questions should help in your efforts to protect your property.

Premises and Personal Security
- Do you have adequate devices installed to control unauthorized entry onto the premises?
- Is there a burglar alarm that reports to a central station or a constantly attended monitoring facility?
- Do you have adequate fencing and gates around the building and parking areas?

- Is there adequate exterior and interior lighting?
- Are there adequate door and window locks?
- Is access to the premises controlled by physical barriers and surveillance?
- Do you require the use of company ID badges?
- Do you have appropriate visitor sign-in, badges, and escort procedures?
- Are check-in and check-out procedures effective in controlling independent contractors and trades people?
- Do you have an inventory control system in place?
- Do you have a comprehensive security policy that outlines procedures for:
  - Threats to personal safety, such as assault, sexual abuse, and robbery?
  - Situations involving drug or alcohol use?
  - Bomb threats?
  - Civil unrest?

– Employee theft?

- Are products and business property that are stored offsite identified and safe?

Accounting Security

- Are cash, bank deposits, and inventory overseen by more than one person?
- Are cash deposits made frequently, to limit the amount of cash on hand?
- Is billing independently reconciled to ensure proper charges, credits, and refunds?

Protection from Theft

- Are your employees trained to recognize shoplifting risks and do they know how to respond?
- Are your employees trained to recognize counterfeit currency?
- Can your employees determine credit card validity?
- Is there a system for employees to report vandalism or theft committed by employees, visitors, vendors, or contractors?
- Is proper security and accountability established for samples, demonstrators, and tools?
- Are valuables secured in adequate lockers and appropriate safes?
- Are office machines and tools marked with identifying etchings or other markings, and are their serial numbers kept on file?
- Are all employees trained in how to respond to a hold-up and in other security measures appropriate for your business?
- Are finished products and merchandise protected from theft and damage?
- Is cash frequently collected from the registers to reduce the chance of theft?

Building/Facilities (Structure, Utilities, etc.)

- Is the building's exterior structure—including all equipment—in good condition, taking into consideration natural perils?
- Are drain pipes, signs, tanks, fences, out-buildings, towers, canopies, trees, etc. secured?
- Is the building's interior structure, including equipment, in good condition?
- Are you sure that the electrical system is adequate and up to date?
- Has the electrical system been upgraded to accommodate new equipment and increased use?
- Is the heating and air conditioning system properly maintained and safely located?
- Is the plumbing system properly installed and adequate?
- Are hazardous operations and concentrations of valuable assets properly segregated?
- Is the roof covering free of leaks?
- Is the roof drainage adequate?
- Has the potential for snow/ice/water accumulation on the roof been considered?

Fire Prevention

- Are all combustibles and flammables stored properly?
- Is the roof covering noncombustible?
- Is the interior finish of walls, floors, and ceiling of a low-combustibility type?
- Are furniture and fixtures of low combustibility?
- Are foamed and rigid plastics used in ducts, pipes, trim, and insulation properly installed and protected by noncombustible materials to reduce smoke and fire risks?
- Is all refuse removed daily?

- Are "no smoking" rules established and enforced?
- Are electric extension cords, tools, and appliances safely used?
- Are smoke alarms in use, and maintained and tested regularly?
- Have you assessed the fire hazards common to your type of business operations (e.g., welding, parts cleaning)?

Fire Protection

- Are your employees trained to respond quickly and correctly when they smell smoke or see a fire?
- Are fire protection devices (extinguishers, etc.) and sprinklers properly installed, maintained, tested, and free of obstruction?
- Are structural openings protected by operable and approved fire doors, dampers, etc., to prevent the spread of fire and smoke?
- Is high-value equipment protected? For example, is the computer room separated from a company's welding operation by adequate fire-resistant construction?
- Are dangerous or flammable raw materials and packing materials safely stored and handled?
- Is high-piled stock segregated from hazardous operations and walls, and properly situated at least 18 inches below sprinkler heads?
- Are there physical and time/space barriers (e.g., firewalls) between people and the hazardous conditions that cause accidents and other incidents?
- Are valuable assets segregated (preferably to other facilities) so that a fire or flood would not wipe out all your major assets?

Source: The Hartford

DOING IT RIGHT

Have floor plans of your facility available both on- and offsite. Physical descriptions of your building and rooms are useful in the event of any emergency and make the jobs of law enforcement and rescue personnel much easier. The plans should indicate features such as windows, doors, water shut-off valves, and electrical breaker boxes. They should also note the location of any communication devices such as televisions, telephones, and computers.

HOME OFFICE SECURITY

Your home may be your castle, but just how safe and secure is your home office? As the number of home-based businesses and telecommuting workers continues to grow, so do the number of homes with computers and other equipment that might be attractive to thieves or that could be destroyed in the event of a fire or natural disaster. Consider the following tips for protecting your home office.

- Take a look at your home through the eyes of a criminal. How vulnerable are you? Your local police department may be able to assist you with a security analysis.
- Duplicate important data and store it offsite. Develop a system for regular back-up procedures for your important business records and customer files to minimize your risk.
- Be sure all doors and windows close tightly and have effective locks.
- Check outside for potential access. Are there shrubs where a criminal could hide? Do trees or a ladder near the house make it easy to access second-floor windows?
- Install exterior lighting using timers and/or motion sensors.

- If you travel, be sure someone will pick up mail, newspapers, and packages so your absence is not apparent to an observer.
- If other people, such as employees and service personnel, have keys to your house, have the locks re-keyed once a year.
- Think about how your business space relates to the living space in your home. Is it distinctly separate and can it have its own locks and other security elements? Or is it integrated with the rest of your home and difficult to segregate?
- Consider an alarm system to protect both your home and your business.

Today's alarm systems can do much more than simply notify police in the event of a break-in. They can monitor your home for fire, water damage, and even power failures. Systems can be zoned to offer different levels of protection in different sections of your house. Chimes can alert you to the opening of exterior doors and windows—particularly important if you work alone in a large house. Closed-circuit cameras allow you to see who is at your door before you open it; for even more advanced notice, a driveway annunciator can sound an interior chime when a vehicle pulls onto your property. Fixed or portable panic buttons can be programmed to notify police with or without an audible alarm.

Shop carefully for a security system. Though they are becoming increasingly affordable, price should be only a small part of your decision. Find out how long the company has been in business; if they have a local office; how their service is handled; how installers and technicians are trained and if they are insured and bonded. Ask about the system's warranty, the cost of monitoring, and the length of contract. Get statistics on the company's history of apprehensions and scare-offs, and ask how many times their system has been beaten. Finally, ask for and check references.

MANAGEMENT TIP

Security badges are meant to prove identity and display access privileges at work. They should never be worn in public when going to lunch, taking a break, or even walking outside. Exposing badges in public permits identity thieves to see your employees' names, office, and possibly their level of security clearance. What's worse is that now the public knows what your badge looks like, thereby increasing the chances of successful forgery. Require employees to always remove and put away their badges when leaving work, even if just for a break.

Source: The SANS Institute

GUIDELINES FOR MAIL CENTER THEFT PREVENTION

Mail is sometimes lost or stolen from company mail centers, or while en route to or from the Post Office. Much of this mail is quite valuable and, needless to say, such losses are costly to a company and its investors. The following are some suggestions for improving theft prevention in your mail center operation.

Know your employees.
Don't put your new hires in your mail center without doing a criminal record check.

Secure your mail center.
Prevent access by unauthorized persons. Keep the mail center locked whenever possible, especially when no one is on duty. Maintain a sign-in sheet for

continued on page 306

GENERAL SAFETY AND SECURITY PROCEDURES
FOR INCOMING/OUTGOING MAIL AREAS

Whether your mailroom is a separate facility, a table in the back room, a corner of your receptionist's desk, or on your kitchen table at home, you need to practice good mailroom security.

- Notify internal and external customers, as appropriate, of steps taken to ensure safety of mail.
- Control or limit access of employees, known visitors and escorted visitors to the mail center with sign-in sheets, badges, and/or card readers. (For large mail operations, include plant, workroom floor, etc.)
- Subject to emergency exit safety requirements, lock all outside doors, and/or prohibit doors from being propped open.
- Require deliveries to be made in a restricted, defined area.
- Restrict drivers' rest areas to an area that is separate from the production/mail center facilities.
- Use video cameras inside and outside the facility/docks, as feasible.
- Keep the area for processing incoming and outgoing mail separate from all other operations, as feasible.
- If a separate processing area is used, it should not be part of the central ventilation system.
- Shut-off points of the processing area's ventilation system should be mapped and should be part of an emergency procedures handout.
- Separate processing area should include appropriate personnel protection equipment and disposal instructions for such equipment, as approved by the CDC.
- Designate and publish/post evacuation routes for emergency situations.
- Conduct training, emergency preparedness drills, and information update meetings, as necessary
- X-ray all incoming mail. (Large mail centers.)
- Maintain a "Suspicious Package Profile."
- Ensure appropriate emergency access numbers are posted by or on every phone. Such numbers should include: call 911; CDC at 770-488-7100; local Postal Inspector; or local police or fire department.
- Maintain updated employee lists (name, address, phone/cell phone), and keep back-up copy off-site.
- Provide only vacuum systems for cleaning equipment, not forced air systems.
- If not already done, alter receiving procedures to require a manifest with all shipments and practice the acceptance of "complete" shipments only.
- Discarded envelopes, packages, boxes should be placed in a covered container and transported to the loading dock for removal. (Ensure local arrangements are in place for disposal of such material.)

Source: United States Postal Service

persons entering and leaving, including times of arrival and departure.

Keep Registered Mail™ separate from other mail.
Document the transfer of Registered Mail by requiring the receiver to sign for custody.

Protect company funds.
If company funds are handled as part of the mail center operations, establish adequate controls to fix individual responsibility for any losses that may occur.

Keep postage meters secure.
Postage meters should be secured when not in use. Check mails periodically to determine if employees are using company postage meters for personal mail.

Vary times and lines of travel between post office and plant.
If currency or other valuable mail is sent or received, check periodically to see if mail messengers are making unauthorized stops or are leaving mail unattended in unlocked vehicles.

Employees caught stealing should be prosecuted.
There is no greater deterrent to a potential thief than the fear that he/she may go to jail. The Postal Inspection Service will extend its full cooperation.

Source: United States Postal Service

The Postal Inspection Service is one of the oldest law enforcement agencies in America and the primary law enforcement arm of the U.S. Postal Service. It is responsible for investigating crimes associated with the mail.

FAST FACT

WHAT ARE THE INDICATORS OF A SUSPICIOUS LETTER OR PARCEL?

A parcel or letter is considered suspicious when it has more than one of the following characteristics:

- No return address or one that cannot be verified as legitimate.
- Excessive postage.
- Handwritten or poorly typed address, incorrect titles or titles with no name, or misspellings of common words.
- Addressed to someone no longer with your organization or not addressed to a specific person.
- Strange return address or no return address.
- Marked with restrictions, such as "Personal," "Confidential," or "Do not X-ray."
- Powdery substance on the outside.
- Unusual weight given its size, lopsided, or oddly shaped.
- Unusual amount of tape on it.
- Odors, discolorations, or oily stains.

Source: United States Postal Service

WORTH KNOWING

If you receive a suspicious letter or package in the mail or by any other means:

1. Handle it with care. Do not shake or bump.
2. Don't open, smell, touch, or taste.
3. Isolate it immediately.
4. Treat it as suspect. Call local law enforcement authorities.

WHEN THE UNTHINKABLE HAPPENS

When a natural disaster, accident, or criminal act causes property damage to your business, doing the right things can control the damage, but doing the wrong things can exacerbate the situation and even increase your losses. If property damage does occur, remember that the damage being done does not necessarily stop once the fire is put out, the water is turned off, and the actual disaster is under control. You need to take immediate steps to protect your undamaged property and to salvage whatever damaged items you can.

- *Verify the safety of the building before entering it.* Don't get hurt: If there's water damage, there's the potential of getting electrocuted; if there's structural damage, walls or ceilings could fall; you could be hurt by debris, broken glass, nails, or other items. Be sure the emergency services personnel have deemed it safe for you to enter the building before you do so.
- Make the necessary notifications, including contacting your insurance carrier, employees, customers, and suppliers.
- If the damage prevents you from accessing your office, find a place to operate, such as a nearby hotel or executive suite complex. Keep all receipts for temporary office space and related costs; these expenses are typically covered by insurance.
- Call the telephone company and arrange for calls to be routed to a location where they can be answered.
- Prevent further damage. While waiting for the insurance adjuster, take whatever immediate steps are necessary to prevent further property damage, such as shutting off water and electricity, boarding up broken windows, covering damaged roofs with tarps, and doing preliminary emergency clean-up.
- Take photographs of the damage. This will assist in your claims process.
- Contact a qualified professional restoration contractor. Be sure to tell the contractor what sort of business property—such as paper and electronic files, business equipment, etc.—you are attempting to salvage. Disaster restoration takes special skills and knowledge; get bids from several professionals before making a final selection. This will not take as long as you might think. Because immediate response is critical, professional restoration companies will usually have someone on site within one to two hours, and be prepared to start work right away.

❧ ❧ ❧

✵ ✵ ✵

CHAPTER 32

Data and Cyber Security

The internet has made it possible for even the smallest of businesses to be "open" 24 hours a day, allows us to communicate instantly with customers and colleagues all over the world, has given us access to more information than we will likely ever have to time study, and much more. But this amazing technology comes with risks to the security of our operation and data.

WHY SMALL BUSINESSES ARE AT RISK FROM INTERNET SECURITY THREATS

Enterprise network security is harder to breach. In recent years many corporations, impacted by internet threats, and in order to comply with strict security measures required by the Sarbanes-Oxley Act and other regulations, have significantly bolstered their network security. As a result, criminals are increasingly turning their attentions toward easier hacker targets—small businesses.

Unprotected systems are easier to find.
Many hackers now have software tools that constantly search the internet for unprotected networks and computers. Once discovered, unprotected computers can be accessed and controlled by a hacker, who can use them to launch attacks on other computers or networks.

Computer security threats are more sophisticated—and more damaging.
Spyware authors are busy creating pernicious programs that resist removal, perpetually mutate, and spread across the internet in minutes. Meanwhile, blended threats, which assume multiple forms and can attack systems in many different ways, are on the rise. Small businesses without adequate, updated security solutions can easily be victimized by these and other threats.

Threats often come from within.

All too often, security breaches don't come from outside the company but from within, either intentionally or unintentionally. For example, an employee may unknowingly download spyware while playing an online game or visiting a web site. Small-business systems are more vulnerable to employee tampering simply because they often lack the internal security precautions of a larger enterprise.

The resulting impact of a security attack is greater.

Small businesses often lack the financial resources that large companies have to bounce back from security attacks. Suppose you're an online retailer and a hacker launches a denial-of-service attack against your web site. Do you have the necessary insurance or funds to recover from the subsequent loss of revenue—not to mention the damage to your business's reputation?

Source: Peter Alexander, "Is Your Biz Safe from Internet Security Threats?", Entrepreneur.com

Forty-three percent of organizations say their information security function is now part of their organizations' risk management function.

FAST FACT

Ernst & Young, November 2006

WORTH KNOWING

If a password is a word that can be found in the dictionary, it may be susceptible to "dictionary" attacks, which is when hackers attempt to guess passwords based on words in the dictionary.

KEEP YOUR NETWORKS SECURE AND YOUR DATA SAFE

Most small-business owners understand that complete, end-to-end network security is something they should have—but it's something they probably don't. And how can they? With security threats coming from a multitude of sources and no end in sight to the new attacks that are frequently launched on both networks and PCs, keeping up with all these threats and figuring out just what to do about them is challenging enough for big companies with dedicated IT staffs. For small businesses, it can be completely overwhelming.

The risks of not adequately securing your business network and PCs are huge, however. Remember: It's not just *your* data that's at risk from attacks from viruses, spyware, hackers, and others. Any customer details stored on your computers—including Social Security numbers, bank account information, and confidential data, such as key sales and marketing data—are at risk as well.

Here are the facts, according to consumer product research organization *Consumer Reports:*

- During a recent 24-hour monitoring period, computer security software firm Symantec recorded 59 million attempts by hackers to gain unauthorized entry into business and home computers.
- One out of four computer users said they had experienced a major, costly problem due to a computer virus, according to a Fall 2006 survey. The average cost per incident was $109. In addition, one out of every 115 people was the victim of a scam e-mail attack, which cost victims an average of $850 apiece.
- To combat viruses and spyware, American consumers spent at least $7.8 billion for computer repairs, parts, and replacement over the past two years.

The Threats

Since security threats continue to evolve, business owners must not only continue to protect themselves from existing threats such as viruses, spyware, and scam e-mails, but also must keep abreast of new threats and understand how hackers will be targeting computers in the future. So what will be the newest threats in the coming years? Here are some trends to watch:

More narrowly defined threats, or
"targeted threats," are becoming common.
These attacks tend to focus on sensitive information from a single company or individual rather than indiscriminately letting a worm loose to find victims wherever they can. The "malware" capable of these attacks is being delivered to users in increasingly sophisticated ways such as in e-mail attachments, embedded in video files or hyperlinks, and even through social engineering tactics that lure, fool, or trick the user to make what seems like a benign action that automatically installs the malware without user help.

Malicious bots are expected to increase.
Bots—short for robots, or software applications that run automated tasks over the internet—are sometimes used to create automated attacks on networks, such as DoS attacks.

Rootkits are becoming an increasing concern.
Rootkits are a set of software tools whose purpose is to conceal processes, files, or system data from a computer's operating system. Rootkits can enable hackers to maintain access to a computer system. Because they can burrow deeply, are capable of modifying parts of an operating system, and can go undetected, rootkits can be particularly challenging to remove.

Zero-day attacks are also on the rise.
A zero-day (also called zero hour) attack takes advantage of computer security holes for which no solution is yet available. They're called "zero day" because they attack between the time a security hole becomes known and the time when a patch to plug the hole is available. As a result, zero-day attacks can spread at an alarming rate.

Identity theft will continue to be a growing concern.
The FTC estimates that 10 million Americans are victims of identity fraud each year. Hackers who gain unauthorized access to computers are often in search of personal identity data they can exploit or sell.

The Solutions

Now that you have some idea what you're up against, is there anything you can really do to protect your business? Absolutely. First, you need to develop a plan that addresses both education and technology. It's critical that you educate your users on what they can do to make sure they're not potentially compromising security (safe user habits for reading and acting upon e-mails can prevent many virus attacks). And make sure unauthorized users (for instance, family or friends) don't use your business's computers.

Next, develop a comprehensive technology plan to address all aspects of security. Talk to your trusted IT adviser. Make a complete list of the security you already have in place, with an eye toward sniffing out vulnerabilities. Develop a plan for complete, end-to-end network protection, and make sure there are steps in place to regularly update your security. Then revisit your plan several times a year to ensure it continues to meet your needs and addresses new security threats that continue to evolve.

Your plan should include the following security essentials:

Antivirus protection

Every PC on your network should have antivirus protection. There are plenty of inexpensive, effective antivirus programs on the market for small and home offices.

Antispyware protection

Spyware has become increasingly malicious, difficult to detect, and difficult to remove. An antispyware program that frequently downloads updated definitions and monitors activity in the background is important, given the insidious nature of spyware.

Firewall

A firewall is designed to block unauthorized access to computers and networks. Firewalls are available in hardware (as standalone network security devices or integrated into network routers) or as software. A software firewall is particularly important for laptop users who travel. Firewall software is usually included in internet security suites, which also offer antivirus, antispyware, and other tools. Some software firewalls are even available in free, basic versions.

Virtual private network (VPN)

A VPN creates a secure "tunnel" between a computer and an unsecured, public network, such as the internet. VPN technology offers an important layer of protection for your business's weakest security link—mobile users. VPN security can be integrated into some network devices, such as intelligent routers, and turned on or off as needed.

Wireless security

If your business uses a wireless network, at a minimum, you should use a password, WEP key, or some other method to block unauthorized users from gaining access.

Secure network hardware

Ideally, your company's network should be protected by routers with comprehensive, built-in security, including integrated firewall, VPN, and an intrusion prevention system.

Data protection

Implementing regular backup procedures is a simple way to safeguard critical business and customer data. Setting permissions and encryption will also help.

Maintaining proper security throughout your network is a big job. If it feels overwhelming, consider hiring an IT person to handle the job. Or outsource network security to an independent contractor or managed service provider.

Source: Peter Alexander, "Crafting a Technology Security Plan," Entrepreneur.com

---

GREAT ADVICE

Protect your customers' information from hackers and thieves by encrypting it. You may already have the necessary encryption programs built into your financial or database software—check your manual to see if your software includes this feature and to learn how to use it. If you don't, consider purchasing an encryption program that will made data unreadable to anyone without a password or key.

One in three workers jot down their computer password, undermining their security.

FAST
FACT

Nucleus Research and KnowledgeStorm, November 2006

COORDINATE ANTI-VIRUS AND ANTI-SPYWARE SOFTWARE

Shielding your computers from viruses and spyware is essential, but when it comes to these programs, more is not necessarily better. It's true that not all programs are equally effective and some will catch malicious code that others miss. But you can cause problems when you install multiple anti-virus and anti-spyware programs.

Because scanning your system for viruses and spyware uses available memory, you may limit the amount of resources left to perform your business tasks if you have multiple programs trying to scan at the same time. It's also possible that one anti-virus or anti-spyware program might mistake the virus definitions in other programs for actual malicious code. If this happens, you could get false positives for the presence of viruses or spyware and it's possible the software that made the mistake could actually quarantine or delete the other software.

So how do you avoid problems while protecting your computers and data?

- *Research your software options before making a decision and installing a program.* When evaluating anti-virus and anti-spyware software, consider the amount of malicious code the software recognizes and how frequently its virus definitions are updated. Also check for known compatibility issues with other software that you may be running on your computer.

- *Limit the number of programs you install.* Look for a package that combines anti-virus and anti-spyware capabilities. The more programs you install, the greater your chance for problems.

- *If you are going to install more than one program, do it in phases.* For example, install the anti-virus software and test it before installing anti-spyware software. If a problem develops, it will be easier to identify the source and determine how to correct it.

- *Watch for problems in your system.* If your computer's performance slows down, you are getting error messages when updating your virus definitions, your software does not seem to be recognizing malicious code, or any other issue develops that cannot be easily explained and corrected, check your anti-virus and anti-spyware software.

USE AWAY MESSAGES WITH CAUTION

If your e-mail system allows you to create an "away" auto response for times when you won't be able to respond to e-mail right away, be careful how you phrase your message. Don't let potential attackers know that you are not home, or, worse, give specific details about your location and itinerary. Safer options include phrases such as "I will not have access to e-mail between [date] and [date]." If possible, also restrict the recipients of the message to people within your organization or in your address book.

THE MOST DANGEROUS THINGS EMPLOYEES DO ONLINE

Opening e-mail attachments from unknown senders
Everybody should know not to do this, right? And most people do. But no matter how often they are warned, some people still can't resist opening an attachment or clicking on a link when they aren't sure it's safe.

Failing to watch for spoofed e-mails that mimic a known sender but include a malicious attachment
People rarely question a file apparently sent by someone they know, even though it may not have been requested or the reason for it isn't adequately explained.

Installing unauthorized applications on company computers
When employees install programs you don't know about and haven't approved, they are increasing the risk of exposing your system to malicious code and security failures.

Disabling security tools
One of the problems with some security tools—such as firewalls—is that they slow a computer's performance. Frustrated employees have been known to figure out how to turn them off and this leaves the system open to attacks. Employees also try to avoid or work around other security features, such as automated virus updates and requests to change their passwords, because they see these functions as annoyances that keep them from doing their "real" work.

Opening HTML or even plain-text messages from unknown senders
Even people who would never click on an attachment may be unaware that e-mails without an attachment are becoming increasingly dangerous. HTML text and images can be infected with spyware and executable code.

Surfing risky sites
Surfing gambling, porn, other sites with objectionable content, and even music and shopping sites wastes time, reduces productivity, increases the risk of a security breach, and may create a hostile working environment for employees that could lead to litigation and/or fines and other sanctions.

Sharing passwords
Trusting employees may give a colleague, friend, or family member their password. Or, despite instructions on how to create and maintain secure passwords, employees will still use passwords that are easy for someone else to figure out and/or will write them down and keep them somewhere near their computers for easy access.

Using an unknown, untrustworthy WiFi network
It's easy for someone on the road to use the closest WiFi connection, perhaps at an airport or a coffee shop, but there's no way to know for sure that such networks are safe and aren't being run by a malicious attacker. Even if an employee is working offline in a public place but has a wireless card attached to his computer, there's a risk a hacker could access the machine and even your corporate network. Wireless cards should be disabled whenever working offline in public places.

Filling out online forms
Hackers use keyloggers and XSS (cross-site scripting) to steal sensitive data. Users are at greater risk of being hacked when they use the same name and password for most of the sites they visit.

Participating in chat rooms and
social networking sites

Business social networking sites allow people to post messages and maintain an online presence—and they put your information at risk. An attacker can use those sites identity your business partners, vendors, and clients simply by viewing your shared connections, and you may be at further risk for virus and other malicious code infections.

Twenty percent of consumers terminated a relationship with a company after being notified of a security breach.

FAST
FACT

Ponemon Institute, December 2005

DEVELOP A DATA BACKUP PLAN

There are two types of businesses: Those that have already lost data and those that will. Businesses without a data backup plan are vulnerable and will likely face a financial or operational problem in the event of data loss. It's estimated that more than 300 million business PCs have a combined 109 petabytes of data—about half of all the corporate data residing on PCs and laptops—that is not backed up regularly. Use the following tips to develop your data backup plan.

Understand your needs

Consider how much data will require backup by examining the current amount produced and stored on all systems and devices. This will determine the type and amount of media needed for backup activities. Also, estimate future data growth as part of a long-term backup strategy. As a general rule, consider that company data will double every 18 months.

Create a backup schedule

Commit to a daily back up routine along with weekly and monthly full back-ups. Critical data includes payroll and HR records; contracts, leases, and agreements; business records including accounting (AP/AR), customer history and orders, and operational data. Once a routine is established, backup can be conducted incrementally where only the data that has changed requires backup because a copy of older data already exists.

Include all data devices

A storage backup routine should encompass desktops, laptops, servers, and other devices including handhelds.

Protect and secure the backup files

Keep portable backup media in a labeled protective case or package, so it stays clean, undamaged, and organized. Scratches and debris on CDs, DVDs, and tape can impact the retrieval and quality of the stored data. Protect storage media in racks or boxes designed to hold them properly and keep them organized. Always store backup copies of files offsite at a location that is far enough away so a disaster cannot destroy the backup and original source of the data.

Source: Maxell

PROTECT YOUR ONLINE SITES

- Choose a web-hosting service with live customer service during normal business hours. Have a telephone number that will allow you to reach a human being if you need to. Avoid companies that offer only online support.
- Keep backup copies of every web site and page you have. Your web designer should keep copies, you should have a copy on your business system, and keep a duplicate on your personal computer for extra insurance.
- Keep a record of all user names, codes, and passwords needed to access your existing web sites in a central location with an offsite backup.
- Identify backup vendors for all critical online services so that you can quickly switch suppliers if it becomes necessary.
- Periodically evaluate your service levels and needs and make changes when necessary, especially as your grow.

GREAT ADVICE

Laptops are a prime target for theft when traveling. To reduce the risk of your laptop being stolen, keep it inconspicuous by keeping it out of sight; transport it in a backpack or tote bag instead of a tell-tale laptop bag; and keep bags containing laptops closed and, when practical, locked.

One in 20 e-mails are infected with malware.
Panda Software, September 2006

FAST FACT

THE MOST OVERLOOKED ASPECTS OF IT SECURITY

- *Physical security.* In many organizations, physical security is often focused more on protecting copiers, printers, and fax machines from theft—not servers or computer equipment. In addition to protecting your facility from an after-hours break-in, pay attention to places where someone might be able to just walk in at any time and make a network attack or other breach. Those places include your shipping and receiving area, the area where smokers take their breaks, and the cafeteria patio. Be sure the people who are in your facility are supposed to be there. Is the copier repairman who stopped by to perform routine service really a copier repairman—or is he looking for an opportunity to steal critical data?

- *Proper disposal of devices, storage media, and sensitive documents.* Are you throwing out the keys to your most valuable information? Before discarding hard drives and other storage media, be sure all the data is erased. The disks and other media should be completely wiped clean—don't just delete files that could be recovered by an attacker. Remember that cell phones and PDAs also contain sensitive information in a file format similar to that used by your PC, so erase that data before discarding those items as well. Finally, shred every piece of paper you throw out so that dumpster divers can't find sensitive information in your trash.

- *Background checks.* Be sure the people on your IT staff aren't eavesdropping, stealing, or worse. Verify education and previous employment. Do a criminal background check. Look for character issues that will reveal potential risk factors. Ask candidates how they safeguard their own data. Finally, continue to monitor employees once they're on board so that you can spot a worker who is going bad over time.

- *Control the at-home user.* Your office system may be secure, but what about the home offices of telecommuters or company executives? What happens if a user's home is broken into and his computer is stolen? Or if the home user leaves the machine connected to the company network and someone else in the household (such as a technologically precocious kid) accesses the system? Conduct a home security audit and train home users on how to protect their computer and the company network.

- *Take advantage of built-in security functions.* Security is big business these days and hardware vendors know it. Many hardware vendors are building security features directly into their devices, giving them out-of-the-box capabilities that are often unexplored or overlooked. However, keep in mind that these built-in technologies are good for consumers but may conflict with your company's encryption and authentication policies and technologies already in place.

- *Analyze trends in security log files.* Log files can be the key to recognizing an attack. External attackers typically use methodical approaches that can be identified as log trends, enabling the IT organization to block or quarantine them. Internal attackers usually leave an audit trail in their logs that can be backtracked and exposed, enabling IT to catch the perpetrators red-handed.

- *Training.* Some of the worst security problems originate from stupid things done by end users—from the seemingly obvious "no-no" of opening attachments from strangers to connecting to the closest WiFi connection while on the road. Security awareness training should be "in your face" and "real," with things like posters, computer-based training, compliance tracking, and face-to-face interactive training. Re-educate users when policies or technologies change.

- *Outsource security functions.* Using third-party services can be a good way to increase security capabilities and save money. Consider outsourcing labor-intensive tasks such as maintaining and upgrading firewalls or doing log file analysis.

- *Encryption.* Use encryption any place where data is portable and/or at risk.

- *Integrate security with software development.* Vulnerabilities and attacks would be less pervasive if developers had better processes for identifying coding problems and other bugs that lead to security woes. Customer demand will drive this, so choose products that are more secure over those that have more features, and software vendors will get the message and develop and deliver more secure products.

Adapted from Dark Reading, *www.darkreading.com*

WORTH KNOWING

The average unprotected computer can be compromised in a matter of minutes.

The average cost of insider data breaches in the United States is $3.4 million per business per year.

FAST FACT

Ponemon Institute/ArcSight, September 2006

ON-SITE TECH SUPPORT SERVICE PROVIDERS

CompUSA
www.compusa.com
800-266-7872

Data Doctors
www.datadoctors.com

Geek Squad (a unit of Best Buy)
www.geeksquad.com
800-433-5766

Geeks On Call
www.geeksoncall.com
800-905-4335

GeeksOnTime
www.geeksontime.com
800-433-5766

PC Pinpoint
www.pcpinpoint.com
720-890-7887

REMOTE TECH SUPPORT SERVICE PROVIDERS

Live Repair/Ask Dr. Tech
www.liverepair.com
914-747-4144
www.askdrtech.com
914-729-6620

PC Pitstop
www.pcpitstop.com

PlumChoice
www.pcpinpoint.com
888-758-6435

THE GROWING PROBLEM OF CYBERBULLING

Bullies used to be limited to tactics such as physical intimidation, postal mail, and telephone harassment. Technology has created a new breed of tormenter—the cyberbully, who uses e-mail, instant messaging, web pages, and digital photos to harass and intimidate. Forms of cyberbullying can range in severity from cruel or embarrassing rumors to serious threats, harassment, or stalking.

If you or an employee becomes the target of a cyberbully, avoid escalating the situation. Responding with hostility is likely to provoke a bully and spur him (or her—bullies may be female) to take the bullying to a higher level. Depending on the circumstances, consider ignoring the issue. Often, bullies thrive on the reaction of their victims and may just shift to a new target if they aren't getting the response they want. Keep a record of any online activity (e-mails, web pages, instant messages, etc.), including relevant dates and times. In addition to archiving an electronic version, keep a printed copy.

Report cyberbullying to the appropriate authorities. Law enforcement agencies have different policies, but your local police department or FBI branch are good starting points. Unfortunately, there is a distinction between free speech and punishable offenses, but let law enforcement officials and prosecutors decide on possible legal ramifications.

❧ ❧ ❧

CHAPTER 33

Take Care of Yourself

RELEASING STRESS

Let's face it, leadership is a highly stressful endeavor. Yet good leadership requires calmness and an ability to rise above the daily stresses and stay cool and collected.

Great leaders are still smiling when all hell breaks loose, and their ability to avoid stress inoculates their entire organization against the enemy from within. So how can leaders (like you) be less affected by stress and lead people by example? To get rid of your own stress (and lead the way to eliminating it in others), you need to adopt some practices that zap stress and keep it from taking control of you. Here are some simple things you can do while you work.

- *Tense up your fists for a few seconds, then gradually relax them to let the stress flow out of your muscles.* If it feels good but doesn't completely eliminate your tension, try this tense-then-release pattern in other muscles (your arms, neck and shoulders, feet, buttocks, stomach, etc.). Breath deeply to enhance the effect.

- *Take a humor break.* Keep a book of jokes or cartoons at hand and stop for a minute to look through it when you need to release the tension. As soon as you find yourself laughing naturally over a good joke, you will discover you've defused the tension and can go back to work with a new, healthier feeling.

- *Make a "minichange" to improve your workplace or working life.* According to Robert Epstein, author of *The Big Book of Stress Relief Games*, "Small changes have BIG outcomes," at least when you make them yourself and they eliminate any of those all-too-common sources of minor irritation.

- *Breathe deeply and calmly ten times.* Yes, ten whole times; don't cheat and stop early.

- *Make a list of things that make you feel good at work.* Keep it at hand (i.e., post it inside the top drawer of your desk) for quick reference when you need it. Next time you start feeling stressed or irritable, check the list and make yourself pick an activity from it to do right away.

Source: Making Horses Drink: How to Lead and Succeed in Business by Alex Hiam (Entrepreneur Press, 2002)

My biggest mistake has been working too hard and putting myself last, and I am still working on correcting it.

—SHARON LECHTER, CO-AUTHOR OF *RICH DAD POOR DAD* AND A FOUNDER OF THE RICH DAD COMPANY

Owning a business is a marathon so take care of yourself like an elite athlete—otherwise, you will fade fast.

—THOMAS FENIG, FOUNDER AND CEO, OUTDOOR LIGHTING PERSPECTIVES

STAYING FIT ON THE ROAD

Whether you travel regularly or rarely, you know that one of the biggest challenges of being on the road is maintaining a healthy diet and exercise schedule. But letting your personal fitness program slide can increase your stress levels, reduce your productivity, and leave you feeling decidedly unhealthy when you get home.

Make No Excuse: Exercise!

You may have to adjust your exercise routine while you're on the road, but there's no excuse for not exercising at all. If you run, take along your running shoes and ask the hotel for guidance on choosing a route. Or put on your workout clothes and find a staircase to climb (but do it safely, ideally with a companion, and check ahead of time to make sure the stairwells are well-lit and that you'll have access to the building on every floor). Even a brisk walk

will be effective. In fact, walk whenever possible—there are no limits to the exercise you can get while exploring new territory. And if you need to have a conversation with someone, do it while walking—it's good for the other person, too.

Many hotels have workout facilities and pools, so check on that ahead of time, and pack the appropriate clothes and shoes. If your hotel doesn't have an exercise room, ask if there's a nearby gym. Or pack a jump rope—it takes up practically no space in your suitcase but provides a healthy cardiovascular workout in the privacy of your room. And remember that exercises such as sit-ups and push-ups require no equipment at all.

Eat and Drink in Moderation

It can take a great deal of discipline to avoid overindulging at mealtime, especially in cities known for exceptional dining experiences. Total self-denial isn't necessary, but moderation will allow you to enjoy yourself without having to pay a hefty price the next day.

Think about what you want to eat before you enter a restaurant and stick to your plan as closely as possible, no matter how many tempting dishes there are on the menu. Certainly savor the local cuisine, but do it in a healthy way. Or don't even look at the menu—just order a healthy meal. Most restaurants will be able to accommodate you.

Eat and drink as close to your at-home schedule as possible. Avoid skipping meals; when you allow yourself to become famished, you'll tend to overeat at the next meal or consume too much in the way of unhealthy snacks. Take your own health-oriented condiments (butter or salt substitutes, special seasonings, fat-free dressings, etc.) and don't be embarrassed about using them discreetly even in fine restaurants. After all, you're the one who has to deal with the consequences of what you eat and drink, not your servers or dinner companions.

Put Yourself First When Scheduling

Certainly you'll have to consider others when making your travel plans, but make your own health and comfort a top priority. If you're flying across several time zones, especially west-to-east, book a daytime arrival. Then head outside and do something active in the natural daylight—it will help your recovery from jet lag.

It's natural to want to maximize your time when you're traveling, but you should include exercise and rest in your schedule. Plan a specific time each day or every other day to do your exercise routines. Avoid going straight from a day of meetings to an important dinner; refresh yourself with a short nap and a shower. End your evenings early enough to allow time to relax and unwind before falling asleep. And even though breakfast meetings can be extremely productive, getting up earlier than you're accustomed to can interfere with your sleep patterns and make you tired and dull for the rest of the day.

While You're on the Plane

Dehydration causes fatigue and airplane cabins are extremely dry. Drink plenty of water (that's water, not coffee, soft drinks, or alcoholic beverages) prior to the flight, while you're en route, and after you arrive. Bring your own water bottle on board and plan to drink at least eight ounces for each hour

you're in the air. While in flight, avoid alcohol and salty foods and eat lightly. Carry your own healthy snacks with you. If you're on a meal flight (rare as they are these days), call ahead and request a low-fat or vegetarian dish.

Relieve the monotony of the flight and do something good for yourself by exercising on the plane. This doesn't mean push-ups in the aisle. Get up and walk the length of the aircraft at least once every hour; it will keep you from feeling stiff when you land and help prevent problems due to poor circulation.

You can also perform discreet exercises while in your seat. For example, relax your jaw and facial muscles by squeezing your eyes and closing your mouth tightly, hold for five seconds, then release. Repeat several times. Open your mouth and "yawn" widely, or mouth the five vowel sounds in an exaggerated way. For shoulders, lift your shoulders then bring them forward and push them down. Then pull them back and return to your starting position. Repeat in the opposite direction. To stretch and relax your back, extend your arms in front of you and lift them over your head. Lead with your arms and let your head and shoulders curl down toward the floor. Curl back up slowly, stretching the spine. Leg exercises can be tricky in the confines of a plane, but try this one if you have room. Place both hands under your right thigh and pull your knee toward

> *The winners in life treat their body as if it were a magnificent spacecraft that gives them the finest transportation and endurance for their lives.*
>
> *Words of Wisdom*
>
> —DENIS WAITLEY

your chest. Extend the leg straight in front as far as you can. Relax, bend your knee and return to the original position. Repeat with the other leg. Exercise your buttocks by tightening and squeezing, hold for five to ten seconds, then release. Keep your ankles, feet, and toes limber by lifting one foot and writing each letter of the alphabet in the air. Repeat with the other foot.

Have Fun

The most important thing to remember is to enjoy yourself and make the most of the time you're on the road. Whether you're traveling for business or pleasure, you'll be more alert, effective, and productive if you stay fit by exercising, eating right and getting adequate rest.

Life is all about people, not about things. As you get older, your friends often die off, so the more friends you can build in your earlier years in your life that are lasting friends, true friends, the more enjoyment you'll have later in your life. I think that friends are much more important than anything else if you want to enjoy your later years.

—ROBERT A. FUNK, FOUNDER AND CHAIRMAN,
EXPRESS PERSONNEL SERVICES

WORTH KNOWING

Common symptoms of stress include rapid heartbeat, headache, stick neck and/or tight shoulders, backache, rapid breathing, sweating and sweaty palms, and upset stomach, nausea, or diarrhea. You may also notice signs of stress in your thinking, behavior, or mood.

GREAT ADVICE

There's no way to avoid an occasional "one of those days"—days when suppliers don't deliver, customers are unreasonable, the computer has a mind of its own, and you can't seem to do anything right. Consider maintaining a special file of complimentary cards and notes from customers. When you're having a bad day, go through your morale-boosting messages to remind yourself of the difference you make for the customers you serve.

THRIVING IN A RAPIDLY CHANGING WORLD

The pace of today's ever-changing world can be overwhelming and unsettling, but if you're prepared it can present a wealth of opportunities. To keep change as a positive element in your business, develop these habits:

- *Accept the certainty of uncertainty.* Our world is filled with ambiguity, shifting priorities, differing expectations, unanswered questions, new ways of doing old things, and phenomenal growth, so accept the certainty of uncertainty—it's here to stay.

- *Become a quick-change artist.* It's natural to resist change and want to maintain a familiar environment, but that path is a dead-end street. Success requires you to abandon the status quo, overcome addictions to your comfort zone, and adapt to new situations and ways of doing things very quickly.

- *Keep learning.* We are all the sum of what we read, hear, and experience. Practice the 30/10 rule: Commit a minimum of 30 minutes each

continued on page 306

TAKING A VACATION

For many business owners, vacations are a mere distant memory of life in the corporate world, where you had plenty of people to cover for you when you took your annual break. But when you're a solo operation, even a husband and wife team, or even have a small team of employees, one of the biggest challenges of being in business may be to find the time to get away long enough to relax and rejuvenate. But vacations are critical, so use the following tips to make sure you get the time off you need.

- *Plan ahead.* Schedule your vacation time far enough in advance that you can plan your work load around your time off. It's also a good idea to coordinate your schedule with your family to make sure that everyone is planning for the same goal.
- *Build a back-up network.* Look for people you trust who can handle work that can't wait while you're gone. If you're a solo operator, develop a strong network of similarly-situated business owners who can help you and who you can help. It's a good idea to draw up a written agreement to protect everyone in terms of the client's status, obligations, and compensation.
- *Notify your regular clients.* About a week before you leave, tell the clients with whom you communicate regularly that you'll be unavailable. You may need to tell them sooner if it means rescheduling some of their work. Most clients understand; they know you need to get away, and they'll usually work with you.
- *Take some of your work with you.* Sometimes a change of scenery is worthwhile even if you can't totally escape your business. Use technology to keep up while you enjoy some time at a resort.
- *Consider several short breaks throughout the year instead of one long vacation.* A Friday-through-Monday break can often be achieved without your clients even being aware that you were gone.

Whether you're one of those people who believes in the value of vacations or you're a workaholic who views them as a waste of time, it's a good idea to structure your business so you can take time off if necessary. Think about what might happen if you become ill or have another emergency that takes you away from your business—you need a plan that will take care of your clients and protect your company.

> *You work to be able to enjoy quality time away from work. Sometimes it is more important to earn more time than money.*

Words of Wisdom

—DON ABBOTT, PRESIDENT,
ABBOTT VIDEO PRODUCTIONS, INC.

day to actively seek out new information and then spend 10 minutes deciding how to apply this new information to your life.

- *Discard your prejudices.* Prejudices can stifle your creativity and limit your ability to respond to change. Open your mind and unhook your prejudices.

- *Watch trends and collect ideas.* Pay attention to what's going on, and create an idea file in which you can stash tidbits that catch your attention for later review and use.

- *Cultivate and maintain a solid resource network.* Never pass up an opportunity to interact with another human being. And remember that networking is a two-way street—it's about getting *and* giving support and assistance.

- *Be a fixer, not a finger-pointer.* Don't just complain about problems; instead, welcome the opportunity for creative problem-solving.

- *Lighten up.* Negativism and its byproduct, stress, cloud judgment and interfere with objectivity. The benefits of optimism and a sense of humor cannot be overestimated in a climate of change and chaos.

- *Stop waiting.* Many people can make an entire life out of getting ready to do something. Change doesn't wait, and the opportunities found in change today may not be there tomorrow. Develop a sense of urgency and couple it with action. The best insurance for tomorrow is the best use of today.

When I was just getting started in business, a man I respected took me aside one day and said, 'You're a bright young man, you've got a lot going for you, but you're probably not going to make a great success out of yourself because you've got a negative attitude. That negative attitude is going to cause you to have a built-in governor.' I didn't really understand the power of a positive attitude, but what he said had a great impact on me because I was very focused on being a success. When I began making a deliberate effort to be positive, the change in my life was remarkable. I liked how I felt when I was positive. The people who worked for me became more productive. And I no longer had a governor stopping me from achieving my goals.

—RUSS WHITNEY, FOUNDER & CEO,
WHITNEY INFORMATION NETWORK, INC.

QUITTING IS NOT THE SAME AS FAILING

Strategic quitting is a conscious decision you make based on the choices that are available to you. If you realize you're at a dead end compared with what you could be investing in, quitting is not only a reasonable choice, it's a smart one.

Failing, on the other hand, means that your dream is over. Failing happens when you give up, when there are no other options, or when you quit so often that you've used up all your time and resources.

Source: Seth Godin, The Dip: A little book that teaches you when to quit (and when to stick), (Portfolio, 2007)

Take care of your body. It's the only place you have to live.

—JIM ROHN, AUTHOR,
SPEAKER, PHILOSOPHER

LEARN TO SAY NO

The word no is the most powerful word you can use, and not being able to say it can bring disaster. Bosses who can't say no will create confusion. You cannot let everyone take next Friday off, you'll have an empty office. You cannot let all of your delinquent accounts enjoy an additional 90 days to pay. Bank officials can't say yes to everyone who applies for a loan. Coaches can't let everyone play, no matter how much the wannabe athletes plead. Protect your schedule, your life balance, your integrity, and your relationships by declining when you need to.

The following tips will help you say no without jeopardizing relationships:

- Assure the person that you respect his or her request, and that your decline isn't personal. "Sounds like a very good project, Joe, but my packed schedule won't allow me to participate."
- Explain why your refusal benefits both of you. Declining membership on a committee, say: "I'm going to be traveling extensively. If I accepted, I couldn't attend meetings or do volunteer work. You'll benefit more by getting someone who will be available."
- Invite the other person to help you make the decision. Let's say your boss gives you a big assignment. Respond with: "Here's a list of what you have me working on already. If I take this new assignment, I'll have to drop something. Please tell me which projects deserve top priority."
- If you can't do everything someone wants, offer some service: "No, I can't be responsible for four Rotary Club programs in February, but I can be in charge of one if that will help."

Source: Bill Lampton, Ph.D., author of The Complete Communicator: Change Your Communication, Change Your Life!

The smartest thing I've ever done is married Kim. It's important to have a true partner in life. Some men like to play 'Me Tarzan, you Jane.' I don't. Kim is my best friend, my business partner, and my wife.

—ROBERT KIYOSAKI, FOUNDER OF THE RICH DAD FAMILY OF COMPANIES

Words of Wisdom

❧ ❧ ❧

SPECIAL SECTION FOR START-UPS

I f you're in the start-up stage—anywhere from "just thinking about it" to "ready to go"—this section is for you. You might want to take a look at the statistics in Section One to remind yourself how important small business is to the U.S. economy. And, of course, use the rest of the information in this book as you're organizing, launching, and running your new venture. Remember, you're getting ready to do something very important—important to yourself, your family, your community, and yes, the country.

❧ ❧ ❧

CHAPTER 34

What Kind of Business Should You Start and Are You Ready?

WORKSHEET FOR STARTING A BUSINESS

You dream of owning your own business, but are you ready to turn that dream into a reality? This worksheet will help you get started. There are no right or wrong answers, but going through the list will help you identify how prepared you are to be in business for yourself and where you need assistance.

Your Reasons for Wanting to Own Your Own Business

1. Do you want freedom from the 9–5 daily work routine? _____

2. Do you want to be your own boss? _____

3. Do you want to be able to do what you want when you want to do it? _____

4. Do you want to improve your standard of living? _____

5. Are you bored with your present job? _____

6. Do you have a product or service for which you feel there is a demand? _____

Some reasons are better than others and none are wrong. Be aware that there are trade-offs when you transition from employee to owner. You might replace your 9–5 routine with one that starts much earlier and ends later. You might find that you don't have the freedom you thought you would. You might also find that even though you're working harder in your own business you are being rewarded both financially and in other ways at a far greater level.

WORKSHEET FOR STARTING A BUSINESS, continued

Self-Analysis

Answer these questions about your personal characteristics:

1. Are you a leader? _____

2. Do you like to make your own decisions? _____

3. Do others turn to you for help in making decisions? _____

4. Do you enjoy competition? _____

5. Do you have will power and self discipline? _____

6. Do you plan ahead? _____

7. Do you like people? _____

8. Do you get along well with others? _____

Your Personal Conditions

1. Are you aware that running your own business may require working 12–16 hours a day, six days a week, and maybe even Sundays and holidays? _____

2. Do you have the physical stamina to handle the workload and schedule? _____

3. Do you have the emotional strength to withstand the strain? _____

4. Are you prepared, if needed, to temporarily lower your standard of living until your business is firmly established? _____

5. Is your family prepared to go along with the strains they too must bear? _____

6. Are you prepared to lose your savings? _____

Your Personal Skills and Experience

1. Do you know what basic skills you will need in order to have a successful business? _____

   _____

2. Do you possess those skills? _____

3. When hiring personnel will you be able to determine if the applicants' skills meet the requirements for the positions you are filling? _____

4. Have you ever worked in a managerial or supervisory capacity? _____

WORKSHEET FOR STARTING A BUSINESS, continued

5. Have you ever worked in a business similar to the one you want to start? _____

6. Have you had any business training in school? _____

7. If you discover you don't have the basic skills needed for your business, will you be willing to delay your plans until you've acquired the necessary skills? _____

Certain skills and experience are critical to the success of a business. It's unlikely that any given individual possesses all the skills and experience needed to start and run a successful business. You'll need to hire personnel to supply the talent and expertise you lack.

Your Business Idea

1. Identify and briefly describe the business you plan to start. _____

2. Identify the product or service you plan to sell. _____

3. Does your product or service satisfy an unfilled need in the market? _____

4. Will your product or service serve an existing market in which demand exceeds supply? ____

_____

5. Will your product or service be competitive based on its quality, selection, price, or location?

Your Market Analysis

1. Do you know who your customers will be? _____

2. Do you understand their needs and desires? _____

3. Do you know where they live? _____

4. Will you be offering the kind of products or services that they will buy? _____

5. Will your prices be competitive in quality and value? _____

6. Will your promotional program be effective? _____

7. Do you understand how your business compares with your competitors? _____

8. Will your business be conveniently located for the people you plan to serve? _____

9. Will there be adequate parking facilities for the people you plan to serve? _____

Planning Your Business Start-Up

1. Have you chosen a name for your business? _____

WORKSHEET FOR STARTING A BUSINESS, continued

2. Have you chosen to operate as a sole proprietorship, partnership, or corporation? _____

3. Do you know which licenses and permits you may need to operate your business? _____

4. Do you know the business laws you will have to obey? _____

5. Do you have a lawyer who can advise you and help you with legal papers? _____

6. Are you aware of:

   Occupational Safety and Health Administration (OSHA) requirements? _____

   Regulations covering hazardous material? _____

   Local ordinances covering signs, snow removal, etc.? _____

   Federal Tax Code provisions pertaining to small business? _____

   Federal regulations on withholding taxes _____

   Social Security? _____

   State Workers' Compensation laws? _____

Risk Protection Considerations

1. Fire _____

2. Theft _____

3. Robbery _____

4. Vandalism _____

5. Accident liability _____

6. Product liability _____

Your Business Premises and Location

1. Have you found a suitable building in a location that is convenient for your customers? _____

   _____

2. Can the building be modified for your needs at a reasonable cost? _____

3. Have you considered renting or leasing with an option to buy? _____

4. Will you have a lawyer check the zoning regulations and lease? _____

WORKSHEET FOR STARTING A BUSINESS, continued

Your Merchandise

1. Have you decided what items you will sell or produce or what service(s) you will provide?

   _____

2. Have you made a merchandise plan based upon estimated sales to determine the amount of inventory you will need to control purchases? _____

3. Have you found reliable suppliers who will assist you in the start-up? _____

4. Have you compared the prices quality and credit terms of suppliers? _____

Creating and Maintaining Business Records

1. Are you prepared to maintain complete records of sales income and expenses accounts payable and receivables? _____

2. Have you determined how to handle payroll records tax reports and payments? _____

   _____

3. Do you know what financial reports should be prepared and how to prepare them? _____

   _____

So that you can plan adequately to fund your business and have sufficient working capital to cover your expenses (at least for the first three months of operation) until your business begins to generate revenue, answer these questions about your finances (use the worksheets on pages 334–336 to calculate your answers):

1. How much money do you have? _____

2. How much money will you need to start your business? _____

3. How much money will you need to stay in business? _____

PERSONAL FINANCIAL STATEMENT WORKSHEET

Assets

Cash on hand   _____

Savings account   _____

Stocks, bonds, securities   _____

Accounts/notes receivable   _____

Real estate   _____

Life insurance (cash value)   _____

Automobile/other vehicles   _____

Other liquid assets   _____

Liabilities

Accounts payable   _____

Notes payable   _____

Taxes   _____

Real estate loans   _____

Other liabilities   _____

Total Assets   _____

– Total Liabilities   _____

Net Worth   _____

START-UP COST ESTIMATE WORKSHEET

Decorating, remodeling   _____

Fixtures, equipment   _____

Installing fixtures, equipment   _____

Services, supplies   _____

Beginning inventory cost   _____

Legal, professional fees   _____

Licenses, permits   _____

Telephone utility deposits   _____

Insurance   _____

Signs   _____

Advertising for opening   _____

Unanticipated expenses   _____

Total start-up costs   _____

MONTHLY EXPENSE WORKSHEET

Your living costs _____

Employee wages _____

Rent _____

Advertising _____

Supplies _____

Utilities _____

Insurance _____

Taxes _____

Maintenance _____

Delivery/transportation _____

Miscellaneous _____

Total monthly expenses _____

ESTIMATED TOTAL CASH NEEDED FOR START-UP AND WORKING CAPITAL

Total start-up costs _____

Total monthly expenses _____ times 3 _____

Total cash needed _____

Adapted from Small Business Administration survey

> *My Rich Dad told me, 'You do not know what you do not know.' To find out what you don't know, you need to start, and begin making mistakes. Mistakes tell you what you do not know.*
>
> —ROBERT KIYOSAKI, FOUNDER OF THE RICH DAD FAMILY OF COMPANIES

Words of Wisdom

Fiction
To be an entrepreneur, you must be born that way.

Fact
Anyone can learn to operate like an entrepreneur.

DO YOU HAVE WHAT IT TAKES TO BE A SUCCESSFUL ENTREPRENEUR?

The Characteristics of Successful Entrepreneurs

- Persistence
- Desire for immediate feedback
- Inquisitiveness
- Strong drive to achieve
- High energy level
- Goal-oriented behavior
- Independent
- Demanding
- Self-confident
- Calculated risk taker
- Creative
- Innovative
- Vision
- Commitment
- Problem solving skills
- Tolerance for ambiguity
- Strong integrity
- Highly reliable
- Personal initiative
- Ability to consolidate resources
- Strong management and organizational skills
- Competitive
- Change agent
- Tolerance for failure
- Desire to work hard
- Luck

Characteristics of Creative People

- Bright
- Adaptable
- High self esteem
- Challenge-oriented
- Idea-oriented
- Inquisitive
- Curious

Sources of Innovative Ideas

- Unsatisfied customers
- Demographic changes in society
- Luck
- Imagination
- Vision
- Problem-solving

Source: Small Business Administration

STARTING A BUSINESS CHECKLIST

❑ Choose a business.

❑ Research the business idea.

❑ What will you sell?

❑ Is it legal?

❑ Who will buy it and how often?

❑ Are you willing to do what it takes to sell the product?

❑ What will it cost to produce, advertise, sell, and deliver?

❑ With what laws will you have to comply?

❑ Can you make a profit?

❑ How long will it take to make a profit?

❑ Write a business plan and marketing plan.

❑ Choose a business name.

❑ See if the business name is available for use as a domain name.

❑ Register the domain name even if you're not ready to use it yet.

❑ Choose a location for the business.

❑ Check zoning laws.

❑ File partnership, corporate, or limited liability company papers with the Secretary of State's office.

❑ File state tax forms with your state Department of Revenue or Treasury Department.

❑ Check your state licensing authorities to get any required business licenses or permits.

❑ Contact the Internal Revenue Service for information on filing your federal tax schedules.

❑ Apply for a seller's permit or resale license, if necessary in your state if you are going to sell tangible personal property. Examples of tangible personal property include such items as furniture, giftware, toys, antiques, clothing, cars, etc.

❑ Contact your state Board of Equalization or its equivalent to see if you are responsible for any fuel, alcohol, tobacco, or other special taxes and fees.

❑ Apply for an employer identification number with your state Department of Labor, Department of Employment, or its equivalent if you will have employees.

WORTH KNOWING

If you are planning to start a retail store, don't base your inventory on impulse items. These items need to be seen to be purchased. When people are in a store to buy something else, they may see an impulse item and decide to buy it—but they wouldn't have gone into the store just to buy that item. Impulse items can increase your sales, but they don't work as the foundation of your retail inventory.

STARTING A BUSINESS CHECKLIST, continued

❑ Find out about workers' compensation if you will have employees.

❑ Register or reserve any federal trademark or service mark.

❑ Register copyrights.

❑ Apply for patent if you will be marketing an invention.

❑ Order any required notices (advertisements) of your intent to do business in the community.

❑ Have business phone or extra residential phone lines installed.

❑ Check into business insurance needs.

❑ Get adequate business insurance or a business rider to a homeowner's policy.

❑ Get tax information such as record-keeping requirements, information on withholding taxes if you will have employees, information on hiring independent contractors, facts about estimating taxes, form of organization, etc.

❑ Open bank account for the business.

❑ Have business cards and stationery printed.

❑ Purchase equipment or supplies.

❑ Order inventory, signage, and fixtures.

❑ Get a business e-mail address.

❑ Get your web site set up.

❑ Have sales literature prepared.

❑ Call for information about Yellow Pages advertising.

❑ Place advertising in newspapers or other media if your type of business will benefit from paid advertising.

❑ Call everyone you know and let them know you are in business.

Source: SBA, Starting a Business Handbook

Fundamentals are the minimum. Distinctive is the difference. Every competitor I have is good—otherwise, they wouldn't be in business. Being good is the entry to the game. To win, you have to be distinctive.

Words of Wisdom

—RANDY PENNINGTON,
PENNINGTON PERFORMANCE GROUP

TIPS TO GO FROM DREAMING TO DOING

Get the point of life
It's short; if you don't do it now, when will you?

Get passionate
Most successful businesses are built on the entrepreneur's passion.

Get a grip on "it"
"It" is what scares you—and "it" is different for everyone. Understand that fear comes with the territory.

Get real
Know that it isn't going to be easy.

Get informed
Talk to people, join associations, and read everything relevant.

Get ready
Set a target date, and create a plan to get you there.

Get support
If you have a network, call on them. If you don't, create one.

Get going
Do at least one thing a day to advance your plan.

Source: Valerie Young, author of the Changing Course *newsletter*

BUYING A BUSINESS

Getting into business for yourself doesn't necessarily require building a company from scratch. If the thought of navigating your way through the start-up process is holding you back, consider taking the entrepreneurial plunge a different way: buy an existing business.

This alternative route to business ownership has some advantages worth considering. It allows you to bypass all the steps involved in creating a business infrastructure because the original owner has already done that. You can take over an operation that is already generating cash flow, and perhaps even profits. You'll have a history on which to build your forecasts and a future that includes an established customer base. And there's generally less risk involved in buying a going concern than there is in creating a whole new company.

Of course, there are drawbacks to buying a business. Though the actual dollar amounts depend on the size and type of business, it often takes more cash to buy an existing business than to start one yourself. When you buy a company's assets, you'll also usually get stuck with at least some of the liabilities. And it's highly unlikely that you'll find an existing business that is precisely the company you would have built on your own. Even so, you jut might find the business you want is currently owned by someone else.

Why do people sell businesses—especially profitable ones? For a variety of reasons. Many entrepreneurs are happiest during the start-up and early growth stages of a company; once the business is running smoothly, they get bored and begin looking for something new. Other business owners may grow tired of the responsibility, or be facing health or other personal issues that motivate them to sell their companies. In fact, some of the most successful entrepreneurs go into business with a solid plan for how they're going to get out when the time comes.

It's a good idea to at least consider buying a business as part of your early planning—especially if the appeal of being in business for yourself is in running the company rather than starting it.

NEGOTIATING TO BUY A BUSINESS

When you've found a business you're interested in buying, don't be the first to mention price. Let the seller name the first figure, and negotiate from there. If there's a broker involved, remember that brokers are the seller's agents and make their money from the commission the seller pays. Though it may not be necessary, consider hiring someone skilled in business acquisitions to represent your interest.

Settling on the price is only the first step in negotiating the sale. The structure of the deal is more important than the actual price. Be prepared to pay between 30 and 50 percent of the price in cash, and arrange terms on the remaining amount. The seller may be willing to hold a note, which assures him of future income. Sellers may also be open to other terms, such as providing benefits like a company car or insurance for a period of time after the sale is completed. Though such agreements may reduce the up-front cash you need, approach them with caution. Have your attorney study the details for legality and liability and be sure they won't cause problems later on—you want your time to be spent running the business not correcting a mistake you made in the acquisition.

Consider including a non-compete clause in your terms of sale—your new business won't be worth much if the seller opens a competing operation down the street a few weeks after you take over his old company.

EVALUATING A BUSINESS

One of the most challenging financial calculations is figuring out what a business is worth. You may want to take the time to research the selling price and terms of recently-sold companies in the industry, and use them as a guide. Or you may value the company based on its after-tax cash flow, or the value of assets if they were liquidated minus the debts and liabilities. You should call on your financial advisors to assist you with working through these calculations.

The figures are only part of the equation. Elements that are not quite so easy to value include the company's reputation and the strength of the relationship the current owner has with customers, suppliers, and employees.

Thorough due diligence is an essential part of the acquisition process. Your pre-acquisition research must include reviewing, auditing, and verifying all the relevant information regarding the business—doing that means you'll know exactly what you are buying and from whom. Use a wide range of professionals to help you during the process. Your accountant will assist you in evaluating the financial statements your banker can help with financing issues; and your attorney should guide you in researching the legal aspects. Consult other experts as appropriate, depending on the industry and specifics involved.

Even as you gather and consider input from your advisors, remember that you are the buyer and the final decision-maker. Once the deal is made, the responsibility for making it work is yours, so don't do anything with which you're not completely comfortable.

Let the seller know your plans for the business. They probably have an emotional as well as a financial investment in the business and will be more comfortable and supportive of the entire process if they feel good about what's going to happen after they leave.

Though you should certainly negotiate for the best price, be willing to pay a fair price. A seller who feels good about the price and terms will make a much more positive contribution to the transition than one who feels ripped off.

Finally, remember that you can walk away from the deal at any point in the negotiation process before a contract is signed.

TURN YOUR HOBBY INTO A PROFITABLE BUSINESS

It sounds like a dream: an activity you love so much, you'd do it even if you weren't getting paid. One way to make that dream a reality is to turn your hobby into a business.

The critical first step is to determine the commercial viability of your hobby. Your friends and family may ooh and ahh over whatever it is you're doing, but when it gets down to the bottom line, will they get out their checkbooks and pay you to do more?

Before you start your business, determine if there is a real market for what you want to do, how best to reach that market, and what you'll need to do to produce a sufficient volume of product.

Remember that with a hobby, you do things when you feel like it—and if you don't feel like working, there are no real consequences. When you're in business, that changes. Customers depend on you. It doesn't matter if you're not in the mood—you must deliver.

HOW DO YOU DISTINGUISH BETWEEN A BUSINESS AND A HOBBY?

Since hobby expenses are deductible only to the extent of hobby income, it is important to distinguish them from expenses incurred in an activity engaged in for profit. In making this distinction, all facts and circumstances with respect to the activity are taken into account and no one factor alone is decisive. Among the factors normally taken into account are the following:

- Do you carry on the activity in a businesslike manner?
- Does the time and effort you put into the activity indicate that you intend to make it profitable?
- Do you depend on income from the activity for your livelihood?
- Are your losses due to circumstances beyond your control (or are they normal in the start-up phase of your type of business)?
- Do you change your methods of operation in an attempt to improve profitability?
- Do you, or your advisors, have the knowledge to carry on the activity as a successful business?
- Were you successful in making a profit in similar activities in the past?
- Does the activity make a profit in some years, and if so, how much profit?
- Can you expect to make a future profit from the appreciation of the assets used in the activity?

Source: Internal Revenue Service

There are some things you don't have to know how it works—only that it works. While some people are studying the roots, others are picking the fruit. It just depends on which end of this you want to get in on.

—JIM ROHN

Words of Wisdom

TIPS FOR CHOOSING A BUSINESS OPPORTUNITY

- Make an honest evaluation of yourself and your abilities.
- Be enthusiastic about the business you'll be operating.
- Be knowledgeable about the product or service with which you will be involved.
- Make a market evaluation of the product or service to be offered.
- Analyze the market trends.
- How many buyers have been in the business and for what period of time?
- Check the skills required to run the business properly.
- Calculate the business opportunity's profitability and financial leverage ratios.
- Determine how much time you need to earn what you do now.
- Check with current operators to see what they are doing now.
- Get the history of the offering company's operation.
- Learn about the service personnel at the parent company.
- Examine the financial standing of the parent company.
- Evaluate the policies and plans of the company with the associations and business groups with which the parent company or seller is involved.
- Find out whether complaints against the company have been registered with the Better Business Bureau.
- Get a status report on the firm from Dun & Bradstreet.
- Have your attorney or CPA evaluate the company.
- Visit the licenser-seller's office at your earliest convenience.

Source: Andi Axman, Entrepreneur Magazine's Ultimate Small Business Advisor

CHAPTER 35

ᐧᐧᐧ

Franchising

WHAT IS A FRANCHISE?

Franchising is often referred to as an industry, but that's incorrect. Franchising is a method of marketing products or services within a structure dictated by the franchisor. When you buy a franchise, you are entering into an agreement either to distribute products or to operate under a format identified with and structured by the parent company. One major advantage of franchising is that you have the opportunity to buy into a product or system that is established, rather than having to create everything yourself. There is, of course, a price for this—in addition to your start-up equipment and inventory, you'll have to pay a franchise fee. Most franchise companies collect ongoing royalties, usually a percentage of your gross sales. Some creative, independent people may find a franchise too restrictive; others appreciate the established systems and the ongoing guidance and support.

TIPS FOR RESEARCHING A FRANCHISE

1.Mine franchisees

It seems like an obvious place to start, but few franchise prospects talk to franchisees, even though they're given names in the Uniform Franchise Offering Circular (UFOC). When you do contact franchisees, choose carefully. Call some franchisees who weren't on the franchisor's recommended list, and if possible, get in touch with some former franchisees. You'll also want to call franchisees who operate in a market and format similar to yours.

Ask tough questions. You want nitty-gritty details on revenue, customer counts, ramp-up times, franchisor support, and line-item costs such as labor, rent, and supplies. With this data, you can create your own P&L projection. Also, visit franchisees at their stores; you'll get more information in person and you'll see the franchise in operation.

2. Dig into the UFOC

The UFOC furnishes tons of franchisor details, but most prospective franchisees barely give this federally required disclosure document a glance. You should use the UFOC as a starting point for further investigation. For instance, if the UFOC lists lawsuits against the company, a franchise attorney can usually obtain the actual lawsuit filings. Be aware that the UFOC's summaries of the suits were written by the franchisor, not an unbiased third party. Read the actual court documents to get a better sense of exactly who's suing and what they allege.

Be sure to ask management probing questions about any revenue or earnings figures found in the UFOC. The FTC's guide to evaluating franchise offers notes that such figures may be averages, which aren't necessarily representative of a typical store, or may have been calculated on a small store base rather than across the entire chain.

One thing few prospective franchisees do is obtain the UFOCs of several competitors in their category of interest. Comparing these side by side can reveal crucial differences in cost, royalty rates, marketing or corporate support.

3. Ramp up research

It's easy to learn more about a franchisor and its management team by cruising the internet. For a small fee, you can check an online news database such as LexisNexis for articles written about the company or its managers. You may find past troubles that have been airbrushed out of a manager's resume, or company missteps written up by a local paper.

A word of caution: Be sure to take what you find online with a grain of salt, and verify what you learn—many sites, blogs, and chat forums have no editors.

Business research companies may also be helpful in vetting a franchisor. Other good sources for a company reputation check include local Better Business Bureaus and state attorneys general, particularly in the 14 U.S. states that regulate franchising: California, Hawaii, Illinois, Indiana, Maryland, Michigan, Minnesota, New York, North Dakota, Rhode Island, South Dakota, Virginia, Washington, and Wisconsin.

4. Meet the management

Ask hard questions of franchisor managers. Walk away from headquarters with a clear sense of just what the company will do for franchisees—and what it won't.

5. Know the market

How does the franchise fit into the competitive picture? It's essential to learn about current players in the sector, their expansion plans, and how many new competitors might be circling.

6. Get advice

Many franchisees cut their research time by using a broker or consultant who has already researched many franchises. But be aware that few consultants work with every franchise out there. Work with several brokers to get exposure to a broader range of franchise options. Run the franchisor's financials by an accountant and have an experienced franchise attorney look over the UFOC.

7. Beat the tom-toms

Many people interact with a franchisor other than the franchisees. These include vendors, corporate store managers, competitors, local media, and of course, customers. All may prove to be good information sources. Many are easy to find, too. For instance, you can interview customers in stores or read their often-unvarnished opinions online at various customer-feedback sites.

Source: Carole Tice, "Find Your Franchise Match,"
Entrepreneur.com

RED FLAGS, GREEN FLAGS

► Red Flag

You heard a pitch for a new business, and after ten minutes you just knew this was it—the perfect business for you. It may, indeed, ultimately turn out to be the business for you, but you can't allow yourself to be pulled in by one sales pitch. There is no love-at-first-sight when selecting a franchise.

► Green Flag

You've visited a good selection of current franchisees, and they've given you favorable information about the franchise. Key questions to ask them: Was the training valuable? Do you enjoy the work? What are the strengths and weaknesses of the business? What were your gross sales last year? And the clincher: If you had it to do over, would you buy this franchise again?

► Red Flag

You've called on franchisees in the system, and they've uniformly told you the franchise is the biggest mistake they've ever made. They've even tried to dissuade you from it. The franchisees know the qualities of the franchise business better than anyone, and you should consider their independent views on the program. Always value the view from the trenches, especially if you're thinking about jumping into the trenches yourself.

► Green Flag

You've taken the franchisor financial statements included in the UFOC to a financial advisor and the franchise agreement to a good legal advisor, and they've both given you the go-ahead.

Source: Carole Tice, "Find Your Franchise Match,"
Entrepreneur.com

Every one of our franchisees should wake up in the morning, look in the mirror, and say, 'There's a whole new world out there today. How am I going to adjust to it?' That is what it takes to be successful not only in this business but in any business.

Words of Wisdom

—Joe McGuinness, Founder, Signs By Tomorrow

WHAT DO FRANCHISORS WANT IN FRANCHISEES?

- Fully 94 percent of franchisors who responded said "good people skills" are either important or very important for prospective franchisees.
- The second most important key to franchisee success is the "ability to be coached"—87 percent of surveyed franchisors ranked it important or very important. Don't misunderstand. An "entrepreneurial mind-set" is also highly valued by franchisors (76 percent ranked it as important or very important). Owning a franchise business, even though it must follow a formula, takes soaring creativity, dogged persistence, and business drive. Successful franchisees must learn to balance the entrepreneurial mind-set with the ability to follow the franchise system.
- The third most important quality to franchisors, with an 86 percent ranking, is "general business skills." That's a huge difference from the ranking for "specific industry skills," which only 29 percent of franchisors consider important. Franchisors value business common sense, a sense of what is important in a successful business. That means paying attention

to financial details, managing cash and cash flow, understanding the importance of promotion and advertising, knowing how to hire employees, focusing on the customer, ensuring quality and consistency of products and services, and striving for excellence in all aspects of your operation. The general business skill that ranks above all others is the art of the sale.

• The next key to success, with 84 percent of franchisors ranking it as important or very important, is "access to capital." Satisfying the capital needs of a newly established business is, without question, a sobering challenge. You need a well-grounded banking relationship with an institution that understands your plans and is prepared to extend your business the credit it needs to succeed.

Source: Andrew A. Caffey, "Are You Franchise Material?," Entrepreneur.com

CONSIDER AN EXISTING FRANCHISE

In your search for a franchise, don't overlook an existing outlet. Though most people think of "buying a franchise" as the purchase of a new franchise, existing franchise operations are regularly bought and sold. It's becoming increasingly common for mid-level managers who leave the corporate world through downsizing to start a franchised operation with the idea of selling it in 10 or 12 years and using that money for their retirement. If you see a franchise you'd like to buy, first go to the owner. The franchisor will probably have to approve the final sale, but your negotiations will primarily be with the individual franchisee.

HOT FRANCHISE OPPORTUNITIES

Senior-care services
As America ages, the senior-care industry is maturing beautifully. Growing 342 units in 2006, established franchises are flourishing and new ones are emerging.

Personal-care services
Baby boomers may be young at heart, but their desire to also look young has spurred the growth of franchises offering laser, skin-care, med-spa, massage, fitness, and tanning services.

Enrichment learning programs for kids
When it comes to learning programs for children, the segment increased by 850-plus units, but 2006 also saw diversification with new types of programs, such as a cooking school and an abacus-learning program. Obviously, the franchising industry remains focused on children—and children's education in particular.

eBay drop-off stores
The largest global online marketplace has been creating opportunities for all, including franchises that list and sell items for those lacking eBay savvy.

Food
Franchises and their customers will never go hungry. Franchises serving up salads and smoothies enjoyed healthy growth last year, a couple of chicken-wing newcomers made their way into this year's listing, and coffee franchises are holding their own (even major players Burger King and McDonald's have upped their gourmet coffee offerings to capture a portion of the coffee profits). Additionally, nonrestaurant food-related franchises are growing: chocolate fondue, food as gifts (like fruit baskets), and wine, to name a few.

New and unique concepts

Hamburgers and pizza will always be American classics, but innovative, original, and sometimes wacky franchise concepts are starting to shake things up. Cereality has made it big with endless hot and cold cereal options, Miami Rice Pudding Co. offers more than 30 flavors of rice pudding, and P.B.Loco keeps things nutty with its extensive line of savory and sweet peanut butters.

Business consulting/staffing

Every business needs help sometimes—and that need is keeping business consulting and staffing franchises growing. The Bureau of Labor Statistics predicts staffing services will be one of the fastest-growing industries over the next five to ten years.

Source: Sara Wilson, "Hot Franchising Trends for 2007," Entrepreneur.com

---

GREAT ADVICE

Consider taking a job in one of the stores of the franchise you're considering. It will give you a great opportunity to see how the company operates.

TEN SIGNS OF A GREAT FRANCHISE

1. Responsiveness during the investigation process.
2. Direct operational training.
3. Other training.
4. Marketing programs.
5. Real estate and construction assistance.
6. Financing assistance.
7. Litigation history (excessive litigation is a red flag).
8. Financial strength of the franchise company.
9. Financial strength of the unit operations.
10. The attitude of the existing franchisees.

Source: Jeff Elgin, CEO, FranChoice, Inc.

TOP TEN U.S. FRANCHISES FOR 2007

#1: Subway
#2: Dunkin' Donuts
#3: Jackson Hewitt Tax Service
#4: 7-Eleven
#5: The UPS Store/Mail Boxes Etc.
#6: Domino's Pizza
#7: Jiffy Lube
#8: Sonic Drive-In Restaurants
#9: McDonald's
#10: Papa John's

Source: Entrepreneur.com

FRANCHISE RESOURCE

If you're considering a franchise, visit the International Franchise Association website at www.franchise.org. You can search for details on more than 1,200 franchises, learn franchising basics, and participate in discussion boards with other franchise seekers and owners.

CHAPTER 36

Writing a Business Plan

BUILD YOUR BUSINESS ON A SOLID PLAN

Does the thought of writing a business plan have about as much appeal as a trip to the dentist? You're not alone—after all, entrepreneurs are doers, they want to be in the middle of the action, not stuck on the sideline dealing with paperwork. But the idea that preparing a business plan is a dull and thankless task is a serious misperception. If you're excited about your business, you should be excited about doing the planning that will make it a success.

A good business plan doesn't have to be formal or complicated but it must be thorough and in writing. The key is to make it as detailed as necessary to give yourself a road map for your company, and it should project at least five years into the future.

Many entrepreneurs, especially solo operators, don't bother writing their plan down, but it's not enough to just have the information in your head. Committing the plan to paper

forces you to think through each step of the process, consider all the consequences, and deal with issues that you might prefer to avoid. It also increases your sense of accountability, even if it's just to yourself—after all, you've written it down, so now you have an obligation to either follow it, or come up with a justification for doing something different. And if you have partners, it reduces the risks of misunderstandings or conflicting goals.

Creating a business plan forces you to think carefully about what you're doing and why. The process is not necessarily sequential; for example, when you develop your market strategies, you'll need to consider both the competitive information and your financial resources, so you may find yourself moving from one section to another and back before you complete the plan.

Another important point to keep in mind is that writing a business plan is not a one-time exercise. This is a tool that you use to run your company every day. If you want to obtain loans or attract outside investors, either in the start-up stage or down the road, you'll need to show a strong plan that you've kept current to demonstrate the viability of your company.

Business plans are not static, and the best plan in the world will come up against unforeseen circumstances. As you write your plan—and later as you work it—you'll probably find that it needs changing. That's OK, but be sure to think your changes through and see how a change in one area will affect the rest of the company. For example, if you make a change in your product, will that affect the packaging? Or if you shift your marketing strategy, do you need to adjust production to meet a change in demand? And how will either of these changes affect your financial situation?

> *You must have long term goals to keep you from being frustrated by short term failures.*
>
> *Words of Wisdom*
>
> —CHARLES C. NOBLE

> *"Would you tell me, please, which way I ought to go from here?"*
>
> *Words of Wisdom*
>
> *"That depends a good deal on where you want to get to," said the Cat.*
>
> *"I don't much care where," said Alice.*
>
> *"Then it doesn't matter which way you go," said the Cat.*
>
> —LEWIS CARROLL, *ALICE'S ADVENTURES IN WONDERLAND*

BASIC ELEMENTS OF A BUSINESS PLAN

Executive summary

This is a very brief overview of the business—almost a synopsis of your entire plan. State the business concept, basic financial points (such as sales projections and capital requirements), and current status of the company. Identify the owners and key personnel, and describe what each one brings to the table. For example, you may have 20 years' experience in the industry, or you may have hired someone with a notable track record or connections who will have a strong impact on your organization. Finally, indicate what the company has achieved so far (this may include patents, prototypes, contracts with customers, and test marketing results).

Business description

Begin with a look at the entire industry, and the various markets it serves. Then describe your company, including your operational structure (retail, wholesale, manufacturing, service provider, etc.), legal form (sole proprietorship, partnership, corporation, or limited liability company), customer base, product(s) and/or service(s), and distribution methods. Emphasize what sets you apart from competitors and other companies in the industry.

Market strategies

First, define the total market in terms of size, structure, growth prospects, trends, and sales potential. Then estimate what you realistically expect your market share to be, and how you intend to reach and capture that share. You also need to outline how you expect to position your company and product in the market, how you will set prices, how you will promote your product, your method of distribution, and the role you will play in your marketing efforts. You may want to use this section to develop your marketing strategy, or maintain that plan as a separate document and simply refer to it here. Either way, you need a comprehensive marketing plan that integrates such elements as sales, advertising in various media, public relations, special promotions, and community activities. The plan should outline what you intend to do, assign a budget and time schedule to the various activities, and include a review process so you can evaluate the success of your efforts and determine if your plan needs any adjustments along the way.

Competitive analysis

Identify current and potential competition, and analyze their strengths and weaknesses. You need to understand the reasons behind their successes and failures so you can fine-tune your own marketing approach. Be specific, detailed and brutally honest; don't let unrealistic optimism, personal bias, or wishful thinking color your view of what the competition truly is.

Design and development plans

Describe the design of your product and outline its development within the context of production and marketing. If your company is built on a new product that you have invented and are developing, this section should include a plan for testing, incremental reviews, and a thorough final evaluation. Be sure your development budget includes material, labor, overhead, capital equipment, professional services, and administrative costs.

Operations and management plans

This section demonstrates how your business will function on a continuing basis. Who is responsible for what aspects of the operation, how will these functions be carried out, and what are your capital and expense requirements? In addition to what will be done, show evidence that you have the necessary and appropriate resources in terms of facilities, equipment, materials, and labor to operate as planned.

Financial components

This is the real backbone of your plan, and should include an income statement, a cash flow statement, and a balance sheet. These reports give you a historical perspective, a forecast for the future, and a clear picture of your current financial situation. Your accountant can help you understand these financial statements, and they can be prepared using any of the popular computer accounting packages on the market today.

I know the price of success: dedication, hard work and an unremitting devotion to the things you want to see happen.

Words of Wisdom

—FRANK LLOYD WRIGHT

Every business plan should be written with a specific audience in mind. While plans are often written to raise money,

Words of Wisdom

other appropriate audiences could include a company's senior management team, company employees, suppliers, strategic partners, or key customers. The Overview section of a business plan must be tailored to answer the specific questions and needs of your audience. It should be especially thorough if you are looking to borrow money from a bank.

—DON DEBELAK, AUTHOR OF *BUSINESS MODELS MADE EASY*

CREATING YOUR BUSINESS MODEL

For investors, a business model is a way to evaluate whether a business will succeed. But for an entrepreneur, it is a tool to create a dynamic business. A successful entrepreneur starts by preparing an initial model and then looking it over, seeing what works and what doesn't, and then changing the model. A model is not a pass-or-fail test to the entrepreneur; it is a building block that leads him or her to a strong, profitable business.

A business mdoel deals with key issues regarding how a company is run that relate to acquiring customers, satisfying customers while making profits, and being able to first maintain and then grow a company's market share. Every business has a model, whether it has been chosen directly or is just the result of how your business is set up. Every business deals in some way with six key elements, whether you are an at-home business, retailer, small service provider, or big manufacturer. Your business must be able to effectively provide all of the following elements or it will quickly fail:

- Acquiring customers
- Offering value to customers
- Delivering products or services with high margins
- Providing customer satisfaction
- Maintaining market position
- Funding the business

Your goal is to create your business model intentionally and with goals in mind. You want to make sure you start with a model that looks promising.

Source: Business Models Made Easy *by Don Debelak*
(Entrepreneur Press, 2006)

RESEARCHING YOUR MARKET

In today's high-tech, online world, it's fairly easy to find the market information you need—in fact, your challenge is going to be sorting through the vast quantities of available information to find what is really appropriate and useful.

Begin the process by simply talking to people—friends and associates who may either be a part of or know something about your potential market. Then go to the library; visit your local chamber of commerce; read general business magazines and industry trade journals; attend trade shows; shop the competition; get on the internet; consult with your nearest Small Business Development Center—just about every major metropolitan area has one. Most communities also have an economic development organization that can help with demographic information; if you can't find such an agency in your area, contact your state Department of Commerce for either information or a referral.

Though much of the information you need has probably already been gathered and is readily available, you may also opt to conduct customized research, typically in the form of surveys. The cost will vary depending on the length and style of the survey, the size of the market sample, and whether the contact is face-to-face, by phone, or by mail. You can either conduct surveys yourself, or hire a market research firm to do it for you. Base your marketing decisions on sound research and information, not on personal preferences. You may or may not be representative of your market, so don't use yourself as a market of one to determine whether something is necessary.

Market research doesn't end once your initial marketing plan is complete. You need to continually study your market, considering how changes in your customer base and your company will affect your marketing strategies. Also, your plan should include a way to track results, so you know what is working and what isn't. The easiest tracking mechanism is to simply ask each customer how they heard about you.

WORTH KNOWING

Distribution is a term that people typically think of as being a sales channel, such as selling through distributors to retailers. But it really means any method you use to get your product to customers. For example, a business that holds seminars for inventors and then sells its products and services at those seminars has a distribution strategy—its seminars. Franchises, store location, and selling through other stores are all distribution strategies.

—*Don Debelak, author of* Business Models Made Easy

PRESENTING YOUR PLAN
TO A LENDER

A business plan is the best indicator a lender has to judge your potential for success. It should be no more than 30 to 40 pages long. Include only the supporting documents that will be of immediate interest to your potential lender. Keep other documents in your own copy where they will be available if you need them. Have your plan bound with a blue, black or brown cover. Make copies for yourself and each lender you wish to approach. Do not give out too many copies at once, and keep track of each copy. If your loan is refused, be sure to retrieve your business plan.

Source: Small Business Administration

HOW TO USE
YOUR SUBCONSCIOUS MIND

The programming tool for unleashing the full powers of your subconscious mind is definition of purpose. The clearer your picture of what you want, the more activity you inspire inside your subconscious system. There are three main ways to put this to work, and they all involve writing.

Continually develop your goals in writing
Paul Meyer, founder of the Success Motivation Institute, says, "If you are not making the progress you'd like to make, it is probably because your goals are not clearly defined." There is power in continually sharpening the definition of your goals on paper. Clarity is power.

Write out your business plan
A written, detailed business plan combines goal setting, action planning, and problem solving. It makes ideas believable.

Create and use daily checklists
Have some organization in your day: see where you need to go and what you have done.

These three action steps have great practical value, but they also serve to communicate to your subconscious mind, in an organized manner, the seriousness of your objectives.

Source: Dan Kennedy, No B.S. Business Success: The Ultimate No Holds Barred Kick Butt Take No Prisoners Tough & Spirited Guide *(Entrepreneur Press, 2004)*

SIX REASONS TO WRITE A BUSINESS PLAN

1. To get financing

No matter how successful a business is, it won't be able to raise money without a business plan with a full set of financial projections for investors, banks, and even potential business partners.

2. To communicate your company's strategy

Employees are much more productive when they have a clear understanding of a business's objective and strategy. You should not minimize this need for communication.

3. As a development tool

A business plan works out the details of how a business concept will be implemented, including the anticipation of problems that might emerge.

4. As a resource planner

New personnel, finances, manufacturing capacity, and inventory are just a few of a company's resources that a thoughtfully prepared business plan can specify.

5. As a standard for evaluation

How do investors and management decide if the company has had a good year? The business plan lays out what a company hopes to accomplish and provides a baseline for determining how well management or the company's owner has done to meet those goals.

6. To set a budget

Monthly revenue and expense budgets are two essential tools for tracking performance and planning during the year. The budget and projections are keys that investors follow closely to judge performance.

Source: Business Models Made Easy *by Don Debelak*
(Entrepreneur Press, 2006)

WORTH KNOWING

A *business plan* is a summary of how a business or entrepreneur intends to organize an entrepreneurial endeavor and implement activities necessary and sufficient for the venture to succeed. It is a written explanation of the company's *business model* for the venture in question.

—*Wikipedia*

TOP TEN BUSINESS PLAN MISTAKES

Most "bad" business plans share one or more of the following problems:

1. The plan is poorly written.

Spelling, punctuation, grammar, and style are all important when it comes to getting your business plan down on paper. Although investors don't expect to be investing in a company run by English majors, they are looking for clues about the underlying business and its leaders when they peruse a plan. When they see one with spelling, punctuation, and grammar errors, they immediately wonder what else is wrong with the business. But since there's no shortage of people looking for capital, they don't wonder for long—they just move on to the next plan. Before you show your plan to a single investor or banker, go through every line of the plan with a fine-tooth comb.

Style is more subtle, but it's equally important. Different entrepreneurs write in different styles. No matter what style you choose for your business plan, be sure it's consistent throughout and that it fits your intended audience and your business.

2. The plan presentation is sloppy.

Once your writing's perfect, the presentation has to match. Nothing peeves investors more than inconsistent margins, missing page numbers, charts without labels or with incorrect units, tables without headings, technical terminology without definitions, or a missing table of contents. Have someone else proofread your plan before you show it to an investor, banker, or venture capitalist. Remember that while you'll undoubtedly spend months working on your plan, most investors won't give it more than ten minutes before they make an initial decision. So if they start paging through your plan and can't find the section on "Management," they may decide to move on to the next, more organized plan in the stack.

3. The plan is incomplete.

Every business has customers, products, and services, operations, marketing and sales, a management team, and competitors. At an absolute minimum, your plan must cover all these areas. A complete plan should also include a discussion of the industry, particularly industry trends, such as if the market is growing or shrinking. Finally, your plan should include detailed financial projections—monthly cash flow and income statements, as well as annual balance sheets—going out at least three years.

4. The plan is too vague.

A business plan is not a novel, poem, or cryptogram. If a reasonably intelligent person with a high school education can't understand your plan, then you need to rewrite it. If you're trying to keep the information vague because your business involves highly confidential material, processes or technologies, then show people your executive summary first (which should never contain any proprietary information). Then, if they're interested in learning more about the business, have them sign noncompete and nondis-closure agreements before showing them the entire plan. Be forewarned, however: Many venture capitalists and investors will not sign these agreements since they want to minimize their legal fees and have no interest in competing with you in any case.

5. The plan is too detailed.

Do not get bogged down in technical details! This is especially common with technology-based startups. Keep the technical details to a minimum in the main plan—if you want to include them, do so elsewhere, say, in an appendix. One way to do this is to break your plan into three parts: a two- to three-page executive summary, a 10- to 20-page business plan, and an appendix that includes as many pages as needed to make it clear that you know what you're doing. This way, anyone reading the plan can get the amount of detail he or she wants.

6. The plan makes unfounded or unrealistic assumptions.

By their very nature, business plans are full of assumptions. The most important assumption, of course, is that your business will succeed! The best business plans highlight critical assumptions and provide some sort of rationalization for them. The worst business plans bury assumptions throughout the plan so no one can tell where the assumptions end and the facts begin. Market size, acceptable pricing, customer purchasing behavior, time to commercialization—these all involve

---

Setting a goal is not the main thing. It is deciding how you will go about achieving it and staying with that plan.

Words of Wisdom

—TOM LANDRY, COACH OF THE DALLAS COWBOYS

assumptions. Wherever possible, make sure you check your assumptions against benchmarks from the same industry, a similar industry, or some other acceptable standard. Tie your assumptions to facts.

A simple example of this would be the real-estate section of your plan. Every company eventually needs some sort of real estate, whether it's office space, industrial space, or retail space. You should research the locations and costs for real estate in your area, and make a careful estimate of how much space you'll actually need before presenting your plan to any investors or lenders.

7. The plan includes inadequate research.

Just as it's important to tie your assumptions to facts, it's equally important to make sure your facts are, well, facts. Learn everything you can about your business and your industry—customer purchasing habits, motivations and fears; competitor positioning, size, and market share; and overall market trends. You don't want to get bogged down by the facts, but you should have some numbers, charts, and statistics to back up any assumptions or projections. Well-prepared investors will check your numbers against industry data or third party studies—if your numbers don't jibe with their numbers, your plan probably won't get funded.

8. You claim there's no risk involved in your new venture.

Any sensible investor understands there's really no such thing as a "no-risk" business. There are always risks. You must understand them before presenting your plan to investors or lenders. Since a business plan is more of a marketing tool than anything else, minimize the discussion of risks in your plan. If you do mention any risks, be sure to emphasize how you will minimize or mitigate them. And be well prepared for questions about risks in later discussions with investors.

9. You claim you have no competition

It's absolutely amazing how many potential business owners include this statement in their business plans: "We have no competition." If that's what you think, you couldn't be further from the truth. Every successful business has competitors, both direct and indirect. You should plan for stiff competition from the beginning. If you can't find any direct competitors today, try to imagine how the marketplace might look once you're successful. Identify ways you can compete, and accentuate your competitive advantages in the business plan.

10. The business plan is really no plan at all.

A good business plan presents an overview of the business—now, in the short term, and in the long term. However, it doesn't just describe what the business looks like at each of those stages; it also describes how you'll get from one stage to the next. In other words, the plan provides a roadmap for the business, a roadmap that should be as specific as possible. It should contain definite milestones—major targets that have real meaning. For instance, reasonable milestones might be "signing the 100th client" or "producing 10,000 units of product." The business plan should also outline all the major steps you need to complete to reach each milestone.

Source: Andrew Clarke, "Top 10 Business Plan Mistakes," Entrepreneur.com

---

Marketplace heroes see the world differently than the rest of us. They bring an edge to everything they do, and that edge is an insatiable desire to compete, improve, and win.

Words of Wisdom

—RANDY PENNINGTON, PENNINGTON PERFORMANCE GROUP

SAMPLE BUSINESS PLANS

These web sites have sample business plans that you can use to become familiar with the format and structure of typical business plans:

BPlans.com
www.bplans.com

Business Resource Software, Inc.
www.businessplans.org

Entrepreneur.com
www.entrepreneur.com/services/sample plans/index.html

Rarely do we find men who willingly engage in hard, solid thinking. There is an almost universal quest for easy answers and half-baked solutions. Nothing pains some people more than having to think.

—MARTIN LUTHER KING, JR.

Order and simplification are the first steps toward the mastery of a subject.

—THOMAS MANN, NOBEL PRIZE WINNING NOVELIST

PROACTIVE VERSUS REACTIVE

There was a time when you could establish and maintain a business by reacting to and meeting changes in tastes, costs and prices. This reactive style of management was often enough to keep the business going. However, today changes happen fast and come from many directions. By the time a reactive manager can make the necessary adjustments, he or she may lose many customers possibly for good.

Proactive planning is the anticipation of future events. Decisions are based on predictions of future states of the environment as opposed to reactions to various crises as they occur. Proactive planning in an unstable, technology driven business environment is critical to continuing success in almost any endeavor. Rather than reacting to the situation as it changes, proactive planning requires that you analyze environmental forces and make resource-allocation decisions. By doing this you will take your business where it needs to be in the next month, year and decade. Barry Worth, a consultant specializing in small business management, puts it this way: "Today's entrepreneur must be a business architect. Anything built in today's business environment must have a step-by-step blueprint or plan on how to achieve success." The blueprint for today's business owner is a business plan.

Source: Small Business Administration

⚜ ⚜ ⚜

CHAPTER 37

Setting Up Your Business

CHOOSING A LEGAL STRUCTURE

One of the first decisions you'll need to make about your new business is the legal structure of your company. This is an important decision that can affect your financial liability, the amount of taxes you pay, the degree of ultimate control you have over the company, as well as your ability to raise money, attract investors, and ultimately sell the business. However, legal structure shouldn't be confused with operating structure. Attorney Robert S. Bernstein, managing partner with the Bernstein Law Firm P.C., explains the difference: "The legal structure is the ownership structure—who actually owns the company. The operating structure defines who makes management decisions and runs the company."

A sole proprietorship is owned by the proprietor; a partnership is owned by the partners; and a corporation is owned by the shareholders. Another business structure is the limited liability company (LLC), which combines the tax advantages of a sole proprietorship with the liability protection of a corporation. The rules on LLCs vary by state; check with your state's Department of Corporations for the latest requirements.

Sole proprietorships and partnerships can be operated however the owners choose. In a corporation, the shareholders typically elect directors, who in turn elect officers, who then employ other people to run and work in the company. But it's entirely possible for a corporation to have only one shareholder and to essentially function as a sole proprietorship. In any case, how you plan to operate the company should not be a major factor in your choice of legal structures. Rather, the decision should be made based on tax and liability issues.

So what goes into choosing a legal structure? The first point, says Bernstein, is who is actually making the decision on the legal structure. If you're starting the company by yourself, you don't need to take anyone else's preferences into consideration. "But if there are multiple people involved, you need to consider how you're going to relate to each other in the business," he says. "You also need to consider the issue of asset protection and limiting your liability in the event things don't go well."

You should also think about your target customers and what their perceptions will be of your structure. While it's not necessarily true, Bernstein says, "There is a tendency to believe that the legal form of a business has some relationship to the sophistication of the owners, with the sole proprietor as the least sophisticated and the corporation as the most sophisticated." You may find that you command more respect from your customers and the community if you have "Inc." after your company name.

Your image notwithstanding, the biggest advantage of forming a corporation is in the area of asset protection, which, says Bernstein, is the process of making sure the assets you don't want to put into the business don't stand liable for the business's debt. However, to take advantage of the protection a corporation offers, you must respect the corporation's identity. That means maintaining the corporation as a separate entity; keeping your corporate and personal funds separate, even if you are the sole

shareholder; and following your state's rules regarding holding annual meetings and other record-keeping requirements.

Is any one of these structures better than another? No. Make your choice on what is best for your particular situation. Do you need an attorney to set up a corporation or a partnership? Again, no. Bernstein says there are plenty of good do-it-yourself books and kits on the market, and most of the state agencies that oversee corporations have guidelines. Even so, it's always a good idea to have a lawyer at least look over your documents before you file them, just to make sure they are complete and will allow you to truly function as you want to.

Finally, remember that your choice of legal structure is not an irrevocable decision, although if you're going to make a switch, it's easier to go from the simpler forms to the more sophisticated than the other way around. Bernstein says the typical pattern is to start as a sole proprietor and then move up to a corporation as the business grows. But if you need the asset protection of a corporation from the beginning, start out that way. Says Bernstein, "If you're going to the trouble to start a business, decide on a structure and put it all together. It's worth the extra effort to make sure it's really going to work."

In real estate, don't trust the landlord's representative. Do your homework.

Words of Wisdom

—MICHAEL CURCIO,
CEO AND FOUNDER, PYROGRILL FRANCHISING, INC.

CHOOSING A LOCATION FOR YOUR BUSINESS

Where should your business be? One expert will tell you location is absolutely vital to your company's success; another will argue that it really doesn't matter where you are—they're both right. How important location is for your new company depends on the type of business, the facilities and other resources you need, as well as where your customers are.

If you're in retail or you manufacture a product and distribution is a critical element of your overall operation, then geographical location is extremely important. If your business is information- or service-related, the actual location takes a back seat to whether or not the facility itself can meet your needs.

Regardless of the nature of your business, before you start shopping for space, you need to have a clear picture of what you must have, what you'd like to have, what you absolutely won't tolerate, and how much you're able to pay. Developing that picture can be a time-consuming process that is both exciting and tedious, but it's essential that you give it the attention it deserves. While many start-up mistakes can be corrected later, a poor choice of location is difficult—and sometimes impossible—to repair.

Types of Locations

The type of location you choose depends largely on the type of business you're in, but there are enough mixed-use areas and creative applications of space that you should give some thought to each type before making a final decision. For example, business parks and office buildings typically have retail space so they can attract the restaurants and stores that business tenants want nearby. Shopping centers are often home to an assortment of professional services—medical, legal, accounting, insurance, etc.—as well as retailers. It's entirely possible that

some version of nontraditional space will work for you, so use your imagination.

Homebased

This is perhaps the trendiest location for a business these days, and many entrepreneurs start at home, then move into commercial space as their business grows. Others start at home with no thought or intention of ever moving. You can run a homebased business from an office in a spare bedroom, the basement, the attic—even the kitchen table. On the plus side, you don't need to worry about negotiating leases, coming up with substantial deposits or commuting. On the downside, your room for physical growth is limited and you may find accommodating employees or meetings with clients a challenge.

Retail

Retail space comes in a variety of shapes and sizes and may be located in enclosed malls, strip shopping centers, free-standing buildings, downtown shopping districts, or mixed-use facilities. You'll also find retail space in airports and other transportation facilities, hotel lobbies, sports stadiums, and a variety of temporary or special event venues.

Mobile

Whether you're selling to the general public or other businesses, if you have a product or service that you take to your customers, your ideal location may be a car, van, or truck.

Commercial

Commercial space includes even more options than retail. Commercial office buildings and business parks offer traditional office space geared to businesses that do not require a significant amount of pedestrian or automobile traffic for sales. You'll find commercial office space in downtown business districts, business parks, and sometimes interspersed among suburban retail facilities. One office option to consider is an executive suite, where the landlord provides receptionist and secretarial services, faxing, photocopying, conference rooms, and other support services as part of the space package. Executive suites help you project the image of a professional operation at a more affordable cost than a traditional office and can be found in most commercial office areas. Some executive suites even rent their facilities by the hour to homebased businesses or out-of-towners who need temporary office space.

Industrial

If your business involves manufacturing or heavy distribution, you'll need a plant or warehouse facility. Light industrial parks typically attract smaller manufacturers in nonpolluting industries as well as companies that need showrooms in addition to manufacturing facilities. Heavy industrial areas tend to be older and poorly planned and usually offer rail and/or water port access. Though industrial parks are generally newer and often have better infrastructures, you may also want to consider any freestanding commercial building that meets your needs and is adequately zoned.

Source: Start Your Own Business: The Only Start-Up Book You'll Ever Need *by Rieva Lesonsky and the Staff of* Entrepreneur Magazine *(Entrepreneur Press)*

GREAT ADVICE

Locate your business in an area that meets both your personal lifestyle and your business requirements. There should be an adequate labor pool and the cost of living and doing business in the area should be acceptable to you and your prospective employees.

ASK THE RIGHT QUESTIONS

Answering these questions for each of the sites you're considering can help you decide on the best location for your business:

- Is the facility located in an area zoned for your type of business?
- Is the facility large enough for your business? Does it offer room for all the retail, office, storage, or workroom space you need?
- Does it meet your layout requirements?
- Does the building need any repairs?
- Do the existing utilities—lighting, heating, and cooling—meet your needs or will you have to do any rewiring or plumbing work? Is ventilation adequate?
- Are the lease terms and rent favorable?
- Is the location convenient to where you live?
- Can you find a number of qualified employees in the area in which the facility is located?
- Do potential customers live nearby? Is the population density of the area sufficient for your sales needs?
- Is the trade area heavily dependent on seasonal business?
- If you choose a location that's relatively remote from your customer base, will you be able to afford the higher advertising expenses?
- Is the facility consistent with the image you'd like to maintain?
- Is the facility located in a safe neighborhood with a low crime rate?
- Is exterior lighting in the area adequate to attract evening shoppers and make them feel safe?
- Will crime insurance be prohibitively expensive?
- Are neighboring businesses likely to attract customers who will also patronize your business?
- Are there any competitors located close to the facility? If so, can you compete with them successfully?

- Is the facility easily accessible to your potential customers?
- Is parking space available and adequate?
- Is the area served by public transportation?
- Can suppliers make deliveries conveniently at this location?
- If your business expands in the future, will the facility be able to accommodate this growth?

Achievement seems to be connected with action. Successful men and women keep moving. They make mistakes, but they don't quit.

Words of Wisdom

—CONRAD HILTON, FOUNDER OF HILTON HOTELS

KEEP YOUR PERSONAL AND BUSINESS RECORDS SEPARATE

Establish a separate checking account and keep track of all cash receipts (deposits) and cash disbursements (checks and payments to suppliers). Avoid using personal credit cards for business expenses. If possible, dedicate one credit card to strictly business use. If you carry balances and mix personal and business purchases together, you may not be able to deduct the credit card interest charges as a business expense. When you use a personal credit card to make a business purchase, record the amount your business owes you back.

Use a good accounting program such as QuickBooks and update your income and expenses at least monthly.

If you will have employees, it is a good idea to use a payroll service to avoid costly penalties for mistakes on payroll taxes. If you prepare the payroll yourself, use payroll tax software. Many accounting software programs offer payroll processing as an add-on.

At least quarterly, touch base with your CPA or other tax advisor as a safety net to be sure you have filed all required forms with federal, state, and local taxing authorities.

Go to the IRS web site and order Form 1518, *IRS Tax Calendar For Small Business and Self-Employed.* This very useful calendar lists filing deadlines for the myriad tax forms that may apply to your business along with other helpful tax hints for the entrepreneur.

If you do not use a CPA or other tax advisor, check with your state taxing authority about free seminars regarding sales tax and other state tax matters.

Source: Brian M. Lewis, CPA

BASIC BOOKKEEPING TIPS

When setting up your bookkeeping system, keep these four points in mind:

1. Competency

To run a small business efficiently, you must become familiar with your bookkeeping system as well as the financial reports it generates. Even if you hire a bookkeeper, it is crucial that you understand the numbers. Successful entrepreneurs are proficient in all areas of their business. Most community colleges offer basic training in financial statements. Sign up for a class so you can make sure you have control of your finances and make sure the money is going in the right places.

2. Computerization

Don't let a lack of computer skills keep you from automating your bookkeeping system. You have to think long term here. A manual system might suffice in the early stages, but it will become more difficult when you grow and it can become very costly as well.

3. When deciding on a computer software package for your bookkeeping system, don't just consider the price

The important issues are:
- The track record of the software system itself.
- The track record of the software manufacturer.
- The amount of technical assistance provided by the manufacturer.

4. Compatibility

Before you make a final bookkeeping software decision, check to see if the system is compatible with the other software you plan to use in your venture.

Source: Rieva Lesonsky, Start Your Own Business

BUSINESS LICENSING, PERMITS, AND IDENTIFICATION

Requirements vary from state to state, from city to city, and for different types of businesses, but here's a checklist of the most common types of legal regulations and requirements that new businesses must take into consideration.

Federal Employer Identification Number (FEIN)

If you plan on hiring employees, you need to let the IRS know by filing Form SS-4 (available from your local IRS office). You may also need to register with your state's Department of Labor.

Federal licenses and permits

Most small businesses won't need any federal licenses or permits, but there are some exceptions: interstate trucking companies, businesses that will be offering investment advice, and businesses involved with meat preparation.

Seller's permit

If you'll be purchasing wholesale merchandise for resale, your state will probably require you to register for a seller's permit or sales tax permit. Check with your state's Equalization Board, Sales Tax Commission, or Franchise Tax Board.

State licenses and permits

Call your state's Department of Commerce to see if your type of business will need a state license. Among those that probably will are building contractors, auto mechanics, hair dressers, and private investigators. Restaurants that serve alcohol will also require a state liquor license.

Local regulations

Again, local licensing requirements vary. Phone your city or county clerk's office for information about exactly what you'll need. If you'll be preparing food, you'll also need to call the governing health department. And, if you'll be doing any remodeling to a commercial space, check building codes to find out if you need to get a building permit.

Business name

If you'll be doing business under a name other than your own, you'll need to file a fictitious name certificate or a "Doing Business As" (DBA). Usually, this is done at the county level, and some states may also require you to publish a notice of the business name in your local newspaper.

Zoning laws

Don't sign a lease without first checking that the space is properly zoned for the use you have in mind. Some cities require all new businesses to get a zoning compliance permit before they begin operating. If you work from your home, verify local zoning ordinances covering homebased businesses. Don't assume that just because your neighbor is working from home, it's fine for you to do so, too. If you live in a condominium or planned community, make sure homebased businesses fall within the community's bylaws.

If you're not sure which agency in your city or state to contact for specific questions about what your business will require, start with unofficial sources of information. The Small Business Administration (SBA), your local chamber of commerce, trade associations, and even other businesspeople should be able to point you in the right direction. Even better is to consult an attorney who has worked with your type of business before.

Source: Carolyn Z. Lawrence, "License & Registration, Please," Entrepreneur.com

DISPLAY LICENSES AND PERMITS

Maintain and display in one central area current copies of applicable licenses, inspection reports, and documentation showing that all required corrections have been completed. This allows customers, staff, and visitors to assess the extent of evaluation and compliance of your facility with regulatory and voluntary requirements. Though specific documents vary by state, the items you display may include:

- Licensing/registration reports
- Fire inspection reports
- Sanitation inspection reports
- Building code inspection reports
- Plumbing, gas, and electrical inspection reports
- Zoning inspection reports
- Results of all water tests
- Evacuation drill records

WORTH KNOWING

The federal tax code treats home offices as commercial buildings. Claiming a home-office deduction is complex; the depreciation is spread over an unrealistically long time; and returning the space to residential use generally entails penalties. In order to qualify for a deduction, a home office must be used exclusively for business—a requirement that ignores the realities of family life and offsets many of the advantages of running a business out of a home.

INSURING YOUR NEW BUSINESS

Be sure the following issues and items are covered.

- *Equipment.* This includes everything you use to operate your business (computers, copiers, printers, telephones, etc.) plus other equipment used to produce products and services.
- *Inventory.* This includes the products you sell and, if you do any of the manufacturing, the materials used to make them.
- *Vehicles.* Any vehicle used for business purposes needs to be insured as such, even if it is personally owned.
- *Customer property.* If you take possession of your customers' property for any reason, it should be insured while in your custody.
- *Fidelity bond.* If you (or your employees) perform work in your customers' homes, a third party fidelity bond will pay for losses due to fraudulent acts such as theft.
- *Workers' compensation.* If you have employees, you need the appropriate coverage as required by your state.
- *Liability.* Base your liability coverage on your potential risks. Consider whether or not you need: professional liability, errors and omissions coverage, liquor liability (for event planners, caterers, etc.), off-premises liability (for when you are working at another location), product/completed operations coverage (if you produce a product or to cover your work after it's done).

Source: M. Beth Parquette,
Parquette-Clement Insurance Services

NAMING YOUR COMPANY

Your company name can be an important marketing tool. A well-chosen name can work very hard for you; an ineffective name means you have to work much harder at marketing your firm and letting people know what you have to offer.

Your company name should very clearly identify what you do in a way that will appeal to your target market. It should be short, catchy, and memorable—and even cute is acceptable in some industries.

Check the name for effectiveness and functionality.
Does it quickly and easily convey what you do? Is it easy to say and spell? Is it memorable in a positive way? Ask several of your friends and associates to serve as a focus group to help you evaluate the name's impact.

Search for potential conflicts in your local market.
Find out if any other local or regional business serving your market area has a name so similar that yours might confuse the public.

Check for legal availability.
Exactly how you do this depends on the legal structure you choose. Typically, sole proprietorships and partnerships operating under a name other than that of the owner(s) are required by the county, city, or state to register their fictitious name. Even if it's not required, it's a good idea, because that means no one else can use that name. Corporations usually operate under their corporate name. In either case, you need to check with the appropriate regulatory agency to be sure the name you choose is available.

Check for use on the World Wide Web.
If someone else is already using your name as a domain on the web, consider coming up with something else. Even if you have no intention of developing a web site of your own, the use could be confusing to your customers.

Check to see if the name conflicts with any name listed on your state's trademark register.

Your state Department of Commerce can either help you or direct you to the correct agency. You should also check with the trademark register maintained by the U.S. Patent and Trademark Office (PTO).

Once the name you've chosen passes these tests, you need to protect it by registering it with the appropriate state agency; again, your state Department of Commerce can help you. If you expect to be doing business on a national level, you should also register the name with the PTO.

TIPS FOR CHOOSING THE NAME OF YOUR BUSINESS

Be sure your company's name conveys the proper message.

- *What does your company's name communicate?* The name of your business should reinforce key elements of your business. Are you upscale, convenient, or a bargain? Your name should tell the tale.

- *Is your name too cute or obscure to mean anything to strangers?* Avoid meaningless initials or cute names that only you understand. And if you're planning to expand, don't limit your business by using a geographic name.

- *Is your name suggestive—which is more abstract—or is it descriptive, telling something about your business, such as what it does or where it is?*

- *How about your competitors?* What approach do they take? Make sure your name distinguishes you from the pack.

Source: Rieva Lesonsky, 365 Tips to Boost Your Entrepreneurial IQ

PROFESSIONAL ADVISORS

As a business owner, you may be the boss, but you can't be expected to know everything. You will occasionally need to turn to professionals for information and assistance. It's a good idea to establish relationships with these professionals before you get into a crisis situation.

To shop for a professional service provider, ask your friends and associates for recommendations. You might also check with your local chamber of commerce or trade association for referrals. Find someone who understands your industry and specific business and appears eager to work with you. Check them out with the Better Business Bureau and appropriate state licensing agency before committing yourself.

The professional service providers you're likely to need include:

- *Attorney.* You need a lawyer who practices in business law, is honest, and appreciates your patronage. In most parts of the United States, there are many lawyers who are willing to compete fiercely for the privilege of serving you. Interview several and choose one with whom you feel comfortable. Be sure to clarify the fee schedule ahead of time, and get your agreement in writing. Keep in mind that good commercial lawyers don't come cheap; if you want good advice, you must be willing to pay for it. Your attorney should review all contracts, leases, letters of intent, and other legal documents before you sign them. He or she can also help you collect bad debts and establish personnel policies and procedures. Of course, if you are unsure of the legal ramifications of any situation, call your attorney immediately.

- *Accountant.* Among your outside advisors, your accountant is likely to have the greatest impact on the success or failure of your business. If you are forming a corporation, your accountant should counsel you on tax issues during start-up. On an ongoing basis, your accountant can help your organize the statistical data concerning your business, assist in charting future actions based on past performance, and advise you on your overall financial strategy regarding purchasing, capital investment, and other matters related to your business goals. A good accountant will also serve as a tax advisor, making sure you are in compliance with all applicable regulations and that you don't overpay any taxes.

- *Insurance agent.* A good independent insurance agent can assist you with all aspects of your business insurance, from general liability to employee benefits, and probably even handle your personal lines as well. Look for an agent who works with a wide range of insurers and understands your business. This agent should be willing to explain the details of various types of coverage, consult with you to determine the most appropriate coverage, help you understand the degree of risk you are taking, work with you in developing risk-reduction programs, and assist in expediting any claims.

- *Banker.* You need a business bank account and a relationship with a banker. Don't just choose the bank you've always done your personal banking with; it may not be the best bank for your business. Interview several bankers before making a decision on where to place your business. Once your account is opened, maintain a relationship with the banker. Periodically sit down and review your accounts and the services you use to make sure you are getting the package that is most appropriate for your situation.

Ask for advice if you have financial questions or problems. When you need a loan or bank reference to provide to creditors, the relationship you have established will work in your favor.

- *Consultants.* The consulting industry is booming, and for good reason. Consultants can provide valuable, objective input on all aspects of your business. Consider hiring a business consultant to evaluate your business plan or a marketing consultant to assist you in that area. When you are ready to hire employees, a human resources consultant may help you avoid some costly mistakes. Consulting fees vary widely, depending on the individual's experience, location, and field of expertise. If you can't afford to hire a consultant, consider contacting the business school at the nearest college or university and hiring an MBA student to help you.

- *Computer expert.* Your computer and data are extremely valuable assets, so if you don't know much about computers, you should find someone to help you select a system and appropriate software, and to be available to help you maintain, troubleshoot, and expand your system as you need it.

You look at any giant corporation, and I mean the biggies, and they all started with a guy with an idea, doing it well.

Words of Wisdom

—IRVINE ROBBINS, CO-FOUNDER OF BASKIN-ROBBINS ICE CREAM

CREATE YOUR OWN ADVISORY BOARD

Not even the president of the United States is expected to know everything. That's why he surrounds himself with advisors—experts in particular areas who provide knowledge and information to help him make decisions. Savvy small-business owners use a similar strategy.

You can assemble a team of volunteer advisors to meet with you periodically to offer advice and direction. Because this isn't an official or legal entity, you have a great deal of latitude in how you set it up. Advisory boards can be structured to help with the direct operation of your company and to keep you informed on various business, legal, and financial trends that may affect you. Use these tips to set up your advisory board:

- *Structure a board that meets your needs.* Generally, you'll want a legal advisor, an accountant, a marketing expert, a human resources person, an expert in your industry, and perhaps a financial advisor. You may also want successful entrepreneurs from other industries who understand the basics of business and will view your operation with a fresh eye.
- *Ask the most successful people you can find, even if you don't know them well.* You'll be surprised at how willing people are to help another business succeed.
- *Be clear about what you are trying to do.* Let your prospective advisors know what your goals are and that you don't expect them to take on an active management role or to assume any liability for your company or for the advice they offer.
- *Don't worry about compensation.* Advisory board members are rarely compensated with more than lunch or dinner. Of course, if a member of your board provides a direct service—for example, if an attorney reviews a contract or an accountant prepares a financial statement—then they should be paid at their normal rate. But that's not part of their job as an advisory board member. Keep in mind that, even though you don't write them a check, your advisory board members will likely benefit in a variety of tangible and nontangible ways. Being on your board will expose them to ideas and perspectives they may not otherwise see and will also expand their own network.
- *Consider group dynamics when holding meetings.* You may want to meet with all the members together, or in small groups of one or two. It all depends on how they relate to each other and what you need to accomplish.
- *Ask for honesty, and don't be offended when you get it.* Your pride might be hurt when someone points out something you are doing wrong, but the awareness will be beneficial in the long run.
- *Learn from failure as well as success.* Encourage board members to tell you about their mistakes so you can avoid making them.
- *Respect the contribution your board members are making.* Let them know you appreciate how busy they are, and don't abuse or waste their time.
- *Make it fun.* You are, after all, asking these people to donate their time, so create a pleasant atmosphere.
- *Listen to every piece of advice.* Stop talking and listen. You don't have to follow every piece of advice, but you need to hear it.
- *Provide feedback to the board.* Good or bad, let the members of your board know what you did and what the results were.

❧ ❧ ❧

CHAPTER 38

Funding Your Business

START-UP FINANCING TRENDS

The landscape for start-up financing has changed considerably over the past few years as both the availability and the cost of various options have been affected by various trends in the industry. Here's a look at some of those trends and how they can help you get money to fund your business.

1. Angel investing will continue to grow

In the late 1990s angel investing came out of the funding closet and entered the financing mainstream when technology companies appeared to provide supernatural returns on investment. It seemed as if everyone knew someone who knew someone who was an early investor in an internet start-up that cashed out just in time. Today, there are about 250,000 angel investors in the U.S. investing in approximately 50,000 small companies each year. The bottom line is, angel investing is here to stay.

2. Valuations and investment terms can't get much better

If you're in doubt that we're living through another start-up financing bubble, consider the following statistic provided by the Center for Venture Research: The yield rate on angel investments (the rate at which investments presented to angels result in funding) increased from 10 percent in 2003 to 23 percent in 2005. (At its historical peak in 2000, the yield rate was also at 23 percent.) Either companies are becoming more worthy of funding, or the bubble is back. Pre-launch start-up valuations involving first-time entrepreneurs have climbed to more than $5 million, rather than their post-bubble levels of $1 million to $2 million. You should expect them to stabilize at $2 million to $3 million in the near future.

3. Business credit scores will supplement personal credit scores

For those seeking debt financing, credit cards continue to be the most popular source of capital. In the past, credit card issuers have traditionally made financing decisions for small-business applicants based largely on the personal credit score of the business owner. More recently, however, credit data for the business itself has been aggregated in data repositories. The Small Business Financial Exchange (affiliated with Equifax), for instance, collects data based on the performance of small businesses on their loans, leases, lines of credit, and credit cards. Banks and other lenders are increasingly using this data to supplement their existing underwriting criteria of the entrepreneur. In fact, almost all the top 20 banks in the United States now use data from small-business data repositories to make lending decisions. This trend should continue as additional credit reporting agencies aggregate business data and the predictive ability of this data becomes clearer.

4. Getting $50,000 in funding continues to be difficult

According to the Global Entrepreneurship Monitor, the average amount of start-up capital used by small businesses in industrialized countries is currently $53,000. But the reality for most entrepreneurs is that credit card financing isn't sufficient for raising $50,000, and angel investors tend to avoid being the only investor in a company that's poorly capitalized.

So where are entrepreneurs getting the money they need? Many turn to relatives and friends to help fill the gap. Some seek government funding, but those options may not be as available as they were in the past. The SBA Microloan Program was originally designed to serve this capital gap, however, funding for the program has been on the chopping block lately and hasn't been aggressively marketed by SBA lenders, so it's unclear whether the program will be revitalized in the future.

Nonprofit microlenders have traditionally struggled to get to scale and compete with banks to serve this niche. There is one promising trend that might help to level the playing field: Microlenders are banding together to convince credit bureaus to include performance of microloans in credit scores, in turn, this will make microloans more viable for those who wish to borrow small amounts in order to build their credit.

5. Low credit scores are no longer a constraint on financing, but patient capital continues to be a critical barrier to success

I've often lamented how the four Cs of credit (cash, credit, collateral, and character) have been reduced to just one C: personal credit score. If you have a good business idea but a mediocre credit score (or no credit score because you're too young or too new to the country), your options in the past were limited. And unless you were willing to bet your home equity on the business, your cost of capital would be considerably higher than it would be for someone with good credit. However, online lenders and non-traditional person-to-person lenders have developed some genuinely unique options for entrepreneurs with poor credit. And while the cost of capital continues to be higher for borrowers with no or low credit even with these new options, the accessibility of credit options has never been easier.

Perhaps a more critical problem is the lack of patient capital (funding from people who don't expect short-term liquidity from their investment) and long-term financing options for entrepreneurs with sub-prime credit. Paying interest rates exceeding 20 percent on loans becomes unsustainable if your business can't generate 20 percent earnings growth. For most start-ups, this is a pipe dream in the short-term (two to three years) but seems more plausible over the long-term (four to six years). In my view, patient capital is one of the most important financing needs for start-ups and among the hardest to find. Unfortunately, I don't see this trend changing anytime soon.

Source: Asheesh Advani, "Start-up Financing Trends for 2007," Entrepreneur.com

---

GREAT ADVICE

Rather than appeal to a prospective investor for money, ask him to review your business plan. If he likes it, he may offer to invest without you having to ask.

SOURCES OF START-UP FUNDS

Your own resources

Do a thorough inventory of your assets. People generally have more assets than they immediately realize. They could include savings accounts, equity in real estate, retirement accounts, vehicles, recreation equipment, collections, and other investments. You may opt to sell assets for cash or use them as collateral for a loan. If you own your primary home, you may want to obtain a home equity loan or line of credit, or refinance to pull out cash. Consider a similar strategy if you have a second home or investment property. Take a look, too, at your personal line of credit: you may be able to fund a significant portion of your start-up costs with credit cards.

Friends and family

The logical next step after gathering your own resources is to approach your friends and relatives who believe in you and want to help you succeed. Be cautious with these arrangements: no matter how close you are, present yourself professionally, put everything in writing, and be sure the people you approach can afford to take the risk of investing in your business. As confident as you might be in the potential success of your business, don't allow any friend or family member to invest money they can't afford to lose.

Partners

Consider using the "strength in numbers" principle and look around for someone who may want to team up with you in your venture. You may choose someone who has financial resources and wants to work side by side with you in the business. Or you may find someone who has money to invest but no interest in doing the actual work. Be sure to create a written partnership agreement that clearly defines your respective responsibilities and obligations. The agreement should also include an exit strategy and succession plan that details what will happen if one of the partners dies or becomes disabled.

Government programs

Take advantage of any local, state, and federal programs designed to support small businesses in general, and your type of business in particular. Make your first stop the U.S. Small Business Administration; then investigate various other programs. Women, minorities, and veterans should check out niche financing possibilities designed to help such groups get into business. You should also check with your local economic development agency for information and referrals.

COMMON BUSINESS FUNDING MISTAKES

1. Investing too little in your own business

When an investor sees that an entrepreneur has invested little or nothing in their own business, it sends a big signal to them that perhaps they don't really believe in their own idea. What constitutes an acceptable investment? Well that depends on a variety of things: What type of business are you starting? Different types of business require different amounts capital—e.g., a medical device company would require more capital than a hair salon. What is the degree of sacrifice represented by the investment. In other words, how much pain will the entrepreneur feel if this business fails?

2. Investing too much in your own business

Believe it or not, you can invest too much in a business. Don't let yourself get trapped into being the only one investing in your deal. If that's the case, there may be a good reason—are you the only one who believes in your business?

3. Paying yourself too much (and/or accruing unpaid salaries)

One of the worst signals an entrepreneur can send an investor is that they're living off the investments of others. When investors see an entrepreneur who has made a limited investment in their business yet are paying themselves $200,000 a year—not from sales revenue, but out of investor capital—they're strongly inclined to pass on the deal. Some entrepreneurs try to get around this by accruing a differential between what they feel is an "affordable" salary and the salary they feel they're truly worth. The difference is expressed as a debt to the business. Investors generally find this offensive and won't invest under such conditions.

4. Not proving sales and sales potential

There's a saying that investors want to see that "the dog will eat the dog food." In other words, if your product won't sell, then you don't have a business. For some reason, a lot of entrepreneurs seeking capital don't seem to understand this concept. Yes, there are cases where businesses need capital before they even have a product to sell, but that's not the issue here. The two things that'll turn off an investor quicker than a cold shower is a business that either has a salable product but has made no effort to sell it, or a business whose product market potential is far less than anticipated.

5. Failure to recognize the "sale-to-value ratio"

Another thing that'll turn off an investor is to see that the entrepreneur has sold off the majority of his business before they've even had their first VC round. What these entrepreneurs fail to realize is the sale-to-value ratio. That is, you never sell too much of your business when the valuation is low. The trick is to sell off only enough to help you get to an important milestone where the value will increase significantly and the next round of capital will buy a lot less of your business.

6. Hiding intellectual property (IP)

Businesses that try and put all their IP into a separate holding company and only license the IP to the company seeking investments don't fool investors. Generally, investors want to know that if management fails to achieve their objectives, the investors have the option to sell the IP and get some of their money back.

7. Incorporating unwisely

A number of entrepreneurs have been fooled into thinking that it's a good idea to incorporate in states like Nevada where there are no state income taxes.

On the surface it sounds like a good idea, but from an investor's standpoint those states often have other laws that are unfavorable to investors and discourage investing. Be sure to investigate whether or not the state you're considering is investor friendly. If not, it may cost you more than you save.

8. Not incorporating at all

Qualified investors won't invest in a DBA—you must have a corporate structure in order to legally sell stock. Generally, investors prefer to invest in "C" corporations because they're the most common form of corporation. In recent years, LLCs have become popular due to their tax incentives. If you decide to go the LLC route, just make sure your lawyer structures the operating agreement to read as much like a "C" corporation as possible. Investors tend not to like LLC investments because they refer to shares as "units" and shareholders as "members."

9. Not having a strong management team

Investors will place strong emphasis on who you've attracted to join you in your vision and whether or not they have invested, contributed, and/or bought or used the product.

10. Not having outside investors

Finally, investors will be looking at who else has invested in your business. How much have they invested? Did they invest more than once? How impressive are your investors? Are they "A" players? As an entrepreneur, you're truly known and respected by the business you keep. If your investors are deemed sophisticated and knowledgeable, then you will be respected and, with any luck, a check will soon follow.

Source: Jim Casparie, "Little-Known Funding Faux Pas," Entrepreneur.com

FINANCING AN IDEA

The truth of the matter is, ideas don't get funded; businesses get funded. That became the mantra of the professional investor community after the dot-com bust of the late 1990s. However, for most entrepreneurs, getting from the idea stage to the business stage requires capital, and it has to come from somewhere. The following tips will help you use your funds wisely as you move from bright idea to booming business.

1. *Create a budget.* Budgets are like oil spills: They expand to fit the space they're allotted. That's why I recommend creating a budget before you raise any money. You may find that the total amount of funding you need is more than you initially thought. Also, when you raise money, your budget will help you make intelligent trade-offs. When I started my business, I decided to hire a web designer as a part-time consultant rather than a full-time employee because I needed to spend money on market research first.

2. *Focus on the critical elements, not the fun stuff.* Entrepreneurs are typically passionate and creative people, but the task of building an early-stage business involves some fairly mundane tasks. For instance, when deciding whether to spend money on designing a logo or doing market research, avoid the temptation to hire a logo designer rather than investing in surveying potential customers. Don't get me wrong, you'll need a logo and a business name to get funding for your enterprise, but market research is more important at the idea stage. And when you speak to members of your target market, you may also discover that the name, logo, and business concept you initially considered is off base.

3. *Brainstorm a list of supporters.* People love to support new business ventures started by people they know. Even if your friends and relatives don't have the financial means to loan you money, they'll want to help you succeed and transform your idea into a business—but you have to ask them first. I know many entrepreneurs who are reticent to ask for help from relatives and friends. Get over it! If you're going to succeed, you'll need to become an expert at asking for help.

4. *Refine your kitchen table pitch.* The "kitchen table pitch" is a modified version of the famous "elevator pitch" for entrepreneurs raising money from relatives and friends rather than from professional investors.

5. *If you can, get resources from a former employer.* If you haven't burned bridges with your former employers, consider approaching them about your idea and asking for their support. You might get free or discounted office space—and possibly financial resources for your new enterprise.

6. *Don't issue founder's stock until you're ready.* There's a lot of misinformation out there about the timing involved with issuing stock to the founders of a business. Some "legal experts" will tell you to do it as early as possible—even before you're certain that your idea will actually become a business. This thinking was developed during the late 1990s when businesses were getting funded very early in the idea life cycle. And even though some investors continue to fund idea-stage businesses, this is not a sufficient reason for you to rush to spend money on legal fees and issuing stock before you know that you'll be devoting your full efforts to the enterprise.

Source: Asheesh Advani, "Financing a Not-Yet-a-Business Idea," Entrepreneur.com

❧ ❧ ❧

CHAPTER 39

Equipping Your Business

WHAT DO YOU NEED?

The equipment you'll need for your new business will depend, of course, on what type of business you're starting. Doing your homework on this topic is an absolute must. Whatever equipment you buy, be sure it will:

- Get the job done profitably.
- Be durable and last long enough for you to get an acceptable return on your investment.
- Operate reliably.

THE PROS AND CONS OF LEASING EQUIPMENT

When making a decision between leasing and purchasing, you need to know the advantages and disadvantage of leasing.

Advantages

- *Minimum cash layout*. By leasing you don't have to finance the entire cost of the equipment; you pay only for what you use and always without a large initial capital outlay.
- *Less stringent financial requirements.* Lessees usually find it easier to obtain financing to lease an asset than to obtain credit to purchase.
- *No equipment obsolescence*. You can ensure that your equipment is always up-to-date by negotiating a short-term lease and exchanging the equipment when the lease runs out.
- *Built-in maintenance*. Depending on the terms of the lease, maintenance can be included, thereby reducing the working capital expenses.
- *Tax advantage*. Lease payments show up as expenses, not as debt on the balance sheet.
- *Greater payment flexibility*. Not only can leases be spread over a longer period than a loan, thus reducing monthly payments—but also they can be structured

to account for variations in cash flow, especially for companies that experience seasonal fluctuations in sales.

- *Expert advice available from the lessor.* This is especially true if the lessor is the manufacturer.

Disadvantages

- *No ownership.* Since lessees do not own their property, they do not accrue tax benefits associated with ownership. In addition, lessees don't build equity in the property, unless a lease-to-purchase option agreement is added to the lease.
- *Higher long-term cost.* While leases generally offer lower monthly payments, they do not offer significant tax benefits nor do they provide equity in the leased property, thus the ultimate cost is often higher than if you purchased the item or property.
- *Non-cancelable lease contract.* Some leases have non-cancelable clauses in the contract or charge a severe penalty for early termination of the lease.

Source: Entrepreneur Magazine's Ultimate Small Business Advisor

---

NEW OR USED?

Should you buy all new equipment, or will used be sufficient? It depends on which equipment you're thinking about. For office furniture (desks, chairs, filing cabinets, bookshelves, etc.), you can get some great deals buying used items. You might also be able to save a significant amount of money buying certain office equipment, such as your copier, phone system, and fax machine, used rather than new. However, for high-technology items, such as your computer, you'll probably be better off buying new. Don't try to run your company on outdated technology.

Shop around for good used equipment. Certainly check out used office furniture and equipment dealers. In addition, check the classified section of your local paper under items for sale, as well as notices of bankrupt companies and companies going out of business for various reasons. Also check eBay and other online auctions for new, used, and reconditioned equipment. Don't overlook new-equipment suppliers, they frequently have trade-ins or repossessions that they're willing to sell at discounts of 75 percent or more.

GREAT ADVICE

Don't buy your computers piecemeal. The ideal setup is a homogenous environment so that all your hardware is either the same or compatible. Your cost of ownership and maintenance needs will be reduced, and this structure makes it easier to expand when the time comes. Stick with major reputable vendors that offer warranties. If you don't have an in-house technician, consider purchasing a service contract.

OFFICE EQUIPMENT

Management and administration are critical parts of any operation, and you need the right tools to handle these important tasks. Your equipment needs will vary significantly depending on your industry and the size of your operation. Consider the following primary basic items.

Typewriter

You may think that most typewriters are in museums these days, but they actually remain quite useful to businesses that deal frequently with pre-printed and multipart forms, such as contracts and government forms.

Computer and printer

You don't necessarily need the "latest and greatest" in computer power, but you need a system with the most current version of Windows, a 2.4GHz Pentium 4 processor or Athlon XP 2100+, 512MG to 1GB RAM, 80GB or more hard drive, CD-ROM drive (48X or better), 56 Kbps modem, and 32MB video card. Ideally, you should have high-speed internet access on a dedicated line.

Software

Think of software as your computer's brains, the instructions that tell your computer how to accomplish the functions you need. There are many programs on the market that will handle your accounting, customer information management, and other administrative requirements. You will also want to take a look at the programs designed specifically for your business or industry. Software can be a significant investment, so do a careful analysis of your needs and then study the market and examine a variety of products before making a final decision. In addition to the software you'll use to run your company, be sure to get an anti-virus package and subscribe to a service that keeps it automatically updated.

Postage meter

Postage meters allow you to pay for postage in advance and print the exact amount on the mailing piece. Many postage meters can print in increments of one-tenth of a cent, which can add up to big savings for bulk mail users. Meters also provide a professional image, are more convenient than stamps, and can save you money in a number of ways. Postage meters are leased, not sold, with rates starting at about $20 per month, or you can get a meter/electronic scale combo for $20 to $120 per month. They require a license, which is available from your local post office. Only four manufacturers are licensed by the United States Postal Service to manufacture and lease postage meters; your local post office can provide you with contact information.

Paper shredder

A response to both a growing concern for privacy and the need to recycle and conserve space in landfills, shredders have become standard in both homes and offices. They allow you to efficiently destroy incoming unsolicited direct mail, as well as sensitive internal documents, before they are discarded. Shredded paper can be compacted much more tightly than paper tossed in a wastebasket, which conserves landfill space.

Other Equipment

Finally, you'll need a photocopier and a fax machine based on your anticipated use. If you're going to accept payment by credit card, you'll also need credit card processing equipment.

SECURITY

Merchandise, office equipment, and cash attract burglars, robbers, and shoplifters. Not only do you need to protect your inventory and equipment with alarms and lighting and through the careful selection of employees, but you also need to ensure your personal safety as well as that of your employees.

Begin by investigating your area's crime history to determine what kind of measures you need to take. To learn whether your proposed or existing location has a high crime rate, check with the local police department's community relations department or crime prevention officer. Most will gladly provide free information on safeguarding your business and may even visit your site to discuss specific crime prevention strategies. Many also offer training seminars for small businesses and their employees on workplace safety and crime prevention.

Common techniques that merchants use to enhance security and reduce shoplifting include mirrors, alarms and video cameras. Technology is bringing the cost of these items down very rapidly, and installing them may earn you the fringe benefit of discounts on your insurance. You can also increase the effectiveness of your security system by posting signs in your store window and discreetly around the store announcing the presence of the equipment.

WHAT'S YOUR SIGN?

What you need to know about signage for your new business:

- Signage is a major component of any business plan and marketing plan. Prior to obtaining any small business loan, all businesses must submit costs associated with signs.
- Signs represent the business's image and brand. A company's sign may be the only thing the customers and clients will recognize so it must be completely representative of the brand and make an impression.
- Companies should purchase signs in two different stages. The first stage is permanent signs for identification and the second is signage for ongoing/promotional purposes. Each stage requires different components; a reputable sign consultant can assist in developing appropriate designs.
- Signs are typically a one-time investment, yet they are visible 24 hours a day, seven days a week. Strong, well-thought-out signs are a very worthwhile marketing investment.
- Signs should always identify, direct, or promote.
- Once you decide on the purpose of a sign (identification, direction, or promotion), determine if it will be permanent or temporary, indoor or outdoor, illuminated, or nonilluminated.
- As part of the design, consider the material for the sign itself (acrylic, aluminum, wood, plastic, and so on).

Sign Trends

- On-site signage has become a more viable component of a company's marketing plan due to their relatively low cost and longevity.
- Digital printing now offers strong-impact

point-of-purchase signs at dramatically lower prices than in the past.

- Digital technology also allows sign consultants to provide solutions for all branding scenarios. For example, signs for a lodge might have a rustic look, while signs for an ad agency can project a modern, high-end image—yet they can be created for essentially the same price.

- In addition to signs on buildings with basic images and lettering, consider magnetic signs that can be affixed and removed from metal surfaces; vehicle wraps (mobile billboards); and digital and interactive signs.

Avoid These Common Mistakes

- Including too much information. Most signs are glanced at for only a few seconds; be sure your message can be read and comprehended in that time. Exceptions are signs positioned where customers are waiting, such as lines at banks and amusement parks or in reception areas.

- Trying to include all product offerings in one sign. Make your signs a concise summary of services and provide additional information in another medium. Because signs are typically glanced at from a distance, too much copy will decrease the size of the print and make them hard to read.

- Failing to get advice from a reputable sign consultant on issues such as color, size, and material.

- Failing to check with the city (or appropriate governmental agency) and landlord to identify sign restrictions, requirements, and ordinances. This applies to both exterior and interior signs. The Americans with Disabilities Act (ADA) has requirements for certain interior signs. For example, signs noting handicapped restroom facilities must be a certain height and size. Inspectors will not allow you to open for business unless these signs are properly designed and installed.

Source: Joe McGuinness, Founder, President, and CEO,
Signs By Tomorrow

APPENDICES

❧ ❧ ❧

Online Resources for Start-Ups and Existing Businesses

Basic Guide to Exporting
www.unzco.com/basicguide/index.html

Center for Women's Business Research
www.womensbusinessresearch.org

Click Z Network
www.clickz.com

Cyber Security Industry Alliance
www.csialliance.org

Dun & Bradstreet
www.dnb.com

Edward Lowe Foundation
www.lowe.org

Entrepreneur
www.entrepreneur.com

ePolicy Institute
www.epolicyinstitute.com

Equifax
www.equifax.com

Experian
www.experian.com

Export.gov
www.export.gov

Family Business Experts
www.family-business-experts.com

Family Business Institute
www.familybusinessinstitute.com

Family Business *Magazine*
www.familybusinessmagazine.com

Family Business Network International
www.fbn-i.org

Free Demographics
www.freedemographics.com

International Reciprocal Trade Association
www.irta.com

International Trade Administration
http://trade.gov/cs/

Inventors Alliance
www.inventorsalliance.org

Jupiter Research
www.jupiterresearch.com

Kauffman Foundation
www.kauffman.org

MarketResearch.com
www.marketresearch.com

National Domestic Violence Hotline
www.ndvh.org

National Safety Council
www.nsc.org

National Venture Capital Association
www.nvca.org

Neilson//NetRatings
www.netratings.com

Occupational Safety & Health Administration
www.osha.gov

ResearchInfo
www.researchinfo.com

Salesopedia
www.salesopedia.com

SANS Institute
www.sans.org

SCORE
www.score.org

Small Business Administration
www.sba.gov

Stat-USA
www.stat-usa.gov

Strategy Targeting Organized Piracy
www.stopfakes.gov

TransUnion
www.transunion.com

Trends Research Institute
www.trendsresearch.com

U. S. Trade Development Agency
www.tda.gov

U.S. Chamber of Commerce
www.uschamber.com

U.S. Copyright Office
www.copyright.gov

U.S. Customs and Border Protection
www.cbp.gov

U.S. Department of Agriculture
www.usda.gov

U.S. Department of Commerce
www.commerce.gov

U.S. Department of Labor
www.dol.gov

U.S. Department of State
www.state.gov

U.S. Patent and Trademark Office
www.uspto

World Intellectual Property Organization
www.wipo.int

Appendixes B and C include additional online resources.

⚜ ⚜ ⚜

Business Education Resources

FREE ONLINE COURSES OFFERED BY THE SMALL BUSINESS ADMINISTRATION

The Small Business Administration offers the following courses online for free. In general, they are self-paced and take about 30 to 60 minutes to complete.

Starting a Business

The Beginning: Developing a Successful Business Plan
Small Business Primer
How to Start a Business
Starting Your Small Business
Business Plan Workshops
Identify Your Target Market
Hot Shot Business Simulation for Young Entrepreneurs

Business Planning

How to Write a Business Plan
Business Plan Workshops
Creating a Strategic Plan

Business Plan Templates
Strategic Planning and Execution

Business Management

Managing the Digital Enterprise
Analyze Profitability
Developing a Successful Business Plan
Business Plan Workshops
Growth Strategies
Valuing a Business
Maintaining an Agile Company

Finance and Accounting

How to Find Start-up Funding
Assessing Financial Needs
Cash Flow
Accounting 101: The Fundamentals

Marketing and Advertising

Building Your Brand

Identify Your Target Market
Advertising Your Business
Promoting Your Business
E-Mail Marketing
Marketing 101: The Fundamentals
Conduct a Marketing Analysis

Government Contracting

Steps to Accessing Contracts and Subcontracts
Guide to Government Contracts

Risk Management and Cyber Security

Computer Security
Surviving Beyond Disaster

E-Commerce

Building Your Web site
Managing the Digital Enterprise

International Trade

Assess Your International Risk
Trade Mission Online
A Primer on Exporting
International Business Opportunities

Federal Taxes

Introduction to Federal Taxes for Small
Businesses
Understanding Taxes
Tax and Accounting Basics
Small Business Tax Workshop
Small Business Tax Center
Small Business Tax Workshop

Small Business Retirement

Retirement Planning

ONLINE UNIVERSITIES AND COLLEGES

An increasing number of universities, colleges, and training providers offer online courses geared to entrepreneurs who need flexibility in their training schedule. The following is a list some of public and private online training facilities that offer courses in business and entrepreneurship. Most of the courses offered by these institutions require a fee.

American Global University
College of Business Administration: MBA
Program
www.americanglobalu.edu

Auburn University
Graduate Outreach Program: MBA Program
www.eng.auburn.edu/gop

California Coast University
www.calcoast.edu

California State University
Dominguez Hills
School of Management: MBA Program
www.mbaonline.csudh.edu

Colorado State University
Distance Education Center: MBA Program
www.biz.colostate.edu/mba/distance/distance.htm

Drexel University
Bennett S. LeBow College of Business: MBA
Program
www.lebow.drexel.edu/Current/Graduate/
Programs/OnlineMBA.php

Grantham University
www.grantham.edu

Honolulu University
MBA Program
www.honolulu-university.edu

Indiana Wesleyan University
  MBA Program
  www.iwuonline.com

Jones College
  (Distance Learning)
  http://dl.jones.edu/

Keller Graduate School of Management
  MBA Program
  www.devry.edu/keller/whykeller/online_
    options.jsp

Pacific Western University
  http://pwu-ca.edu

Rensselaer Polytechnic Institute
  Lally School of Management and Technology
  MBA Program
  www.pde.rpi.edu

University of Baltimore
  Merrick School of Business: MBA Program
  www.ubonline.edu

University of London
  MBA in International Management
  www.londonexternal.ac.uk

University of Maryland University College
  MBA Program
  www.umuc.edu/mba

University of Phoenix
  www.onlineuop.com

University of Texas at San Antonio
  College of Business: MBA Program
  www.business.utsa.edu/mbaonline

Western Governors University
  www.wgu.edu

RESOURCES FOR SMALL BUSINESS COUNSELING AND TRAINING

U.S. Small Business Administration (SBA)

The SBA was created in 1953 as an independent agency of the federal government to aid, counsel, assist, and protect the interests of small-business concerns, to preserve free competitive enterprise and to maintain and strengthen the overall economy of the United States. Through an extensive network of field offices and partnerships with public and private organizations, the SBA delivers its services to people throughout the United States, Puerto Rico, the U.S. Virgin Islands, and Guam. Learn more at www.sba.gov.

Service Corps of Retired Executives (SCORE)

SCORE is a resource partner of the SBA dedicated to entrepreneur education and the formation, growth and success of small businesses nationwide. There are more than 10,500 SCORE volunteers in 389 chapter locations who assist small businesses with counseling and training. SCORE also operates an active online counseling initiative. Learn more at www.score.org.

Small Business Development Centers (SBDCs)

This training resource is a cooperative effort of the private sector, the educational community, and federal, state, and local governments. It is SBA's largest resource partner and an initiative that enhances economic development by providing small businesses with management and technical assistance. There are more than 1,100 SBDC lead and service centers located around the country. Learn more at www.sba.gov/sbdc.

Women's Business Centers (WBCs)

WBCs represent a national network of more than 80 educational centers designed to women start and grow small businesses. WBCs operate with the mission to level the playing field for women entrepreneurs, who still face unique obstacles in the world of business. Learn more at www.sba.gov/services/counseling/wbc/serv_cnsling_wbc.html.

GENERAL SMALL BUSINESS AND ENTREPRENEUR ASSOCIATIONS

These associations are a great resource for entrepreneurs. You will want to consider membership in some; others will be a source of information and referral.

American Management Association (AMA)

AMA is a global nonprofit, membership-based association that provides a full range of management development and educational services to individuals, companies, and government agencies worldwide, including 486 of the Fortune 500 companies. Each year, thousands of business professionals acquire the latest business know-how, valuable insights, and increased confidence at AMA seminars, conferences, current issues forums, and briefings, as well as through AMA books and publications, research, and print and online self-study courses.

American Management Association
1601 Broadway
New York, NY 10091
Phone: (212) 586-8100 or (800) 262-9699
www.amanet.org

The Chiefl Executive Officers (CEO) Club

The CEO Club is a nonprofit organization comprised of chapters in the U.S., Korea, United Arab Emirates, and China, which creates a nurturing environment for CEOs dedicated to improving the quality and profitability of their enterprises through shared experience and personal growth. Members must be CEOs of businesses that have above $2,000,000 in annual sales; the average club member has $20,000,000 in annual sales. Chapters each meet eight times a year for a half-day luncheon program. The morning is spent in roundtables and a speaker usually concludes the program. Each chapter also holds social sessions.

CEO Clubs, Inc.
47 West Street, Suite 5C
New York, NY 10006
Phone: (212) 925-7911
www.ceoclubs.org

Edward Lowe Foundation

Founded by Edward and Darlene Lowe, the Edward Lowe Foundation envisions a society that actively embraces and encourages entrepreneurship as the source and strategy for economic growth, community development, and economically independent individuals. The foundation supports entrepreneurship by focusing on second-stage entrepreneurs and the belief that they are vital to the U.S. economy. The foundation also believes that these entrepreneurs have the best opportunity to succeed if they learn from their peers. To that end, it develops and delivers programs and information that help communities appreciate and support the growth of these entrepreneurs.

A second-stage business is defined by the foundation as: privately held; past the startup stage and focused on growth; facing issues of growth rather than survival; generating between $750,000 and $50 million in annual revenue or has that range of working capital in place from investors or grants; employing between 10 and 99 full-time equivalent employees, including the owner.

Edward Lowe Foundation
58220 Decatur Road
P.O. Box 8
Cassopolis, MI 49031-0008
Phone: (800) 232-5693
www.lowe.org

Entrepreneurs' Organization (EO)

A global community of entrepreneurs who are the founder, co-founder, owner, or controlling shareholder of a company that grosses more than $1 million annually. EO has chapters in 40 countries.

Entrepreneurs' Organization
500 Montgomery St., Suite 500
Alexandria, VA 22314
Phone: (703) 519-6700
www.eonetwork.org

Office Business Center Association International (OBCAI)

The OBCAI is the nonprofit trade association for the office business center industry.

Office Business Center Association International
15000 Commerce Parkway, Suite C
Mount Laurel, NJ 08054
Phone: (800) 237-4741 or (856) 439-1076
www.execsuites.org

Independent Insurance Agents and Brokers of America (IIABA)

The IIABA is a national alliance of 300,000 business owners and their employees who offer all types of insurance and financial services products. Unlike company-employed agents, IIABA agents and brokers represent more than one company, so they can offer clients a wide choice of auto, home, business, life, and health coverages as well as retirement and employee-benefit products.

Independent Insurance Agents and Brokers of America
127 S. Peyton Street
Alexandria, VA 22314
Phone: (800) 221-7917
www.iiaba.org

National Association for the Self-Employed (NASE)

The NASE is a leading resource for the self-employed and micro-businesses. The association focuses on providing a broad range of benefits to help its members successfully compete in the market, drive the growth of this vital segment of the economy, and put the smallest of businesses on a more equal footing with their corporate counterparts.

National Association for the Self-Employed
P.O. Box 612067
DFW Airport
Dallas, TX 75261-2067
Phone: (800) 232-6273
www.nase.org

National Association of Professional Employer Organizations (NAPEO)

The NAPEO is a trade association representing more than 370 professional employer organizations nationwide. NAPEO's members represent more than 70 percent of the industry's revenues and range in size from start-up PEOs to large, publicly held companies with years of success in the industry.

National Association of Professional Employer Organizations
901 N. Pitt Street, Suite 150
Alexandria, VA 22314
Phone: (703) 836-0466
www.napeo.org

Small Business Service Bureau, Inc.

The Small Business Service Bureau, Inc. provides members with products and services ranging from group insurance programs to vendor discounts.

Small Business Service Bureau, Inc.
Phone: (800) 343-0939
www.sbsb.com

Young Entrepreneurs Association (YEA)

The Young Entrepreneurs Association is a non-profit organization aimed at Canadian business owners aged 35 and under. It provides members with the opportunity to learn from one another and to take advantage of peer support and mentorship as they grow their businesses.

Young Entrepreneurs Association (YEA)
1027 Pandora Ave.
Victoria, BC, Canada V8V 3P6
Phone: (888) 639-3222
www.yea.ca

ONLINE RESOURCES FOR ENTREPRENEURSHIP AND SMALL BUSINESS INFORMATION

Kauffman eVenturing

Geared to those who are building companies that innovate and create jobs and wealth, Kauffman eVenturing is the trusted guide for entrepreneurs on the path to high growth. The site provides original articles written by entrepreneurs for entrepreneurs, and aggregates "the best of the best" content on the web related to starting and running high-impact companies.

www.eventuring.org

MAGAZINES FOR ENTREPRENEURS

Barron's

The indispensable guide to what's happening on Wall Street and all the international markets: Who won, who will win, what happened and what's to come.

Business 2.0

Business 2.0 informs readers on what is working today in management, technology, marketing and other areas; provides comprehensive industry coverage including emerging technologies, business models and trends, and includes strategies of groundbreaking companies and how to put them to use.

BusinessWeek

Each issue of *BusinessWeek* features in-depth perspectives on the financial markets, industries, trends, technology, and people guiding the economy. Draw upon *Business Week*'s timely incisive analysis to help you make better decisions about your career, your business, and your personal investments.

Entrepreneur

The small business authority helping to manage and grow your business. *Entrepreneur* contains great articles, tips, and information on everything an entrepreneur needs to start and grow a business.

Fast Company

The how-to magazine that keeps managers abreast of emerging business trends and ideas. *Fast Company* is the magazine that sets the idea agenda for the future of business.

Financial Times

The leading newspaper of international business, finance, politics, and economics; covers events shaping the global economy.

Forbes

Forbes is filled with the latest news dealing with politics, people, sports, and finance, all from a business perspective.

Fortune

Fortune speaks the language of the street: Wall Street, Silicon Valley, Madison Avenue, and everywhere in between, providing innovative business ideas and indepth strategies and analysis.

Harvard Business Review

Thought-provoking ideas on managerial excellence from the best in the business.

Inc.

The magazine for growing companies, *Inc.* provides managers with the hands-on tools and information needed to grow small to mid-size companies.

Kiplinger's Personal Finance

Sound advice to enhance your personal finance position.

Money

Tips and strategies to make the most of your money.

Newsweek

Newsweek magazine brings readers the latest news of the world, with a heavy emphasis on political, business, and international news stories.

Smart Money

Spending and investing from the *Wall Street Journal*.

The Economist

The news and business publication written expressly for top business decision-makers and opinion leaders. Each issue explores the links between domestic and international issues, business, finance, current affairs, science, technology, and the arts.

Wall Street Journal

Every business day, over 1.5 million readers turn to the *Wall Street Journal* for knowledge they depend on to live well, advance in their careers, and increase their income. You'll discover ideas and insights on new technologies, trends, and investment intelligence.

WIRED

WIRED delivers a glimpse into the future of how technology is shaping innovation, business, entertainment, culture, and communications.

To subscribe to any of the above, go to www.magazines.com or call (800) 624-2946.

TEN ESSENTIAL ELEMENTS OF AN ENTREPRENEURSHIP PROGRAM

Here's what to look for to make sure you'll be successful in your entrepreneurial studies:

1. Experiential learning
2. Approachable professors
3. Mentorship programs
4. Faculty experienced in entrepreneurship
5. Interdisciplinary program offerings
6. Community involvement
7. Partnerships with entrepreneurial organizations
8. Innovative and creative environment
9. Graduate support
10. A school that fits who you are

TOP 25
ENTREPRENEURIAL COLLEGES
FOR UNDERGRADUATES
(Statistics for 2006)

 # 1 University of Arizona, Tucson, AZ
Eller College of Management McGuire Center for Entrepreneurship
http://entrepreneurship.eller.arizona.edu

 # 2 Syracuse University, Syracuse, NY
Department of Entrepreneurship and Emerging Enterprises
http://whitman.syr.edu/eee

 # 3 DePaul University, Chicago, IL
College of Commerce, DePaul Entrepreneurship Program
http://ent.depaul.edu

 # 4 Temple University, Philadelphia, PA
The Fox School of Business Innovation & Entrepreneurship Institute
http://sbm.temple.edu/iei

 # 5 University of Dayton. Dayton, OH
L. William Crotty Center for Entrepreneurial Leadership
www.sba.udayton.edu/entrepreneur

 # 6 Drexel University, Philadelphia, PA
LeBow College of Business
www.lebow.drexel.edu

 # 7 Fairleigh Dickinson University, Madison, NJ
Rothman Institute of Entrepreneurial Studies
www.fdu.edu/rothman

 # 8 University of North Dakota, Grand Forks, ND
http://business.und.edu/entr

 # 9 University of Illinois, Chicago, Chicago, IL
Institute for Entrepreneurial Studies
www.uic.edu

 # 10 Babson College, Babson Park, MA
The Arthur M. Blank Center for Entrepreneurship
www.babson.edu/eship

 # 11 Xavier University, Cincinnati, OH
Williams College of Business Entrepreneurial Center
www.xu.edu/entrepreneurial_center

 # 12 Brigham Young University, Provo, UT
Marriott School Center for Entrepreneurship
http://marriottschool.byu.edu/cfe

 # 13 Loyola Marymount University, Los Angeles, CA
The Entrepreneurship Program
www.lmu-entrepreneurship.org

 # 14 University of Southern California, Los Angeles, CA
Marshall School of Business, Lloyd Greif Center for Entrepreneurial Studies
www.marshall.usc.edu/entrepreneur

 # 15 Chapman University, Orange, CA
Argyros School of Business and Economics
www.chapman.edu/argyros

 # 16 Columbia College Chicago, Chicago, IL
Arts Entrepreneurship and Small Business Management
www.colum.edu

 # 17 Rowan University, Glassboro, NJ
Center for Innovation and Entrepreneurship
www.rowan.edu/cie

 # 18 Baruch College, City University of New York, New York, NY
Zicklin School of Business, Lawrence N. Field Center for Entrepreneurship
http://zicklin.baruch.cuny.edu/centers/field

 # 19 Miami University, Oxford, OH
Richard T. Farmer School of Business, Thomas C.

Page Center for Entrepreneurship
www.sba.muohio.edu/pagecenter/pagecenternew

 # 20 University of Alabama, Tuscaloosa, AL
C&BA Entrepreneurship Program
www.cba.ua.edu

 # 21 University of Notre Dame, Notre Dame, IN
Mendoza College of Business—Gigot Center for
Entrepreneurial Studies
http://gigot.nd.edu

 # 22 Clarkson University, Potsdam, NY
School of Business
www.clarkson.edu/business/undergrad/entrepre-
neur/index.html

*# 23 Northern Kentucky University, Highland
Heights, KY*
Fifth Third Bank Entrepreneurship Institute
http://ei.nku.edu

 # 24 Iowa State University, Ames, IA
Pappajohn Center for Entrepreneurship
www.isupjcenter.org/

 # 25 University of Iowa, Iowa City, IA
The John Pappajohn Entrepreneurial Center
www.iowajpec.org

Ranking for 2006 by Entrepreneur and Princeton Review

TOP 25 ENTREPRENEURIAL COLLEGES FOR GRADUATES
(Statistics for 2006)

 # 1 Syracuse University, Syracuse, NY
Department of Entrepreneurship & Emerging
Enterprises
http://whitman.syr.edu/eee

 # 2 DePaul University, Chicago, IL
DePaul College of Commerce Entrepreneurship
ent.depaul.edu

 # 3 Northwestern University, Evanston, IL
Larry & Carol Levy Institute for Entrepreneurship
www.kellogg.northwestern.edu

*# 4 California State University—San Bernardino,
San Bernardino, CA*
Inland Empire Center for Entrepreneurship
iece.csusb.edu

 # 5 University of Washington, Seattle, WA
Center for Innovation and Entrepreneurship
www.bschool.washington.edu

 # 6 University of Arizona, Tucson, AZ
McGuire Center for Entrepreneurship: The Eller
College of Management
entrepreneurship.eller.arizona.edu

 # 7 Temple University, Philadelphia, PA
The Fox School of Business Innovation &
Entrepreneurship Institute
sbm.temple.edu/iei

*# 8 Monterey Institute of International Studies,
Monterey, CA*
Fisher Graduate School of International Business
fisher.miis.edu

 # 9 Indiana University, Bloomington, Bloomington, IN
Johnson Center for Entrepreneurship and Innovation
www.kelley.indiana.edu/jcei

 # 10 University of Louisville College of Business, Louisville, KY
IMBA—The MBA for Entrepreneurial Thinking
business.louisville.edu

 # 11 University of California—Los Angeles, Los Angeles, CA
Harold and Pauline Price Center for Entrepreneurial Studies
www.anderson.ucla.edu/

 # 12 University of Illinois—Chicago, Chicago, IL
Institute for Entrepreneurial Studies
http://uic.edu/cba/ies/

 # 13 Tulane University, New Orleans, LA
Freeman School of Business, Levy-Rosenblum Institute for Entrepreneurship
www.freeman.tulane.edu/lri

 # 14 Rensselaer Polytechnic Institute, Troy, NY
Lally School of Management and Technology
http://lallyschool.rpi.edu

 # 15 Pennsylvania State University, University Park, PA
www.entrepreneurship.psu.edu

 # 16 University of Dayton, Dayton, OH
L. William Crotty Center for Entrepreneurial Leadership
http://sba.udayton.edu/entrepreneur/

 # 17 Wake Forest University, Winston-Salem, NC
Babcock Graduate School of Management, Angell Center for Entrepreneurship
www.mba.wfu.edu

 # 18 Simmons College School of Management, Boston, MA
www.simmons.edu/som

 # 19 Fairleigh Dickinson University, Madison, NJ
Rothman Institute of Entrepreneurial Studies
www.fdu.edu/rothman

 # 20 Boston University, Boston, MA
The Entrepreneurial Management Institute
http://bu.edu/entrepreneurship

 # 21 Southern Methodist University, Dallas, TX
Cox School of Business Caruth Institute for Entrepreneurship
http://caruth.cox.smu.edu

 # 22 Babson College, Babson Park, MA
The Arthur M. Blank Center for Entrepreneurship
www.babson.edu/eship

 # 23 University of Virginia, Charlottesville, VA
Darden Graduate School of Business Administration
www.darden.edu

 # 24 University of North Carolina—Chapel Hill, Chapel Hill, NC
The Kenan Flagler Business School
www.eship.unc.edu

 # 25 University of San Francisco, San Francisco, CA
USF Entrepreneurship Program
www.entrepreneurshipprogram.org

Ranking for 2006 by Entrepreneur and Princeton Review

ONLINE RESOURCES FOR SMALL BUSINESSES

The following sites contain information and advice on various topics of interest to small business owners. Many offer free or fee-based e-newsletters and articles. Most carry advertising from suppliers of possible interest and many also sell their own products. It is important to be a responsible and discriminating consumer of the advice and products.

BNET
www.bnet.com
A range of newsletters, white papers, articles, and other information for business.

Business.com
www.business.com
A business-to-business search engine and directory.

CEOExpress Company
www.ceoexpress.com
Resources for busy executives.

Entrepreneur
www.entrepreneur.com
Newsletters, articles, links, and products for start-up and established business owners.

Forbes
www.forbes.com
The web site for *Forbes* magazine with information for business leaders.

Inc.com
www.inc.com
The web site for *Inc.* magazine with advice, tools, and services for business owners.

Morebusiness.com
www.morebusiness.com
Business articles, e-newsletters, and products.

SCORE Counselors to America's Small Business
www.score.org
Small business advice for entrepreneurs

StartupNation
www.startupnation.com
Articles, discussion boards, and more for entrepreneurs.

U.S. Chamber of Commerce
www.uschamber.com
The world's largest business federation.

U.S. Small Business Administration
www.sba.gov
Information and assistance for small businesses.

Yahoo! Small Business
www.smallbusiness.yahoo.com
Learn about Yahoo! products, such as domain names, web site hosting, e-mail, and more. Browse a large library of business articles.

SCORE'S FIVE TIPS FOR USING COLLEGES AND UNIVERSITIES TO HELP YOUR BUSINESS

1. Volunteer your company to be a business school case study. You'll learn much about your company in the process and get good ideas for the future.

2. Obtain management and technical assistance from one of more than 50 Small Business Development Centers. Check the U.S. Small Business Administration web site at www.sba.gov for locations.

3. Participate in special programs. Many colleges and universities sponsor venture capital forums, entrepreneurship centers, and family business programs.

4. Work with the business school to offer internships to graduate students.

5. Find out what expertise is on a business school's staff. You may find just the right person to hire as a consultant or serve on your board.

Source: SCORE, www.score.org

⚜ ⚜ ⚜

Source Contact Information

The following companies, publications, and individuals are mentioned in the *Small Business Almanac*. The contact information was current at the time the book was published.

ASSOCIATIONS AND RESEARCH GROUPS

Center for Women's Business Research
1411 K Street, NW, Suite 1350
Washington, DC 20005-3407
202-638-3060
www.womensbusinessresearch.org

The ePolicy Institute
2300 Walhaven Ct., Suite 200A
Columbus, OH 43220
800-292-7332, 614-451-3200
www.epolicyinstitute.com

International Reciprocal Trade Association
140 Metro Park Drive
Rochester, NY 14623

585-424-2940
www.irta.com

National Venture Capital Association
1655 N. Ft. Myer Dr., Suite 850
Arlington, VA 22209
703-524-2549
www.nvca.org

BOOKS AND PUBLICATIONS

Caffey, Andrew A., *Stay Out of Court! The Small Business Guide to Preventing Disputes and Avoiding Lawsuit Hell* (Entrepreneur Press, 2005)

Caplan, Suzanne, *Second Wind: Turnaround Strategies for Business Revival* (Entrepreneur Press, 2003)

Debelak, Don, *Business Models Made Easy* (Entrepreneur Press, 2006)

Dunn, Michelle, *Entrepreneur Magazine's Ultimate Credit and Collections Handbook:*

The Check Is in the Mail! (Entrepreneur Press, 2006)

Feltenstein, Tom, *The 10-Minute Marketer's Secret Formula: A Shortcut to Extraordinary Profits Using Neighborhood Marketing* (Entrepreneur Press, 2005)

Hiam, Alex, *Making Horses Drink: How to Lead and Succeed in Business* (Entrepreneur Press, 2002)

Kautz, Gerhard, *Take Your Business Global: How to Develop International Markets* (Entrepreneur Press, 2004)

Kennedy, Dan, *No B.S. Business Success: The Ultimate No Holds Barred Kick Butt Take No Prisoners Tough & Spirited Guide* (Entrepreneur Press, 2004)

Kiyosaki, Robert T. with Lechter, Sharon L., *Before You Quit Your Job: 10 Real-Life Lessons Every Entrepreneur Should Know About Building a Multimillion-Dollar Business* (Warner Business Books, 2005)

Levinson, Jay Conrad Levinson and Lautenslager, Al, *Guerrilla Marketing in 30 Days* (Entrepreneur Press, 2006)

Parker, George, *MadScam: Kick-Ass Advertising Without the Madison Avenue Price Tag* (Entrepreneur Press, 2006)

Pennington, Randy, *Results Rule!* (Wiley, 2006)

Weil, Debbie, *The Corporate Blogging Book,* (Portfolio Hardcover, 2006)

Whitney, Russ, *The Millionaire Real Estate Mindset* (Doubleday, 2005)

Whitney, Russ, *Building Wealth: Achieving Personal and Financial Success in Real Estate and Business without Money, Credit, or Luck* (Simon & Schuster, 2006)

CONSULTANTS AND OTHER EXPERTS

Abbott Video Productions, Inc.
Don Abbott, President
12856 Banyan Creek Dr.
Fort Myers, 33908
239-415-4690
www.abbottproductions.com

Anderson Business Advisors, PLLC
Greg Boots, Partner
20819 72nd Avenue South, Suite 110
Kent, Washington 98032
800-706-4741
www.andersonadvisors.com

Bernstein Crisis Management, LLC
Jonathan Bernstein, President
180 S. Mountain Trail
Sierra Madre, CA 91024
626-825-3838
www.bernsteincrisismanagement.com

BizStats.com
316 Pennsylvania Avenue SE, Suite 403
Washington, DC 20003
www.bizstats.com

Brian M. Lewis, CPA
1681 Maitland Ave.
Maitland, FL 32751
321-439-4778
www.brianlewiscpa.com

Business Advantage International, Inc.
D. Allen Miller
101 South 2050 East
Layton, UT 84040
801-444-9919
www.gotoBAI.com

Davis, Charlene
Business Writer
www.cdavisfreelance.com

Jowaisas Design
Elizabeth Jowaisas, Principal
www.jowaisas.com

Parquette-Clement Insurance Services
M. Beth Parquette, President
4673 Fernway Drive
North Port, FL 34288
941-429-8855

Pennington Performance Group
Randy Pennington, President
4004 Winter Park Lane
Addison, TX 75001
800-779-5295, 972-980-9858
www.penningtongroup.com

Publicity Hound, The
Joan Stewart
3434 County KK
Port Washington, WI 53074
262-284-7451
www.publicityhound.com

Sanderson & Associates
Rhonda Sanderson, President
1052 W. Fulton Street, Suite 3W
Chicago, IL 60607
312-829-4350
www.sandersonpr.com

Signs By Tomorrow
Joe McGuinness, President, CEO
8681 Robert Fulton Dr.
Columbia, MD 21046
800-765-7446
www.signsbytomorrow.com

WordBiz.com, Inc.
Debbie Weil
Blogging Consultant
3601 Newark St. NW
Washington DC 20016
202-363-5705
www.debbieweil.com, www.BlogWriteForCEOs.com

ENTREPRENEURS

Berger, Ron, Chairman and CEO
Figaro's Italian Pizza, Inc.,
1500 Liberty Street SE
Salem, OR 97302
503-371-9318
www.figaros.com

Curasi, Paul A., D.V.M., owner
University Animal Hospital
9357 University Blvd.
Orlando, FL 32817
407-657-7297
www.uahvet.com

Curcio, Michael, CEO and Founder
Pyrogrill Franchising, Inc.
734 Cable Beach Lane
North Palm Beach, FL 33410
561-626-2813
www.pyrosgrill.com

Evanger, Jim, Co-Founder and CEO
Designs of the Interior (DOTI), Inc.
18–3 East Dundee Rd., Suite 208
Barrington, IL 60010
847-713-2622, 888-382-7488
www.doti.com

Fenig, Thomas, Founder and CEO
Outdoor Lighting Perspectives

1238 Mann Drive, Suites 100/200
Matthews, NC 28105-7591
704-841-2666, 877-898-8808
www.outdoorlights.com

Funk, Robert A., Founder and Chairman
Express Personnel Services
8516 NW Expressway
Oklahoma City, OK 73162
800-222-4057, 405-840-5000
www.expresspersonnel.com

Gordon, Julian, Founder and President
American Ramp Systems
Division of Gordon Industries, Inc.
202 West First Street, Boston, MA 02127-1110
800-649-5215
www.americanramp.com

Jansma, Michael, President
GEMaffair.com
P.O. Box 1900
Largo, FL 33779
727-588-9300
www.gemaffair.com

Kiyosaki, Kim, author, real estate investor, and a
founder
The Rich Dad Company
www.richdad.com
www.richwoman.com

Kiyosaki, Robert T., author, investor, and a founder
The Rich Dad Company
www.richdad.com

Lechter, Sharon, author and a founder
The Rich Dad Company
www.richdad.com

Lev, Gary, President and CEO
LTS LeaderBoard Tournament Systems Ltd.
21043-2591 Panorama Dr.

Coquitlam, British Columbia V3E 2Y0
604-468-2211, 800-411-4448
www.ltsleaderboard.com

Mitten Rosenberry, Lois
Children's Discovery Center and Discovery
Express
3905 Talmadge Rd.
Toledo, OH 43606

Murphy, Chris, President
Murphy Lighting Systems, Inc.
621 Brookhaven Drive
Orlando, FL 32803
407-895-7475
www.murphylighting.com

Whitney, Russ, Founder and CEO
Whitney Information Network, Inc.
1612 E. Cape Coral Pkwy
Cape Coral, FL 33904
239-542-0643
www.wincorporate.com

Woods, David, CEO and President
Adventures in Advertising Franchise, LLC
800 Winneconne Ave.
Neenah, WI 54956
920-886-3700
www.exploreaia.com

Index